Charles Prestwood Lucas

West Africa

Charles Prestwood Lucas

West Africa

ISBN/EAN: 9783744753135

Printed in Europe, USA, Canada, Australia, Japan

Cover: Foto ©Andreas Hilbeck / pixelio.de

More available books at **www.hansebooks.com**

HISTORICAL GEOGRAPHY

OF WEST AFRICA

LUCAS

London
HENRY FROWDE
OXFORD UNIVERSITY PRESS WAREHOUSE
AMEN CORNER, E.C.

New York
MACMILLAN & CO., 66 FIFTH AVENUE

A

HISTORICAL GEOGRAPHY

OF THE

BRITISH COLONIES

BY

C. P. LUCAS, B.A.

OF BALLIOL COLLEGE, OXFORD, AND THE COLONIAL OFFICE, LONDON

VOL. III

WEST AFRICA

WITH MAPS

Oxford

AT THE CLARENDON PRESS

1894

Oxford
PRINTED AT THE CLARENDON PRESS
BY HORACE HART, PRINTER TO THE UNIVERSITY

PREFACE

A GREAT part of the historical matter comprised in this book has been compiled by Mr. R. L. Antrobus of the Colonial Office, who has also revised the pages relating to St. Helena, of which island he was acting Governor in 1889-90. My warm acknowledgements are due to him, as also to Sir A. W. L. Hemming, K.C.M.G., of the Colonial Office, and Sir G. T. Carter, K.C.M.G., Governor of Lagos, who have been good enough to look through the pages relating to West Africa. I must also acknowledge the kind assistance given to me by, among many others, Sir W. Brandford Griffith, K.C.M.G., Governor of the Gold Coast; Sir F. Fleming, K.C.M.G., Governor of Sierra Leone; and Mr. R. B. Llewelyn, C.M.G., Administrator of the Gambia. Any opinions expressed in the book are mine alone.

C. P. LUCAS.

December, 1893.

Digitized by the Internet Archive
in 2008 with funding from
Microsoft Corporation

http://www.archive.org/details/westafrica03lucauoft

CONTENTS

SECTION I.

GENERAL INTRODUCTION.

		PAGE
CHAP. I.	The British Colonies and Dependencies in Africa	1
CHAP. II.	Early Exploration of Africa down to the opening of the route round the Cape of Good Hope	8

SECTION II.

THE WEST AFRICAN DEPENDENCIES.

CHAP. I.	Introductory—The West Coast of Africa	30
CHAP. II.	Early European Trade and Settlement on the West Coast of Africa	38
CHAP. III.	The African Companies and the Slave Trade	70
CHAP. IV.	English, French, and Dutch on the West Coast of Africa, 1660-1821	96
CHAP. V.	The Rise of the British West Coast Settlements	114
CHAP. VI.	The last Twenty Years in West Africa	138
CHAP. VII.	The Gambia	157
CHAP. VIII.	Sierra Leone	170
CHAP. IX.	The Gold Coast	197
CHAP. X.	Lagos	217
CHAP. XI.	The Niger Protectorates	229
APPENDIX.	Oil Nuts and Seeds of British West Africa	243

SECTION III.

The Islands in the South Atlantic 247

LIST OF MAPS

1. Map of Africa, showing its geographical position and political divisions . . . . . *To face Page* 1

2. Map of the West Coast of Africa, showing European dependencies . . . . ,, ,, 31

3. Map of the North-West African Settlements, with inset showing Freetown Harbour. . . ,, ,, 157

4. Map of the Gold Coast, and Lagos . . . ,, ,, 197

5. Map of the Niger Delta, St. Helena, and Ascension . . . . ,, ,, 229

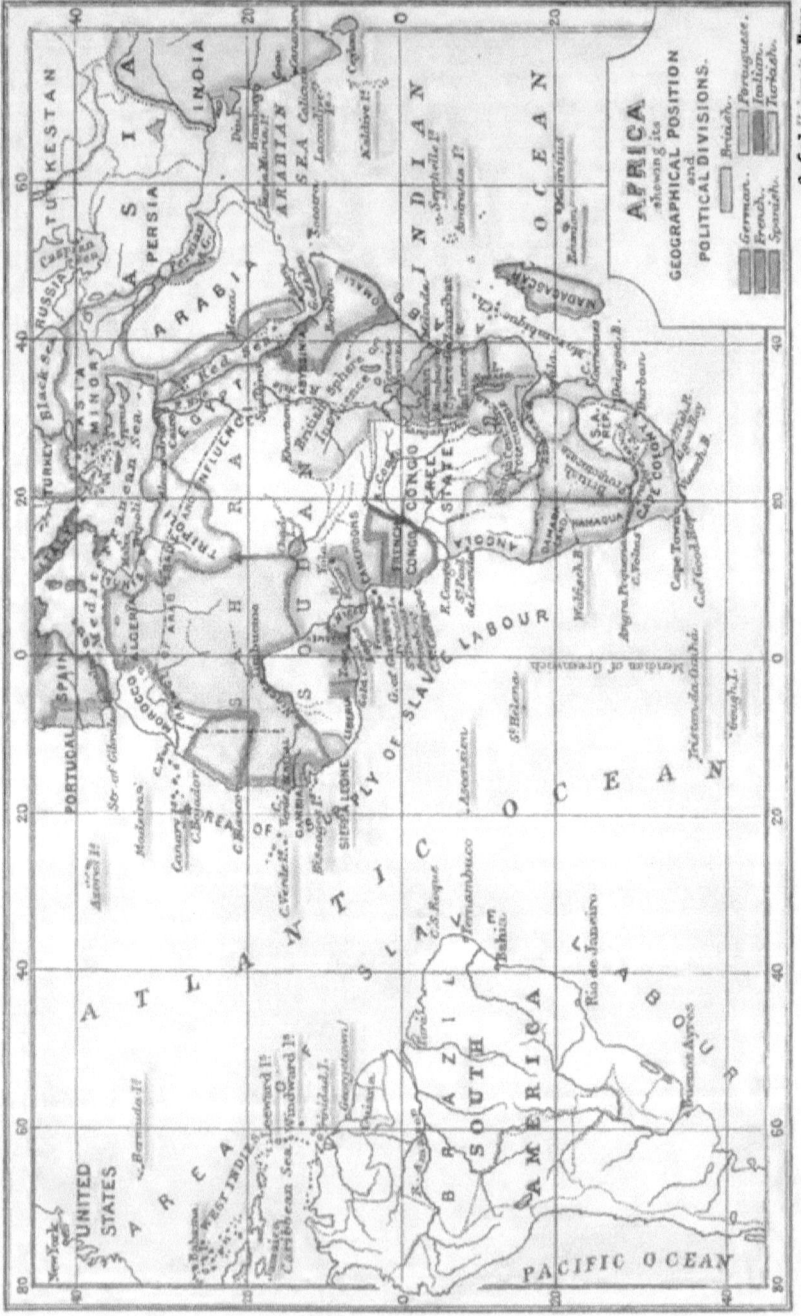

HISTORICAL GEOGRAPHY

OF

THE BRITISH COLONIES.

VOL. III.

WEST AFRICA.

SECTION I.
GENERAL INTRODUCTION.

CHAPTER I.
THE BRITISH COLONIES AND DEPENDENCIES IN AFRICA.

AFRICA has been the scene of some of the earliest as of some of the latest phases in the growth of the British Empire. Within its limits may be traced and found almost every possible factor in the history of colonisation. It contains samples of the trading station, the military outpost, the Protectorate, well or ill defined, the tropical dependency governed from home, the self-governing colony where Europeans reproduce European life and strength. Here is the prime source of the slave trade and negro slavery, the land which has contributed that dark and dismal strain to colonial history. Nowhere have the numberless difficulties, which arise when white men make a home among coloured races, been more accentuated than in Africa. Here trading companies played a great part in the past, and this is the field

CHAPTER I.

SECTION I. of their latest operations. Africa has at once the healthiest and the most unhealthy of climates. The western coast is the white man's grave; the southern peninsula is one of the sanatoria of the world. Nearly every colonising race has left its mark on Africa. In old times, on its northern shores, Phœnicians and Carthaginians, Greeks and Romans, in turn traded, settled, and ruled. In modern days, the continent has known Portuguese, Dutch, French, English, and Danes, Spaniards too in a less degree; while the last few years have brought to its shores Germans, Italians, and the Belgian founders of the Congo Free State.

Central position of Africa.
On the outstretched map of the world Africa holds a central position. Hence, since the opening of modern history, it has been in touch with all the other parts of the world. It has received the overflow of other lands; it has been the feeder of other lands; along its coasts have been the ways of men going to the East, the West, or the South. By the Red Sea or round the Cape is the route to southern Asia, and in history, as in geographical position, the eastern side of Africa has been the western limit of the East Indies. In like manner the West Coast of Africa, with its northerly islands, was the starting-point for the tropical lands of the New World, the place from which for many generations those lands drew their labour supply [1], the eastern limit of the West Indies. Take the map, view the water on the earth's surface as bounded by land, instead of viewing the land as surrounded by water, look on the Indian Ocean lying between Africa and Asia, on the Atlantic lying between Africa and America, regard Africa as in either case forming one side of a great lake, so will be realised the true position of this continent in the story of the movements of mankind. Even the great islands of the southern ocean,

---

[1] It will be seen below that the West Coast of Africa was always within the sphere of the Dutch and French West India companies, not within that of the East India companies.

AFRICAN COLONIES AND DEPENDENCIES.

Australia and New Zealand, have been, to some extent, connected with Africa; for the Cape is the southernmost outpost of the Old World, the point by which, before the Suez Canal was made, ships came and went between Europe and the Antipodes.

Thus it is that, down to our own times, Africa has been in the main a place on the way, not a final goal; and this is one great reason, perhaps the greatest, why its opening and development has been so slow, why it has been pre-eminently the dark continent.

Great Britain owns many possessions in Africa; and, outside her colonies and dependencies, British protection and British influence now cover great areas of a once unknown land.

British possessions in Africa.

The following table gives, as far as it can be given, a list of the British colonies, Protectorates, and Spheres of influence, their date and mode of acquisition, their size in square miles, and the results of the last census.

	Name of dependency.	How acquired.	Date.	Area in sq. miles.	Population (1891 census for the Colonies).
West Africa	1. Gambia	Settlement and cession	1618 } 1816 }	3,550[1]	14,266[2]
	2. Sierra Leone	,,	1787	24,000[1]	74,835[3]
	3. Gold Coast	Settlement	1618	40,000[4]	1,500,000[4]
	4. Lagos	Cession	1861	1,100[5]	85,607[5]
	5. Territories of Royal Niger Company	Declaration of Protection	1884-5	500,000[6]	25,000,000[6]
	6. Niger Coast Protectorate	,,	,,	10,000[6]	
Total West Africa				578,650	26,674,708

[1] Including the Protectorate.
[2] Population of the colony only.
[3] Population of the enumerated districts of the colony only.
[4] Estimated area and population of the colony and Protectorate only.
[5] Incomplete estimate of the area and population of the colony and Protectorate only.
[6] The very roughest estimate only.

4 HISTORICAL GEOGRAPHY OF THE COLONIES.

SECTION I.

	Name of dependency.	How acquired.	Date.	Area in sq. miles.	Population (1891 census for the Colonies).
South and Central Africa	1. Cape Colony	Conquest and Settlement	1806	221,311	1,525,739
	2. Basutoland	Cession	{ 1868 1884 }	10,293	218,902
	3. Natal	Conquest and Settlement	1840–1843	20,461	543,913
	4. Zululand	Conquest and Cession	1887	9,000	142,686
	5. British Bechuanaland	Occupation	1885	51,000	60,386 [1]
	6. Bechuanaland Protectorate	Treaties and Proclamation	from 1885	386,000 [2]	?
	7. Sphere of operations of British South Africa Co. and British Central Africa Protectorate	,,	from 1888	500,000 [2]	?
	Total South and Central Africa			1,198,065	?
East Africa	1. Zanzibar and Pemba [3]	Declaration of Protection	1890	} 750,000 [2]	?
	2. Sphere of operations of Imperial British East Africa Company	Treaties and Proclamations	1886–90		
	3. Somali Protectorate [4]	,,	1887		
	Total East Africa			750,000	?
Islands	1. Ascension	Occupation	1815	34	160 [5]
	2. St. Helena	,,	1651	47	3,877 [6]
	3. Tristan da Cunha	,,	1816	20	[1893] 52
	4. Mauritius [7]	Conquest	1810	708	371,655
	5. Seychelles [7]	,,	1794	100 [5]	16,592
	6. Minor dependencies of Mauritius [7]	,,	1810	100 [5]	3,224
	Total of Islands			1,009	395,560
	Grand Total Africa			2,527,724	[Incomplete]

[1] Exclusive of the native population in the Gordonia district.
[2] The very roughest estimate only.
[3] No account will be given in this work of the Sultanate of Zanzibar, as it is an independent state, though under the direct protection of Great Britain.
[4] See vol. i. of this work under 'British Dependencies at the mouth of the Red Sea.' Under the same heading is placed the island of Socotra, whose area has been credited to the minor Asiatic dependencies.
[5] Estimate only.   [6] Civil population only.
[7] These have been described in vol. i. under the head 'British Dependencies in the Indian Ocean.'

The older African possessions of Great Britain are, in the main, strips of coast, peninsulas, and islands; whereas the Protectorates and Spheres of influence, the results of latter-day dealings in Africa, include inland territories stretching far into the recesses of the continent.

In past times, neither in Asia nor in Africa did the English strive after a continental dominion. Children of the sea, coming from an island home, seeking to secure trade routes in tropical waters and trading stations in tropical lands, they laid hold here and there of the outskirts of the continents, of places which their ships could take and keep, where in time of peace the natives living near and the foreigners passing by would bring their wares, and which in time of war would keep the waterways of the world open to Englishmen and their friends. It is only of late, since steam and telegraphs have made communication swift and sure, since explorers have gone further and further afield, tracing rivers to their source and finding well-watered provinces where our fathers on their maps placed wastes of sand, that, keeping pace with European rivals and pressed forward, as of old, by trading companies, the English have moved their line more and more inland.

There is no more striking feature in the history of the British empire, no point more characteristic of the race, than the extent to which Great Britain holds, so to speak, the keys of Africa. On the north, Gibraltar, all but an island, commands the entrance of the Mediterranean and the empire of Morocco, where Tangier was also once in British keeping. Malta lies over against the central promontory of the North African coast, watching the site which in the days of old gave Carthage so much strength and so great a name. Cyprus is not too far from the Suez canal to be reckoned as in a sense an outpost of Africa, although the present British occupation of Egypt has for the time being diminished its importance in this respect. Aden, Perim, Socotra, and the Somali Protec-

The British hold on Africa.

torate keep north-eastern Africa and the mouth of the Red Sea secure for British trade. Next come Mombasa and the great territory in which the Imperial British East Africa Company have been at work, stretching from the sea to the inland lakes.

In mid-ocean, but yet within African limits, the beautiful Seychelles Archipelago, with its harbour of Mahé, is a British dependency. Lower down and close to the mainland coast, the island of Zanzibar, now under direct British protection, is still, as it has ever been, a great emporium of East African trade. Further south again, the late arrangements with Portugal secure access by the Zambesi and Pungwe rivers from the coast to Nyassaland, and to the plateau of Mashonaland, where the British South Africa Company have their sphere of operations.

Out at sea lies the British colony of Mauritius with its invaluable harbour of Port Louis, perhaps the best in the Indian ocean, a stronghold and coaling station on the direct line from the Cape to India. Then comes the living place of English in Africa, the southern peninsula, whose coast is all British from above Sordwana Point on the eastern to the mouth of the Orange river on the western coast, and whose inland frontier has now been carried far into the interior to territories already named. Going up the western coast, we find Walfisch Bay, the one harbour on many miles of barren coast, held by the Cape Colony. Further north, the islands of St. Helena and Ascension are British. In the angle of the gulf of Guinea, the Niger Protectorates command the mouth and lower basin of the greatest river of West Africa. Next come Lagos, the Gold Coast, and Sierra Leone, island, coast stations, and peninsula, with ever-growing protected territories; and lastly, at the mouth and on the lower waters of the Gambia, near the westernmost point of Africa, the English still hold, under the guise of a Crown colony, the earliest scene of their West African trade. Thus do British possessions

encircle Africa. Every motive has been at work, every agency CHAPTER
has been employed. The interested merchant, the disinterested I.
enemy of the slave trade, those who would safeguard native
races, those who hold them to be a mere stumbling-block in
the white man's path, the missionary, the military expert, the
colonist, and the passer-by, one at this point, another at that,
have for good or evil brought the English into Africa; and
out of it has come a great and complex dominion with an
estimated area of two and a half million square miles.

CHAPTER II.

EARLY EXPLORATION OF AFRICA DOWN TO THE OPENING OF THE ROUTE ROUND THE CAPE OF GOOD HOPE.

SECTION I.

It has been shown that the central position of Africa on the map of the world has tended to make it a land to be skirted, called at, and passed by, rather than a final resting-place; and that therefore, until a comparatively few years ago, the great mass of the interior was, as far as Europeans are concerned, a sealed book. This cause, however, has operated only since the discovery of America and of the route to India round the Cape; a further explanation must, therefore, be given for the fact that, in earlier days also, outside the limits of the Mediterranean, this great continent, so closely connected with Europe and Asia, ever remained an unknown quantity. The explanation will be found in the geographical configuration and natural features of Africa, which make it singularly difficult of entry whether by land or by sea.

Main geographical features of Africa.

The four main characteristics of an accessible land are, shores broken by bays and estuaries, an absence of mountain barriers along the coast, navigable rivers forming waterways into the interior, and, when the interior is reached, no long stretch of desert making communication between the habitable districts either difficult or altogether impossible. Moreover, even if a country be accessible, climate is a further factor to be considered, and an unhealthy coast-line bars to a great extent the way inland.

Tried by these tests, Africa is in every respect found wanting. The outline of its inhospitable coast is rounded and unbroken. The many peninsulas and indentations, which make the shores of Europe and Asia so strikingly irregular, are here conspicuous by their absence. The sea does not run into the land, the land does not jut out into the sea. With the exception of the huge Gulf of Guinea, which has nothing of the nature of an estuary or arm of the sea, there are practically no gulfs or bays; and the only well-defined projection is the great southern peninsula, comprising nearly half the continent. There are hardly any natural harbours; and bars at the mouth, or rapids and cataracts inland, obstruct the navigation of the rivers. There is no long series of level plains and grassy prairies; and the mountains, though they rarely rise to any extraordinary height, for the most part run parallel and near to the sea. Finally, where the continent is widest, the great desert of the Sahara, sandy and waterless, nearly one thousand miles in breadth, cuts off North from South and East from West, stretching from the Atlas mountains to the Sudan and from the valley of the Nile to the Atlantic.

Speaking generally, it may be said that Africa is simply one great compact table-land of moderate elevation, surrounded by a comparatively narrow belt of low-lying territory[1]. In the extreme north and the extreme south, where the continent projects beyond the tropics, this strip of coast-land is not unhealthy; but elsewhere, along the eastern and western sides, it is so fever-stricken, so deadly to the white man, as to be hopeless from the point of view of European settlement and dangerous even for Europeans to cross. Behind it rise the edges of the plateau, sometimes taking the form of mountain ranges, which present steep and high escarpments on the side towards the sea.

[1] It has been compared to a pie-dish turned upside down, the great plateau and the low-lying belt being represented respectively by the inverted basin and the rim. The configuration of the Deccan is, on a smaller scale, similar to that of the southern half of Africa.

SECTION I.

Thus the physical features of the continent help to explain why Africa, which in dim ages past gave birth to the wondrous civilisation of Egypt, and at a later date to the mercantile greatness of Carthage, is now the least civilised of all the quarters of the globe, and why, as known in Greek and Roman history, it comprised little more than the Valley of the Nile and the comparatively small tracts of fertile country bordering on the Mediterranean, lands which belong rather to Europe and Asia than to the continent of which they geographically form part.

Early exploration of Africa. Phœnician and Carthaginian voyages.

It would be beyond the scope of this book to discuss how far in classical and pre-classical times Africa was explored, what were the bounds of Libya, as it was then called, and where the tribes and races, whose names are recounted by Herodotus, had their dwelling-place. There seems no reason to doubt the far-famed voyage of the Phœnicians about 600 B.C., who, at the command of Necho, king of Egypt, started from the Red Sea, sailed round Africa, and within three years returned to Egypt by the Straits of Gibraltar, telling to an unbelieving world that, in the course of their travels, they had the sun on their right hand. But it was a barren enterprise, fraught with danger, real and imaginary; it opened no fresh trade route; and, if the southern Cape was passed this once, no subsequent voyagers in ancient times seem to have sailed so far again. In the same passage of Herodotus[1] we read of one Sataspes, a Persian of noble birth, but a convicted criminal, who was sent by Xerxes with a Carthaginian crew to sail round Libya from west to east. Though more than a hundred years had passed since the former venture, this task was imposed as an alternative to a lingering death; and, daunted by the difficulties and currents of the West African coast, the

---

[1] Hdt. iv. 42. 3. The statement that the Phœnicians had the sun on their right hand proves that they crossed the Equator into the southern hemisphere.

unfortunate man turned home again and met his fate. Yet to the trading nations of old, to the Phœnicians and their Carthaginian descendants, Africa was not wholly a blank. Down the Red Sea went the Phœnician merchants to bring back to the Mediterranean world the spices of the East. The coast of East Africa was, it would seem, included with the shores of Asia under the general name of Ophir; while Aden, close to Africa, was a great emporium of merchandise, and found a place in later Greek geography with Perim and Socotra—the island of Dioscorides[1].

CHAPTER II.

Nor on the West was all dark beyond the Pillars of Hercules—the gates of the inland sea. Outside them was placed the Phœnician city of Gades—in oldest days a centre for an Atlantic traffic, as it was in after times the port of entry for the riches of Spanish America. The Canary Islands and Madeira, the legendary Isles of the Blest, were most probably known to the Phœnicians and Carthaginians, and possibly were within the limits of their sea-going trade[2]. Along the coast of Morocco, Hanno, the Carthaginian, in 450 B.C. planted a series of colonies; and he himself sailed

---

[1] See vol. i. of this work, pp. 54-5, chap. on 'The British Dependencies at the mouth of the Red Sea.' Alexander the Great was said to have planted a Greek colony in Socotra.

[2] As to how far the Canaries and Madeira were known to the nations of antiquity, see Heeren's Historical Researches, Asiatic and African Nations; Humboldt's Kosmos; Mr. Major's introduction to the Conquest of the Canaries (published for the Hakluyt Society, 1872), &c., &c. Gibbon, in his first chapter, has the following characteristic note: 'M. de Voltaire, unsupported by either fact or probability, has generously bestowed the Canary islands on the Roman empire.' In the reign of Augustus, Juba, king of Mauretania, sent an expedition to explore the Fortunate islands. A fragment of the report of the expedition, preserved in Pliny's Natural History, gives to one of the islands the name of Canaria, 'so called on account of the great number of large dogs therein.' Nivaria, the name of another island, according to Mr. Major, 'clearly indicates the snowy peak of Teneriffe, almost constantly capped with clouds,' the origin of the name being the same as that of the West Indian island of Nevis. (See vol. ii. of this work, p. 133 and note.) Madeira, the 'wooded' island, was shown on a Genoese map dated 1351, under the title of Isola de la Legname, or 'Island of Wood' (Major's Discoveries of Prince Henry the Navigator, 1877, chap. 5).

12 *HISTORICAL GEOGRAPHY OF THE COLONIES.*

Section I.
south down Africa to the Senegal and Gambia, if not as far as Sierra Leone. From Herodotus it may be inferred that Carthage trafficked by sea with the Gold Coast, and on land, owing to her command of the caravan routes of the Sahara, with Upper Egypt on the one side and the countries of the Niger on the other. In short, antiquarian researches have tended to show that in old days the Semitic settlers on the Mediterranean shores knew something of the northern half of Africa —more at any rate than Europeans knew before the days of Prince Henry of Portugal[1]; and the aggry beads, which are to this day found in West Africa, have been held to be of Egyptian or Phœnician make, and to be evidence of a trading connexion between the North and West of Africa in very early times[2].

Africa in Roman times.
The Old World ran its course. Egypt, the Phœnician cities, Carthage with all her wealth and all her dependencies, the fair Greek settlement of Cyrene, all the northern coast of Africa became merged in the Roman empire. But along the coast-line only that empire extended. In Africa, as in Asia[3], the Romans were in no sense pioneers of civilisation among savage races; they were not explorers of strange lands; they kept within well-known limits and ruled where others had gone before; the shores of the Mediterranean were under their government and within their ken; but over the great mass of the African continent brooded deeper darkness than ever.

---

[1] Reference should be made to Heeren's Historical Researches, African Nations. Hanno's Periplus is given in Appendix 5, to vol. i. 2nd ed. Among the passages in Herodotus from which Heeren draws his deductions are Bk. iv. chaps. 181–5, and chap. 196. It is worth noticing that one of the colonies which Hanno founded on the Morocco coast was called Acra—the name of the present seat of Government on the Gold Coast.

[2] It is said that no English manufacturer has been able to imitate these beads sufficiently well to deceive the native women. See Winwood Reade's Story of the Ashantee Campaign, pp. 8–10.

[3] The expedition to Arabia in the reign of Augustus perhaps forms an exception to this statement.

Centuries passed, and at length the Arabs brought a new life into Africa, a force which is not yet spent, a religion which is still spreading. The year of the Hegira was 622 A.D.; and so great was the strength of the new religion, so irresistible was the onward movement of the followers of Mahomet, that, by 709 A.D., the whole of the North African coast had been overrun and subdued, and the two following years saw bands of Saracens cross into Spain, and give to the northern pillar of Hercules a new Arab name, Gebal Tarik, now modernised into Gibraltar[1].

CHAPTER II.

The Arabs in Africa.

Nowhere has the Arab race and the Arab religion been so successful as in Africa. 'The northern coast of Africa,' wrote Gibbon, 'is the only land in which the light of the Gospel, after a long and perfect establishment, has been totally extinguished[2]'; and in the interior, at the present day, to the north of the Equator, Christianity has hardly a foothold, whereas the religion of the Moslems is all in all. Elsewhere, in Europe and in Asia, Mohammedanism has long been a deadening creed of fatalism and decay; but here, in the dark places of the world, it has overlain the fetish worship of the negroes, and is still a living force, full of fire and energy, awakening the hearts and inspiring the lives of men. Nor was this Arab movement a mere religious crusade. It was a gradual importation, lasting through centuries, of an Eastern language and Eastern manners and mode of life into the inmost parts of Africa. Coming at first as missionaries, the Arabs planted their schools in the negro towns. Arabic became the language of education and the means of intercourse between distant tribes. In every town a Moslem quarter grew up, and larger and larger bands of converts followed their Sheikhs to holy wars. Hence have arisen the Mahdis of the Sudan at the present day; and the intensity of their fanaticism, and the

---

[1] See vol. i. of this work, p. 8.
[2] Chap. li.

SECTION I.

strength of their following, show how completely the Arabs have dominated North and Central Africa and its peoples.

Egypt was from the first as much Asiatic as African: ancient geographers hesitated whether to place it in Asia or in Africa. 'By its situation,' to quote Gibbon's words, 'that celebrated kingdom is included within the immense peninsula of Africa, but it is accessible only on the side of Asia, whose revolutions, in almost every period of history, Egypt has humbly obeyed[1].' The Phœnicians and Carthaginians, the chief colonists of the African coast, the only explorers of the continent so far as in ancient times it was explored, were of Semitic origin; and the Arabs again were an Asiatic and Semitic race. Thus, down to the opening of modern history, so far as Africa was leavened from without, the leaven came from Asia rather than from Europe. But, unlike the Phœnicians, the Arabs were not a seagoing race; they colonised by land; they did not come in here and there to holes and corners of the coast; they did not abide in trading stations by the sea; on their camels they 'navigated the great dry ocean'[2]; their road was through the desert, their sphere was the great inland plateau, the length and breadth of northern Africa.

Their work, as has been said, is still going forward; and thus, ever since the fifteenth century, ever since the time when the nations of modern Europe, having become, in a sense, solidified at home, began to send forth ships and men to other parts of the world, Africa, outside the southern peninsula, has been subjected to a double process, to two moulding influences, simultaneous but, for geographical reasons, wholly independent of each other. The manners and the religion of the East are being spread in the interior, while Christianity and the civilisation of the West are being introduced by sea.

[1] Chap. i. p. 161 (1862 ed.).
[2] See Winwood Reade's Story of the Ashantee Campaign, p. 12, from which the preceding passage has mainly been taken. The camel is not a native of Africa, but was brought in by the Arabs.

While the centre of Africa was being gradually transformed into an Eastern land, the very existence of the continent, beyond the narrow limits of antiquity, was unknown to Europe. The break-up of the Roman empire left Europe in darkness and chaos, in travail while modern nations were being formed and brought to birth, hardly holding its own against the great movement from the East which was taking Africa captive, slowly and painfully working out within its own limits a new and brighter order of things. In the Dark Ages and in the Middle Ages, Africa was to the Western peoples of Europe almost as unknown as America; it was a world beyond the horizon, waiting to be revealed when the fullness of time had come.

Chapter II.

Whatever riches came into Europe from without came from the East. From the East Genoa and Venice drew their stores of merchandise. India and China were the goal of travellers like Marco Polo. To the East men's minds and eyes were turned, as to the birthplace of the human race, the source of light and life; and when the haze, which had so long enshrouded Africa, gradually lifted before the rising sun of modern history, it disclosed to the expectant gaze of Western peoples not so much a new continent as a new road to the Indies.

The modern exploration of Africa was due to the desire to find a new way to the East.

French writers in past times claimed for their countrymen the honour of discovering or rather re-discovering the Gold Coast. Norman sailors from Dieppe, it was asserted, sailed thus far as early as 1364, and built a fort at Elmina in 1413. But the claim must be disallowed, as not being based on any solid foundation, and there is no question that the Portuguese were the pioneers of European discovery, trade, and settlement along the West Coast of Africa.

French claims to have been the first modern explorers of Africa.

If, however, these early French visits to the Gold Coast must be dismissed as an idle tale, it is certain that the first European settlement in the Canary Islands, which comes within the range of modern history, was of French origin.

First settlement in the Canaries.

16 *HISTORICAL GEOGRAPHY OF THE COLONIES.*

SECTION I.

Before the fifteenth century opened, these islands had been reached by Genoese and Portuguese sailors; and, in 1344, don Luis de la Cerda, of the royal house of Castile, obtained a grant of them from the Pope under the old name of the Fortunate Islands, taking himself the title of Prince of Fortune. Nothing, however, came of these high sounding words, and it was not till the year 1402 that the Canary Islands, or rather some of them, were colonised from the West of Europe. In that year, Jean de Bethencourt, a Norman baron, whose estate lay not far from Dieppe, sailed from Rochelle with a small company, and established himself in the island of Lanzarote, as it was afterwards called, whence he extended his dominion over other of the islands, reducing the natives to vassalage, and bringing them to the Christian faith. He was engaged in his work of conquest and colonisation for some three years, and finally went home in 1405, leaving his nephew to govern in his stead. Bethencourt's backing came principally from Castile, and to the King of Castile he did homage as his over-lord; but, some years after his departure, his nephew, on leaving the colony, ceded his uncle's rights first to the Castilians, and subsequently to Prince Henry of Portugal. Thus for a while the sovereignty of the islands was claimed by both Spain and Portugal, until a treaty of 1479 gave them to the Crown of Castile, in whose possession they have remained down to the present day [1].

And in Madeira.

North of the Canaries, and further from the coast of Africa, the island of Madeira is reputed to have been the scene of a mediæval settlement, or rather of a mediæval romance, the hero of which was an Englishman. The story runs that, in the reign of Edward III, about the year 1344, a young man named Robert Machin eloped with Anne d'Arfet or Dorset, a lady of noble birth; and, sailing from the port of Bristol for France, was carried out to sea as far as Madeira.

---

[1] See Mr. Major's edition of the Conquest of the Canaries (Hakluyt Soc. 1872), and Helps' Spanish Conquest in America, Bk. I. chap. i.

There the lovers soon died; but one of the survivors of the company, after a period of captivity in Morocco, was brought to Portugal, and the report of his adventures contributed to the re-discovery of the island in 1419-20 by the captains of Prince Henry the Navigator[1].

In the list of men of all times, who have done good work in the world, few names stand as high as that of Prince Henry of Portugal. His character was pure and disinterested to a wonderful degree, and his life is well summed up in the motto which he took for himself, 'Talent de bien faire[2].' He combined intense love of science with practical ability in peace and war. He had religious enthusiasm to carry him forward, and a calm steadfastness, which made him content to sow, leaving to later generations the fruits of his patient work. Beyond all others, he was the father of modern discovery, the man who taught the European world to brave the perils and win the secrets of the great dim ocean, the first and well nigh the noblest figure in modern history. He was born on Ash Wednesday in the year 1394, almost exactly a century before his countrymen found their way round the Cape of Good Hope. His father was King John the First of Portugal, a patriot king 'of good memory': his mother was a Plantagenet princess, Philippa, daughter of John of Gaunt, Duke of Lancaster. Thus Portuguese and English blood mingled in his veins; he drew life from two widely different races, but each destined in their time to lead the world in discovery and colonisation; and, if from his father he inherited the chivalrous daring of the Southerner, his English mother gave him tenacity of purpose and constancy of mind. In 1415, he made his name at the taking of Ceuta, the southern pillar of Hercules, from the Moors; and,

CHAPTER II.

Prince Henry the Navigator.

---

[1] See Mr. Major's Discoveries of Prince Henry the Navigator, 1877. The story of Robert Machin has given to a village of Madeira the name of Machico.

[2] 'Talent' meant 'desire' or 'aspiration.' See Mr. Major's Discoveries of Prince Henry the Navigator, p. 43.

SECTION I.

having there struck a strong blow for Christianity and for Portugal, having given his country a firm footing in Africa, having widened by contact with the Arabs his knowledge of geography and commerce, he set his mind more and more as a patriot, as a religious enthusiast, as a scientific discoverer, to explore the coast of Guinea and find a new road to the Indies. At the extreme south-west of Portugal, near the port of Lagos, the bare rocky promontory of Sagres—the Sacrum Promontorium of the Romans—looks out on to the Atlantic; and here, at the end of Europe, on the brink of the outer ocean, Prince Henry, in or about the year 1418, stationed himself and built his observatory. Here, year after year, he studied maps and the stars, sending ship after ship down the African coast, unfaltering in his convictions, unmoved by failure, gradually lifting the veil from land and sea.

The first Portuguese voyages down the West African coast.

Great were the difficulties with which he had to contend, slow and laborious was the progress of discovery. Cape Non, i.e. Cape 'Not,' Cape No Further, near the southern boundary of Morocco, then marked the horizon; and beyond it for 1100 miles, to the mouth of the Senegal, stretches an inhospitable coast, without harbours and without rivers. He had to train his sailors to face the real dangers of these desert shores, and the still greater perils with which the human imagination ever credits the unknown.

In 1418, two members of his household, driven out to sea by a storm, reached the little island of Porto Santo, and in the following year the neighbouring land of Madeira was discovered. Steps were taken to colonise these islands, and the first governor of Porto Santo, a man named Perestrello, deserves mention as having been the father-in-law of Columbus[1].

---

[1] Columbus married the daughter of Perestrello after the latter's death, and with his wife visited and spent some time in Porto Santo. The first of the Azores (so called from the hawks which were found there) was discovered in 1431, and the larger islands of the group between 1440 and 1450.

In 1434 a great step forward was taken. Cape Bojador, the 'bulging' cape, off which the Atlantic currents ran perilously strong, was doubled in that year; and the Portuguese sailors now began to work their way southward along the barren coast of the Great Desert. An expedition, sent out in 1441, brought back some Moorish captives; and the hopes, which were thus raised, of catching and converting the heathen led to the issue of a papal Bull, granting to the Portuguese an exclusive right to the possession and dominion of all the lands which they might discover from Cape Bojador to the Indies. In the following year, two of the Moors were exchanged for ten negro slaves and some gold dust—first instalments of the two baleful products, the existence of which subsequently brought such untold misery upon West Africa. More slaves were obtained from the bay of Arguin in 1443; and, in 1444, a syndicate or company seems to have been formed at the port of Lagos, the first of many companies established by different nations for exploiting the West Coast of Africa. The principal figure in it was Lanzarote, a late retainer of Prince Henry's household, whose name is borne by one of the Canary Islands[1]; and its firstfruits were 200 slaves, of whom Prince Henry received one fifth by way of royalty.

Chapter II.

Cape Bojador rounded.

Beginning of the negro slave trade.

As yet the land of the negroes had not been reached, and such slaves as were brought to Europe had been procured through the Moors of the Desert. In 1445, however, Dinis Diaz passed the mouth of the river Senegal, discovered Cape Verde—the westernmost point of Africa, and came back to Portugal with four negroes whom he had taken in their own country.

The Senegal and the coast of the Sudan reached.

The Senegal divides the Sahara from the Sudan. It marks with sharp contrast the boundary between the dry, bare waste of northern desert, the home of wandering tribes of brown-skinned men, and the fixed dwelling-places, the

[1] See above, p. 16.

20   HISTORICAL GEOGRAPHY OF THE COLONIES.

SECTION I.

towns and cornfields, of the negroes who dwell upon its southern bank. Thus at last, after years of toilsome voyages, the Portuguese had reached a settled and a watered land, a country which gave promise of great wealth, and which, difficult as it had been to reach, was after all not far from home. The French are now masters of the Senegal; and the northernmost British possession in West Africa is on the Gambia river some 240 miles farther down the coast.

The Gambia reached.

The first Portuguese to reach the Gambia were the members of an ill-fated expedition, which started in 1446, and nearly all of whom, including their leader Nuño Tristam, perished at the hands of the natives. It was left to a young Venetian,

Cadamosto. named Cadamosto, acting under Prince Henry's guidance, to explore the river ten years later in two voyages undertaken in 1455 and 1456[1], to fight and to trade with the negroes, and to leave a full account, for the benefit of afterages, of the scenes and results of his travels.

Death of Prince Henry.

Prince Henry's life was by this time drawing to a close. Though much work had been done, much still remained; and he was not destined to see the full results of his long unselfish devotion to the cause of science and discovery. But, ere he died, he had taught his countrymen their lesson; he had trained them to press on to the south, to reach year after year some new cape, some new river, some further landmark on the African coast. He had made the way comparatively easy for after-comers; for, by the time of his death, men's hearts were hardened and their imaginations fired to seek and to find new lands of promise. He died in November, 1460, in the 67th year of his age.

When the Portuguese thus lost their great counsellor, the furthest point reached on the western coast of Africa was the mouth of the Rio Grande, which still belongs to Portugal,

---

[1] On the second voyage, Cadamosto discovered the Cape Verde Islands. An earlier date is sometimes assigned to their discovery.

and which is situated midway between the Gambia and Sierra Leone. The latter peninsula, the Mountain of the Lions, so called from the noise of roaring thunder, lies about 500 miles to the south of the Gambia. It was sighted shortly after Prince Henry's death, in 1461 or 1462; and its discoverer, Pedro de Cintra, sailed on as far as Cape Mesurado, in what is now the territory of Liberia. Then for a few years little progress was made, for men missed the master-mind which had so long given them guidance. But the rulers of Portugal inherited, with the blood, something of Prince Henry's spirit, and the work of exploration had now been carried on long enough to have become commercially profitable. In 1461, a fort was begun on the island of Arguin to give protection to the trade in gold; and in 1469, King Alfonso, nephew of the great prince, from his conquests in North Africa surnamed the African, farmed out the traffic of the African coast to Fernando Gomez for five years, on condition that in each of these five years 300 miles of coast should be explored, beginning from Sierra Leone. No time was lost in carrying out the contract. Passing on from Sierra Leone, explorers skirted the shores to which the name of the Grain Coast was afterwards given, and which are now included in the Liberian Republic: they rounded Cape Palmas, where the coast-line turns north-east and east into the Gulf of Guinea: they sailed by lands known in after years as the Ivory Coast, the Gold Coast, and the Slave Coast: they found and christened the islands of Fernando Po, St. Thomas, and Annobon[1]: and, within two years, they carried the Portuguese flag across the Equator, into the

CHAPTER II.

Sierra Leone sighted.

The fort of Arguin.

Fernando Gomez.

The Guinea Coast discovered.

The Equator passed.

---

[1] Fernando Po, supposed to have been discovered at this time, and at first called Formosa, was subsequently christened after the name of its discoverer. The island of St. Thomas was sighted on St. Thomas's Day, 1470; and the island of Annobon, which lies south of the Equator, is said to have been discovered on New Year's Day, 1471. Hence the name Anno Bom, Good Year.

southern hemisphere. Cape St. Catherine, two degrees south of the equinoctial line, was the furthest point reached before the death of King Alfonso, which took place in the year 1481.

In one of these expeditions, probably in 1471, two commanders whom Gomez had sent out, Joao de Santarem and Pedro de Escobar, first landed on the Gold Coast—in Portuguese phrase the coast of La Mina, and there trafficked for gold at a village named Sama. When in ten years' time King John the Second succeeded his father Alfonso on the throne of Portugal, one of his first acts was to build and garrison a fort at a neighbouring point on this same coast, which was given the name of San Jorge de Mina, and is known as Elmina at the present day. This, the first European settlement on the West Coast of Africa, is now in British hands, being one of the principal stations of the Gold Coast colony. Commerce was thus following in the track of exploration, but exploration went on fast and far; and in 1484 Diogo Cam reached the Congo, where his just and kindly dealings won the hearts of the natives, and in a few years' time brought about a rapid spread of the Christian faith.

In the twelfth and thirteenth centuries, there was through Europe a widely spread belief, that somewhere in the far East a great Christian king and conqueror held sway, a champion of the true religion against Moslem and infidel. This legendary potentate, who was a kind of Will o' the Wisp to mediæval travellers, was given the name of Presbyter or Prester John; and, at a much later date, the legend was localised, and Prester John identified with the King of Abyssinia[1]. At the time when the Congo was reached,

---

[1] The story of Prester John has been analysed by Sir Henry Yule in Cathay and the Way Thither (vol. i. pp. 173-82) in the Hakluyt Society's Series, and also in his Book of Marco Polo (2nd ed. 1875, vol. i. pp. 229-33).

a tale came to Portugal, from negro sources, of some monarch in Central Africa, whose description seemed to tally with that of Prester John; and, fired by the accounts which he received, the Portuguese King determined once for all to make every effort to find a way to the East.

CHAPTER II.

Two expeditions were sent out, one by sea, the other by land. The first discovered the Cape of Good Hope but did not cross the Indian sea: while the travellers, who were sent by the overland route, successfully accomplished the object of their journey and reached India.

The first expedition started at the end of August in 1486. It consisted only of two small ships of fifty tons each, with a still smaller boat as tender, but it was led by a strong, determined man, Bartholomew Diaz[1], one of a family of explorers. Sailing past the newly discovered Congo, tacking and turning with the wind, Diaz reached Cape Voltas, the Cape of 'turns,' near the mouth of the Orange river. Driven southwards from thence by storm for thirteen days, he beat up again east and north hoping to find land. He found it at length, but the coast was now stretching in an easterly instead of southerly direction, for, without knowing it, he had rounded the southernmost point of Africa. The land which he sighted was the shore of Vleesch or Flesh bay, near the Gouritz river. Sailing still east, he set up a cross on a small island in Algoa bay, which still bears the name of Santa Cruz or St. Croix; and subsequently reached the mouth of the Great Fish river, which in modern times was long the eastern limit of the Cape Colony. Here he turned back, not of his own will but in deference to the fears of his crew; and, on his return journey along the coast, he sighted, first of modern sailors, that great landmark since so familiar in both history and geography, which now out of all the numberless points of land on the

Bartholomew Diaz rounds the Cape.

---

[1] He was related to Dinis Diaz mentioned above, p. 19.

24 HISTORICAL GEOGRAPHY OF THE COLONIES.

SECTION I.

earth's surface has appropriated the generic name of 'the Cape.' At the time, the tempest-tossed sailor christened it the Stormy Cape; but, on his return to Portugal in December 1487, the King, from promise of good things to come, gave it a more cheering name—the Cape of Good Hope.

India reached by the Portuguese overland.

Some eight months after Diaz had started on his voyage to the south, two men were sent out, whose mission it was to make their way into the Indian seas by an overland eastern route. Their names were Pedro de Covilham and Alfonso de Payva. Journeying by Naples and Rhodes to Alexandria and Cairo, they reached the shores of the Red Sea and crossed over to Aden, then a great entrepôt of eastern trade, and described, a few years later, by the Bolognese traveller Ludovico di Varthema as 'the rendezvous for all the ships which come from India Major and Minor, from Ethiopia, and from Persia[1].' Here the two travellers parted company; Payva went to Abyssinia; and Covilham, taking passage in an Arab ship, reached Cananore on the Malabar coast, from whence he went to Calicut and Goa—the first Portuguese who ever landed in India. From Goa he crossed over to Eastern Africa, examined the gold mines at Sofala, and gathered news of the island of Madagascar, styled by the Moors the island of the Moon. Returning to Egypt in 1490, he heard of the death of his fellow traveller, and met with messengers sent by King John to learn how his journey had sped. By one of them he sent the cheering message 'that the ships, which sailed down the coast of Guinea, might be sure of reaching the termination of the continent, by persisting in a course to the south; and that, when they should arrive in the eastern ocean, their best direction must be to enquire for Sofala and the island of the Moon.' Thus Portuguese sailors rounded the Cape, and a Portuguese traveller reached India. One link alone was yet to be forged in the chain of

---

[1] See the Travels of Ludovico di Varthema [Hakluyt Soc. Ed. 1863, p. 60]. Varthema visited Aden in 1503.

discovery, one last task was yet to be performed: the ships which came from the West had still to work their way up the south-eastern coast of Africa, and, turning over the Indian Ocean, to complete the sea route to the East. Some few years passed before the goal was reached. Troubles at home in Portugal, and the sickness of the King, delayed its fulfilment; and the New World beyond the Atlantic was discovered five years before the toil and daring of the Portuguese was finally crowned with success.

In 1495, King John 'the perfect prince' was succeeded by his cousin Manuel 'the Fortunate.' Like his predecessors, the new ruler of Portugal was staunch to the cause of discovery, and in 1497 he sent Vasco da Gama on his far-famed voyage. Bold, resolute, resourceful, ruthless, Da Gama seems to have combined the best and worst qualities of his time and race, the courage which ensured success, the cruelty which darkened it. On March 25, or on July 8, for accounts differ [1], he sailed with four ships, his starting-point being a chapel some four miles from Lisbon, which had been set up by Prince Henry for the spiritual comfort of outward-bound sailors, and where King Manuel subsequently built the church of Bethlehem or Belem. After prayer and absolution, the expedition set sail, amid the tears and forebodings of the people of Lisbon, for the way was dark and dangerous, and the Portuguese nation did not share the high hopes of the Portuguese King. In November they doubled the Cape; and, after encountering storm and tempest and the southern sweep of the Mozambique current [2], on

CHAPTER II.

The voyage of Vasco da Gama.

---

[1] See the Three Voyages of Vasco da Gama, edited for the Hakluyt Society by the Hon. H. E. J. Stanley, 1879, pp. 37, 52, notes. The other dates of the voyage are also variously given.

[2] This current flows south between the island of Madagascar and the African coast; and, in consequence of it, the Portuguese named the point on the mainland opposite the southern end of Madagascar, Cape Corrientes. Sir G. Birdwood in his Report on the Old Records of the India Office, pp. 158, 162, points out that this current had been an obstacle to the southward voyages of the Arabs on the east of Africa, just as on the west coast the currents off Cape Bojador had been an obstacle to the Phoenicians and Carthaginians sailing south.

SECTION I.

Christmas Day they again sighted land, and called it Natal in honour of the birthday, the dies Natalis, of the Christian religion. Sailing on up the East African coast, they came to the island of Mozambique, to **Mombasa**, and Melinde, which they reached on **Easter Day, April 15, 1498**; and, taking a pilot from this last-named place, they went eastward over the ocean, until, on May 17, they came within view of the long-sought shores of India. Three days later, on May 20, they anchored off the town of Calicut. The return journey was by the same route. Melinde was reached early in January, 1499; on March 20 following, the Cape was again doubled; and, at the end of August or the beginning of September, they sailed into the Tagus honoured of all men. Thus the work was done at which generations had toiled, and the new way to the Indies was opened up at last.

Thenceforward, until in our own days the cutting of the Suez canal brought back the commerce of nations to its old channel, the high road between East and West was no longer by the overland and Red Sea route, but across the southern ocean and round the southern cape.

Thus Africa was opened and closed again; its fate was sealed for centuries; its coasts were to be visited, its gold exported, and its natives enslaved; but it was to be merely a handmaid to the far East and the far West, seeing the coming and going of men, with all its vast interior unheeded and unknown.

The beginning of Modern history.

Modern history dates from the fifteenth century. Its birthplace was Portugal, its father Prince Henry the Navigator. The time had come, the chosen people, and the man. The discovery of America and the rounding of the Cape must not be regarded as isolated events, standing alone in solitary grandeur. They were but incidents, though the most striking incidents, in a world-wide movement. The century, which ended with the great deeds of Columbus and Vasco da Gama, had seen the last lingering remains of the Roman empire swallowed up, when in 1453 Constantinople was taken by the Turks. The book of the past was then at length finally closed, the eastern half of the ancient Mediterranean world was merged in Asia, and the western half, cut adrift from its old moorings, turned its back on bygone days and found in itself a new starting-point for the future.

As the centre of life shifted westward, it passed through the peninsula, which on one side looks on to the inner sea, on the other on to the open ocean, and which was thus marked out on the map to be the connecting link between the old and the new. Here, at this western outpost of the then known world, in the land between the Mediterranean and the Atlantic, in the corner of Europe which nearly touched Africa, where the Arabs and their religion first crossed into Europe, the West began to assert itself against the East; modern history was made; nations were formed, and gathered strength by constant struggle within a limited area against an alien people and an alien creed; and Spain and Portugal came to lead the world. Of these two, Portugal, lying more securely on the western side of the peninsula, became a country, and her inhabitants became a nation, at an earlier date than was the case with Spain; and, having done their work at home, the Portuguese, like all young peoples, began to make themselves felt abroad. But they lived in a narrow land, shut in on the west by the sea, on the north and east by the growing Spanish Kingdoms; their only outlet was towards the south, on the south was welcome war against the Moorish enemies of their faith, and so they pressed forward into Africa.

'Portugal,' says Professor Freeman, 'led the way among European states to conquest and colonisation out of Europe. She had a geographical and historical call so to do. Her dominion out of Europe . . . was not actually continuous with her own European territory, but it began near to it, and it was a natural consequence and extension of her European

SECTION I.

advance. The Asiatic and American dominion of Portugal grew out of her African dominion, and her African dominion was a continuation of her growth in her own peninsula[1].' The southward expansion of Portugal was the natural outcome of circumstance and of geographical position, and in this sense the African discoveries of the Portuguese were the outward and visible sign of a national movement. But, if the movement was national, it was not popular. The people of Portugal may have been glad to fight near home for the Cross against the Crescent, but there was no popular enthusiasm for Atlantic voyages. When two-thirds of a century had been spent in tracing out the coast of Africa, when only one crowning act remained to be done, when the discovery of America for Spain might naturally have awakened the spirit of national rivalry, it was against the people's will and amid ill-omened lamentations that Vasco da Gama was sent out to sail to India. It was the princes and rulers of Portugal who pressed on discovery, it was their personal followers who did the deeds. The nation shared the glory of the enterprise and its rich results, but they shared it in spite of themselves.

Among these princes who proved so strong and true, one figure stands out above all others. 'The grand impulse to discovery was not given by chance, but was the deeply meditated effort of one master-mind[2].' From Prince Henry the Navigator came all the inspiration and all the guidance. The names of explorers, who were great when he was gone, are better known to the world than his; but, tried by the highest standard, he takes the first place. Scientific and far-seeing as Columbus was, he went to work when new coasts and islands had been already found, when technical and general knowledge had made some way, when sailors had begun to trust the sea; and, after all, in sailing to America,

---

[1] Freeman's Historical Geography of Europe, chap. xii. sect. 3.
[2] Thus Washington Irving writes of Prince Henry of Portugal in the Life and Voyages of Columbus, bk. i. chap. 3.

he cast his bread upon the waters and found it after not so many days. Prince Henry, on the other hand, made the first beginning; he told his captains where to go and what they would find; he taught them to despise fabulous dangers, to overcome those which were real; they came back year after year and proved his words, and then he doggedly worked out some further problem.

In the course of human affairs it must needs be that great movements will come, but honour to the men by whom they come. If ever the agency of individual men can be traced in history, then the hand, which drew back the curtain and let in the bright light of day on more than half the world, was the hand of Prince Henry of Portugal.

BOOKS RELATING TO THE SUBJECT OF THIS CHAPTER.

Among many standard works, the following are mentioned for convenient reference :—

HELPS' *Spanish Conquest in America*, Book I.

MAJOR'S *Discoveries of Prince Henry the Navigator* [1877].

Sir G. BIRDWOOD'S *Report on the Old Records of the India Office* [1891].

SECTION II.

THE WEST AFRICAN DEPENDENCIES.

CHAPTER I.

INTRODUCTORY—THE WEST COAST OF AFRICA.

SECTION II.

THE West African dependencies of Great Britain are at present divided into six Colonies or Protectorates:—(1) The Gambia, (2) Sierra Leone, (3) the Gold Coast, (4) Lagos, (5) the territories of the Royal Niger Company, and (6) the Niger Coast Protectorate.

The tabular statement given above on page 3 shows, as in the case of other parts of the empire, how and when these West African possessions were acquired by Great Britain, and what is their present area and population; but the statement is approximate only, and, if taken by itself alone, might be to some extent misleading. As a matter of fact, these dependencies have been built up bit by bit during the course of three centuries, and the same process is still going on. They consist partly of British territory, and partly of districts which are only under British protection or within the range of British influence. The Colony and Protectorate of the Gambia, and the Colony and Protectorate of the Gold Coast, have grown out of the operations of a trading Company formed in 1618, which

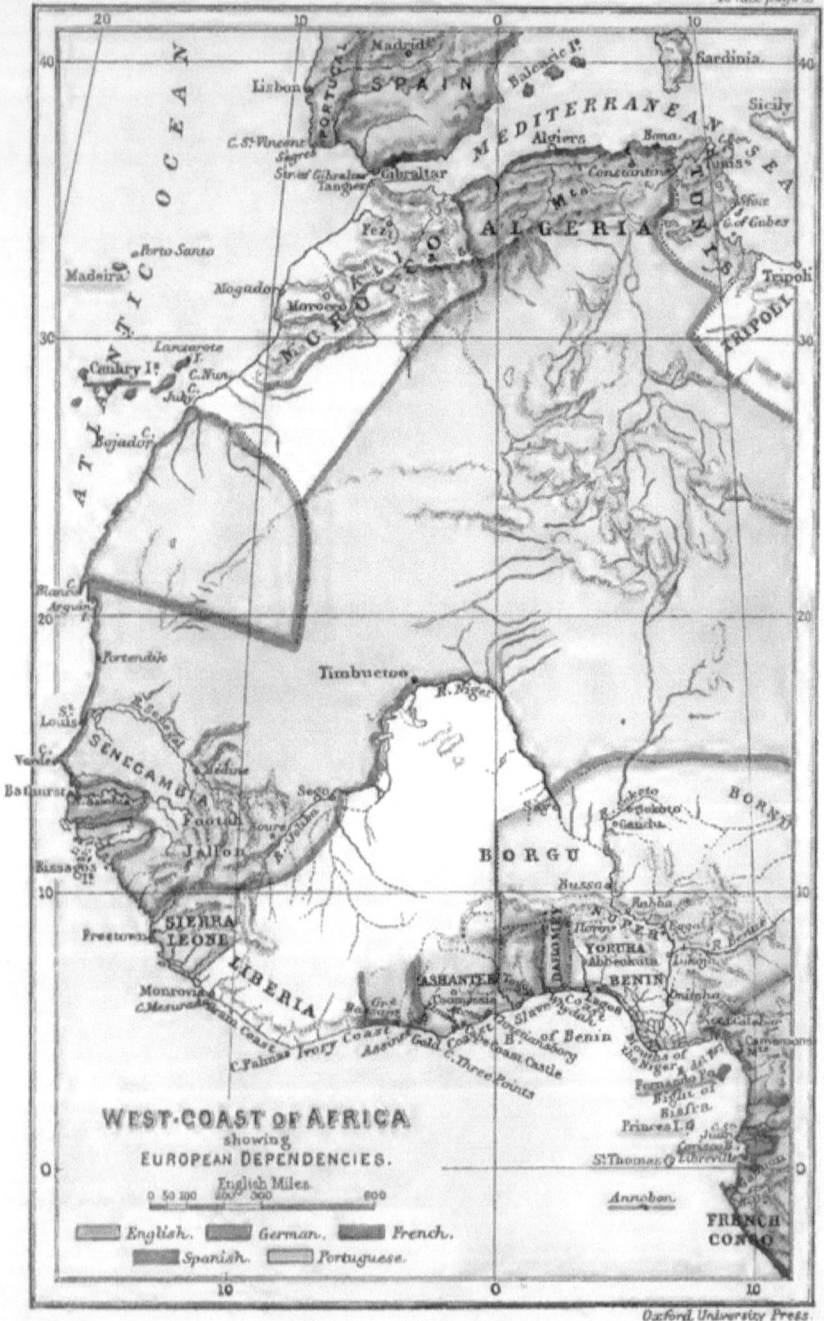

set up one fort upon an island in the Gambia[1], and another at Cormantine upon the Gold Coast. The peninsula of Sierra Leone was first acquired in 1787, by a company formed for the purpose of establishing a colony of liberated African slaves in their native country, and has since been a nucleus from which British rule has gradually been extended over the adjacent territories. The Colony and Protectorate of Lagos date only from 1861, when the native ruler of Lagos, unable to prevent his land from being used for the purposes of the slave trade, was compelled to cede it to the British government. The territories of the Royal Niger Company, and the Niger Coast Protectorate, are still later acquisitions, having only been definitely secured to Great Britain since 1884-5.

CHAPTER I.

The Gambia, which is about a hundred miles south of Cape Verde, the westernmost point of Africa, and Sierra Leone, some 500 miles further down on the same section of the coast, look westward over the Atlantic. The other dependencies are upon the coast of the Gulf of Guinea, and face for the most part towards the south. The two groups are separated by some 700 miles of coast: but they are all to the north of the Equator, and in that portion of West Africa which is sometimes called Upper Guinea.

Two main groups of British dependencies on the West Coast of Africa.

When in the fifteenth century the Portuguese explored the western coast of Africa, they gave the name of Guinea 'to all the countries they successively discovered from the river Senega to that of Camarones[2], ... and many have

The 'Guinea' coast.

---

[1] This fort, Fort James, was abandoned after the abolition of the slave trade, and it would perhaps be more accurate to say that the present colony on the Gambia dates from 1816 than from 1618. See below, pp. 58, 98, 117, 157.

[2] From the Introduction to the Description of the Coasts of North and South Guinea by John Barbot, Agent General of the Royal Company of Africa and the Islands of America at Paris, written in 1682, and published in Churchill's Voyages, vol. v. The writer also remarks that ' Ptolemy, in the second century, says, concerning the name of Guinea, that it is a word of the country, and signifies hot and dry.' But the natives are strangers to the term, as Barbot points out; and a name meaning hot

SECTION II.

since extended this name of Guinea to the country still southward ... as far as Cape Negro in 16° of south latitude.' The English and the Dutch, both of whom adopted the name, are said to have differed very much in the extent to which they applied it. During the seventeenth and eighteenth centuries, however, when the term was most in vogue, it seems to have been used by both the two trading nations to cover much the same area as had been assigned to it by the Portuguese. The Guinea Coast began at the mouth of the Senegal or at Cape Verde, and extended to the head of the great bay which is still called the Gulf of Guinea. At the present time, if used at all, the name is usually confined to the northern shores of the Gulf, where the gold was found from which 'guineas[1]' were coined; but in geographical works it is sometimes employed to denote the whole of the coast between the Sahara or Great Desert on the north, and the South African or Kalahari Desert on the south; and this long extent of coast-line is again divided into Upper and Lower Guinea by the Equator.

British West Africa is all North of the Equator.

North of the Equator is the land of gold. North of the Equator too is that part of the African continent which stretches out furthest towards America. When the coast of Africa had once been explored, and when the New World had been discovered, gold for Europe and slaves for the American colonies were the two great attractions which brought European traders to the West Coast of Africa.

and dry, however appropriate to the Sahara, would be singularly inappropriate to Guinea, which is notoriously damp. The etymology of the name Guinea seems to be quite uncertain.

[1] Guineas will be found referred to in Pepys' Diary. 'Lord Braybrooke, in his edition of the Diary, vol. iv. p. 11 (1890), gives the following note on the subject: 'Guineas took their name from the gold brought from Guinea by the African company, who, as an encouragement to bring over gold to be coined, were permitted, by their charter from Charles II, to have their stamp of an elephant upon the coin. There were likewise five-pound pieces, like the guinea, with the inscription upon the rim, like the crown piece.'

Consequently the peoples, who followed the Portuguese in Africa, stopped short at the Equator; or, if sailing to the East, they no longer skirted the mainland, but shaped their course straight for the southern Cape. Thus West Africa, south of the Equator, remained till latter days an undisputed part of the Portuguese dominions; and it was only in the northern hemisphere that French, Dutch, Danes, and English plied their trade and built their factories. The term West Africa, therefore, as far as the British colonial empire is concerned, is confined to the northern half of the continent.

Again, when reference is made to European trade and settlement in this part of the world, it is usual to speak not of West Africa so much as of the West Coast of Africa, or more shortly of the 'West Coast.' This geographical limitation represents actual historical facts. More than four centuries have passed since Prince Henry's ships came sailing into African seas, yet it is still on the coast alone that Europeans have established a firm footing. The British settlements are almost entirely coast settlements, forts and stations by the sea. The trade of the Gambia, of the Gold Coast, and of Lagos is at present almost entirely confined to the low-lying districts of the coast; and, if the products, which are shipped at Sierra Leone, have of late years come from a greater distance inland, if the Niger brings down the commerce of the western Sudan to be carried to Europe in British ships, this trade developement is of comparatively recent date, indicating, it may be, the extension of British influence, but not as yet in any true sense the spread of British colonisation into the interior of Africa.

The three great rivers of Upper Guinea are the Senegal, the Gambia, and the Niger. The Senegal and the Gambia rise within a short distance of each other, little more than 200 miles from the sea-coast, upon the northern or north-eastern slopes of the mountainous country of Footah Jallon, which lies to the north of Sierra Leone; they then flow north

SECTION II.

and west, until they empty themselves into the Atlantic, the Senegal about 140 miles to the north, and the Gambia about 100 miles to the south, of Cape Verde, the westernmost point of Africa. The Niger, on the other hand, starts in an easterly direction and takes a semicircular course. Flowing first towards the north-east, to the borders of the great desert and the far-famed city of Timbuctoo, it there turns due east for some 200 miles; subsequently, taking a sharp bend towards the south-east, it continues in that direction as far as the junction with the Benue river; and finally, flowing due south, it pours itself by many mouths into the sea at the head of the Gulf of Guinea, the length of its whole course being about 2500 miles. Of these three rivers, the Senegal is obstructed by a dangerous bar at its mouth and by sandbanks along its channel. The Gambia, although navigable by ocean-going vessels for about 250 miles from the sea, does not lead beyond the coast region. The Niger alone gives access to the interior; but its mouth is barred to ships of any considerable size, and it is only of late years that the tribes who dwell along its banks have come to terms with European peoples and given facilities for trade. There are other smaller rivers in this region, many in number, but they are no more than local streams; they flow only from the outside edge of the great plateau, and water only the coast-line—the West Coast of Africa.

The present partition of the West Coast.

The whole of this coast, from Cape Bojador to the Equator, has now, with the exception of Liberia, been divided between different European powers.

The northernmost part, extending from Cape Bojador[1] to Cape Blanco, is claimed by Spain. From Cape Blanco round Cape Verde, to a point rather over 30 miles north of the peninsula of Sierra Leone, the coast belongs to France, with the two following exceptions—1. The Gambia river, with the

---

[1] According to the latest maps, the Spanish claim begins north of Cape Bojador and near the southern boundary of Morocco.

strip of land immediately adjacent to its mouth and lower waters on either side, is British; and 2. between Cape Roxo on the north and the mouth of the river Cajet on the south, a small and unimportant section of the coast-line has been recognised as belonging to Portugal. It includes the estuary of the Rio Grande, the southernmost limit of Portuguese exploration at the time of Prince Henry's death[1], and it is the only part of the mainland of Africa north of the Equator which is still owned by Portugal.

The English colony of Sierra Leone extends for 220 miles between the French territory and the independent Republic of Liberia.

Beyond Liberia, the French again hold the line of the shore as far as the Gold Coast, where the British colony and Protectorate extends for 350 miles from west to east, ending at a point some little way beyond the mouth of the Volta river. Here, within narrow limits, the German Protectorate of Togoland intervenes, bounded on the east by another strip of French territory, which forms part of the sea-board of the savage Kingdom of Dahomey and includes the stations of Grand Popo, Kotonou, and Porto Novo. At the eastern limits of this latter Protectorate, marked by the Ajera creek, the British colony of Lagos begins, and extends as far as the Benin river, whence the Niger Protectorates carry on the British line to the extreme end of the Gulf of Guinea. Here the British sphere in West Africa ends, and, from the Rio del Rey southward, the region of the Cameroons has been assigned to Germany, until a point is reached about $2\frac{1}{2}°$ north of the Equator. The French equatorial possessions then begin, and stretch into the southern hemisphere as far as the river Congo. This last great tract of coast includes the Gabun and Ogowe rivers, but at one point in the line the Spaniards intervene, holding or claiming to hold Cape San Juan, and Corisco island and bay.

[1] See above, p. 20.

36 HISTORICAL GEOGRAPHY OF THE COLONIES.

SECTION II.

From this enumeration of the various European possessions in West Africa, it will be noticed that, as in old days the forts and factories of different peoples along this coast were interspersed one with another, so, at the present time, the different nations break each other's line at this point and at that, and no one of them has consolidated its dependencies so as to form a continuous stretch of territory. North of the Congo there are six separate strips of coast belonging to France, four to Great Britain, two to Germany, two to Spain, one to Portugal, and one to the Liberian Republic. The French own the longest extent of coast-line and claim dominion over the largest area, but the English have the advantage of being more centralised, and of holding stronger positions. Their dependencies do not extend very far north or very far south. They are all between 14° and 4° North latitude, all between the westernmost point of Africa and the head of the Gulf of Guinea. The mouths and lower basins of two out of the three great rivers, the Gambia and the Niger, are in British keeping; the best harbour on the mainland coast is the British harbour of Sierra Leone; and the rich Gold Coast belongs to Great Britain. Even if, by the late partitions of Africa, the French have acquired a predominating share of the 'Hinterland,' the fact remains that the main outlets of trade and the richest sections of the coast are left in British hands [1].

The English hold the strongest positions on the Coast.

Special characteristics of the respective British dependencies.

Each of the British dependencies in West Africa has its own special characteristic features, which have caused it to be included within the limits of the British empire. The Gambia has its wide, deep, and navigable river. Sierra Leone has its unrivalled harbour, valued for Imperial as well as for local purposes; it has streams which bring the produce of the coast-belt down to the sea; and it has easier

---

[1] According to the Statesman's Year Book for 1892, the total area of the French dependencies and Protectorates in West Africa north of the Equator, including the Sahara but excluding the Gabun, is 2,140,000 square miles.

land routes to the interior than are to be found at any other point in British territory. The Gold Coast, which possesses none of these advantages, whose rivers are rendered comparatively useless by bars and rapids, whose shores are harbourless and surf-bound, has yet the stores of precious metal which gave it its name in earliest times. Lagos—the lagoon colony—is placed at the outlet of a unique network of lakes and rivers, by which the trade of many miles of coast is brought to be shipped to Europe in exchange for European wares. Lastly, the Niger, difficult as it is for ocean steamers, carries boats and launches far into the interior; it gives access to thickly peopled regions of wide extent; and its Delta is the most central point on the western side of Africa.

But, though each dependency has its particular value, they have more in common than they have apart. In the seventeenth and eighteenth centuries, the forts and factories on the Gambia and the Gold Coast, although separated by more than 1,200 miles, were controlled by the same company; and twice within the nineteenth century[1] the Gambia and Sierra Leone have been united with the Gold Coast under one Governor-in-Chief. None of these places are colonies in the true sense of the word. At none of them can an Englishman live and thrive. They are all tropical dependencies. They are all cursed with the same malarious climate. All are, in the main, of the nature of trading stations by the sea, scenes of barter and exchange rather than fields of production. All have been concerned with the rise and the fall of the slave trade; and, in these brighter days, all, if the gold of the Gold Coast be excepted, send the same kind of produce, chiefly palm oil, to the country which has the good or bad fortune to own them as dependencies.

[1] From 1821 to 1828, and again from 1866 to 1874.

CHAPTER II.

EARLY EUROPEAN TRADE AND SETTLEMENT ON THE WEST COAST OF AFRICA.

SECTION II.

IN a preceding chapter it has been seen that the fifteenth century brought with it the dawn and sunrise of modern history; that the races of Western Europe then became consolidated into nations, and, led by strong men, began to enlarge their borders and work their way slowly over the sea; that the African coast, nearly continuous with Europe, was the earliest scene of discovery and exploration; and that, therefore, on this coast were placed the first forts and factories in the history of modern trade and modern colonisation.

Antiquity of European settlements in West Africa.

Newfoundland, which is commonly regarded as the oldest British colony, dates back its colonial existence to 1583, when Sir Humphrey Gilbert annexed but did not settle the island; but the Portuguese built their fort at Elmina in 1481, almost exactly a hundred years earlier, and more than 300 years before any European settlement was planted in Australia. The first point to notice, therefore, in the case of the West African dependencies is their comparative antiquity.

Variety of European peoples, which have traded and settled in West Africa.

Again, because this part of the world is near to Europe, and because it was in consequence early found out and explored, therefore nearly every colonising nation has had part and lot in its history. As the Spaniards were followed into the West Indies by English, French, Dutch, and Danes, so the same four nations dogged the footsteps of the Portuguese in West Africa; and, in the seventeenth and eighteenth centuries, when the system of tropical plantations worked by slave labour was in full force, West Africa formed one and the same sphere of colonial enterprise with the West Indies and Brazil. The Dutch West India Company monopolised not only the eastern coasts and islands of America, but also the West African coast from the tropic of Cancer to the Cape. While attacking the Portuguese in Brazil, the Dutch attacked them also in Angola, and wrested from them their fort of Elmina on the Gold Coast. The sphere of the French West India Company, again, included at one time the coast of Senegambia and Guinea. In short, as long as the slave trade lasted, the very existence of West Africa, as far as Europe was concerned, was bound up with the plantation colonies of the New World, and West African history was the complement of West Indian.

Close connexion between West Africa and the West Indies.

The only great colonising nation, which was not represented on the coast, was the Spaniards, just as the Portuguese alone were not to be found in the West Indian islands. The celebrated papal Bull of 1493, which had no binding force on later comers, marked off the eastern world for the Portuguese, and the western world for the Spaniards; and, though the former found their way to Brazil and the latter to the Philippines, they respected in the main each other's sphere of trade and settlement, and the Spaniards did not acquire their present little West African possessions of Fernando Po and Annobon till as late as the year 1778.

The Spaniards had no dealings in West Africa.

Even if it were possible, which is not the case, to treat the story of West Africa separately from that of the West Indies, it would be found that they have much in common. In the one case the Portuguese, in the other the Spaniards, ran their course. In either case, the northern nations of Europe came in gradually on the outskirts, trading, plundering, fighting side by side, making efforts at first spasmodic, afterwards more sustained, gathering boldness and strength as the Latin

European trade and settlement in West Africa and in the West Indies contrasted and compared.

SECTION II.

The climate of the West Indies is more favourable to European settlement than that of West Africa.

The West Indian Colonies have been producing colonies to a greater extent than West Africa.

peoples drooped and declined. In both cases the work done was, at the outset, rough and ready to the last degree; but, for the following reasons, the West Indies took definite form and shape in the history of European colonisation to an extent which has never been the case with West Africa.

West Africa and the West Indian islands are in the same latitudes, they both lie within the tropics, and are the nearest tropical lands to Western Europe, West Africa being the nearer of the two; but, while the West Indian islands have a comparatively healthy climate, the West African coast is notoriously unhealthy for Europeans, and even its native inhabitants suffer from the constant malaria of the low-lying shores. Hence, while the West Indies became a sphere of European settlement, and, as far as the British race is concerned, have been one of the very few tropical parts of the world where colonists from Great Britain have made a home, the West Coast of Africa has been from first to last hardly suitable even for the temporary residence of Europeans. European traders perpetually came and still come to West Africa, but they have as perpetually gone away again; they find no suitable resting-place for wives and families; they build up no society; they buy and sell; but, speaking generally, they never settle and never colonise. Under these conditions, the connexion of Europeans with West Africa has had no stability, no element of permanence, such as is to be found on the other side of the Atlantic.

Again, the West Indian colonies are places which have always been producing colonies. The first settlers grew tobacco, and sugar subsequently became the universal product. The settlements were plantations where systematic agriculture was carried on to supply the European markets; and the result of slavery was to extend, though at the same time to stereotype, the cultivation of the ground. West Africa on the contrary produced, it is true, and still produces gold in some districts; and, at the present time, it sends palm oil and similar commodities to Europe; but its products are in the main jungle products; there are few or no sugar, coffee, or tobacco plantations; the ground is not cultivated under European management on a definite system; there are no regular agricultural settlements, just as there are no great mining centres.

Further, whereas slavery in the West Indies promoted cultivation within certain limits, in West Africa it retarded it. The discovery of America converted the African coast into a great hunting-ground for procuring slave labour for the American colonies. It was impossible to develop a part of the world which was perpetually being drained of its labour supply. It was impossible at one and the same time to make war and peace, to burn villages, to kill and transport their inhabitants, and to build up agricultural communities or to carry on legitimate trade. At first Europeans trafficked with the West African natives, only kidnapping a few here and there. Then the slave trade became the one absorbing industry of the coast, with the result that West Africa was in a perpetual state of war, and the European dependencies in West Africa were simply so many fortified posts. Then came a time when forts and settlements on the coast were mainly valued, at least in the eyes of the English, for the nobler purpose of putting down the slave trade; and finally the stage has been reached, at which honest *bona fide* commerce has reasserted itself, and the West Coast settlements have become places at which Europe and Africa supply each other's wants. Thus there has been a want of continuity in the economic, as in the political, history of West Africa; there has been on the whole no steady commercial developement, just as, north of the Equator, there has been no long uninterrupted ownership of any large area by one and the same European people.

Once more, stress has already been laid on the fact that Africa is on the way to other parts of the world, and never

CHAPTER II.

Slavery promoted agricultural settlement in the West Indies, the slave trade retarded it in West Africa.

The West Indies were less a place

was, in past times, a final goal—an end in itself. Its coasts were explored to find a way to the East, and the discovery of the way to the East coincided with the discovery of America. In connexion with this point of view, it is interesting to notice a parallel to the history of West Africa in the early history of the smaller West Indian islands. Most of these little islands were constantly changing hands, whereas the continent, over against which they lie, was continuously owned by the same power. The reason was that, though quite close to America, they were not actually part of it. They were but the threshold of the New World, and there was something better beyond. Consequently the Spaniards passed them by, treating them as detached parts of their property, and after-comers owned, disowned, shared, and monopolised them in turn, just as they took up from time to time this or that point on the West Coast of Africa. But, if not actually the goal, these islands were close to it; the ownership therefore became gradually more and more continuous. West Africa, on the other hand, is far from the East, and, the more scientific navigation became, the more men passed it by, as being a little off the straight road. So the first owners, the Portuguese, in great measure neglected it; later peoples strayed into and out of it; and the one permanent element in its history was the slave trade, which turned it towards America instead of towards the East, and which at the same time made it less than ever a final resting-place, and more than ever a part of the world to be visited, raided, devastated, and left. In a word, the history of the European dependencies on the West Coast of Africa is a story of traffic not of settlement, a chronicle of broken and disjointed enterprise; its central feature is the slave trade; the New World was discovered, and West Africa was sacrificed to America.

The colonial history of Portugal flowed in a parallel channel to that of Spain. Side by side the two countries rose to greatness, side by side they gained their empires.

Beyond all other nations who conquered and colonised, they were the counterpart of each other; they coincided in time; their main lines of action were the same; the world was shared between them; and the real differences in the characters and methods of the two peoples have been to some extent obscured by the strong family resemblance which either bore to the other. Yet the points of divergence are striking and suggestive; and, as each nation took its own route over the sea, the varying circumstances of either course brought out and intensified the special national characteristics.

CHAPTER II.

compared as colonising peoples.

Portugal is a small country, Spain is a large one. The Portuguese were traders even more than conquerors, the Spaniards were conquerors alone. The Spaniards overran a Western continent, the Portuguese took and held positions which gave them command of the Eastern seas. The Spanish conquest of America was in a sense a single act. With the exception of the little islands on the north-west of Africa, the Canaries and Azores, there was nothing between the Old World and the New. There was nothing halfway in the geography; it was all or nothing in the history. The Portuguese, on the other hand, reached the East after a long series of coasting voyages, and their way to the Indies of necessity continued to be round the shores of an intermediate continent. The Spanish route was a line for a conquering race, the Portuguese route was a line for a trading race. So also when they reached the end of their voyages. The Spaniards found, it is true, two great empires, Mexico and Peru; but they were isolated organisations, which could be broken in pieces; and outside them were virgin lands, whose inhabitants were physically and politically weak. The Portuguese found Eastern kingdoms and Arab traders, a commerce of long standing, peoples not to be swept away but to be partially coerced by force of arms, partially beguiled by specious treaties, a scene for planting factories on coasts and islands, to form the nucleus of a great overlordship, but not an all unconscious world to be conquered, ruled, and enslaved.

Great as is the extent of Central and South America, it is compact as compared with the numberless peninsulas and islands of the East. There was nothing compact in the territories which the Portuguese claimed for their own. Their sphere extended from Brazil to Japan. It included West and East Africa, the Red Sea, India, the Eastern islands, and the China seas. A great nation might weld half America into connected provinces of a continental dominion, but how could a people numerically weak do more than hold points of vantage in all the lands and waters of the East?

They could not do so; their commercial instincts led them not to do so; and their previous training, as Heeren points out[1], told in the same direction. For, as compared with the Spaniards, the Portuguese were, in the field of trade and colonisation, a trained race. For years and generations they had been feeling their way, exploring by slow degrees, doing a little and again a little, finding out the worth or worthlessness of new countries, learning to refuse the evil and to choose the good. Had the Spaniards at one stroke discovered the Gold Coast with its signs of precious metal, as they discovered the gold and silver of America, they might have stayed and poured in floods of adventurers to look for Eldorado on the Upper Niger; but the Portuguese came gradually to the place, they built a fort to keep it for their own, and then they went on their way to the East—to the lands where merchants had already found more than gold.

It is true that, when at length they came to the East, their rate of progress was even faster than that of the Spaniards

[1] In the Manual of the History of the Political System of Europe and its Colonies, Tr. 1834, vol. i. pp. 39, 40.

in America. In less than twenty years from the date of Vasco da Gama's first voyage, in 1515, when Albuquerque died, they were at the height of their power, at least as strong, though not perhaps as showy, as ever they were in after years; and the extraordinary rapidity with which they pressed forward, when once they had reached the Indies, contrasts strangely with the slow and hesitating movements of their earlier voyages down the African coast. They moved so fast, and went so far, because they were in one sense less thorough, as in another they were more thorough, than the Spaniards. They did not conquer whole countries, but contented themselves with forts and towns and districts of limited size. 'The Portuguese established themselves in the Indies,' writes Pyrard de Laval[1], who visited Portuguese India in 1608-10, 'at first partly by war as in some places, and partly by friendly commerce as in others. The latter was the most successful means, for they have with difficulty taken towns by force, as they did Goa and some others'; and he adds later on, 'under all these treaties and agreements the Portuguese have managed to become masters of the Indian seas.'

Such was the nature of the Portuguese power, as compared with the power of Spain. Theirs was a sea, not a land dominion, a monopoly of trade rather than a military empire. This was the reason why, in every hole and corner of the world, the Dutch followed them up with such unrelenting pertinacity. Like was drawn to like, a small people to a small people, traders to traders. In the East, in Brazil, in West Africa, the Netherlanders, far more purely commercial than the Portuguese themselves, hunted them as rivals in trade rather than as foes of their religion and their race. The national quarrel of the Netherlands was with Spain, not with Portugal; but the Portuguese held the very places

CHAPTER II.

Characteristics of the Portuguese dominion. It was an empire of trade and therefore specially attractive to the Dutch.

---

[1] Voyage of Pyrard de Laval, translated and edited (for the Hakluyt Society) by Albert Gray, 1888, vol. 2. pt. 1. chap. xv.

Section II. which the Dutch longed to hold, for the self-same reasons; and the union of the Crown of Portugal with that of Spain, in the year 1580, gave to the bold sailors of the seven United Provinces a political excuse for attacking the Portuguese dependencies, which exactly coincided with their commercial instincts. Philip the Second interdicted his rebellious subjects from trading with Lisbon, from whence Dutch vessels had hitherto carried the imported wealth of the Portuguese Indies to other countries of Europe. The Dutchmen's answer was to go to the Indies themselves, and to wrest from the Portuguese the Spice Islands with all their wealth. At home the Netherlanders fought for life and liberty with Spain. Abroad they won a trading dominion at the expense of Portugal.

The Portuguese in Brazil. Spain, as has been noticed, secured the Philippines in that half of the world which had been assigned to Portugal; and Portugal owned Brazil within what was or was supposed to be the Spanish sphere. The possession of Brazil was a very important factor in the colonial history of Portugal, and especially important in connexion with the West Coast of Africa. The Portuguese claim to it dated as far back as 1500, when Cabral, the commander of the second voyage to India, was carried to its coasts by storm and wind. Neglected while the East, with all its dazzling wealth, absorbed the attention of Portuguese statesmen and Portuguese adventurers, it grew as their Eastern dominion declined; until in course of time it became the soundest and strongest of the Portuguese dependencies, the one part of the world which was really colonised by Portugal, the one part of the world where they formed a territorial dominion, and where they proved more than a match for the Dutch.

Position of the Portuguese in West Africa. Now, bearing in mind that the Portuguese were essentially a commercial people, and bearing in mind also that they owned Brazil as well as the East, we can take true stock of their position on the West Coast of Africa.

After the voyages of Vasco da Gama and Cabral, the Portuguese government sent year after year a series of expeditions to the Indies. Their main object was to extend and consolidate their Eastern trade. They left behind them their fort of Elmina on the gold-bearing Guinea coast, stations on the Congo, and other more or less isolated footholds on the Atlantic side of Africa. They were undisputed masters of these seas, for there was none to contest their supremacy; and, having no call to safeguard the scenes of their earlier discoveries, they devoted all their energies to exploiting the coasts and islands of Asia. During the first half of the sixteenth century they built up their world-wide empire, while the nations which were afterwards to supplant them were slowly growing from youth to manhood, slowly training for the coming time. But, as the century went on, Brazil, at first despised, began to attract the attention of the home government, and the introduction of sugar-planting into that country brought about a demand for African slave labour. Africans were wanted too to supply the place of the natives, whom the Spaniards had killed out in their American dependencies. Thus West Africa became the field of a great traffic in black men, and the owners of West Africa, having a keen eye to business, supplemented the wealth which they drew from the East by becoming carriers of labour to the West.

Chapter II.

Beginning of the Portuguese slave trade, especially in connexion with sugar-planting in Brazil.

In short, there came to be three distinct branches of Portuguese trade, and three distinct spheres of the Portuguese empire. Goods were imported from the East; slaves were transported from West Africa through Portugal to America; and, with the help of the labour thus obtained, sugar was grown in Brazil and brought back to Europe. Gold, ivory, pepper, and cottons, were also obtained from the Guinea coast; but, as far as West Africa was concerned, the trade in men quite dwarfed all other kinds of commerce. Heavy merchant ships carried the East Indian trade: in the Western

SECTION II.

The Province of Angola.

traffic smaller craft were employed, the swift-sailing caravels.

When Dutch and English began to intrude into West Africa, they found the Portuguese most firmly established at the Gambia and near Cape Verde, at Elmina on the Gold Coast, and in the southern province of Angola. The early Portuguese explorers fared well in the kingdoms of the Congo; and Angola, which lies to the south of that great river, was the strongest dependency of Portugal in West Africa, the part of the coast which became and remains to this day most exclusively Portuguese. Lying due east of Brazil, it was a great recruiting-ground for slaves; and here, in 1578, San Paulo de Loanda was founded, a town of no small importance in the colonial history of Portugal, especially in connexion with the war in Brazil. The old writer, Pyrard de Laval, who has been already quoted, notes that, 'the possessions of the Portuguese, as well on this side the Cape of Good Hope, at Angola, Guinea, and the adjacent islands, as in Brazil, are held in a different manner from the East Indies: for in the former places they are sovereign lords, for the most part, like the Spaniards in the West Indies, without other competitors, having fortresses both on the coasts and within the country which mostly belongs to them and is being continually conquered by them[1]'; and in the same chapter, referring to a silver mine in the interior of Angola, he writes that 'the Portuguese there and those of Mozambique and Sofala wish to join from the one side and the other to conquer it, and reach this mine to work it[2].' These passages imply that, by the beginning of the seventeenth century, the Portuguese in West Africa, as in Brazil, had obtained some measure of territorial dominion; and Angola was, up to a point, colonised on much the same lines

---

[1] Vol. ii. pt. 1. ch. xvi.
[2] Linschoten speaks of this mine in much the same way. See the Voyage of Linschoten, vol. i. p. 32 (Hakluyt Soc. ed. 1885).

as Brazil. Like the South American country, it was made a receptacle for convicts, including Jews who had fallen under the ban of the spiritual tribunals; and these forced settlers, together with Jesuits and traders, gave to Loanda a considerable white population. But in no part of West Africa, not even in Angola, did the Portuguese really rule any great extent of territory. A coast of which 'the greatest wealth is that of slaves[1]' might be widely raided, and dotted over with traders' forts; but solid evidence of a strong dominion was to be found in the American land to which the Africans were sent, not in Africa itself[2].

CHAPTER II.

Two years after the town of Loanda was founded, in 1580, Portugal was annexed to Spain. The annexation gave a death-blow to the Portuguese power. The national vigour, which had carried the sailors of this small nation in triumph to the uttermost parts of the world, was sapped when the country which they had made great became the dependency of a foreign crown. Weighted with its own overgrown empire, absorbed in European wars, the Spanish government could but contribute to the decay of its new dominions. As in a great household, amid a number of useless dependants, the means of the owner are wasted and frittered away, so from sheer size, from simple want of adequate control, the Spanish Portuguese dominions fell to rack and ruin in spendthrift wastefulness. Then, little by little, new European peoples, of straitened means and careful habits, stepped into the places of their more brilliant predecessors, and, taught by what had gone before, built up lasting empires on the ruins of what had once belonged to Spain and Portugal.

Annexation of Portugal by Spain—the death-blow to the Portuguese empire.

A pathetic story is that of the Portuguese. No other nation in modern times, except perhaps the Dutch, rose from such small beginnings to so much greatness. No other nation,

---

[1] From Pyrard de Laval, as above.
[2] E. g. in 1578, the year in which Loanda was founded, a Portuguese fort at Accra on the Gold Coast was taken and destroyed by the natives.

SECTION II.

except perhaps the Spaniards, fell from so much greatness into such deplorable decay. Cast in a smaller mould than the Spaniards, they win more sympathy, for they lost their power through being annexed by Spain, and the determined patriotism shown by their colonists in Brazil bore striking witness to the strength and courage of the race. In Africa was played the first bright act of their colonial history. In Africa the last act seems to be drawing sadly towards the close. The dependencies of Angola and Mozambique tell only of poverty and weakness, of a nation whose sun has set, of political and social decay. Yet something is due to the memory of a very splendid past; and those who rule where the Portuguese were once all powerful, who trade in the lands and sail on the seas which they had made their own, may well find excuses for the people who led the van of modern enterprise so boldly and so well, who piloted Europeans into Africa and the East.

Early English enterprise in West Africa.

When new worlds were discovered, the English were among the first to bestir themselves; but they reconnoitred only and then drew back again, as though, conscious of weakness, they wished to husband their resources and bide their time. Thus Cabot discovered North America in 1497; but, beyond the Newfoundland fisheries, nothing came of the discovery for the space of a hundred years. English ships, again, found their way to the West Indies as early as 1516, but no English settlement was formed in any of the islands until the year 1623, when St. Kitts was first colonised. The same was the case in regard to the West Coast of Africa.

Projected voyage to Guinea in 1481.

In 1481, the year in which the Portuguese founded the Castle of St. George at Elmina, an attempt was made by two Englishmen to fit out a fleet for the coast of Guinea. Hearing of their preparations, King John of Portugal at once sent an embassy to England to remonstrate; and, so great was the name of Portugal at the time, so strong the respect for the papal Bull[1] of 1442 by which the Portuguese discoveries were safeguarded, that the English King, Edward the Fourth, agreed to the demand that the fleet should be dissolved and the expedition given up.

CHAPTER II.

Years went on. Cabot made his famous discovery. English fishermen sailed summer after summer to the Newfoundland Banks. Writers[2] hinted at the possibility of finding a north-western route to the Portuguese Indies and far Cathay. But the first half of the sixteenth century passed away, barren of outward and visible results, though, under strong King Henry the Eighth, an English navy was being formed, and English seamen were being trained in the science of navigation[3].

One English voyager alone is recorded to have visited the Guinea coast before 1550. We learn from Hakluyt[4], that, in the years 1530-2, 'Old Mr. William Hawkins of Plymouth,' father of the more famous Sir John Hawkins, 'a man for his wisdom, experience, and skill in sea-causes, much esteemed and beloved of King Henry the Eighth,' made three voyages to the coast of Brazil, thus travelling far beyond the limits which bounded British enterprise at the time. In the course of these voyages 'he touched at the river of Sestos upon the coast of Guinea, where he trafficked with the negroes, and took of them elephants' teeth and other commodities which that place yieldeth.' The short chronicle of this venture contains more than one point of interest. It is noteworthy that the first English trader, who touched at the Guinea coast, belonged to a family so renowned in the naval annals of Great Britain; it is noteworthy too that he visited West Africa, not, like his son, to kidnap Africans, but for the purposes of honest trade; and again, the fact, that he went there on the way to Brazil, illustrates the growing importance

William Hawkins' voyages in 1530-2.

---

[1] See above, p. 19.   [2] E.g. Robert Thorne, in 1527.
[3] Reference should be made on this point and on the subject of the beginnings of English maritime enterprise to Doyle's History of the English in America, vol. i. chap. 4.   [4] Vol. iv. pp. 198-9 (1811 ed.).

SECTION II.

Windham's voyage in 1553.

of this South American colony of Portugal, and its close connexion with the West Coast of Africa.

After 1550 began a series of English voyages to the coast of Guinea. What is called in Hakluyt[1] 'the first voyage to Guinea and Benin' took place in 1553, the year in which Willoughby and Chancellor sailed to find a north-east passage to the Indies, when Willoughby's life, like many others since, was sacrificed to Arctic exploration, and Chancellor, returning home through Russia, opened a new field for British trade. In that year some merchant adventurers in London equipped 'two goodly ships' to sail to the West Coast of Africa. Their commander was Captain Windham, who had already made two voyages to the coast of Barbary, and with him was associated a Portuguese named Pinteado. Pinteado, we read, was a man who had been 'sometime in great favour with the King of Portugal, and to whom the coasts of Brazil and Guinea were committed to be kept from the Frenchmen.' He is described as 'a man worthy to serve any prince,' as 'a wise, discreet, and sober man, as well an expert pilot as a politic captain.' Through no fault of his own, he had fallen into disgrace at the Portuguese court; and, finding his way to England, he led Englishmen into Portuguese Africa. Unfortunately he was 'evil matched with an unequal companion,' for Windham was a violent and headstrong man, who would have none of Pinteado's guidance, jealous, like his crew, of one of foreign blood. By him Pinteado was 'most vilely used,' and in consequence the expedition proved a dismal failure. They 'fell in with the great river of Sesto,' sailed as far as Benin, and obtained 150 lbs. of gold on the Gold Coast; but both the commanders lost their lives, 'and of seven score men came home to Plymouth scarcely forty, and of them many died.' Thus ended the first ill-omened trading voyage to Guinea; but, nothing daunted, English merchants sent out more ships in the very

[1] Vol. ii. pp. 466-9.

next year in charge of Captain John Lok, who reached the
Gold Coast, and brought home a cargo of 400 lbs. of gold,
a quantity of 'grains' or Guinea pepper[1], and 250 elephants'
teeth. Other voyages followed. In 1555, William Towrson
brought back gold dust and ivory, in spite of being attacked
by the Portuguese; and, in 1556, the same captain joined
forces with French traders on the West African coast, but
found them indifferent allies; and, after beating off a Portuguese squadron near Elmina, with difficulty defended
himself against another French vessel, which took advantage
of his crippled condition.

Voyages of Lok and Towrson.

It will be noted, in connexion with these early voyages to
Guinea, that constant mention is made of the French as
trading and privateering in African waters, and that the
Portuguese were not able to prevent either French or
English from intruding into their domain. Even if the
Portuguese had been much stronger than was really the case,
it was impossible that their cruisers could keep watch over
the whole coast of West Africa; and, as a matter of fact,
they were beginning to be found out, just as a few years
later the inherent weakness of the Spanish power in America
was exposed by Drake and his fellow freebooters. The
chronicler of Windham's voyage refers almost contemptuously
to the Portuguese monopoly of the African trade, speaking
of West Africa as a promising field for British enterprise, 'if
the same be not hindered by the ambition of such as, for the
conquering of forty or fifty miles here and there and erecting
of certain fortresses, think to be lords of half the world[2].'
Seventy years before, a remonstrance from the King of
Portugal had sufficed to scare away the English from
Africa; but neither hard words nor hard blows were likely

Weakness of the Portuguese in West Africa.

---

[1] Grains of Paradise, Guinea grains, or Melegueta pepper, the seeds of the Amomum Melegueta, are a kind of spice, now used in this country chiefly in the preparation of medicines for cattle and to give artificial strength to cordials, spirits, &c. [see Encyc. Brit. s. v.].

[2] Hakluyt, vol. ii. p. 464.

SECTION II.

in future to have much effect, for a generation was springing up in England, in Holland, and in France, which could gauge the strength and weakness alike of Spain and Portugal, and which intended to share the good things of the East and West. As modern discovery began in Africa and was the work of Portugal, so the northern traders and freebooters, who eventually broke up the Spanish and Portuguese empires, first tried their prentice hands in the Guinea voyages at the expense of the Portuguese.

Slave-trading had no place in the earliest English voyages to Guinea.

It is satisfactory to find that slave-catching was not a feature of these early English voyages. Guinea pepper, ivory, and gold, were the objects of the expeditions. From the constant mention of the Sestos river, on what was then called the Grain Coast and is now the Liberian Republic, it would seem that Guinea pepper was much prized in these days, for we read that 'Betwixt the river de Sestos and the Cape das Palmas is the place where all the grains be gathered [1].' The first Englishman who was concerned in slave-trading was Sir John Hawkins, who, in 1562, carried off 300 negroes from Sierra Leone and sold them to the Spaniards in Hispaniola. This fact, we are told and would like to believe, met with no encouragement from Queen Elizabeth, who is reported to have said on hearing it, that 'if any Africans should be carried away without their free consent, it would be detestable and call down the vengeance of Heaven upon the undertaking [2]'; but, inasmuch as she lent Hawkins one of her own ships, the 'Jesus' built at Lubeck, for his next slave-trading voyage in 1564, and probably shared the profits; inasmuch as she gave him a coat of arms on which a negro bound in chains was a prominent feature, it may well be doubted whether her remonstrance, if it was ever made, amounted to more than a 'pious opinion.' Hawkins, who was a freebooter of the

Sir John Hawkins was the first English slave-trader.

---

[1] Hakluyt, vol. ii. p. 486.
[2] Quoted in Bandinel's History of the Slave Trade (1842), p. 36.

most pronounced type, combined with the slave trade plundering of Portuguese vessels on the Guinea coast; and, when he took his negroes over to America, he compelled the Spaniards to buy them by force of arms. He was almost the first of the many English sea-captains, as bold as they were unscrupulous, who set at nought and finally broke up the power of Spain and Portugal. As yet, however, state policy required that adventurers of this class should not be directly countenanced by their sovereigns, and for a few years more the Portuguese seem more or less to have held their own against English and French interlopers in West Africa, offering a reward of 100 crowns for every Frenchman's head[1]. But their strength was on the wane, and their doom was sealed, when the Portuguese king died without heirs, and all his dominions became the property of Philip the Second of Spain. Thenceforward, the many enemies of Spain were *ipso facto* enemies also of Portugal, and open authorised attack soon took the place of unauthorised and spasmodic hostility.

In 1588, the year of the Armada, Queen Elizabeth, being then at war with Spain, gave a patent to 'certain merchants of Exeter and others of the west parts and of London for a trade to the river of Senega and Gambra in Guinea,' conferring upon them a monopoly of the traffic of these two rivers and the intermediate coast for the space of ten years. Thus, rather more than a century after the first British expedition to Guinea had been contemplated and given up, a company was formed to trade with West Africa under the direct sanction of the Crown. The preamble of the patent recited that the merchants who applied for it had been 'persuaded and earnestly moved' to that course 'by certain Portugals resident within our dominions,' and the document went on to state that the voyages which were contemplated under it 'will also be a great succour and relief unto the present distressed estate

Incorporation of the first English company to trade with West Africa, 1588.

---

[1] Barbot, p. 113.

SECTION II.

of those Portugals.' Thus, as a Portuguese sailor piloted the first British expedition to Guinea, so the first Guinea company originated, it would seem, with representations made by Portuguese residents in England. Possibly they were refugees, who preferred exile from their own country to living at home under Spanish rule; and their case may be quoted as one among many which illustrate how much England has owed to the aliens who have settled on her shores. The voyages [1] undertaken under this patent had no connexion with the slave trade, nor did they result in any settlement being formed upon the coast. The account of one of them, entitled in Hakluyt [2] the 'voyage of Richard Rainolds and Thomas Dassel to the rivers of Senega and Gambra adjoining upon Guinea,' in 1591, throws considerable light upon the state of Senegambia at this time. The Portuguese had apparently almost entirely disappeared from the Senegal [3], and were chiefly to be found in the negro towns of Porto d'Ally and Joala [4] between that river and the Gambia, and in the Gambia itself, 'which is a river of secret trade and riches concealed by the Portugals.' The settlers consisted in the main of 'banished men or fugitives' from Portugal or Spain, colonists of the same type as was to be found in Angola [5] and Brazil. They were, according to this English, probably a biassed, account, hated by the natives, being esteemed 'a people of no truth'; and, so far from exercising any real dominion over this part of the coast, the writer states that 'in all these places hereabouts, where we use to trade, they have no fort, castle, or place of strength, but only trading by the negroes' safeconduct and permission.'

The French were apparently more in evidence on the

Rainolds' voyage, 1591.

---

[1] Bandinel, p. 38, mentions three voyages in 1589, 90, 91.
[2] Hakluyt, vol. iii. pp. 2–7.
[3] The account says, 'In the river of Senega no Spaniard or Portugall used to trade.'
[4] Now Portadal or Sali and Joal, both in French territory.
[5] See above, p. 49.

Senegal than any other European people, and they had been trading there for many years past, whereas the English were quite new-comers[1]. The list of commodities, which attracted European traders, included all the ordinary West African products; but no mention is made of slaves, and the natives appear to have been sufficiently masters of the situation to prevent their country from being raided in order to supply the labour market of the Spanish and Portuguese colonies in America.

CHAPTER II.

In 1592, the year after this voyage, another patent was granted by Queen Elizabeth to Mr. Thomas Gregory of Taunton and others 'for traffic between the river Nonnia (Nunez) and the rivers of Madrabumba and Sierra Leona on the coast of Guinea[2].' This patent, like the former one, was granted for ten years, and it covered a strip of coast-line further south than before. It will be noted that, as Exeter merchants are specified in the first patent, so a Taunton merchant is specified in the second, for the West country towns at this time and for many years afterwards led the way in British enterprise beyond the sea.

Patent of 1592.

The seventeenth century came in. James the First took the place of Elizabeth. An age of settlement succeeded to a time of adventure; trading companies grew and multiplied; and the English began in real earnest that long competition for trade and dominion in all parts of the world, which is still being actively carried on—nowhere more actively than in Africa.

In 1618, a royal Charter was granted to an English Company, which was formed for the purpose of 'adventuring in the golden trade' in West Africa. The company, of which Sir Robert Rich (afterwards Earl of Warwick) was the chief promoter, was styled the Company of Adventurers of London trading into Africa; its operations were directed

Incorporation of the 'Company of Adventurers of London trading into Africa,' 1618.

[1] See marginal note to this voyage in Hakluyt, p. 2; 'our trade hither began 1587.'   [2] Hakluyt, vol. iii. p. 7.

SECTION II.

Beginning of British settlement in West Africa.

at once to the Gambia and to the Gold Coast; and for protection, as much against other Europeans as against the natives, one fort[1] was erected on the Gambia, and another at Cormantine on the Gold Coast. These were the earliest British settlements in West Africa.

The gold-bearing districts of West Africa are the Gold Coast, and Bouré on the Upper Niger; and a large proportion of the gold from the Bouré mines used, till a few years ago, to find its way to the sea by the Gambia river. At the beginning of the seventeenth century, the accounts given by mediaeval writers, such as Edrisi and Leo Africanus, coupled with reports brought over the desert by the merchants of Morocco, credited Timbuctoo, which lies northeast of Bouré on the Niger and much further inland, with being a great mart for the trade in gold. Consequently the efforts of the newly formed company were mainly directed to reaching that place by way of the Gambia, which was then supposed to be one of the mouths of the Niger, anticipating the attempts which have been made of late years to penetrate into the interior by the same route.

Thompson's expedition up the Gambia.

An expedition was sent out under a leader named George Thompson, who sailed up the Gambia as far as a place called Kassan, and, leaving his ship there, continued his journey up-stream in boats. In his absence the Portuguese and half-breeds, jealous of any intrusion into their own special river, seized the vessel and massacred the crew[2]. Thompson, however, contrived to send news of the

---

[1] This was perhaps Fort James; but if so, it was rebuilt in 1664. See p. 68.

[2] Jobson's account of what happened, given in the Golden Trade (1623), is as follows: 'The ship was betrayed, and every man left in her his throat cut by a few poor dejected Portingals and mulattos, whom they gave free recourse aboard, being only banished people and for the most part runnagados from their country.' He constantly calls the Portuguese 'the vagrant Portingall,' confirming the earlier description of the character of the Portuguese settlers on the Gambia, which has been quoted above, on p. 56.

disaster to his employers who despatched another ship, and went on his way again with eight companions. In 1620, the company sent out two more vessels in charge of Captain Richard Jobson, who was greeted on arrival in Africa with the news that his predecessor had been killed, it would seem by one of his own men. Notwithstanding, he too pushed up the Gambia, passed the falls of Barraconda, more than 250 miles above Bathurst, and reached a point called Tenda in the narrative, when, for reasons not fully explained, he gave up hope of reaching Timbuctoo, turned back, and came home to England. Thus ended the first attempt to find a way into the interior by the line of the Gambia, and no similar effort was again made by this route for a hundred years.

Chapter II.

Jobson's voyage.

In the account, which Jobson wrote of his expedition[1], he mentions a negro trader on the Gambia who came to him, bringing women to be sold for slaves. The answer given was, that Englishmen did not deal in any such commodities, that they did not buy and sell one another, 'or any that had our own shapes.' Up to this time, such Englishmen as had gone to Africa had, with the exception of Hawkins, kept clear of slave-trading. The settlements in Virginia and the Bermudas were still in their infancy; there were as yet no British colonies in existence in the West Indies; and, even after St. Kitts, Barbados, and other islands had been colonised, any slaves that were brought over were imported not so much in British vessels as in Dutch. The second African company, which received its charter from Charles the First in 1631, is said to have supplied slaves to the West Indies, but it was not till after 1660 that the English began to take any leading part in the African slave-trade.

The company of 1618 was not a slave-trading company

The company of 1618 was formed to traffic in produce, not in men; and, although it was incorporated under royal charter,

Nor was it backed by the government.

[1] Entitled The Golden Trade—a discovery of the river Gambra and the Golden Trade of the Ethiopians, 1620–1. London, 1623.

60 HISTORICAL GEOGRAPHY OF THE COLONIES.

SECTION II.

it received no further backing from the Government than the British North Borneo company, the Royal Niger company, or any other of the chartered companies of the present day. Indeed, in one respect it was less favoured by the Crown than modern companies, for the territories, in which the latter carry on their trade, are recognised as being under British protection or within the limits of exclusive British influence; whereas this first African company had no rights as against foreign nations, and, in sending ships to the Gambia, its promoters trespassed on what had ever been a Portuguese preserve. The building of a fort was a step beyond what had been achieved in former ventures; but the foothold thus obtained was very precarious, and a much later date than 1618 must be assigned to the first permanent British settlement on the Gambia.

Early French colonial enterprise.

It has been seen that the French claimed to be the earliest explorers of the West Coast of Africa, and that the first colony in the Canary islands was planted by a Norman noble[1]. It has been seen too that English voyagers to the Guinea coast in the middle of the sixteenth century found French vessels[2] there, busily plying their trade, and that the Portuguese apparently regarded Frenchmen at this time as the most dangerous of the various intruders into the charmed circle of their African dominions[3].

The world has never known bolder or better seamen than those who sailed west from the Norman and Breton ports. They were among the very first visitors to the Newfoundland fisheries; and, led by Jacques Cartier, they had, in the first half of the sixteenth century, discovered and explored the St. Lawrence. Many, if not most, of them belonged to the Huguenot party; and, as the shade of religious persecution grew darker over France, they turned their eyes towards foreign lands, to find places of refuge no less than new openings for industry and trade.

[1] See above, pp. 15–6. [2] See above, p. 53. [3] See above, pp. 52–55.

The French were the first to make the beginnings of colonies on soil which belonged to Portugal and Spain, and the Portuguese had good cause to fear them and to offer rewards for every Frenchman's head. In 1555, under the counsel and advice of the great Huguenot leader Coligny, a band of French colonists was sent to Brazil, and established themselves at Rio Janeiro. The scheme was wrecked by religious discord, and by the mismanagement of the commander Villegagnon; and, in no long time, the settlers were all driven out of the country. Enough however had been done to make the French for the time being more formidable than any other Europeans to the Portuguese, who dreaded French men and French ships not only in Brazil, but also in West Africa with which Brazil was so closely and constantly connected. About the same time occurred the episode of the Huguenot colony in Florida, planted by Ribault in 1562, savagely extirpated by the Spaniard Menendez in 1565, and again, in two years' time, avenged with terrible thoroughness by the French adventurer Domenic de Gourgues. The story of the ill-fated settlement is so dramatic, that its real importance is almost lost sight of in the setting of the tale. As a matter of fact, though it was cut short in its infancy, the colony was a bold attempt—the boldest for many long years—to give a rival European people a foothold within the range of the Spanish dominions; and, had it succeeded, France might well have disputed with Spain the sovereignty of Central America.

In West Africa, though the French went trading along the Guinea coast, their main sphere of operations was and always has been the country of the Senegal. The narrative of Rainolds' voyage to Senegambia in 1591, which has already been quoted[1], states that 'the Frenchmen of Dieppe and Newhaven have traded thither above thirty years, and commonly with four or five ships a year, whereof two

Chapter II.

Attempted French settlements in Brazil and Florida.

The French in West Africa.

---
[1] Above, p. 56.

62 HISTORICAL GEOGRAPHY OF THE COLONIES.

SECTION II.

small barks go into the river Senega.' On the other hand, it is added that 'the Frenchmen never use to go into the river of Gambra,' the trade of which was left in the hands of the half-breed Portuguese. The power, which the French always possessed above other European nations, of ingratiating themselves with native races, was as conspicuous in their dealings with the negroes of Senegambia, as it was at a later date in their relations to the North American Indians or to the Caribs of the West Indian islands [1]. 'In all places generally they were well-beloved, and as courteously entertained of the negroes as if they had been naturally born in the country. And very often the negroes come into France and return again [2].' Coming after the Portuguese, and not at first concerned to kidnap slaves, they must, in the eyes of the natives, have presented a pleasing contrast to their predecessors, who were represented in West Africa by the scum of Portugal. It is only surprising that, having so good a start, they kept themselves almost entirely to the region of the Senegal, and did not compete with English and Dutch further south on the coast of the Gulf of Guinea. By the year 1626 [3], a French West African company had been formed, entitled the 'compagnie libre de Dieppe et Rouen,' which had an agency on the Senegal. It was contemporaneous with the beginning of French colonisation in the West Indies, for the first West Indian colony of France was planted in St. Kitts in 1625, and in 1626 Richelieu incorporated the 'company of the islands of America.' Accordingly, in a short time, the trade of the Rouen company developed into a slave trade for supplying labour to the West Indian plantations, and in 1664 it was merged in the reconstituted French West India company.

Fighting for their lives and homes against Philip the

[1] See vol. ii. of this work, p. 50 note.
[2] From the same narrative as above, Hakluyt, vol. iii. pp. 2-7.
[3] Raynal gives 1621 as the approximate date of the first French settlement on the Senegal.

EARLY EUROPEAN TRADE AND SETTLEMENT. 63

Second, the Dutch were somewhat later in coming to West Africa than either the English or the French; but, when once they appeared on the scene, they proved the most determined and deadly foes to Portugal. In 1581, the Seven United Provinces proclaimed their independence, and the first recorded Dutch voyage to Guinea was made in 1595. In that year one Bernard Ericks or Erecksen of Medenblik sailed to West Africa, 'running along the whole Gold Coast, where he settled a good correspondence with the blacks for carrying on the trade with them in future times[1].' The natives welcomed the Dutchmen, as bringing them better and cheaper goods than were sold by the Portuguese, and looked to them as possible deliverers from the only Europeans of whose oppressions they had as yet had much experience. They had still to learn that the Hollanders in their turn would prove hard task-masters, and, like the Portuguese, would resent dealings with other nations than themselves.

This first visit to the Gold Coast gave promise of good things to come, and, in after years, it was to this part of West Africa that the Dutch mainly devoted their energies. But, before they planted any fort or established any factory on the coast of Guinea, they secured a foothold further to the north off Cape Verde, buying, in 1617, the island of Goree from its native ruler.

The early Dutch voyages, like those of the French and English, were private enterprises, not directly supported by the government; but, in 1621, the States General incorporated the Netherlands West India company, and gave it a monopoly of trade on the West Coast of Africa as well as on the other side of the Atlantic. The English never formed one company to include both the West African and the American trade. The French did not take such a step till 1664. The Dutch, therefore, were the first of the

CHAPTER II.

The Dutch in West Africa.

The Dutch West India company.

[1] Barbot, bk. 3. chap. 7.

SECTION II.

three peoples to treat West Africa as purely subsidiary to America and the West Indies. They showed their usual sagacity in thus early consolidating their forces. They had one great East India company and one great West India company. The sphere of the former was east of the Cape of Good Hope, the sphere of the latter was west of the Cape.

As far back as 1542, the Dutch had been trading in contraband fashion off the Spanish main, and their first settlement on the coast of Guiana dated from 1580[1]. In 1609, Hudson had in their service sailed up the famous river which still bears his name; and at its mouth, in 1622, the year after the West India company was formed, a Dutch settlement was established under the name of New Amsterdam, the forerunner of the present great city of New York. But in East and West alike trade not settlement was the aim of the Dutch, and in East and West alike they saw clearly that their own profits could only be secured at the expense of the Portuguese. Consequently, in 1623, their West India company began a Thirty Years' war in Brazil; and in connexion with that war, as well as with a view to securing the carrying trade to the West Indies, they went to work with grim and dogged determination upon the West Coast of Africa.

War between the Dutch and the Portuguese.

The French and the English in Africa rather avoided than courted conflict with the Portuguese. In the East Indies the Dutch themselves did not as a rule invite collision. But on the Guinea Coast, as in Brazil, they made straight for the centre of the Portuguese dominions, for the Gold Coast, where the fort of Elmina had stood for nearly a century and a half; and there they fought it out with their commercial rivals, with the subjects of the king whose sovereignty they had themselves cast off for ever. At a very short distance to the east of Cape Coast Castle they built, in 1624, a fort at

---

[1] See vol. ii. of this work, pp. 39, 52, 268.

a place called Mouree, and named it Fort Nassau. It would seem from Barbot's account to have been built by the Government and handed over to the West India Company; but the point is immaterial, for the Government of the Netherlands was a government of traders; the great merchant companies were national concerns; and the Dutch East and West India Companies were but the States-General under another name. In the following year, 1625, they attacked Elmina, but were repulsed with heavy loss; and twelve years passed before they finally succeeded in wresting it from the Portuguese.

Founding of Fort Nassau at Mouree.

In January 1637, Count Maurice of Nassau arrived in Brazil to take command of the Dutch forces in that country. Not long after his arrival, he learnt from the governor of Mouree that an attack on Elmina would probably prove successful; and, acting on the information, he sent a fleet of nine vessels over the Atlantic with eight hundred men on board. Their commander effected a landing in the neighbourhood of Elmina, after four days' siege the Portuguese garrison capitulated, on August 29, 1637, and the famous castle of St. George passed for ever out of the hands of its original owners. The other Portuguese forts on the coast followed suit, Fort St. Anthony at Axim, which ranked next in importance to Elmina, being taken in January 1642; and a treaty with the newly-restored King of Portugal secured to the Netherlands the fruits of war [1]. Thus the Portuguese were practically driven from the Gold Coast, and the Dutch for the time being lorded it in their place. The blow came from America, not from Europe. It came as an incident in the Brazilian war. It was dealt by a West India Company, belonging to a nation of carriers, to a people who saw more

Taking of Elmina.

---

[1] The main treaty between Portugal and the Netherlands was in 1641, and therefore the fort of St. Anthony would seem to have been taken subsequently to it; but the dates are very uncertain. Barbot himself says in one place it was taken in 1642, and in another in 1643.

SECTION II. clearly than their contemporaries that West Africa was the natural recruiting-ground for the labour required in the plantations of the New World, and that wealth was to be made by the slave trade. Bosman, the Dutch historian of the Gold Coast, says that 'the Portuguese served for setting dogs to spring the game, which, as soon as they had done, was seized by others[1].' His words were applicable to Portuguese history elsewhere than in West Africa, but they applied most fully to the Guinea coast. These Europeans were indeed hunters—of human game; and, when the slave trade was becoming most profitable, other nations—above all the Dutch—supplanted the Portuguese.

We have traced the beginnings of English, French, and Dutch enterprise upon the West Coast of Africa. It remains to notice two other peoples who, though later comers, made some show on the coast before the seventeenth century ended. One of them, the Danes, held their ground and played a considerable part in West African history down to our own times. The other, the Brandenburghers, made but a short stay.

The seventeenth century was a notable time in Northern Europe. Its earlier years saw the victories of Gustavus Adolphus, the great King of Sweden. Its later years saw the formation and growth of the Prussian power. The striking success of the Dutch in foreign parts seems to have awakened a spirit of adventure amongst the peoples of the North, and traders set out from the lands which bordered upon the Baltic to try their luck beyond the sea. Notices of the Swedes on the West Coast of Africa occur in old writers, and in 1642 a colony of Courlanders settled in the West Indian island of Tobago[2].

---

[1] From A New and Accurate Description of the Coast of Guinea, by William Bosman, chief factor of the Dutch at the castle of St. George d'Elmina. [English Translation, 2nd ed. 1721, p. 2.] Bosman was on the coast at the end of the seventeenth century

[2] See vol. ii. of this work, p. 254.

The Danes formed an East India Company as early as CHAPTER 1618, but they did not establish themselves in the West Indies till 1671, when they occupied St. Thomas; and their West India Company was not incorporated till 1734.

The Danes in West Africa.

It is difficult to determine the precise date when they began to plant factories on the West Coast of Africa. Their principal fort, Christiansborg near Accra, which is now the seat of government of the British Gold Coast colony, was certainly in existence in or shortly after the year 1660; and, to judge from its name, given 'in honour of their King then reigning[1],' it was built before Christian the Fourth of Denmark died, in 1648, and was succeeded by his son Frederick the Third. It is stated in one account that it was originally the site of a small Portuguese station, from which the Portuguese were expelled by the Swedes, and that in 1657 the Swedes were in their turn driven out from this and other neighbouring posts by a Danish expedition[2]. The King, who was ruling in Denmark in 1657, was King Frederick. His reign lasted from 1648 to 1670, and he gave his name to another fort—Fort Fredericksborg—which stood on what was known as the Danish Mount close to Cape Coast Castle, in a position commanding the English fort at the same place. It was at a comparatively early date handed over to the English, and by them renamed Fort Royal. These were the two principal strongholds of the Danes in West Africa; but, when in 1850 all their possessions on the Gold Coast were finally sold to Great Britain, their sphere extended from Christiansborg on the west to Quittah on the east, taking in the mouth of the Volta river, and comprising the greater part of the eastern district of the present Gold Coast colony[3]. In early times, as in latest

---

[1] Barbot, p. 183.
[2] See Meredith's account of the Gold Coast of Africa, 1812, p. 197, note.
[3] See the map attached to the Parliamentary Paper of 1850, entitled Papers respecting the Danish possessions on the Coast of Africa; and see below, p. 126.

days, the Danes do not seem to have prospered greatly in Africa. They were there side by side with stronger European powers, and they hardly held their own against the negroes, who, in the later years of the seventeenth century, deprived them for a while of their fort of Christiansborg and transferred it to the Portuguese. They played apparently, though on a smaller scale, the same part as was played by the Dutch, feeding the markets of other nations rather than supplying any wants of their own. Their West Indian island of St. Thomas was, like the Dutch islands of St. Eustatius and Curaçoa, a distributing centre; and its owners in West Africa, as on the other side of the Atlantic, seem to have contented themselves with a modest share of the carrying trade between the Old World and the New.

The Brandenburghers in West Africa.

In the early years of the seventeenth century, the Mark of Brandenburg was united to the Duchy of Prussia; and, under Frederic William, the great Elector, who ruled from 1640 to 1688, the newly-formed state grew in strength and independence, until in 1701 his son took the title of King. Late in the great Elector's reign, some Dutch merchants, chafing against the monopoly of the Netherlands West India Company [1], are said to have instigated him to incorporate a company for trading on the West Coast of Africa. The result was that, in 1682 [2], a fort which, like the Danish fort at Cape Coast, bore the title of Fredericksburg, was built at Cape Three Points, towards the western end of the Gold Coast, between Axim and Elmina. Two smaller outlying forts were also built very slightly to the east; and, some three years later, a fourth station is said to have been established

---

[1] Compare the case of the Portuguese merchants in England, above, pp. 55-6.
[2] The dates connected with the Brandenburg Company are very variously given. According to Bosman, the Brandenburghers were in West Africa before 1674. Raynal says they sold their forts to the Dutch in 1717, Barbot, in 1720. Bosman speaks of them also as the Embden Company.

far to the north near Cape Blanco, on the island of Arguin, which, from the earliest Portuguese times[1], had been a favourite place for European factories. Forty years was the life of this German episode in West African history. As time went on, the Prussian people and the Prussian Government had more than enough on their hands at home to engross their energies, without competing for the doubtful advantages of West African trade. In or about 1720, the Brandenburg forts were sold to the Dutch; and, under its new masters, Fort Fredericksburg became Fort Hollandia.

[1] See above, p. 21.

CHAPTER III.

THE AFRICAN COMPANIES AND THE SLAVE TRADE.

Section II.

The Slave Trade was

By the middle of the seventeenth century, the African slave trade had become gradually recognised in Europe as a legitimate kind of commerce. It is a subject of which it is difficult to write. The details are so revolting, the inevitable accompaniments of the traffic were so horrible, that any sober estimate of its causes and effects may appear at the present time as an attempt to condone the wickedness of white men, and to explain away the sufferings which for so many years they inflicted upon

the result of economic causes.

a lower and a coloured race. Yet, in good truth, the slave trade, in its origin and in its developement, was due to natural, to economic causes. It was the necessary outcome of time and place.

Slavery indigenous to Africa.

The place, from which the slaves were transported, was a land where slavery always was, and still is, one of the normal conditions of native life. Europeans are not responsible for the beginning of slavery and slave-raiding in Africa. Their responsibility consists in having utilised an existing system for their own interest, in having intensified its evils, and in having forcibly transported thousands and tens of thousands of human creatures to a new scene of slavery beyond the seas. The Europeans in Africa have been spoken of above in metaphorical terms as hunters of human game; but these words do not quite correctly represent what actually happened. No doubt black men, from the time of the first Portuguese voyages onwards, were constantly kidnapped by white; but such cases were the exception, the ordinary rule being that black men raided black men, and sold their victims to the agents of Dutch, French, or English companies. It was the business of these companies to buy slaves from middlemen, not to catch them themselves. They had factories on the coast, which in most cases they simply leased from native chiefs. They were there more or less on sufferance, and they dealt with negroes for negroes, just as they dealt and deal with them for gold dust and palm oil. It was a trade, though an infamous trade. It was familiar to, countenanced by, and welcome to the stronger native races. In it and through it the European sank to the African level, but he did not actually import into Africa a system which was not there already.

CHAPTER III.

The Europeans in Africa were slave traders rather than slave catchers.

Now let us turn to the other side of the Atlantic, to the place to which the slaves were carried. Here was a great expanse of rich tropical lands, which had become the property of European peoples. These lands, it was found, were especially adapted for the plantation system, and most of all for growing sugar. If their riches were to be developed, coloured labour had to be supplied, for white labour was found wanting in all respects. But coloured labour was not to be procured on the spot. The natives of America either were weakly and easily exterminated, as proved to be the case in Hispaniola, or they were, like the West Indian Caribs and the North American Indians, a limited number of fierce, intractable savages. Hence, if tropical America was not to be left a desert, the importation of a strong black race from beyond the sea was an absolute necessity. Immediately beyond the sea, directly over against the West Indies, lay the West Coast of Africa. It was inevitable, therefore, that from Africa should come

The slave trade led to the developement of the West Indies.

SECTION II.

the labour supply for the New World. The slave trade thus served a useful purpose. Without it, the West Indian islands and the mainland of tropical and sub-tropical America would not have been cultivated. Without it, these lands would not have been colonised, would not have been peopled with a race admirably suited to the climate. Nor were the conditions of living in the New World widely different from those of Africa. The blacks, it is true, were carried into slavery; but slavery had been universally prevalent in the land of their birth. In Africa the weaker negro races were slaves of the stronger, in America they were slaves of European masters. They were set to profitable work in their new homes, they formed part of organised communities, they exchanged spasmodic and useless servitude for the settled routine of plantation life.

Circumstances which led to the slave trade.

As long as the world lasts, there will ever be abundant evidence that some races are superior to others; and, as long as such evidence exists, there must be consciousness of superiority among some races and of inferiority among others. It is not a long step from this position to the assumption, that the white man should always rule and the black man should always serve; and from such an assumption may easily be deduced a further conclusion, that force should be used to ensure service, to make the coloured man fulfil the purpose for which he might be presumed to be most suited by nature. This in past times was the apology for slavery.

The discoveries of the fifteenth century for the first time brought the peoples of Western Europe

From the days of the Romans down to the fifteenth century, the peoples of Western Europe were never brought into contact with uncivilised coloured races. They fought and traded with Eastern nations, but they fought and traded with them as equals. The Saracen was at least as civilised as the Crusader, the Moor was more civilised than the Gothic noble of Spain. If Christians took Mohammedans captive,

Moslems in their turn owned Christian slaves; and the competition between East and West was a competition between rival races and rival religions, neither of which could claim any marked outward superiority over the other. The result of the discoveries of the fifteenth century was to bring Europeans for the first time face to face with multitudes of human beings on an obviously lower level than themselves, the more promising among them being child-like and childish, the less promising, little removed from the beasts that perish. Even where a civilisation was found, like that of the Aztecs, it was clearly based on savagery and paganism, attracting the animal instincts of the invaders, their lust, and their avarice, but not in any way appealing to any higher sense or suggesting favourable comparison with European types of life. Into these strange new worlds of Africa and America there came white men from beyond the seas, bold, strong, enthusiastic, but withal half-civilised themselves, fierce and brutal, fanatical to the last degree, the law of whose life was force. Bond-service and villeinage had long been an integral element in the social system of Europe, and slavery was countenanced at once by custom and by religion. The roughest and rudest specimens of rough and rude peoples, in a rough and rude time, found themselves in the presence of men and women who feared, who admired, who in some cases adored them as almost divine. Was it possible that any other result should follow from the meeting of races, than that the incomers should be masters, and the natives should be slaves? To prevent slavery and the slave trade there was nothing but the instinct of humanity, which exists to some extent at all times and in all peoples, but which, being the most progressive of all human feelings, is weakest in a dark and fighting age; and policy, which dictated to occasional leaders of privateering or trading expeditions kindness to the children of the soil, as being likely to bring more gain in the future. On the other side

CHAPTER III.

into contact with distinctly lower races.

Characteristics and motives of the first European adventurers into Africa and America.

were ranged not only the lowest impulses—greed, luxury, and sensual slothful enjoyment—but also higher motives, strangely enlisted on the side of wrong. The enslaving of the body might, it was thought, bring about the saving of the soul. So Prince Henry of Portugal rejoiced over the firstfruits of kidnapping in West Africa, and the Pope contributed his blessing. Las Casas, noblest of philanthropists, yearned to save the miserable remnant of worked-out Indians from the inhumanity of his countrymen, and hence he suggested to the Spanish government the African slave trade as the lesser of two evils.

The Spaniards and the Portuguese.

The Spaniards and Portuguese, the first two peoples who found their way to Africa and America, and who went ravening among negroes and Indians, had a strong strain of ferocity in their national character. Their training had hardened and intensified their disposition, and they became ruthless, masterful fanatics. Of all Europeans, they were least likely to deal out either just or kindly treatment to those who crossed their onward path. In their case too, as in that of other peoples, the adventurers who went to distant lands were in large measure men who had sinned against society at home. Condemned criminals were sent out from Spain to conquer and colonise America. Convicts and outlaws formed a great proportion of the Portuguese settlers in Africa [1]. At all times, even in an age of steam and of telegraphs, it is difficult for a government constantly to keep full control over its subjects beyond the seas. In the early days of discovery and adventure, control of any kind was well nigh impossible. Thus the worst specimens of cruel peoples went in and out among natives; the new conditions of their lives encouraged all their vices; they became more and more familiarised to constant brutality; their bad deeds were done, before the news of them reached the ears of the government at home; and laws and regulations, framed for restraining their inhumanities, were framed for men who were out of sight and out of reach.

[1] See above, pp. 49, 56, 58 note.

Of these two peoples the Portuguese were the slave traders. They owned in Africa the source of supply, and they supplied not only the Spanish colonies but also their own great dependency of Brazil. The slave trade was well suited to the Portuguese, and the Portuguese to the slave trade. By it they combined oppressive ownership of lower races with a form of commerce. It was not only not abhorrent to them, but exactly suited their inclinations.

The Portuguese were by nature and position slave traders.

It is not unfair to say that the Northern races of Europe are on the whole more humane than the Southern, and the sense of freedom was far stronger in England or the Netherlands than in Spain or Portugal. The first English traders to Africa, as has been seen[1], would have nothing to say to enslaving the natives, and Hawkins was almost a solitary instance of an English slave trader for many long years. How came it then that our own countrymen, in their turn, to their eternal disgrace, meddled with this filthy traffic, and carried it to dimensions which it had never before attained? There were two all-powerful causes at work. The first was that they became habituated to dealing with natives, and deteriorated in consequence. The second was that they owned colonies in the West Indies. The first Englishmen came and looked on Africa and the Africans and went their way; others came and came again; they grew accustomed to what had at first disgusted them; they saw day by day what other Europeans had done and were doing; they became infected with the conditions of West African life, as with the malaria of the West African climate; they touched pitch themselves and were defiled. At the same time, while constant contact with coloured men was bringing about the necessary result of lowering the European character, Barbados and the other West Indian islands, Virginia and her sister colonies, were calling out for labour for their plantations. It was impossible to depend on white

The Northern peoples of Europe and the slave trade.

Causes which led to the English slave trade.

[1] See above, pp. 51, 54, 59.

labour, forced or free. The quantity to be obtained was not sufficient, the kind was obviously unsuited to the climate. As philanthropy combined with interest to substitute negro labourers for the natives in the Spanish colonies, so the same combination of motives dictated the employment of coloured workmen in the plantations of the tropical and sub-tropical colonies of Great Britain, in preference to English, Scotch, or Irish employés, whether they were convicts, or political prisoners, or free men under contract of service for a term of years. But to import free East Indian labour in those days was out of the question. The age was not one for a carefully regulated system of indentured Coolies, such as was devised when negro slavery had become a thing of the past. The English had barely even a foothold in India. They had no command whatever of the labour market of that country; and, if they could have procured the labourers, the expense of carrying them to America would have been prohibitive. They were obliged to turn to Africa, and in Africa the workman was a slave and could only be procured as a slave. Englishmen were therefore face to face with the alternatives of carrying their own slaves, or of leaving the traffic in the hands of some other European nation. Humanity was not likely to be served by the latter course, and the former course offered a new and profitable opening for British merchants and British sailors. Thus it was in the natural order of things that the English became slave traders.

Results of the slave trade. It is impossible then to resist the conclusion, that the slave trade was inevitable, and that it provided the material by which tropical America was developed and was colonised, and without which developement and colonisation would have been impossible. But such an admission involves no denial of its hideous atrocities, or of the evil which it brought on every country and every people which had part and lot in its wickedness and its shame. In America, it produced conditions of life, which were only partly remedied by nothing short of social revolution, which have left to this day a blight on the lands to which Africans were carried, which have created difficulties of race and colour, of political and social economy, which make the present anxious and the future all uncertain. In Africa, it stereotyped savagery, it paralysed industry, it created such monstrosities as the negro power of Dahomey, it made the land which Europeans first visited in modern history the darkest and most degraded part of the world. But, worst of all, it tainted and lowered the peoples of Europe, it ran directly counter to freedom, to humanity, to every noble impulse of growing races and moving times, and it left a mark of infamy on English history, which no chronicler can minimise and no apologist erase.

The slave trade began when the sailors of Prince Henry of Portugal brought back negroes from Africa to Europe, at first obtaining them through the Moors, and afterwards carrying them off from their own country. The Pope received these firstfruits of the traffic, which was sanctified as a possible means of saving souls; and Prince Henry himself encouraged it, taking by way of royalty a certain proportion of each batch of slaves. It is due, however, to the Prince's memory to record, that he framed regulations to prevent as far as possible any excessive cruelty on the part of the Portuguese slave dealers, and laid down that slaves were to be procured only by barter with the Moors at the island of Arguin, instead of being hunted and kidnapped along the African coast.

Indeed the guilt and shame of the slave trade, with all its horrors, must be laid on the nations which took part in it, rather than on their rulers or statesmen. Cardinal Ximenes refused to countenance it[1]. Leo the Tenth, who

Beginnings of the slave trade.

Early denunciations of the traffic.

---

[1] Apparently however not so much on grounds of humanity, as for financial reasons, and because of the supposed warlike character of the negroes. See Helps' Spanish Conquest in America, vol. i. pp. 504–6.

SECTION II.

filled the papal chair in the years 1513-22, issued a Bull against slavery. Charles the Fifth, in 1542, prohibited the traffic for the time being, and ordered that all the slaves in Spanish America should be set free; and Queen Elizabeth, again, is said to have rated the first English slave trader, John Hawkins[1]. It is true that such prohibitions were temporary and spasmodic, and that, as a rule, the various European governments authorised the trade. But they followed in the matter, they did not lead; they were overborne by economic forces, and by national interests; and, when they interfered, the interference was frequently on the side of humanity

Slaves imported into Portugal.

Before Prince Henry died, some 700 or 800 negroes were, it is said, imported every year from Africa into Portugal; and, as America was not discovered for another thirty years, the number of slaves in Portugal at the end of the fifteenth century must have been considerable. Reasons of economy, if not of humanity, must sooner or later have put an end to the employment of slaves in Europe, where there were too many white workmen already on the spot to make black labour profitable. Consequently, if the New World had not been discovered, the slave trade would probably never have amounted to more than supplying the great houses of Spain and Portugal with a limited number of black domestic servants.

The discovery of America led to a great extension of the slave trade.

But America was discovered; and, as the Spaniards began to work the mines of Hispaniola, the necessity for stronger workmen than the native Indians became apparent. Accordingly, as early as 1503, some Africans appear to have been imported into the island from Portugal. Eight years later, in 1511, King Ferdinand formally authorised their importation in larger numbers; and from this time onward, for three centuries, a constant current of forced black labour poured from Africa into the New World.

[1] See however, above, p. 54.

The papal decree, which divided the World between Spain and Portugal, had an important bearing on the slave trade. Under its terms, Africa was closed to the Spaniards, and therefore they were left dependent upon other peoples for the supply of slaves to their American colonies. Consequently, the Portuguese, English, French, and Dutch slave traders always had a twofold object, at once to find workmen for their fellow-countrymen in America and the West Indies, and to secure the gainful monopoly of carrying slaves to the dependencies of Spain. This second branch of the trade led to international difficulties, and the Assiento or contract with the Spanish government for the supply of slaves became a prominent feature in the political history of the eighteenth century.

CHAPTER III.

The Spaniards were dependent on other nations for slaves for their colonies.

Before 1600, the slave trade was almost exclusively in the hands of the Portuguese. They stood alone among European nations, as owning the whole of West Africa. They supplied the wants of their own colonists in Brazil, and of the Spanish colonists in the West Indies. They were the only licensed slave dealers, all others were trespassers and smugglers. It is true that we read of Charles the Fifth giving, in 1517, a patent to a Flemish courtier, which authorised him to import annually four thousand negroes into the West Indian islands; but the Fleming, it must be presumed, had an understanding with the Portuguese government, or otherwise it would have been impossible to carry out the terms of his contract; and, as a matter of fact, he sold his monopoly to a Genoese syndicate, from whom it passed into Portuguese hands.

The slave trade in the sixteenth century.

At first, it would seem that the slaves were as a rule not carried direct across the Atlantic, but brought back to Portugal, and there trans-shipped for America; and, about the year 1539, some 10,000 or 12,000 slaves are said to have been sold annually[1] in the Lisbon slave market. As years

The slaves were at first exported through Europe to America.

---

[1] This statement is made in Bryan Edwards' History of the West Indies, vol. iii. p. 202, note; but, as Bandinel points out, in quoting the passage, Edwards does not cite any authority for it.

80 HISTORICAL GEOGRAPHY OF THE COLONIES.

SECTION II.

went on, however, and as the European settlements in America grew and multiplied, the direct trade between Africa and America increased, with the result that the slavers and their ships and freight rarely came into European ports, where they might have been inspected and supervised by the governments, under whose authority they plied their trade.

Sugar-growing in Brazil and the West Indies gave a great impulse to the slave trade.

A demand for miners first brought Africans to America, but it was the rise of the plantation system, and most of all the development of sugar-growing, which gave the greatest impulse to the slave trade. Before the middle of the sixteenth century, the cultivation of the sugar-cane became an important industry in Brazil; and from that country, about the year 1640, a Dutchman is said to have introduced into the English colony of Barbados the art of sugar-making [1], which the Brazilian colonists had turned to good account. From this time onward, the West Indian colonies absorbed an ever-growing number of negro slaves. In Hispaniola, sugar plantations took the place of silver mines; over half of the island French rule was substituted for Spanish; Africans multiplied, where native Indians had been exterminated; and the desolated land became, under the name of St. Domingo, the most prosperous agricultural settlement in the West Indies. To Jamaica, once a neglected dependency of Spain, sugar-planting and negro labour gave wealth and power, and for many years Kingston harbour was a great distributing centre of the slave trade. Barbados became and has ever remained a marvel for the density of its population and the developement of its soil; and into every island in turn working colonists were imported, to grow sugar for European markets, and to make money for European owners of American lands and African men.

The Dutch and the slave trade.

Before the West Indies were thus transformed, the Portuguese in Africa, like the Spaniards in America, had had

[1] See vol. ii. of this work, pp. 64 and 178.

their day; and their trade monopoly had been broken in pieces by the Dutch. Unlike the English and the French, the Dutch appear to have gone to Africa with the deliberate intention of engaging in the slave trade. The English and French became slave traders rather by force of circumstances; in the first instance, because their countrymen wanted negroes; subsequently, because they found West Africa given over to this traffic to the exclusion of all other forms of commerce, and because the profit to be derived from slave-trading became more and more in evidence. The Dutch, on the contrary, were slave traders from the first. They were essentially a nation of middlemen, a carrying people; and, though they required a certain number of slaves for their own colonies, especially for Guiana, yet their main object was not so much to supply labour to Dutch planters in the West Indies, as to take and keep for themselves the general transport trade across the Atlantic. They took over or tried to take over the business from the Portuguese; and, as soon as they had ousted the latter, they turned their arms against the English, as likely to be the most dangerous competitors in their own special line.

The year 1640 may be given as the date at which the English began to export negroes to their American colonies, but twenty years passed before the British slave trade became an established fact. It was the time of the Civil War, a series of years well suited for privateering, ill suited for systematic commerce—even for commerce in slaves. Jamaica was not taken by Cromwell's soldiers till 1655, and Barbados, the restive Cavalier colony, imported slaves and exported sugar in Dutch ships. The trade in negroes from Africa was, we read, up to the year 1660 'little known to the English[1].' Unhappily the knowledge soon came, bringing

The English and the slave trade.

---

[1] From the Universal History quoted in the note to p. 66 of vol. ii. of this work. See also pages 178 and 181 of that volume as to the extent to which the Dutch, prior to 1660, managed the carrying trade of Barbados.

SECTION II.

The slave trade was part of the commercial system of Great Britain.

bitterness and sorrow to after-generations. Cromwell was not the man to leave the carrying trade of Great Britain and her colonies in the hands of a rival nation; and the first of the Navigation Acts, which was passed by the Government of the Commonwealth in 1651, was directed against the Dutch. His measures were continued after his death, and the British slave trade came into being as an integral part of a national commercial policy.

The company of Royal Adventurers.

In 1662, the third African company received its charter from Charles the Second, under the title of 'The company of Royal Adventurers of England trading to Africa.' It was under distinguished patronage, one of the members being the King's brother, the Duke of York, afterwards James the Second; and it contracted to supply three thousand slaves annually to the British colonies in the West Indies. Thus the slave trade was sanctioned by the Government in the most direct and formal manner, and the Royal family of England thought it no shame to take part in the traffic. The time when Englishmen refused to deal in human beings had passed away. Evil communications had corrupted good manners, and now the carrying of negroes from Africa to America had become a matter of prime interest to the British government and the British nation. The company was not successful. The Dutch were in force on the West Coast of Africa, thwarting and injuring their English rivals. Their depredations brought on open war from 1665 to 1667; and, in 1672, the adventurers were glad to surrender their charter to the Crown, and to dispose of their property and interest to

The Royal African company.

the fourth African company, incorporated in the same year under the title of the Royal African company of England.

The new company is said to have numbered among its members the King himself, as well as the Duke of York. Its charter was most comprehensive, conferring upon it exclusive rights over the whole coast of Africa, from the port of Sallee in South Barbary to the Cape of Good Hope, for

AFRICAN COMPANIES AND THE SLAVE TRADE.

CHAPTER III.

a term of one thousand years, and prohibiting all other British subjects from even visiting the coast without a licence from the company. The total capital subscribed was not very large, amounting to £111,000[1]; but every effort was made to develope the British African trade and to compete successfully with the Dutch. The forts on the coast were strengthened and increased in number. Gold, dyewoods, and ivory were imported into England, as well as slaves into the English colonies; and English manufacturers were encouraged to produce woollen goods, in order to prevent the necessity, which had hitherto existed, of having recourse to the markets of the Netherlands for cargoes to be exchanged for the commodities of West Africa[2]. At the time when the Royal African company was incorporated, the Dutch, according to one account[3], still exported ten times as many slaves as the English; but they gradually lost ground, overweighted with their own dependencies, and finding a richer and more fruitful field for commerce in the East Indian islands than on the West Coast of Africa.

North of the Gold Coast, their place was taken by the French, who thus in Africa, as elsewhere, came into rivalry with the English.

The Royal African company was not long permitted to enjoy its monopoly. In 1689, the Declaration of Rights, presented to and accepted by William and Mary upon their accession to the English throne, virtually abolished the exclusive privileges which had been granted; and, in 1697, the private traders succeeded in inducing Parliament to give formal sanction to the abolition, and to throw open the

The monopoly of the company abolished.

---

[1] This sum seems a considerable one for the time, but Meredith in his Account of the Gold Coast of Africa, with a brief history of the African company (1812), p. 255 note, observes: 'The small stock which the company had, and their great desire to establish themselves as speedily as possible in opposition to the Dutch, sufficiently account for the hasty and unskilful manner in which some of their forts were constructed.'

[2] See Bryan Edwards, vol. ii. p. 54.

[3] See Bandinel, p. 53.

SECTION II.

African trade to all British subjects. The statute took effect from June 24, 1698, and remained in force for fourteen years, till June 24, 1712. It empowered any British subject to trade from England or from the American plantations to Africa, but it enacted that all traders should pay an ad valorem duty of 10 per cent. on any exports to Africa, the proceeds of which were to be applied by the company to the maintenance of the forts and garrisons upon the coast, which gave protection to all alike.

Up to this date the English slave traders had in the main confined themselves to supplying slaves to the British colonies; for, though in 1689 the African company entered into an agreement with the Spanish government to supply the Spanish colonies in the West Indies with negroes from Jamaica, the French were, at the end of the seventeenth century, the principal importers of slaves into Spanish America. Official returns published in 1789, in the report of the Privy Council on the Trade to Africa[1], showed that, in the years 1679–1688, the English imported 46,396 negroes into the colonies, the African company shipping slaves between 1680 and 1688 at a rate varying from 5,000 to 9,000 per annum; that, in the period from January 1680-1 to February 4, 1688-9, 15,872 slaves were sold in Jamaica by the company, at an average price per slave of £13. 1s. 9d.; and that, between 1698 and 1707, the company and private traders combined landed in the plantations about 25,000 negroes per annum. Thus, by the beginning of the eighteenth century, the British slave trade had grown to very large dimensions.

Statistics of the British slave trade at the end of the seventeenth century.

The Peace of Utrecht and the Assiento contract.

From the year 1713 onward, the English took the lead in catering for the colonies of other nations in addition to their own. In July of that year the peace of Utrecht was signed, the twelfth article of which confirmed the famous Assiento contract already concluded in the preceding March.

[1] Part iv. Tables No. 5 and No. 25.

The origin of the Assiento has already been stated[1]. It was an agreement between the Spanish government and a foreign nation to supply the Spanish colonies in America with negro slaves. The French had held it, and now it passed into the hands of the English company 'with the same conditions on which the French enjoyed it or at any time might, or ought to enjoy the same[2].' Its terms were that, during the thirty years for which it was to last, the company were to import 144,000 Africans into Spanish America, being at the rate of 4,800 slaves per annum. They were at the same time given liberty to import during the first twenty-five years as many more negroes as they could sell, fixing in all cases their own price, except at certain specified ports; and they were also allowed to send one ship every year to the Spanish colonies with a cargo of ordinary goods[3]. In return for these privileges, they were to pay in advance a sum of money to the King of Spain, together with a royalty on each slave imported and sold: and, in addition, one quarter of their profits was assigned to the Spanish Crown, and one quarter to the King of England. Clearly the contract was expected to be most lucrative, but as a matter of fact it proved quite the reverse. In 1739 the company owed a considerable sum to the King of Spain, who in consequence threatened to cancel the bargain. This difficulty was one of the main causes of the war which broke out shortly afterwards between Great Britain and Spain, during which the Assiento was suspended; and, though the peace of 1748 provided that it should be renewed for four more years, it was finally determined after two years by a convention signed in 1750, the Spanish government paying £100,000 by way of compensation.

[1] See above, p. 79.
[2] Treaty of Utrecht, Art. 12.
[3] The Treaty of Utrecht also gave the company a concession of land on the river Plate for the purposes of their traffic. This part of South America was one of the principal importing centres of the slave trade.

86 HISTORICAL GEOGRAPHY OF THE COLONIES.

SECTION II.

Dissolution of the Royal African company.

The Act, which gave the African company the proceeds of the ad valorem duty on exports to Africa, expired in 1712; and thereafter, while the trade remained open to all British subjects, the expense of keeping up the forts fell upon the company alone. Unable to bear the constant loss which ensued, they petitioned Parliament in 1729, and the House of Commons passed resolutions to the effect that the African trade ought to remain open to all, that it ought not to be taxed for the upkeep of the forts, that the forts should be maintained 'as marks of the possessions of Great Britain,' and that an allowance should be made for their maintenance[1]. The sum of £10,000 was accordingly voted for this purpose, and a similar grant was made annually, with two or three exceptions, for the next twenty years. Still the company did not thrive, and, in 1749, a further memorial was presented to Parliament. The result was two Acts of Parliament, one passed in 1750, the other in 1752. The preamble of the former Act[2] recited that 'the trade to and from Africa is very advantageous to Great Britain, and necessary for supplying the plantations and colonies thereunto belonging with a sufficient number of negroes at reasonable rates, and for that purpose the said trade ought to be free and open to all His Majesty's subjects'; and it went on to enact that all His Majesty's subjects trading to Africa 'shall for ever hereafter be a body corporate and politic in name and in deed by the name of the Company of Merchants trading to Africa.'

The Company of Merchants trading to Africa.

Such was the system devised to take the place of the old African company. A new corporation was formed, but it was prohibited from trading in a corporate capacity; its membership was open to all British traders to Africa on payment of a fee of 40s; and its affairs were to be managed by a com-

---

[1] See the report of 1789, part 1, paper entitled: 'An account of the most material proceedings that have been had in the House of Commons relative to the African trade.'

[2] 23 Geo. II. cap. 31.

mittee of nine, elected annually by the members, three to be chosen in London, three in Bristol, and three in Liverpool. The second Act [1], which supplemented the first, provided for 'making compensation and satisfaction to the Royal African company of England for their charter, lands, forts, castles, slaves, military stores, and all other their effects whatsoever.' The compensation was paid, and the Royal African company ceased to exist from April 10, 1752. To its successor Parliament allowed from £10,000 to £15,000 a year, wherewith to keep up the African forts for the public service; and for the next 55 years, down to the abolition of the slave trade, the grant averaged £13,000 per annum. After the Abolition Act had been passed, the subsidy was increased to £23,000; and finally, in 1821, the company was dissolved and the forts taken over by the Crown.

Dissolution of the last African company.

In the narrative of these African companies there is much to interest and much to admonish. It is evident that slave-trading, under the conditions which were imposed upon the companies, was not as a rule a paying business. The profits, which were derived from it, were not sufficient to cover the cost of maintaining the stations in Africa; and bankruptcy was only averted by a system of Parliamentary subsidies. The Royal African company did not depend on slaves alone, but dealt also in various African products; and, when it secured the Assiento, the most profitable item in the bargain was found to be the right to send a single ship every year to the Spanish colonies with a cargo of other goods than negroes. There were two reasons why the slave trade did not pay. The first was, that it was in its essence an utterly unsound kind of commerce. The great requisite for *bona fide* healthy trade is peace, the slave trade on the contrary implied a state of war. It was dealing in captives, its marts were so many prisons, its agents were so many gaolers, it was produced by

The slave trade was not profitable to the companies

(a) because it was economically unsound;

---

[1] 25 Geo. II. cap. 40.

88 *HISTORICAL GEOGRAPHY OF THE COLONIES.*

SECTION II.

war and kept up by war, it depended on a set of conditions utterly opposed to progressive development of lands and peoples. A thriving trade in some agricultural or mineral commodity brings in its train other subsidiary sources of wealth; but the profit derived from trading in men was paid, so to speak, out of capital, and was acquired only by draining a continent of its labour supply and checking all legitimate industries. The second reason was, that the companies engaged in the traffic were in the eighteenth century face to face with unlimited competition. In old days a charter as a rule implied exclusive privileges; but, during the greater part of its existence, the Royal African company was expressly prohibited from enjoying any monopoly; and the association of merchants which took its place was forbidden to trade at all as a corporate body. Why, in an age of monopolies, was free trade in the case of Africa not only not discountenanced but actually insisted upon by the British government and the British nation? The answer is, that the numbers interested in the African trade were too great for any chartered company to contend with and exclude. The London, Liverpool, and Bristol merchants were determined that no company should have exclusive rights to trade to or from the West Coast of Africa; and, strong as was their opposition to any monopoly, the opposition of the American colonists was still stronger. To the planters in the West Indian islands cheap labour was a necessary of life. Barbados thrived, while the carrying trade was open to all nations and negroes were imported by the Dutch. Its prosperity waned, when the Navigation laws broke down freedom of transport, and when English African companies for a while, though only for a while, monopolised the slave trade. The law of 1750, whose preamble has been quoted above, recited that the African trade ought to be free and open, with a view to supplying the plantations 'with a sufficient number of negroes at

(b) because no monopoly was allowed.

Reason why monopoly was prohibited.

The Planters required cheap labour.

reasonable rates.' In short, the success of the plantation system, as based on slavery, was, as was afterwards demonstrated in the case of the Southern States of the Union, closely bound up with free trade.

Trade, colonisation, and territorial acquisition are the main factors in building up an empire; but the history of the British colonies teaches, among many other lessons, that trade may at times retard instead of promoting colonisation, and does not necessarily bring about ownership of soil. The colonisation of Newfoundland was perpetually prohibited through the agency and in the interests of Devonshire and Dorsetshire merchants, who feared that any scheme for settling the island would interfere with the fishing trade. Similarly, in the case of West Africa, even if the climate had permitted of settlement, not only would the conditions, under which the slave trade was carried on, have been opposed to the formation of organised colonial communities, but commercial interests in England, and planting interests in the West Indies, would have been ranged against any system giving to English settlers in Africa command of the African trade. The same reasoning explains the attitude of the British government towards West Africa. In no part of the world were its dealings more tentative. In no part of the world was there greater reluctance to proclaim dominion, and to exercise the immediate supremacy of the Crown. It has ever been a rule of British colonial policy to lean to indirect in preference to direct government control, to incorporate companies and declare Protectorates, but to keep the Government as far as possible in the background, and to be chary of incurring the full responsibilities of national ownership. The British connexion with West Africa was, and still is in the main, a trading connexion. What the traders wanted was protection for, but no restriction on, their trade. They wanted forts to be maintained, and factories to be kept open; but they had no wish for a local

CHAPTER III.

Trade does not always lead to colonisation.

As shown in West Africa.

Policy of the British government with regard to West Africa.

SECTION II.

administration, which would regulate their dealings by fixed rules. Hence no pressure was put upon the Government to annex territory and to exercise sovereignty; and the British parliament was well content with subscribing to keep up a trade which was a matter of national interest, without also pursuing a policy of annexation.

It has been noticed that, in 1729, the House of Commons resolved that the West African forts ought to be maintained 'as marks of the possessions of Great Britain.' The original resolution was to the effect that these forts were necessary for securing the African trade, and the substitution of the words quoted may be taken as an indication of some feeling at the time in favour of asserting British sovereignty. But, when African affairs were again brought to the notice of Parliament in 1749, the phrase was struck out, and protection of trade remained the only reason alleged for the intervention of Government. Again, after the peace of 1763, the northern part of West Africa, including the Gambia, was placed under the direct control of the Crown; but twenty years later it was handed back to the company; and, even after the company had been dissolved in 1821, and the forts on the Gold Coast placed under a formally organised colonial administration, they were, six years later, once more transferred for a while to the custody and control of African merchants: so hesitating was the action of the Government, so entirely was West Africa considered to be a sphere of British trade, not an integral part of the British dominions.

Statistics of the slave trade in the eighteenth century.

It is very difficult to asertain even approximately the number of negroes whom the slave-traders carried off year by year from Africa to the New World. It has been seen that, at the beginning of the eighteenth century, the total annual number carried into the plantations in British vessels was estimated at 25,000.[1] The possession of the Assiento

---

[1] See above, p. 84.

does not seem to have led to any increase in the British export, for between 1713, the date of the treaty of Utrecht, and 1733, the average number annually exported by the English was estimated at 15,000, and for the next twenty years, from 1733 to 1753, at 20,000.

In 1768, 1787, and 1798 the total number of slaves exported from West Africa by all nations was estimated roughly at 100,000 per annum. At the first of these three dates, after the peace of Paris in 1763 had left England at the height of her power, and before she was crippled by the war with the United States, the proportion carried in English ships was reckoned at from 40,000 to 60,000. At the second date specified, after the independence of the United States had been recognised by the peace of 1783, the English were credited with 38,000, against 31,000 carried by the French, 25,000 by the Portuguese, 4,000 by the Dutch, and 2,000 by the Danes. Lastly, in 1797, when during the wars of the Revolution France had for a while lost her share in the trade, the numbers were distributed as follows, English 55,000, Portuguese 25,000, Americans 15,000. From these figures one dismal fact at any rate is made clear, that Englishmen stood pre-eminent among the slave-traders of the eighteenth century: so far had they fallen since the time when the first African explorers gave out that Englishmen did not buy and sell 'any that had our own shapes[1].'

The story of the Abolition of the slave trade has often been told. For many years before it came to pass, there had not been wanting powerful protests against the traffic. The influence of religion was in England thrown, as has not always been the case, into the scale of humanity; and, even before the seventeenth century ended, two ministers at least had in their writings denounced the wickedness of trading in human beings. They were Godwin, a clergyman of the

---

[1] See above, p. 59.

SECTION II.

Church of England, author of the 'Negro's and Indian's Advocate,' who had seen in Virginia the fruits of the slave trade, and Richard Baxter, the great Nonconformist **divine**.

In 1750 Montesquieu, in the 'Esprit des lois,' wrote against **slavery in** every form; and, at a later date, his countrymen Lafayette, Condorcet, and others, who formed the Society of the Amis des Noirs, made common cause with the English enemies of the trade. In 1761 the Quakers began to protest, **the** Wesleyans followed suit, and Bishop Warburton from the pulpit proclaimed the slave trade to be contrary to all law human and Divine. In the years 1769–1772 occurred the celebrated trial, brought on at the instance of Granville Sharp, when Lord Mansfield and his brother judges decided that a slave on setting foot **in** England became free and could not be carried back to slavery. Four years later, in 1776, the first—an ineffectual—resolution against the slave trade was moved in the **House** of Commons; and, in 1788, owing to the efforts of Granville Sharp, Clarkson, Wilberforce, and others, who had formed themselves into a private society for the Abolition of the trade, the Committee of the Privy Council for Trade and Foreign Plantations was directed by **Order** in Council to hold an enquiry into the subject. **The** evidence which was taken, and which was presented to the House in 1789, contained, as might have been expected, many contradictory statements, and the witnesses on behalf of the slave-traders maintained that the traffic was carried on with all humanity. But the real test of a system is whether or not gross abuses can be practised under it, and, tried by this standard alone, the slave trade stood in the light of abundant evidence hopelessly condemned. The horrors of the Middle Passage were duly entered in print, and the evidence went further to prove that the mortality among the English sailors employed on the slave ships was very **high**, so that the cause of the negro slaves was helped by compassion for the men who were paid to carry them into slavery. Even before the report was issued, the majority of leading English statesmen had definitely pronounced against the trade. Among them were Pitt, Fox, Burke, Grey, and Lord Grenville, while at a later date the names of Canning and Brougham were added to the roll of Abolitionists. The evil was dying, but it died hard. The city of London placed humanity before vested interest, and petitioned for abolition; but the merchants of Liverpool, backed by Lord Thurlow, used every effort on the other side. The opposition took the usual course. First it was contended that the trade needed no amendment or regulation. Then its supporters agreed to regulation but opposed abolition. Then accepting the inevitable, they contended that the abolition should be gradual. Finally the tide of healthy public feeling carried all before it, and swept away for ever obstacles, objections, and delays.

The end would no doubt have come sooner, had the question arisen in less troublous times. But the days were those of the French Revolution, when the terms liberty, brotherhood, and the like became unattractive to moderate-minded men, and when the thoughts of statesmen were engrossed with more immediate problems. Hence Wilberforce and his colleagues year after year moved their resolutions and brought in their bills, without coming much nearer to the final goal. In 1787, the first settlement of Sierra Leone was founded, to be a nucleus of freedom in the land of bondage. In 1788, at the instance of Sir W. Dolben, a law was passed putting an end to over-crowding and other abuses on board the slave ships. In 1792, the King of Denmark gained for himself the glory of being the first European sovereign to prohibit his subjects from any longer engaging in the slave trade. In 1794, the Congress of the United States forbad the exportation of slaves from the States to any foreign country. In 1805, an Order in Council was issued in Great Britain, closing any newly acquired colonies to the slave trade. This proclamation was supplemented in the next year by two laws, one prohibiting British subjects from carrying slaves to any foreign country or colony, the other making it illegal for any new vessels to be employed in the traffic; and at length, in 1807, after Pitt had died and Fox had died, without seeing the end of the wearisome parliamentary struggle, Lord Grenville's Act for the abolition of the slave trade, emanating, be it noted, from the House of Lords, was carried through both Houses and received the Royal assent. By this Act the African slave trade, as far as Great Britain, her subjects, and her colonies were concerned, became, from May 1, 1807, 'utterly abolished, prohibited, and declared to be unlawful'; and the same Act broke for ever the chain, which had so long linked together in an unlovely bond the history of West Africa and that of the West Indies.

'The evil that men do lives after them,' but the doers are spared by death from seeing and feeling the full consequences of their crimes. For peoples there is no such merciful dispensation. They reap in bitterness what they have sown, they cannot cancel the past, or lightly regenerate scenes of former misrule. For a century and a half the English had taken a foremost place in keeping the West Coast of Africa as a preserve for catching, buying, and selling men. They had discouraged peace and the arts of peace. They had encouraged raiding and war. They had invited the native races to prey on one another; and, though in the end they abolished the slave trade and reversed their policy, they could not undo the mischief which that policy had wrought. West Africa was left as a dead weight on their hands, profitless, helpless, well nigh hopeless, disorganised, demoralised, with its natural barbarism artificially intensified. Eighty years and more have passed since the date of the Abolition Act, English lives have been lost, and English money has been spent, in trying to bring peace and order and industry into lands which were taught to know none of these things. Yet the end of it all is that civilisation has made but little way, that industry is hardly more than trade in jungle produce, and that, even in these brighter and healthier days, men sometimes wonder whether the game is worth the candle, whether England gives any real benefit to or derives any real benefit from her possessions on the West Coast of Africa.

CHAPTER IV.

ENGLISH, FRENCH, AND DUTCH ON THE WEST COAST OF AFRICA, 1660-1821.

SECTION II.

DOWN to the present century, the slave trade was the central point in West African history. All other events were grouped round it, and its exigencies determined the relations of the various European powers to each other in Africa. For this reason it seemed necessary to give a continuous sketch of its rise and fall, which must now be supplemented by some notice of the wars, the treaties, and the international dealings which it involved.

The seventeenth century. Struggle between the Dutch and English in West Africa.

North of the Gulf of Guinea, the English have from first to last been brought most into contact and conflict with the French. On the coast of the Gulf of Guinea their chief rivals till little more than twenty years ago were the Dutch. It will be remembered that the company of 1618 established themselves at two points in West Africa, on the Gambia, and at Cormantine on the Gold Coast[1]. The fort at the latter place, a few miles to the east of Cape Coast Castle, was kept up in spite of the dissolution of the company; and, with some minor factories on the same coast, was in British hands in the year 1662, when the new company of Royal Adventurers took over the African trade of Great Britain. Hard by Cormantine was Mouree, where, as we have seen[2], the Dutch in 1624 built their first stronghold in Guinea. Thus side by side the two peoples planted themselves upon the Guinea coast. The

[1] Above, pp. 57-8.   [2] Above, p. 65.

English had the priority in time, but the Dutch had a definite national policy, which carried them forward far faster than their rivals. That policy was not merely to break down the Portuguese monopoly, but to substitute for it a monopoly of their own, no less exclusive in theory and more effective in practice. The first part of the programme was carried out by the taking of Elmina. The second part involved dislodging the English. With this end in view, Dutch cruisers were kept on the coast for the express purpose of preventing the English from trafficking with the natives; and, whether there was war or peace in Europe between Great Britain and the Netherlands, there was constant strife between Dutch and English traders on the West Coast of Africa. The strength of the Dutch consisted in having their resources concentrated in the hands of a single powerful company; and it was the recognition of this fact by their rivals, which led to the incorporation in 1662 of the British Company of Royal Adventurers trading to Africa. At the same time, the grievances of the British traders, and the wrongs which they had suffered in Africa, were strongly pressed upon the King and Parliament. A list was made of the ships which had been taken by the Dutch, and the British minister at the Hague was instructed to demand compensation. None could be obtained; the Dutchmen in West Africa proved more vigorous and more aggressive than ever; and an address from the British merchants to both Houses of Parliament in 1664, praying for immediate and effectual redress, produced only ineffectual remonstrances[1]. Eventually war was formally declared by Charles the Second

---

[1] In Pepys' diary, however, will be found an opinion that the wrongs done by the Dutch were not very serious after all. Under date May 29, 1664, he gives a conversation with Sir W. Coventry on the subject, who 'seemed to argue mightily upon the little reason that there is for all this,' and expressed an opinion that the loss suffered by the Guinea company 'did not amount to above £200 or £300.' (Lord Braybrooke's edition of Pepys' diary, vol. ii. p. 53.)

98 HISTORICAL GEOGRAPHY OF THE COLONIES.

SECTION II.

against the Netherlands at the beginning of 1665, and thus questions arising out of the Guinea trade brought on open hostilities between the two leading naval powers of Europe.

The Dutch war of 1665.

It was a memorable struggle—this war which originated on the West Coast of Africa. It was fought out on the sea, on the coasts of England and Holland, in African waters, in the East Indies, on the Hudson river, on the shores of Guiana, and among the West Indian islands. The great Dutch admiral De Ruyter was everywhere, at one time on the Guinea coast, at another raiding the Leeward Islands and threatening Barbados, and again sailing up the Thames and Medway, while Monk hard pressed could scarce keep London safe.

English successes.

Long before the two governments had finally broken with each other, their subjects in foreign parts had come to open warfare. For a while the flowing tide was with the English. In the autumn of 1663, an expedition was sent out to West Africa to protect British trade. Its commander, Captain Holmes[1], took all the Dutch forts upon the Gold Coast with the exception of the two strongest, the fort at Axim and the Castle of Elmina. Off Cape Verde, he laid low the twin forts Nassau[2], which the Netherlanders had built on the island of Goree; and at the Gambia, he founded Fort James on an islet in the river, about 20 miles from its mouth, 'for the principal seat of the English commerce and to secure their new conquests over the Hollanders on this coast[3].' The conquests however were short-lived. In the summer of 1664 Holmes sailed west for the Hudson, where the days of the Dutch colony of New Netherlands were rapidly being numbered; and almost immediately De Ruyter made good his countrymen's losses in Africa, recovering every Dutch fort

English reverses.

---

[1] Afterwards Admiral Sir Robert Holmes. See Dict. of National Biography, s. v.
[2] One on the hill and one on the plain (Barbot, p. 20).
[3] Barbot, p. 74.

on the coast except Cabo Corso or Cape Coast Castle, and in addition taking the English stronghold at Cormantine. 'I hear fully,' writes Pepys in his Diary on December 24, 1664, 'the news of our being beaten to dirt at Guinny by De Ruyter and his fleet[1].'

The war ended with the peace of Breda in 1667, the terms of which were that either side should keep the fruits of its conquests. Accordingly, in America, the English colony of Surinam became the property of the Dutch, and the New Netherlands on the Hudson passed into English hands and became the State of New York[2].

In West Africa, the net result was that the English lost Cormantine and gained instead Cape Coast Castle, and that the Royal Adventurers, crippled by the losses which they had suffered and the expenses of the war, made way in 1672 for a new company, the Royal African Company of England.

The ninth clause in the treaty of Breda deserves special notice, as illustrating the condition of affairs at this time upon the West Coast of Africa. It enacted that 'Whereas in countries far remote, as in Africa and America, especially in Guinea, certain protestations and declarations and other writings of that kind, prejudicial to the liberty of trade and navigation, have been emitted and published on either side by the governors and officers in the name of their superiors,' any such declarations should be null and void, and trade and navigation should be free as before the war. Even with the help of the submarine cable, it is still found no easy task at times to prevent governors and officers 'in countries far remote' from issuing proclamations, which go beyond the instructions and the wishes of their superiors at home; it may be well imagined, therefore, that in the seventeenth

Chapter IV.

The Peace of Breda.

---

[1] Lord Braybrooke's ed. vol. ii. p. 124.
[2] The terms of the peace of Breda were not finally carried out till after a second war with the Dutch, which broke out in 1672, and ended in 1674 with the peace of Westminster, confirming the former treaty.

SECTION II. century, on the West Coast of Africa, fire-eating Dutch and English captains protested loudly from their ships and forts, and backed up their protestations with gun and sword, regardless of the responsibilities which they were entailing on their respective governments. There is no rivalry more unscrupulous, no jealousy more bitter than that between traders of different races in foreign parts, and the servants of the Dutch West India Company on the one hand and the English Adventurers on the other hammered at each other, until their quarrels and reprisals brought on a world-wide war.

Position of the English on the Gold Coast after the peace of Breda.

When peace was restored, the Dutch were in a far stronger position than the English; but, with the incorporation of the Royal African company, British prospects improved. Forts were built at Accra, Dixcove, Winnebah, Secondee, Commendah, and Annamaboe on the Gold Coast: and further to the east, on the Slave Coast, a post was established at Whydah,

Cape Coast Castle kept and strengthened.

the chief centre of the slave trade. Cape Coast Castle itself was at the same time strengthened and enlarged, until it ranked second only to the Dutch stronghold at Elmina; and here the Agent General of the British company resided, with the title of 'General of Guinea from Sierra Leone to Angola[1].' Thus the English drew up level with the Dutch in West Africa, and more than a hundred years passed before any serious difficulty again arose between the two nations in African waters.

The French in Senegambia.

North of the Gold Coast, Dutch and English alike had to reckon with the French, who, under Louis the Fourteenth and his minister Colbert, were making a bold bid for colonial trade and colonial empire. Following the example of the Dutch, Colbert, in 1664-5, incorporated two great exclusive companies, one for the East and one for the West. The West India company, in which the old Dieppe and Rouen company was merged[2], was given the sole right to trade, in

[1] Barbot, p. 170.   [2] See above, p. 62.

America from Canada to the River Amazon, in Africa from Cape Blanco to the Cape of Good Hope. The scheme, formulated as it was by a far-seeing statesman, and backed by a strong despotic ruler, contained all the elements of success; but want of stability and continuity in the colonial policy of the French government proved fatal to this, as to many other well-planned projects. **Nine** years only passed, before the company broke up in 1673–4; the West Indian colonies were taken over by the Crown, **and** various minor companies handled the West African trade.

Colbert's **measures, however, seem to** have given an impetus to French enterprise **in** Africa, **and** the results of **the war** between France and the Netherlands, which lasted from 1672 **to 1678,** strengthened **the position of the French in** the **region of** Cape Verde. **Here was** the island of Goree, the earliest Dutch possession in West Africa, lately taken by the English, and promptly recovered by De Ruyter. In 1677, the French admiral D'Estrées took **the** forts on the island and burnt them to the ground, sailing away subsequently over the Atlantic to attack the Netherlanders again in the West Indian island of Tobago[1]. In the following year, by the peace of Nimeguen, Goree was **ceded to** France, **and the old Dutch fort of** Nassau **on the** plain was rebuilt **by its** new owners under the name of Fort St. Francis or **Vermandois.** This incident, small in itself, was one which shaped to a large extent the future course of West African history. Henceforward the operations **of the** Dutch were mainly confined to the Gold Coast[2], **while, north of the** Gambia, French influence was consolidated in the country of the Senegal. Goree, which is at the present time a fortified outpost of the **great French** naval station of **Dakar** on Cape **Verde,** became, from the date of the treaty of Nimeguen,

Goree taken by the French from the Dutch.

---

[1] See vol. ii. of this work, p. 256.
[2] It is not quite certain, however, whether the Dutch **still retained for** a while a fort on the island of Arguin.

SECTION II.

one of the most important strongholds, if not the most important, of the French in West Africa, subordinate only to St. Louis on the Senegal, which was, as Barbot tells us, the usual residence of the Director or General Agent of the French company. In addition, the French had a station on the Gambia, at a place called Albreda over against the English Fort James; and about the same date, in 1685, they appear to have carried on trade in the Bissos or Bissagos islands, lower down the coast, off the mouth of the Rio Grande, though here, as on the Gambia, they were less successful than the English.

French policy in West Africa.

The short life of the French West India company has been taken as an illustration of the fault, which more than all others marred the colonial enterprise of France, the want of a continuous settled policy, as opposed to a series of schemes generally well conceived, often brilliantly executed, but on the other hand rarely persisted in for a long time on the same lines, modified, amplified, or reversed, according to the whims and caprices of the French rulers for the time being. Curiously enough this criticism does not apply to the main course of French history in West Africa. Here they seem to have from the first marked out for themselves a well-defined sphere. That sphere was the Senegal river and the surrounding districts, and they kept themselves on the whole steadily within its limits. Judged at the present time, with reference alike to past history and to future prospects, the French in Senegambia have on the whole achieved distinct success, as compared not only with the work of rival European nations in West Africa, but also with their own doings in other parts of the world. This result may be attributed to the fact, that on the African coast they measured their interests correctly, and moved forward neither too fast nor too far. Though their traders were among the first to exploit the Guinea coast[1], there were no French forts or

---

[1] See above, pp. 15, 53, 60.

factories to be found there. They did much better, as Barbot points out, in 'driving their trade by shipping only along the Gold Coast and in other parts of Guinea properly so called, without the charge of such settlements ashore[1].' Once, in the years 1701–4, they established a station at Assinee, immediately to the west of the present Gold Coast colony, at a point in the coast to which they have reverted in the present century; but the experiment proved unsuccessful. They had to beat off the Dutch, they were at variance with the natives, they attracted little or no trade, and, after two or three years, the fort was abandoned.

While the French were making way on the Senegal and at Cape Verde, the English held a strong position on the Gambia. Fort James, which Holmes had founded, ranked second among the British forts to Cape Coast Castle. It was 'the next best fortification to Cape Coast Castle of all that are to be found on either the north or the south coasts of Guinea[2]'; and, with this one exception, it was the head settlement of the Royal African company of England. Several smaller factories on various branches of the river were subordinate to it, and its importance was shown by the fact that it was garrisoned by sixty or seventy white men in addition to 'gromettoes[3].' Thus, towards the end of the seventeenth century, Senegambia was divided much as it is at the present day, the French being found mainly on the Senegal, and the English mainly on the Gambia. But neither river belonged exclusively to either French or English. An islet in the Senegal, which bore the name of 'L'Ile aux Anglois[4],' told that the English had at one time or another

The English on the Gambia.

---

[1] p. 168. Barbot contrasts favourably the results of their trading in Guinea without having factories on shore, with the costliness of their establishments in Senegambia.

[2] Barbot, pp. 74, 75.

[3] Gruméte in Portuguese means a ship boy. The word constantly occurs in the early notices of West Africa. See also below, p. 180.

[4] Barbot, p. 18.

a footing on the Senegal; on the Gambia, on the other hand, the French had their factory of Albreda, while Dutch and Portuguese also came trading up this latter river[1].

War between the French and English in West Africa.

There was no rest for the English in West Africa. War with the Dutch on the Gold Coast was followed by war with the French in Senegambia. In 1692, an English expedition from the Gambia took Goree and St. Louis from the French; but St. Louis was retaken at once, and Goree in the following year. In 1695 came the turn of the French, who levelled Fort James to the ground. It appears to have been soon rebuilt, for it is stated to have been again twice[2] taken by the French between the peace of Ryswick in 1697 and the treaty of Utrecht in 1713. In the eleventh article of the latter treaty, mention is made of some outstanding French claim in connexion with the capitulation of the 'castle of Gambia.'

The eighteenth century.

This then was the position of affairs on the West Coast of Africa in the early years of the eighteenth century, that century of great wars and of the slave trade. North of the Gold Coast, the two leading nations were the French and the English. They alone had fortified posts on the Senegal and Gambia and the adjoining coasts, though there were Dutch and Portuguese traders also on the scene, who possibly maintained some factories of small account. On the Gold Coast there was a strange medley of nations, but among them the Dutch and the English held the strongest forts, while the French had no fortification at all.

Characteristics of European occupation in West Africa.

West African history was slowly shaping itself according to the course of events in Europe, the English gaining strength on the Gold Coast as compared with the Dutch, and in Senegambia competing, sometimes defeated, sometimes

---

[1] The English however were far stronger on the Gambia than other Europeans. Writing in 1682, Barbot (p. 75) speaks of the French as 'having an inconsiderable trade here in comparison of the English, who are almost as good as masters of the river.'

[2] Probably in 1702 and 1709, but the dates are not very clear.

triumphant, with the French. But the story of West Africa cannot be rightly understood, without bearing in mind that no European people at this time or for many long years afterwards had any dominion on the Coast. It is true that the Portuguese had claimed lordship over land and sea, and that the Dutch professed to have taken over their inheritance, attempting in the days of their strength to treat other Europeans as unlicensed interlopers. But, as a matter of fact, no European nation held in these times any territorial possession in West Africa. There were no West African colonies with adjoining Protectorates, such as exist at the present day. The competition between French, Dutch, and English was for trade, not for sovereignty. The forts and factories were built on soil which belonged and was recognised as belonging to natives. West Africa was owned by negroes, who admitted European traders; and no part of it, except possibly some small islets such as Goree[1], was definitely conquered by or sold or ceded to any European government. As the British empire in India began with factories set up by permission of Indian princes, as, in China, European agencies at Canton existed only on sufferance, so in West Africa French, English, Dutch, Danes, and Brandenburghers enjoyed no ownership, no sovereign rights. Near the English Fort James on the Gambia stood the French fort of Albreda; hard by Cape Coast Castle was the Dutch fort of Mouree; at Accra, English, Dutch, and Danes had each their fortified factory. There was no exclusive possession, for none were landlords, all were tenants from year to year. Ships of all nations, on entering the Gambia, were wont to salute the King of Barra, who owned the mouth of the river, and to pay a toll of one bar of iron. On the Senegal, the French company paid to the native rulers both import and export duties[2]; and, when in

CHAPTER IV.

---

[1] See above, p. 63.
[2] See Barbot, pp. 18, 43. In the former passage Barbot says: 'The

SECTION II. 1872 the English took over the Dutch forts on the Gold Coast, it was found that the Dutch were still paying an annual subsidy to the King of Ashantee, which, though stated not to have been of the nature of a rent or tribute, had been paid from time immemorial to the neighbouring chiefs, and was at least evidence of insecurity of tenure[1]. In fact, these payments were intended in one form or another simply to safeguard trade: companies were concerned, not governments: factories were in case, not colonies: ownership or no ownership, trade was the one thing needful, and without the goodwill of the natives no trade could be carried on[2].

British factories in West Africa in the middle of the eighteenth century.

The Treaty of Utrecht, by confirming the grant of the Assiento contract to the Royal African company, placed the English in front of their rivals on the West Coast of Africa. Out of this contract arose war with Spain[3], but no serious complication on the coast with either French or Dutch is recorded until the time of the Seven Years' War. The schedule of the Act of 1752[4], which completed the dissolution of the African company, enumerated the forts of the company according to a survey which had been held in 1749. They were nine in all; eight on or near the Gold Coast, viz. Cape Coast Castle, Commendah, Secondee, Dixcove, Tantumquerry, Winnebah, Accra, and Whydah; and James island, as it was styled, on the Gambia. There were no doubt also subsidiary factories, but none others that were garrisoned or fortified.

French here, for the privilege of their factory and trade, pay to the King of Senega sixteen in the hundred for hides, . . . the Portuguese paid but ten when they traded here, and but little for other commodities.'

[1] See Parliamentary Paper, c. 670 (1872), 'correspondence relative to the cession of the Dutch settlements on the West Coast of Africa,' and see below, pp. 133-4.

[2] Meredith in his Account of the Gold Coast of Africa (1812), pp. 103-4 note, writes: 'We appear to claim no right of conquest in Africa, as far as it respects the natives. The company pay ground-rent and water-custom at most of their settlements. The forts have been maintained for the purpose of trade only.'

[3] See above, p. 85.

[4] 25 Geo. II. cap. 40. See above, p. 87.

The Seven Years' War began in 1756. In Africa, as elsewhere throughout the wide world, English and French struggled for the mastery, and in Africa, as elsewhere, the former nation gained at the expense of the latter. In 1757, a small French squadron, under a commander named De Kersaint, made a half-hearted attempt on Cape Coast Castle. There were but thirty white men in the garrison, together with some mulattos; the Dutch at Elmina would gladly have seen their dangerous neighbours dispossessed; the natives were probably indifferent, possibly hostile to the English. But the English agent at the fort, Bell by name, had the nerve and resolution which the Frenchman seems to have lacked; and, after a short and fruitless attack, De Kersaint[1] followed the usual course taken by naval officers in West Africa, whether successful or unsuccessful, of sailing off with wind and tide to the West Indies. At this time, the chief article of export to European markets from the Senegal and the coast to the north of that river was gum-arabic. The trade was entirely in the hands of the French, and British merchants were driven to securing their supplies of gum at second-hand through the Dutch. Chafing under the annoyance thus caused, an English Quaker merchant, called Cumming, who had visited these countries and made friends with one of the leading native princes, laid before his government a scheme for driving the French out of Senegambia—a feat, which he reconciled to his Quaker conscience as being capable of achievement without loss of blood. His views were adopted, and an expedition was sent to the Senegal, to which St. Louis capitulated in 1758. The same force attempted unsuccessfully to reduce Goree, but later in the year a second expedition under Commodore Keppel took this island also.

CHAPTER IV.

War between the French and English in West Africa, 1756.

---

[1] He was possibly the same officer as the De Kersaint to whom the English in Demerara capitulated in 1782.

SECTION II.

The peace of 1763.

Thus for the time being the French were entirely driven out of West Africa[1].

In 1763 the peace of Paris was signed. The tenth article restored Goree to France 'in the condition it was in when conquered,' but confirmed to Great Britain, 'in full right,' 'the river Senegal with the forts and factories of St. Louis, Podor, and Galam, and with all the rights and dependencies of the said river Senegal.' Judged by the light of subsequent events, it was a stupid, ill-advised provision, one of those compromises inevitably leading to future trouble, for which the English seem to have a perfect genius, and examples of which might be almost indefinitely multiplied from the annals of colonial history.

Treaties should be the end, not the beginning of strife. There must, it is true, be a certain amount of compromise, but the arrangement need not be so framed as to invite further friction. By this very treaty of Paris Great Britain took the whole of Canada; yet, as though deliberately to sow the seeds of future dissension, the French fishing rights on the coast of Newfoundland were fully confirmed, and the islets of St. Pierre and Miquelon were ceded to France. In West Africa, if Great Britain had kept all her conquests, the connexion of France with this part of the world would have been for the time being, and might have been for all time, completely broken; if, on the other hand, the French forts had all been given back, French and English spheres of influence in Africa might have been definitely marked off with some hope of finality. As it was, the Senegal was taken, and Goree was left, a position near enough to the Senegal to make the recovery of the river an ever-present object to the French, and strong enough to facilitate that recovery at a convenient season.

[1] An account of these operations on the West Coast of Africa will be found in Smollett's History, chaps. xxvii and xxix. See also the Annual Register for 1758, p. 75, to which there is an interesting note.

After the peace of Paris was signed, the forts on the Senegal were at first handed over to the company of merchants. Very shortly afterwards, however, by an Act of 1765, the British Government assumed the direct control of the West African coast from Barbary as far south as Cape Rouge or Roxo. For the time being, therefore, both the Senegal and the Gambia were placed directly under the Crown, the company being still left in possession of the forts on the Gold Coast. In 1775 war was renewed, and in the following year the French retook St. Louis, which, with its dependencies on the Senegal, was ceded to France by the treaty of Versailles in 1783[1]. The same treaty guaranteed in full right to the French the forts of Arguin and Portendik to the north of the Senegal; but, by a provision bearing a family resemblance to the treaty rights of the French in Newfoundland, the English were allowed to engage in the gum-trade on this section of the coast from the mouth of the river St. John to the bay of Portendik, though prohibited from forming any permanent settlements. Another clause in the treaty guaranteed to the English their possession of 'Fort James and of the river Gambia,' which was immediately afterwards by Act of Parliament again transferred from the Crown to the company. Thus the French recovered the whole of their possessions in Senegambia; and a few years later, in 1787, they still further strengthened their position by acquiring from the natives Cape Verde and Dakar.

The peace of 1783.

Meanwhile the English were also involved in war with the Dutch; and, repulsed from Elmina in 1781, they subsequently took the Dutch forts at Commendah and Accra[2]. Peace between the two peoples was patched up by the treaty of 1784, the seventh clause of which provided for a settlement

Peace of 1784 between

---

[1] The clause in the treaty—clause ix, which ceded the Senegal to France, also restored to the French the island of Goree which had been taken by the English in the course of the war.

[2] Accra, with four smaller forts, was taken by Captain Shirley of the *Leander*, apparently sometime in 1782.

SECTION II.
the Dutch and the English.

of the differences which had arisen between the English African company and the Dutch West India company, 'relative to then avigation on the coasts of Africa, as also on the subject of Cape Apollonia.' The forts were duly restored in the following year.

The Wars of the French Revolution.

The last great struggle came on between England and France, and West Africa was involved in the war. In 1800, and again in 1804, the English took Goree, and in 1809 St. Louis also; but the treaties of 1814 and 1815, which, as far as West Africa was concerned, revived the peace of Versailles, gave them back to France, and in 1817 the English evacuated them for the last time.

The French on the Gambia.

In 1786, in spite of the treaty of Versailles, the French re-established themselves at their old post of Albreda on the river Gambia. They justified their action by contending that, though the treaty guaranteed the Gambia to Great Britain, the river only began at James island, which is really about twenty miles from the mouth, and that therefore they were free to build a fort at or slightly below that point. After 1814 they returned to Albreda, and maintained their position there down to the year 1857, when they finally left the river, as a set-off against the abandonment by the English of their trading rights at Portendik.

Before the eighteenth century had quite passed away, two events occurred in West Africa, which were signs of the coming time. In 1787, the year in which the first British colonists were sent to Australia, a beginning was made of a settlement at Sierra Leone. It was intended to be an asylum for negroes, who had been brought over or had found their way over to England from America or the West Indies, and who, on landing in England, had gained their freedom, and gaining it had been left to starve. For their benefit, a tract of land was bought from the natives on the peninsula of Sierra Leone; and, at the instance and under the charge of private philanthropists, but at the expense of the Govern-

The founding of the Sierra Leone settlement.

ment, a detachment of black freemen was sent to the scene of what is now perhaps the best known of the West African colonies of Great Britain. This settlement, the story of which will be told hereafter, was a wholly new departure, and marked in more ways than one that the tide was beginning to turn. The descendants of Africans, who had been carried into bondage in the New World, now came back through England to liberty in the land of their fathers; and, twenty years before the slave trade was abolished, a colony was planted in the midst of the slave traders' domain, the essence and object of which was freedom. The settlement again was established on a spot definitely ceded to Great Britain, and over which therefore the British government could exercise sovereign rights. The King of the country, by a treaty concluded in 1788, proclaimed himself a liege of the King of England; and the Act of 1791, which incorporated the Sierra Leone company, spoke of them as holding the ceded land from the British Crown. The African company had no lot or part in the undertaking. It was the outcome of a new policy. It was inspired with a new spirit. It was intended to be, and it became, a home of law and liberty under British protection and British rule. It was the first-fruits of colonisation, as opposed to the old fort and factory system, the beginning and the end of which was private trade.

CHAPTER IV.

As these traders' factories, with the system of which they were the outcome, were the negation of colonies, so and for the same reasons they were a bar to discovery and exploration, to the developement and opening up of Africa. They were a chain of posts by the sea, receptacles for men and merchandise brought by the natives from the interior, not intended to be points from which European influence and protection might extend inland, but, on the contrary, standing protests against any interference with the savagery which reigned supreme, and upon the continuance of which the slave trade depended. Only along the rivers had Europeans

African exploration and Mungo Park.

SECTION II.

gone to any distance from the sea, and, at the end of the eighteenth century, hardly more was known of the interior of Africa than had been known two hundred years before. Some advance had been made by the French on the Senegal between 1697 and 1720, when André Brue, Director of the French Senegal company, carried French influence as far up the river as Médine, 625 miles from St. Louis; and, about the same date, an English exploring expedition was sent up the Gambia. But, whatever scanty knowledge experts may have thus gained, to the ordinary public Africa was a sealed book, and the great West African river of the Niger was wrapped in a kind of legendary obscurity, such as even in our own time shrouded the sources of the Nile. A note to the Annual Register of 1758[1] runs as follows: 'The river Senega or Senegal is one of those channels of the river Niger, by which it is supposed to discharge its waters into the Atlantic ocean. The river Niger, according to the best maps, rises in the east of Africa, and, after a course of 300 miles nearly due west, divides into three branches, the most northerly of which is the Senegal as above, the middle is the Gambia or Gambra, and the most southern Rio Grande.' Such was the authorised view of the waterways of West Africa, written at the time when England was well nigh making the world her own. Three centuries had passed since Europeans first came to West Africa, and the net result was the most hopeless ignorance of all beyond the coast. The reason was, that Africa had never been valued for itself, never been more than skirted by traders, whose interest it was to keep the veil undrawn.

Exactly at the time when the settlement at Sierra Leone was founded, the African Association, formed to promote discovery in Africa, began to send out explorers to the north and west of the continent. The dangers were great, the results were small, and one and another lost their lives. At

[1] p. 75; reference has been made to this note, above, p. 108, note.

length, in 1795, they secured the services of Mungo Park, the father of modern African exploration, and the first of Europeans to reach the upper waters of the Niger. In 1795, and again in 1805, the first time in the employ of the Association, the second time in that of the Government, Park made his way from the Gambia to the Niger. From the second expedition he never returned, but lost his life in attempting to follow the Niger down to the sea. It was left for those who came after to complete what he began, and to disprove his own theory that the Niger and the Congo were one. Long and bright as is the list of African explorers, no other name holds quite the same place in African history as his. A Scotchman from the Vale of Yarrow, he was the forerunner of other Scotchmen, too many to recount, who, as explorers and missionaries, one after another spent their lives for Africa. The fact, that the scene of his exploits was West Africa, may well have contributed with other motives to deter the British government from relinquishing their hold upon this part of the continent; but, over and above what he was, and over and above what he did, his record is chiefly interesting because it embodied the movement of the time. The spirit, which stirred up the African Association to promote discovery, was the same spirit as that which fired Clarkson and Wilberforce against the slave trade, and which gave birth to the Sierra Leone colony. It meant the awakening of Africa, and of the minds of Europeans about Africa. It meant the revolt of good feeling and common sense against a system, which shut up this great land against light, and freedom, and knowledge, and intercourse between peoples. Men had begun to ask why should these things be? How was it that all these years had gone and left Africa undeveloped, uncared for, and unknown? The old order was brought up in judgement and was condemned, and at length into Africa there came from Europe, with a mass of evil, some little leaven of good.

CHAPTER V.

THE RISE OF THE BRITISH WEST COAST SETTLEMENTS.

SECTION II.

Modern history of West Africa.

WITH the abolition of the slave trade in 1807, the close of the wars between French and English in 1815, and the dissolution of the African company in 1821, we enter upon the Modern history of West Africa, or rather of Europeans in West Africa. The line is sharply drawn between the old and the new, more sharply than in other parts of the world. Nowhere else, perhaps, was there such a complete break, such an entire reversal of policy and system. The slave trade disappeared. The connexion between Africa and America was severed. Companies gradually made way for Governments. Forts and factories leased from natives developed into settlements, colonies, and Protectorates, stretching further and further inland. Europeans ceased to war perpetually with each other, or to encourage strife between negro tribes. Their objects and their dealings were changed. Only there remained the same unhealthy lands, the same savage races, long made more savage by the slave trade, and now further demoralised by gin.

The change, which was gradually wrought in and for West Africa, resulted in more pronounced interference by the British government; but it must not be overlooked that in this, as in every other phase of English history, private pioneers first showed the way. Private associations led the battle against the slave trade, and originated the scheme of a free negro colony at Sierra Leone. A private association first sent out Mungo Park to explore the interior of the continent. It was on the second occasion only that he was sent by the Government.

CHAPTER V.

A world-wide empire, like that of Great Britain, whose growth has been due more to private agency than to the policy of kings and statesmen, includes various places and provinces, which, if the choice had from the first rested with the Government, would never have become dependencies of the British Crown. Trade springs up in one form or another. Vested interests come into being. Protection is demanded for those interests; and ever-growing pressure is brought to bear upon the Ministry of the day to endorse the acts of irresponsible citizens. Even if the original tie be broken, subsidiary links still hold fast. It is found impossible wholly to cut adrift from what has gone before. It is always difficult for a Government to draw back, most of all in the sphere of foreign and colonial policy. Foreign powers and native races do not distinguish between a people and its rulers. Whatever Englishmen do in strange lands, whatever engagements they make, whatever responsibilities they incur, all is eventually credited to the British government. Hence ministers are driven to accept the inevitable, and often, when roundly charged with being aggressive, are, if the truth be known, going forward with heavy hearts, only because greater misery would be caused by turning back.

Public Policy and Private Interests.

When the slave trade was abolished, the main interest which Great Britain had in West Africa entirely disappeared. There was apparently no strong reason why even the semblance of a connexion between these two parts of the world should any longer be maintained. The Government was most anxious to withdraw if possible. Even as late as '1865, a select Parliamentary Committee reported 'that all further extension of territory, or assumption of government, or new treaties offering any protection to

SECTION II.

native tribes would be inexpedient; and that the object of our policy should be to encourage in the natives the exercise of those qualities, which may render it possible for us more and more to transfer to them the administration of all the governments, with a view to an ultimate withdrawal from all, except, probably, Sierra Leone.' Yet, as a matter of fact, territory has been extended; government has been assumed; a long series of treaties has been made, perpetually enlarging the sphere of British protection; until, at the present day, the British government is far more deeply and far more definitely involved in West Africa, than ever it was in the days of the slave trade.

Causes which, after the abolition of the slave trade, kept the English in West Africa.
1. The practical impossibility of immediate withdrawal.

This result has been mainly due to two causes. In the first place, human nature being what it is, the English had been too long on the coast to leave it all at once. Even the Danes and the Dutch, who had for many years fallen behind in the race of nations, kept a hold on the Gold Coast, the former people till 1850, the latter till 1872. Much more then was it impossible for the leading European power in West Africa by one act to dissolve for ever a connexion which was two centuries old. But, unless the knot was cut, unless a wholesale severance was at once effected, it was absolutely certain that a people which was still growing, still moving forward, would, by mere force of circumstances, be carried along the thorny path which leads to annexation, to sovereignty whether directly proclaimed or partly veiled under the guise of a Protectorate.

2. Philanthropy.

In the second place, as England had been most deeply tainted with the guilt of the slave trade, so she was beyond all other nations pledged to wipe it out. Philanthropy is essentially aggressive, and a nation instinct with the philanthropic spirit moves forward fast and far. Sierra Leone was the outcome of a new-born love for the human race. If all the forts on the Gold Coast had been given up, if the Gambia had been left for ever, if Liverpool traders had ceased to send ships to Guinea, this one settlement, it may safely be asserted, would still have been retained, and would have become a nucleus for a British dominion in West Africa. The English went for generations to Africa to follow up the slave trade. Then they went again to put it down. Thus new interests were created and took root, until in our own time West Africa has marched with the rest of the world, and the competition of European powers, coupled with the revival of chartered companies, has, for the time being, put an end to looking backward.

In the year 1791, there are said to have been forty European forts in West Africa, established for the purposes of the slave trade. Of these forts, fifteen belonged to the Dutch, fourteen to the English, three to the French, and four to the Danes and the Portuguese respectively. On the abolition of the slave trade, the English company abandoned Fort James on the Gambia, but the increased Parliamentary subsidy enabled them to maintain their forts on the Gold Coast and at Whydah, the number of which seems to have been twelve, when the company came to an end in 1821. The Government determined to keep up four forts only with a civil and military establishment, not formally relinquishing the others, but practically leaving them to take care of themselves. The four in question, taken from west to east, were Dixcove, Cape Coast Castle, Annamaboe, and Accra, the distance from Dixcove to Accra being about 130 miles. Meanwhile, some British merchants, who removed from the Senegal and Goree, when at the end of the great war those settlements were given back to France, had established themselves, in the year 1816, on St. Mary's island at the mouth of the Gambia. The new colony was named Bathurst after Earl Bathurst, who was then Secretary of State for the Colonies, and was taken over by the Government at the same time

Chapter V.

Policy of the British government after 1821.

Reduction in the number of forts on the Gold Coast.

Foundation of Bathurst on the Gambia.

SECTION II. as the Gold Coast forts. Both the one and the other were placed under the government of Sierra Leone, which had become a Crown colony on January 1, 1808; and the whole formed for administrative purposes a single colony, under the name of the West Africa Settlements.

Thus, for the moment, all vestiges of company rule were swept away, and the various disjointed dependencies were united under one administration and under the direct control of the Crown. It was too good a change to last. Behind *Difficulties with the Ashantees.* the Gold Coast is the once powerful negro kingdom of Ashantee, which had risen on the ruins of other native powers, and which was, in the early years of the present century, extending its supremacy to the seaboard over the Fantee tribes, who claimed and received the ground-rents of Cape Coast Castle. In 1807, the Ashantees besieged Annamaboe, and, playing off the Dutch against the English, extorted from the latter an acknowledgement of their suzerainty over the coast tribes and a promise to pay to their King tribute or rent for the forts. Two new invasions took place, in 1814[1] and 1816 respectively, in the latter of which Cape Coast Castle was blockaded. In 1817, the company, sending an embassy to the Ashantee capital Coomassie, made a treaty, under which the authority of the King of Ashantee over the coast and its native inhabitants was duly recognised, while he on his side accepted an English resident at his capital. In the next year, 1818, the British government interfered for the first time directly in Gold Coast affairs, and sent an envoy, Mr. Dupuis, to Coomassie, who made a fresh treaty with the King. The company appear to have resented the interference of Government in what they considered their own sphere. Their agents rejected Dupuis' treaty, and at the same time refused to carry out the terms of their own, with the result

---

[1] In the invasion of 1814, the Ashantees took the fort of Winnebah, and killed its commandant Mr. Meredith, the author of 'An Account of the Gold Coast of Africa.'

that their own dissolution **was hastened, and the** Government **was, after 1821, left face** to face with a fresh Ashantee invasion, unhappily justified by English breach of faith.

The first governor of the united West Africa Settlements was Sir Charles McCarthy. Under-rating, as Englishmen times without number have under-rated, the strength of the savage forces opposed to him, he led an expedition, consisting chiefly of native auxiliaries, across the Prah into Ashantee in January 1824, when he was utterly defeated and lost his life. The Ashantees advanced on Cape Coast Castle, **and** withdrew after a while, only to make, in 1826, a fresh invasion into the eastern districts behind Accra. On this occasion, however, **they were so** signally defeated[1] as not to give further active trouble for a space of a generation; and, in 1831, a tripartite treaty was signed between the Ashantees, the English, and **the** native allies of the English, which for the time being assured peace and free traffic between the coast and the interior. The Ashantee King relinquished his claim to dominion over the Fantees, and the English governor was recognised as the future referee and arbitrator in the case of native quarrels.

The treaty of 1831.

Some **time** before this treaty was signed, the British government had become heartily tired of their newly-acquired dependencies on the Gold Coast, which had involved war and expense, without corresponding national benefit. An attempt was made to meet the cost of occupation by the imposition of heavy customs duties, but the only result was to divert trade from the British stations to the neighbouring free ports of the Dutch and Danes. Under these circumstances it was, in 1825, decided to keep military possession of two forts only, Cape Coast Castle and Accra. Next year it was proposed to give up **one or** other of these two, preferably

---

[1] The victory of the English is **stated** to have been mainly due to the use of rockets, which had not been previously employed upon the coast, and which the Ashantees took **to** be real thunder and lightning.

SECTION II.

Accra; and finally, in 1827, the governor of the West Africa Settlements was instructed that, after a short interval had been allowed for the merchants on the Gold Coast either to remove or to make arrangements for staying at their own risk, every fort would be evacuated, every garrison would be withdrawn, and all civil government would be discontinued.

The Merchants' government on the Gold Coast.

But the Government was not destined to rid itself of the Gold Coast. The merchants took over the forts, but they took them over with what was tantamount to British protection, and with the security of a Parliamentary grant. In October 1828, it was definitely arranged that the government of the forts should be vested in a committee of London merchants trading to the Gold Coast, under whom five of the residents at Cape Coast and Accra should form a local Council of Administration and a court of Justices of the Peace. The London committee was to be chosen by the Government, and the names of the local councillors were to be approved by the Secretary of State. The authority of the merchants was not to extend beyond the limits of the forts. Cape Coast and Accra were to remain nominally dependencies of Sierra Leone, so that British law would there be still in force, and felonies and misdemeanours would be tried before the Sierra Leone courts. No rules or appointments were to be made without the sanction of the Government. The ports were to be free to all; and a Parliamentary subsidy of £4000 per annum was to be allowed for the maintenance of garrisons and fortifications [1]. Thus the Gold Coast once more passed into the hands of merchants, but the merchants were strictly tied down. The Government nominally retired from the coast. Virtually it retained the control, and, with the control, the burden of responsibility.

When a country is uncivilised, a rough and ready administration, depending on persons more than on rules, generally

[1] See the correspondence contained in a House of Commons paper, dated Feb. 17, 1830, Sierra Leone, No. 57.

works better at the time, and certainly prepares the ground better for the future, than a fully organised and strictly scrupulous system, whose principles and regulations have been derived from and are only fitted to more advanced communities. There are parts of the world at the present day, which probably thrive better under a chartered company, or under native rulers advised by British residents, than if they had been at once constituted Crown Colonies. Similarly, the merchant government of the Gold Coast achieved for the time a distinct success.

The local governor, Captain George Maclean, was a strong, energetic man, of singular ability in dealing with native races. He it was who brought about the treaty of 1831, called by the Ashantees 'the treaty of Maclean.' Though the money at his disposal was not more than the £3500 or £4000 annually voted by Parliament[1], though his forces consisted only of a hundred native troops or police, though the authority and jurisdiction entrusted to his colleagues and himself was presumed to be bounded by the walls of the forts, yet, as a matter of fact, to quote the guarded words of the select Parliamentary committee of 1842, he acquired 'a very wholesome influence over a coast not much less than 150 miles in extent, and to a considerable distance inland, preventing within that range external slave trade, maintaining peace and security, and exercising a useful though irregular jurisdiction among the neighbouring tribes.' Maclean, in short, created what is now known as the Gold Coast Protectorate. Before his time, the relations of English and Dutch alike with the natives, when not openly hostile, had been confined to purchasing security for trade by periodical payments. His authority, on the other hand, became recognised as practically supreme over all the country lying between the coast and the Ashantee kingdom, while with that kingdom he maintained for ten years unbroken peace. Thus confidence in English rule and English justice

[1] From 1834-9 the grant was only £3500.

grew up among the savage inhabitants of the Gold Coast. Their inhuman customs became sensibly modified; and Wesleyan missionaries began to spread the knowledge of the Christian religion, making their way even to the Ashantee court itself.

But West Africa could not be wholly civilised in ten or twelve years, and meanwhile public opinion was moving on in England. Reports came home that the merchants and their representatives on the Gold Coast tolerated domestic slavery, and furnished supplies to the factories and vessels of foreign slave dealers. These charges against the system were supplemented by personal accusations against Maclean himself. In 1840, Dr. Madden, a commissioner of West Indian experience, was sent out on a mission of enquiry, and on his return the affairs of West Africa were submitted to a select Committee of the House of Commons. The Committee's report bore strong testimony to the good which had been done under Maclean's administration. They recognised, however, that the time had come for a change of system; and they held that greater confidence would be felt in the character and impartiality of the government, if it were 'rendered completely independent of all connexion with commerce,' and 'placed in direct and immediate communication with the general government of the empire.' Accordingly, they recommended that the government of the British forts upon the Gold Coast should be resumed by the Crown; that several of the forts which had been previously abandoned, such as Apollonia, Winnebah, and Whydah, should be again occupied, and that others should be reconstructed; that the informal jurisdiction which had grown up outside the forts should be more accurately defined; that the Gold Coast should in future be no longer even nominally dependent upon the government of Sierra Leone; and that the Gambia should also be severed from the latter government.

These recommendations were convincing proof of the progress which had been made since 1828. In that year the Government handed over the Gold Coast to a semi-private association, because they could make nothing of it themselves. They now felt the necessity of taking it back again, not merely because there were flaws in the merchants' administration, but much more because that administration had brought about a new and better order of things. English influence had during these years become paramount on the Gold Coast. The natives had learnt to look to, and to trust, the English as arbitrators, as rulers, and as judges. It was time to endorse the good which had been done, no less than to amend the defects resulting from want of adequate organisation and from the continuance of a régime which by working successfully, had created a demand for a stricter and more formal administration.

The Gold Coast again taken over by the Crown. The Committee's report was in the main adopted by the Government. In 1843, the Gambia, by this time including, in addition to Bathurst, McCarthy's island and other strips of ceded territory, was constituted a separate settlement from Sierra Leone; and the Gold Coast was also given its own Governor or Lieutenant-Governor, though it remained a nominal dependency of Sierra Leone till 1850. All the Gold Coast forts were taken over by the Crown; and—most important provision of all—a Judicial Assessor was appointed, holding within the forts a commission as Justice of the Peace, and exercising beyond their limits a jurisdiction which, in the terms of the Committee's report, was based on the principles but not bound by all the technicalities of British law, wherever by voluntary agreement the native chiefs agreed to submit to such judicial control. The first of these judges was Maclean himself, and his appointment proved that the Government had resolved to continue the system which he had originated. Two Acts of Parliament, passed in the same year, gave legal

SECTION II.

The Foreign Jurisdiction Act.

The French at Assinee.

sanction to the new arrangements. The first[1], 'An Act to enable Her Majesty to provide for the government of Her Settlements on the Coast of Africa and in the Falkland Islands,' recognised by its title the fact that the Crown owned West African settlements, and empowered the Queen to legislate for their good government by Order in Council. The second[2], the Foreign Jurisdiction Act of 1843, legalised the exercise of British authority and British jurisdiction beyond the limits of British territory, wherever by treaty or by usage such authority and jurisdiction had already come or might afterwards come into being. It was from this latter Act that the Judicial Assessor on the Gold Coast derived his powers. Under the jurisdiction thus constituted the natives on the coast lived and prospered in security and peace; and in 1844, the year after the Act was passed, the Fantee tribes in the British Protectorate executed an agreement known as the 'Bond,' by which they renounced human sacrifices, and agreed that all cases of murder, robbery, and other serious crime, should be tried by the officers of the Queen.

Just at the time when these changes were taking place, the French, it is interesting to note in passing, began to gain a footing on the coast of the Gulf of Guinea. In 1843, they established a post at Assinee, at the western extremity of the Gold Coast, near the spot where, in the early days of the eighteenth century, there had been a short-lived French factory[3]; and one of the native kings of the district is stated to have accepted French protection. They came, it would seem, in the hope of exporting gold; and, although little resulted from the enterprise at the time, for a few years later the station was said to have been virtually abandoned, they never entirely lost their hold on the district, which is now definitely recognised as being under French influence. From 1843, therefore, may be dated the time when English and French

[1] 6 and 7 Vic. cap. 13.   [2] 6 and 7 Vic. cap. 94.   [3] See above, p. 103.

became rivals and neighbours in Guinea, as they had long been in the regions of the Senegal and the Gambia.

Extension of the British power on the Gold Coast.

As the success, which had attended the informal authority exercised by the merchants' government over the coast districts, created the want of a more regular administration, and led to the direct intervention of the British government; so the progress, which resulted from the new system, in turn revealed its defects, and invited further changes and better-defined authority. In 1847, the area of territory under British protection on the Gold Coast was estimated at 6,000 square miles, with a population of not less than 275,000. To protect and police this large province, it was proposed to form a local military corps; to develope it, roads were required; and the improving condition of the natives called for schools and means of education. Before, however, any further advance could be made, it was necessary to devise means of raising a revenue. The problem was one of great difficulty. Placed between the European forts on the sea-board and the Ashantee kingdom inland, the natives of the coast region had, under Maclean's influence, accepted British protection and become amenable to British justice. But they were not subjects of the British Crown, and their territory was not British territory. No Protectorate even had ever been formally proclaimed. The existing order had grown up out of voluntary agreements and treaties of friendship. It had not been created by any specific act of the British government. Consequently, when, in 1849, Lord Grey, then Secretary of State for the Colonies, suggested that the protected territory should be definitely ceded to Great Britain, with a view to placing the revenue and administration upon a sounder basis, he was dissuaded from any such step by representations that the assumption of territorial rights and the imposition of taxation would cause widespread alarm and distrust among the tribes concerned. Nor were the British merchants in favour of a system which involved customs duties at the ports and restrictions

SECTION II.

Purchase of the Danish forts by the British government.

Separation of the Gold Coast from Sierra Leone.

on their trade; while, over and above questions of native interests on the one hand and merchant interests on the other, there was a further difficulty, arising from the presence of foreign nations on the coast. The Dutch and Danish forts still stood side by side with the English, and the Dutch and English spheres of trade were hopelessly intermixed. Any attempt, therefore, to impose customs duties at English ports, promised to be, as it had already proved, of little avail, unless the Dutch adopted the same tariff; and, although the Netherlands government were inclined to co-operate, their officials on the coast, being themselves traders, successfully obstructed any combined action. So matters stood in the year 1850. In that year two important steps were taken. The first was buying out the Danes from the coast. By this measure the British government obtained exclusive authority over the Gold Coast from Christiansborg eastward, and brought under its influence the tribes of Akim—a large and fertile territory, and of the district watered by the Volta river and its tributaries. The second was the issue of a charter, formally constituting the Gold Coast a separate government from that of Sierra Leone.

Thus the Gold Coast Colony and Protectorate, as it is now called, was gradually being evolved, slowly taking form and shape as a dependency of the British Crown. The purchase of the Danish possessions not only eliminated for ever one of the two European nations which had long shared with Great Britain the control of the sea-board, but it transferred to the British Crown 'in full property and sovereignty' a certain number of existing forts, and exclusive, if ill-defined, rights of protectorate over a large extent of 'Hinterland.' It added to British sovereignty as well as to British trade and influence. It increased the responsibilities of the British government. That government still went forward, recognising its responsibilities and strengthening its position. A Supreme Court of Justice was established; a small local military force, the Gold Coast Corps, was formed; a military road was carried for forty miles into the interior towards the Ashantee capital; domestic slavery among the protected tribes, while not absolutely prohibited, was greatly restricted[1]; and, in 1852, the Governor, calling the native chiefs together, under the high-sounding title of 'the Legislative Assembly of Native Chiefs upon the Gold Coast,' induced them to agree to a poll-tax in consideration of the advantages derived from the protection of Her Majesty's Government. This was one more distinct step in advance. British protection was thereby formally proclaimed as an existing fact, and taxation was levied as the legitimate consequence. Shortly afterwards, notwithstanding that no customs union with the Dutch had yet been framed, a small duty was levied on imports at the British settlements on the coast.

CHAPTER V.

As on the Gold Coast, so elsewhere in West Africa, the British policy in these years was a progressive policy. In 1850 and 1853, further cessions were obtained on the Gambia, forming the district now known as British Combo; in 1861, the limits of the colony of Sierra Leone were enlarged by the acquisition of British Quiah and British Sherbro; and in the same year an entirely new dependency was added, the island of Lagos being ceded by its native king in full sovereignty to the British Crown.

British progress in West Africa.

The annexation of Lagos.

Lying to the east of the Gold Coast, in the Bight of Benin, commanding the one outlet of many miles of rivers and lagoons, from which it takes its name, Lagos, in the words of the British Consul, had for some years been 'the haunt of piratical slave dealers[2].' In the course of its crusade against the slave trade, the British government had, by a treaty of 1851, bound over the native king of the island to abolish the export of slaves and to expel the slave traders

---

[1] Domestic slavery in the Gold Coast Protectorate was subsequently abolished by two local ordinances passed at the close of the Ashantee war of 1873-4.
[2] See the Parliamentary paper relating to the occupation of Lagos, 1862.

from his territories. As the slave trade declined, healthy commerce grew; and, with its growth, came a demand for greater security of life and property. Under an impotent native ruler such security was not to be obtained; and it was felt that, if slave-dealing in the Bight of Benin was to be completely suppressed, if the aggressive barbarism of the neighbouring kingdom of Dahomey was to be held in check, Lagos, the key of the coast, must be in British keeping. Accordingly the negro king Docemo, on August 6, 1861, was induced to sign a treaty of cession, and the senior Naval Officer on the station, with the British Consul, took possession of the island in the name of Queen Victoria.

The story of the cession of Lagos illustrates what took place everywhere else along the coast of West Africa. British philanthropy warred against the slave trade; British interests followed close on the heels of philanthropy; native chiefs were bound over by treaties; treaties implied supervision by the stronger of the contracting parties; and in the end philanthropy and interest combined to bring in sovereignty or Protectorate. In the case in point the results were far-reaching. The acquisition of Lagos took the British government beyond the Gold Coast towards the head of the Gulf of Guinea, towards the Oil Rivers and the Delta of the Niger. It marked the formal beginning of a new ring of trade and settlement. It was a fresh centre round which Protectorates would gather. In 1861, Lagos was the furthest British outpost on the Guinea coast. In 1891, it was almost the nearest point in a great sphere of British influence, which covers the whole basin of the Lower Niger.

The Committee of 1865.

In the year 1865, a select Committee of the House of Commons inquired into and reported upon 'the state of the British establishments on the Western Coast of Africa.' It was a strong committee, and the report was brief and decided. Recognising 'that it is not possible to withdraw the British government wholly or immediately from any settlements or engagements on the West African coast,' the committee laid down, in words which have already been quoted[1], that all further extension of sovereignty or of Protectorate was inexpedient, and that the object to be kept in view was the ultimate withdrawal of the Queen's Government from the coast, with the probable exception of the settlement of Sierra Leone. It was recommended that McCarthy's island on the Gambia should be no longer occupied, the British settlement on this river being confined as much as possible to its mouth; and that all the West African settlements should, with a view to efficiency and economy combined, be placed once more under the government of Sierra Leone.

Such a report was a flat contradiction of the policy which had been carried out, or, to speak more accurately, which had insensibly grown up for some years past; but the causes of the apparently sudden reversal are not far to seek. Political feeling in England was at the time running counter to annexation, to intervention in foreign lands, and to any addition to the great burden of foreign and colonial responsibilities, which pressed so heavily on the British nation; and the taking of Lagos, which was rightly described in the Chairman's draft report as a strong measure, invited a protest against the movement, of which that acquisition was the latest and most significant result. On the Gold Coast the course of events had been far from smooth. The presence of the Dutch was ever a standing difficulty. The native poll-tax, owing mainly to difficulties of collection, had proved a failure. The merchants, glad of British protection but impatient of British taxation, thwarted the operation of the poll-tax, resented the imposition of import duties, and wished to revert to the irregular system of Maclean. An outbreak took place at Accra; and twice, in

Reasons for its report.

Difficulties on the Gold Coast.

---

[1] See above, pp. 115-6.

VOL. III.   K

SECTION II.

1853 and in 1863, the Ashantees again appeared in arms. Meanwhile the original and all-powerful reason for the maintenance of British influence in West Africa was fast disappearing. Hardly any country, except Cuba, was left into which slaves were still imported; and, as the demand for slaves became extinct, the slave trade was bound to die a natural death. These were the motives which inspired the well-meaning report of 1865. But Committees of the House of Commons cannot stop the working of natural causes. Neither peoples nor individuals ever stand still. They either go forward or they go back; and if a white race, not decaying in itself, keeps a hold among and is brought into daily contact with natives, it must, by a law of being which overrides all Parliamentary dicta, neither stand still nor go back, but extend its influence and widen its empire. When the Committee prefaced their report with the admission that the British settlements and engagements in West Africa could not at once or wholly be abandoned, they practically gave up their case; for, impossible as was immediate and total abandonment, it was perhaps less impossible than for the English to remain in Africa without still going forward. Their recommendations therefore were for the most part still-born.

Sierra Leone made the centre of Administration for the British dependencies in West Africa.

Though Sierra Leone was, as they suggested, made in 1866 the seat of government for all the West African dependencies of Great Britain, this change was nothing but a mere shuffle of the cards, which were duly re-shuffled in the course of a few years.

Cession of the Dutch forts on the Gold Coast to Great Britain.

As far as the Gold Coast was concerned, it was patent that, if any satisfactory administration was to be established, some arrangement must first be come to with the Dutch. The forts of the two peoples still stood, as they had stood for the last two hundred years, in and out of each other along the coast. No line was drawn, on one side of which were the Dutch, and on the other the English. No Protectorate or Sphere of influence was definitely marked out for either people, except that the English power had extended inland far beyond the Dutch, and that the purchase of the Danish possessions had placed the eastern end of the coast under exclusive British control.

The headquarters of the English were still at Cape Coast Castle. The headquarters of the Dutch had ever been a few miles off, at the old historic fort of St. George d'Elmina. English interests had suffered greatly from the neighbourhood of the Dutch. The Dutch settlements, in their turn, for many long years past had not prospered; their trade had dwindled; attempts to grow cotton and tobacco and to work gold mines had all failed; and, instead of bringing in revenue, like the Netherlands Indies, to the mother country, the West African possessions of Holland cost her some £10,800 per annum. Under these circumstances, both governments were ready to come to terms; and, in March 1867, a convention was signed, to take effect from the following January, by which the Sweet river, flowing into the sea between Cape Coast and Elmina, was made the boundary line, all the Dutch forts to the east of that river being ceded to the English, and all the English forts to the west being ceded to the Dutch. The same convention provided for a uniform customs tariff, the want of which had in former years been the main obstacle to raising a revenue at the ports.

This partition improved the position of the stronger party —the English, but the Dutch found that it only added to their embarrassments. The natives, who were transferred to British protection, accepted the transfer; but behind the Dutch section of the coast the tribes defied the authority of their new protectors, and on the coast itself the position was equally hopeless. One of the ceded forts, Commendah, was destroyed by a Dutch fleet in their efforts to take possession of their new property against the will of the inhabitants; another, Dixcove, was shortly afterwards plun-

132 HISTORICAL GEOGRAPHY OF THE COLONIES.

SECTION II.

dered and destroyed; and all along the seaboard the Netherlanders were little better than prisoners in their own forts. In 1870, the Fantees from the British Protectorate invaded the Elmina territory, destroyed some sixty villages, and blockaded the castle of Elmina itself; and, in despair, the Netherlands government negotiated for the cession of all their settlements to Great Britain, glad to leave the Guinea Coast for ever, on receipt of an indemnity for the bare value of whatever stores might be handed over to their successors. A convention to this effect was signed at the Hague on February 25, 1871; and, on April 6, in the following year, the British governor of the West Africa settlements made his formal entry into Elmina. There, in the hall of the castle, in the presence of the native chiefs and their followers, he received from the representative of the Dutch government the ancient baton of the fortress, the symbol of the once far-reaching power of Holland upon the West Coast of Africa, and which claimed to have been De Ruyter's own. The old tower still stood, which had been reared nearly four centuries back by Portuguese hands, a stern memorial of a distant past, surviving both its former and its latter owners. For 235 years it had been a Dutch stronghold, and now the Dutch too went their way, and the English reigned in their stead. One nation after another had come to the Gold Coast, seeking gold and slaves, and of them all, Portuguese, Dutch, Danes, Brandenburghers, and English, in the end the English alone were left. It was, we may venture to think, an instance of the survival of the fittest. When the age of the slave trade was past, when the time had come not to traffic merely but to govern, it was well that the residuary legatees of the Castle of St. George should be a people who, with all their faults, could give rule which was not oppression, and protection which was more than a name.

Not once or twice only in the colonial history of Great Britain have the English, by taking over the possessions of another European power, become involved in difficulties with a native race. The Ashantee war of 1873-4, the most serious native war which has as yet befallen the British government in West Africa, followed close upon, and was, as far as can be judged, the direct result of, the cession of the Dutch settlements.

CHAPTER V.

The Ashantee war of 1873-4.

At the close of the seventeenth century, there were two great native kingdoms behind the line of European forts on the coast, named Denkera and Akim, the former having Elmina as its port, the latter Accra. Behind them again was the Kingdom of Ashantee. These three states and their dependencies occupied the low-lying country between the sea and the plateau of the interior. They were pagan states, Mohammedan propagandism not having penetrated to the coast region; and, though it is not known exactly how the various kingdoms came into being, their inhabitants were and are supposed to be of the same or of kindred origin[1]. To the native potentate of Denkera the Dutch at Elmina paid rent or tribute for the ground on which their fort stood, and the Europeans at Accra seem in old times to have paid a similar rent to the King of Akim.

The Ashantee kingdom grew at the expense of its neighbours. In the year 1719, on the plea of an insult offered by the King of Denkera to one of the wives of the King of Ashantee, an Ashantee army invaded the territory of the Denkeras, who were supplied with arms and ammunition by the Dutch and assisted by the people of Akim. The war ended in both Denkera and Akim becoming subject to Ashantee, in Dutch cannon being carried off to Coomassie, and, what was in the end more important, in the Ashantee

---

[1] There is a tradition that the Ashantees and Fantees were originally one people, but, being compelled on an expedition to separate in order to find food, the Fantees derived their name from eating the plant 'fan,' and the Ashantees (the initial A is hardly sounded) acquired theirs from eating one called 'shan' (Keith Johnston's Africa in Stanford's Geographical Series, p. 141).

King obtaining the paynotes[1], which the Dutch had given to the ruler of Denkera as a guarantee for their rent. From this time onward the Dutch paid a small annual sum to Ashantee, and, with the natives of the Elmina district, kept up an alliance and friendship with the Ashantee King. Years went on, and the power of Ashantee still grew; its conquered subjects revolted in vain; new territory was annexed; and a strong dominion was formed, the profession of which was war, and its main source of wealth the slave trade.

In 1807, the year in which the British government abolished the slave trade, the Ashantees first came into direct conflict with the English, and a succession of wars and treaties followed, some notice of which has already been given[2]. No longer finding a market for slaves, the Ashantees turned to arts of peace, to silk-weaving in narrow webs, to manufactures in gold, iron, and pottery. They traded with the Mohammedan tribes of the interior, and from the coast they imported salt, rum, and fire-arms. It was all-important to them to have access to the sea; and, short of obtaining a foothold of their own on the coast, they relied on their long-standing alliance with the Dutch at Elmina for an outlet to their country. Hence, it was no light matter to them that Elmina should pass into the hands of another European power, known as the protector of the coast tribes, strong enough to discontinue at will the stipend, of no small significance, if trifling in actual amount, which the Dutch had paid from time immemorial to the Ashantee King, and able to block the routes from Ashantee to the sea-board. There were also subsidiary causes of friction. The native chiefs of Elmina were at feud with the Fantee tribes of the British Protectorate; they began to resent the transfer from Dutch to British control, and openly intrigued with emissaries of the Ashantee King. The latter meanwhile was being pressed

---

[1] These notes were apparently 'payable to bearer.'
[2] See above, pp. 118, &c.

by the representatives of the British government to release some German and Swiss missionaries, held captive at Coomassie since 1869. So war broke out. On April 6, 1872, the Dutch forts were ceded; and in January 1873, a force of 40,000 Ashantees crossed the Prah and entered the British Protectorate. Advancing slowly, in April and June respectively they defeated the Fantees in two engagements; and, after coming within three miles of Cape Coast Castle, they laid siege to Elmina. Fortunately a British man of war had just arrived at the port, and the seamen and marines, joining the West India forces, inflicted, under Colonel Festing's command, a crushing defeat on the invaders. After this engagement the Ashantees made no further attempt upon the forts; but, as they still held their ground within the borders of the British Protectorate, it was determined to take measures which would not only drive them back for the time but also give security against a periodical recurrence of similar invasions. A twofold advance was organised. Captain (afterwards Sir John) Glover, who was then administering the government of Lagos, was sent to the eastern districts of the Gold Coast to raise native levies and with them march by a flank movement upon Ashantee; and Sir Garnet Wolseley came out from England in October to Cape Coast Castle, to take charge of the main attack. Operating at first only with the colonial troops and native allies, Wolseley forced the Ashantees into retreat; and, having constructed a road to the Prah, he crossed that river into Ashantee territory on January 20, 1874, at the head of a mixed force, including some 1800 white soldiers lately sent out from home. On January 31, the Ashantees were severely defeated at Amoaful, about sixteen miles south of Coomassie; and, after another engagement at Ordasa on February 4, the English on the evening of the same day occupied Coomassie. The Ashantee King fled into the bush and refused to make terms. His town was therefore burnt down

SECTION II. on February 6, and the expedition moved back at once to the coast, followed some six days later by Glover and his Houssa troops, who had made their way up from the east in time to pass through the deserted ruins of Coomassie. On his homeward march, Wolseley was overtaken at a place named Fommana by Ashantee envoys, who, on February 13, signed a treaty of peace to which the King afterwards affixed his mark. Under its provisions the Ashantees renounced all claims on the Protectorate, and promised to abandon human sacrifices, to pay an indemnity of 50,000 oz. of gold, to secure trade, and to keep up a good road to the Prah.

Such was the outcome of this short, sharp campaign. For a while, it was doubted what impression the burning of Coomassie had made upon the Ashantee King and his people, and some years later a fresh invasion of the Gold Coast was seriously apprehended. In 1881, a native chief, who had escaped from Coomassie, took refuge at Elmina, and Ashantee messengers arrived to demand his surrender, bearing the threatening symbol of a golden axe. The demand was as a matter of course rejected; but an attack was expected to follow upon the refusal, and the forces on the coast were strengthened in anticipation. The Ashantees, however, in their turn took alarm, made full apology, and paid an indemnity of 2,000 oz. of gold.

The power of Ashantee had, in fact, been effectually broken by the war. The reigning King had been deposed, the vassal tribes revolted, and thus the one strong native organisation behind the Gold Coast became, for purposes of aggression, a thing of the past. Commercially, as well as politically, the gain was great. Hitherto, the Ashantee kingdom had not only threatened the very existence of the European settlements, but also effectually cut them off from trade with the interior. The routes were now thrown open, and a free current of commerce flowed between the native tribes of the forest-belt and the English merchants of the coast.

At the close of the Ashantee war the English in every sense held the field. On the Gold Coast—the historic centre of European settlement in West Africa—British influence was paramount, disputed by no European rival, by no native potentate. The great war between Germany and France was more than enough to engross all the attention and to tax all the resources of the French. At its outbreak they suspended for the moment their settlement at Assinee; and negotiations, which were opened in 1870, for a mutual exchange of French and British territory in West Africa, and for the demarcation of the Sphere of influence of either power, were prematurely cut short.

<small>CHAPTER V.

End of the Ashantee War.

The English predominant in West Africa.</small>

It was the course of events, not the designs of any government, which had carried the English on. They had warred with the natives only in self-defence. They had taken the place of other European nations, only with those nations' free and full consent. Yet, within ten years from the date when the Parliamentary Committee of 1865 recommended retrenchment and withdrawal, they had become more distinctly than ever before the leading European power on the West Coast of Africa.

Recent occurrences had given special prominence to the Gold Coast; and its administration was in 1874 once more severed from that of Sierra Leone. The settlements on the Gold Coast and at Lagos were constituted one colony, under the name of the Gold Coast Colony; while Sierra Leone and the Gambia, still under one government, kept the family title of the West Africa Settlements. Since that date further decentralisation has taken place. Lagos was separated from the Gold Coast in 1886, and the Gambia was cut off from Sierra Leone in 1888. At the present time, therefore, the lines of British administration in West Africa run in a direction diametrically opposed to the policy of concentration which was suggested by the Committee of 1865.

<small>*Administrative changes in the British West Africa settlements.*</small>

CHAPTER VI.

THE LAST TWENTY YEARS IN WEST AFRICA.

Section II.

The new movement in Africa.

In the preceding pages the story of European trade and settlement on the West Coast of Africa has been told down to the days of the present generation. Rival companies and rival nations came and went, until at length the tangle seemed to be unravelled, and some finality to have been attained. Yet, just when the conditions became simplified, and when the field was to some extent cleared—possibly for the very reason that a clearance had been made—there was a new and great outpouring from Europe into Africa. This latest chapter in African history is very far from being closed; but it is possible to trace to some extent the leading features of the movement, its causes and effects, and to compare the new 'scramble for Africa,' as it has rightly been termed, with the scrambles of former times.

Its causes.

Nations take to colonial enterprise for the most opposite reasons; sometimes in consequence of a great failure, sometimes in consequence of a great success. When a people, vigorous and high-spirited, has, in the pride of its strength not in the course of natural decay, experienced a serious loss or defeat, it instinctively looks for some fresh path to greatness, seeking out a new world to redress the balance of the old. When the English lost their American colonies, they

Activity of the French;

found compensation in colonising Australia. When the French were defeated by the Germans in the war of 1870, and deprived of their provinces of Alsace and Lorraine, they turned to foreign venture with redoubled energy, and set themselves to extend the bounds of their colonial empire. The interval in either case was very short. The peace of 1783 recognised the independence of the United States: in 1788 Englishmen were settled in New South Wales. The war between France and Germany ended in 1871: within the next five or six years the French were bestirring themselves in foreign parts, notably in Africa. Both cases, it will be noticed, were instances of peoples, which already had large colonial possessions, making further additions to their empires; and in both cases extension of dominion was the result of a great defeat and of a national failure.

But colonisation is often due to the opposite cause, to national success. History shows that the time when a nation first begins to send its sons over the ocean to found colonies and to acquire dependencies is, as a rule, the time when it has finished its constructive work at home. As soon as Portugal had taken its present form and shape, as soon as it became a country and a nation, Portuguese enterprise began to overflow into Africa. The great Spanish empire in America came into being immediately after, and, in a measure, as the direct outcome of, the consolidation of Spain by the union of Arragon and Castile. The Dutch subjects of Philip the Second threw off their allegiance to the Spanish Crown, and formed themselves into the United Netherlands; they won their freedom and built up their country; and out of it there grew a trading dominion in East and West. England, as we now know it, as an island power of the West, not as an appendage to the continent of Europe, dates from the time of the Tudors; and from the time of the Tudors we date, if not our colonies, at least the beginnings of the colonial movement. Young, self-made peoples, like young, self-made men, instinct with self-reliance, with the new-born exultant sense of strength and life, must find some outlet for their energies; and, when they have worked out their salvation at home, they take their ways into foreign lands and

CHAPTER VI.

over distant seas. The result of the Franco-German war was to finish the task of consolidating the German nation. The Germans have always been an emigrating race; but, placed as they are in the heart of Europe, the most continental of continental peoples, they owned, till the last few years, no colonial dependencies[1]. The war made them one great people. When it ended, they wanted new openings; and they found them outside Europe—in the Pacific and in Africa.

The same law of national life, for it amounts to no less, has operated in the case of Italy. United Italy, like United Germany, is trying her prentice hand at colonial annexation. In short, national consolidation within Europe has almost implied national aggrandisement in other parts of the world.

Consciousness of loss, then, in the case of the French, sense of work done, of union, and strength in the case of the Germans, has been a motive force; and, as one and the other has moved, competition has sprung up in which other peoples have joined, resulting in a race between nations for the waste places of the world. In Africa, a few years back, these waste places were chiefly to be found. This was the one unappropriated continent. Long as Europeans had been there, European colonisation had made but little way inland; and, even in the healthy South, settlement had not moved very far from the sea. Meanwhile explorers, from Livingstone to Stanley, had been busy filling up the great blank map; and, as their discoveries awakened curiosity and gave attractiveness to Africa, the missionary came in and the trader, forerunners of companies and governments, skirmishing in front of the main body of European advance.

The secret of the Niger had long been known. Mungo Park died in the belief that the Niger was one with the Congo[2]; and, acting on this theory, the British government

---

[1] The Brandenburg forts on the West Coast of Africa hardly deserve to be classed as 'colonial dependencies.'
[2] See above, p. 113.

sent out two exploring expeditions in 1816. One was intended to make its way from the West Coast to the Niger, starting from the Nunez river between the Gambia and Sierra Leone. The other, under Lieutenant Tuckey, aimed at following up the Congo from its mouth. Neither expedition proved successful; and, in 1821, a new attempt was made to penetrate into the Western Sudan from the north. This time the leader was Clapperton, a fellow countryman of Park's. Starting from Tripoli, he reached the central basin of the Niger, Lake Chad, and the native kingdoms of Bornu and Sokoto, and came back by the way he went in three years' time, with largely increased knowledge of Central Africa, though the course of the great river was not yet fully determined. Setting out again at the end of 1825, from Badagry near Lagos in the Bight of Benin, he reached Bussa on the Niger, the scene of Park's death, and passing on north to Sokoto, died there himself in April 1827, leaving his work still unfinished.

His mantle fell on Lander, his servant and companion on his last journey. In 1830, Lander took again the same route from Badagry to Bussa, and thence followed the Niger down to the sea. Thus the mystery of one of the African waterways was solved at last, and it was proved that the Oil Rivers, already well known to European traders, were in most cases but the many mouths of one great stream.

The head waters of the Niger are not very far from those of the Senegal; its Delta is to the east of the Bight of Benin. In its long semicircular course it compasses nearly the whole land of Guinea, and links the two spheres of European influence in West Africa, the land of Senegambia, and the coast which looks south over the Gulf of Guinea. Were the river from source to mouth in the hands of a single European nation, that nation would command in course of time the whole of the Western Sudan. But, both on the coast and inland, there has ever been a line of divergence between

CHAPTER VI.

SECTION II.

Upper and Lower Guinea; and, while the masters of the Senegal—the French—now control the Upper Niger, its lower basin belongs to the English—the leading power on the Gulf of Guinea. Exploration went on simultaneously in north and south. While Clapperton and Lander were at work on the Lower Niger, Laing from Tripoli in 1826, and Caillé from the Rio Nunez in 1827, made their way to Timbuctoo. Subsequently, however, to Lander's discovery, British enterprise was mainly devoted to pushing up the Niger from its mouth, the chief promoters being Liverpool merchants under the leadership of Macgregor Laird, whose first voyage of exploration was made in 1832. The unhealthiness of the country, and the hostility of the inhabitants, for many years retarded the opening of the Niger to continuous and settled trade; but, for a while, the Government supported Laird and his colleagues in their work, sending steamers up the river to make treaties for the furtherance of commerce and the suppression of the slave trade, and once more, in 1849, despatching an expedition from Tripoli into the Sudan. On this last occasion, the German traveller Dr. Barth made his way to the Benue, the great eastern tributary of the Niger, at a higher point than had yet been reached.

The National African company.

The impulse given by discovery gradually died away. The Niger was left in the main to private traders, who competed one with another; and, while tales of new-found lands and waters were coming home from the Nile and the Zambesi, from Central and Eastern Africa, comparatively little was heard of the Niger for many years by the outside world. At length, in the face of growing foreign competition, all the English firms, who traded in these regions, combined their resources and their efforts in the year 1879, forming one large company under the name of the United or National African company. This combination was a part and no small part of the new European movement in Africa.

It is worth while to consider, with special reference to West Africa, how far the latest phase of European trade and settlement has been parallel to or has differed from the enterprise of the seventeenth and eighteenth centuries.

Comparison of the latest phase of European trade and settlement in West Africa with previous phases.

Africa, in past times, it must be once more repeated, had for Europeans only a subsidiary value. Europe, in Professor Seeley's phrase, 'expanded,' into the East and West, into Asia and America; and Africa, the central continent, was taken on the way. The East and the West were gradually exploited, parcelled out, and appropriated. A new continent in the South, Australia, to which Africa again was on the way, was found and opened up. Economic conditions changed, the spirit of humanity grew strong, fresh scientific forces were discovered, and Africa lost its subsidiary value. It was less wanted than before as a place of call. It was no longer requisitioned for labour. Thus it became more isolated from other continents, while at the same time it attracted more curiosity, according as other parts of the world were more fully known and taken up. Hence it was that explorers and traders began to go to Africa for its own sake, not for the sake of Asia or America. They no longer skirted its shores, but went far inland, proving, as they went, that this great section of the world's surface had been unduly ignored by former generations. Then Western Europe, having once more reconstructed its own map by a series of wars, of which the Franco-German war was the greatest, sent out yet one more wave of expansion, which flowed into Africa, no longer, as in Portuguese times, streaming rapidly by its coasts, but bidding fair to flood its interior. In a word, the last few years have seen the beginning of the conquest or colonisation of Africa, in the same sense that other parts of the world have been conquered or colonised from Europe. In old days, Europeans touched at this or that point in Africa, they held forts in Africa, they had factories in Africa. Now they own, as Sovereigns or as

Africa treated as a continent.

SECTION II.

Protectors, great stretches of the continent. They are building up African dominions, as they built up empires in America or in the Eastern or Southern seas. Africa, in fact, it may almost be said, has at length been recognised as a continent, and is being dealt with on continental lines.

West Africa especially illustrates this point. It was in former times the West Coast and nothing more; geographically a part of Africa, but, as far as Europeans were concerned, wholly unconnected with the main body of the African continent, and rather regarded as an outlying part of America. In the last few years this has ceased to be the case. It is true that European settlement in West Africa, such as it is, and direct European rule are still confined to the coast-line; but, on the other hand, European claims, and in some cases European outposts, have been carried far into the interior. The rivalry between Europeans is no longer merely for the occupation of some particular island, promontory, or harbour, but for the control of vast river-basins and of countries greatly exceeding their own in size. Moreover, in the demarcation of European Protectorates, Africa has been considered as a whole, Western Africa being meted out with some reference to the rest of the continent. The great extension of French territory, for instance, in Senegambia and Guinea is not an isolated fact. It is at once intended to counterbalance the spread of English and German power elsewhere in Africa, and part of a scheme and a policy, which looks to including the Sahara and the Western Sudan on the one hand and the North African provinces of Algeria and Tunis on the other in one continuous Sphere of French influence.

The Dutch and the Germans compared in reference to West Africa.

This same point of view may be further illustrated by noting what European peoples were once strong in Africa, and who are they that now prevail. The Portuguese are still there, but with only a shadow of their former strength; the English are there; the French are there. One European

power, the Dutch, for many years the strongest of all, has CHAPTER
now no place at all in Africa, though the Dutch race is VI.
perpetuated in the south, under English or Republican
government. On the other hand, the Germans, who, except
for the few years when the Brandenburghers traded on the
Guinea Coast, never had any footing in Africa, have lately
taken a prominent position among the Europeans who are
in so lordly a manner slicing up the continent. The Dutch,
as has been seen, were above all others a trading and
carrying people. They went to Africa, at any rate to West
Africa, as carriers; and, when the carrying trade over the
Atlantic came to an end, their connexion with West Africa
gradually died away. Weak as Holland is, when compared
with Great Britain or France or Germany, she still holds her
East Indian and West Indian possessions; but, since West
Africa has ceased to be what it once was, the scene of
a series of depôts from which ships fetched human wares,
she has left the Guinea Coast apparently for ever. Meanwhile
a new power, Germany, has made its appearance. The
Germans, no doubt, like all other peoples, look in their
colonial enterprises to securing trade for the mother country;
but they have taken their place in Africa under and in full
harmony with the new set of conditions. They have come
there as a continental people to a continent, not as a sea-
going merchant people to a coast. They have come, not,
like the Prussians of old, to build and hold on sufferance
small factories, but to rule or claim to rule, to protect or
claim to protect large areas of territory. They belong as
distinctively to the new order of things, as the Dutch belonged
to the old.

In this new order one most striking feature is the re- *The New*
generation of chartered companies. There was a time when *Birth of Chartered*
the colonising nations of Europe, the Dutch, the French, and *Companies.*
the English, worked almost entirely through the medium
of such companies. That phase, like many others, passed

SECTION II.

away. When in India the rule of the Crown supplanted that of the East India company, when in Canada the territorial rights of the Hudson Bay company were ceded to the newly constituted government of the Dominion, it seemed as though, even in the British empire, the very heart and home of private enterprise, the day of chartered companies had gone for ever. Yet, within a very few years, they have risen again to play a great part, doing in modern guise the same work which was done on the whole so successfully of old.

The mission of chartered companies is to go in front of nations, into lands not yet ripe for direct European rule; to exploit, to trade, to organise in rough and ready fashion, preparing the way for fuller administration by the State. They have found of late a new life in Africa; and here, among others, the Royal Niger company, the Imperial British East Africa company, and the British South Africa company, are not unworthy successors of the great historic companies of the past. Of these three, the Niger company, having its sphere in Western Africa, suggests comparison with the old West Africa companies, of which some account has been given in the preceding chapters. In former times, a charter nearly always implied monopoly of trade. At the present day, a British chartered company is as a matter of course prohibited by the letter of its charter from setting up any commercial monopoly. But, as has been already pointed out, in the eighteenth century the trade with West Africa was carefully kept free and open to all British subjects, and therefore the terms under which the West Africa companies of that time traded were, in one important respect, similar to those by which the present Niger company is bound. In other respects, however, the conditions were widely dissimilar. The older companies had no territorial rights outside the forts and factories, and even the forts and factories did not belong in full ownership either to them or

The Royal Niger company compared with the old West Africa companies

to the nation which they represented. There was a certain trade in existence, and for carrying on that trade depôts were necessary. The Government, seeing that large commercial interests were involved, voted annual subsidies towards the upkeep of the depôts. But it sought no sovereignty, and it conferred no sovereignty; it regarded West Africa as a foreign land outside the sphere of British rule, jurisdiction, or protection. Very different is the case of the Royal Niger company. It is empowered not to trade merely but to govern [1], and the territories subject to its government have been declared to be under the Protectorate of Her Majesty the Queen. The company is something more than a syndicate of British merchants engaged in foreign trade. Its work represents the progress of British influence, the growth for good or evil of the British Empire. It means that Africa is gradually being made, as it never was made in old times, a dependency of Europe; and that the methods, by which European dominions were established in Asia and America, are being repeated in the great land which lies between the East and the West.

In a sense, indeed, these methods are more than being repeated, for it would be difficult, for instance, to find a parallel in other times and other continents to the Congo Free State.

The Congo Free State.

This State is the outcome of an International Association, though, owing to the fact that the King of the Belgians has from the first been the leading spirit in the enterprise, it is gradually becoming more and more exclusively a Belgian dependency. In 1876-7 Stanley traced the Congo down to its mouth; and, after his return, the International Asso-

---

[1] Sir William Anson in The Law and Custom of the Constitution, part ii. chap. 5, sec. 5. subsec. 3, says that the charters granted to companies, 'as the North Borneo company or the three great companies for the Niger, East, and South Africa . . . enable the companies to acquire territory and to make ordinances and exercise jurisdiction over it subject to the approval and continuous supervision of the Secretary of State.'

148 HISTORICAL GEOGRAPHY OF THE COLONIES.

SECTION II.

ciation of the Congo was formed to open up and develope the resources of the river-basin. Thus the Congo Free State came into being, whose neutrality was assured by the Berlin Conference of 1885, the navigation of the river, its tributaries, and its outlets being declared to be free to the merchant ships of all nations. Here the explorer came first, the company followed, and out of it grew a state. But the state was, in part at any rate, the product of international action, and its existence testifies at once to the new growth of companies and associations, and still more to the extent to which Africa has become of late years an object of general European attention. Not only have Europeans hurried into Africa, as though it were a newly discovered world; not only have they jealously marked out their respective claims, like so many miners at a gold field; but they have already found occasion to combine as well as to compete, to frame international arrangements, to guarantee neutral ground, and to safeguard to all comers the waterways into and out of a continent, which forty years ago, except in the extreme north and the extreme south, was held of small account and attracted little interest.

French and English in West Africa.

In a despatch dated March 30, 1892, and addressed by Lord Salisbury to the British ambassador at Paris[1], will be found a summary of the relations existing at that date between Great Britain and France in West Africa. It runs as follows: 'The colonial policy of Great Britain and France in West Africa has been widely different. France, from her basis on the Senegal coast, has pursued steadily the aim of establishing herself on the Upper Niger and its affluents. This object she has attained by a large and constant expenditure and by a succession of military expeditions. . . . Great Britain on the other hand has adopted the policy of advance by commercial enterprise.

[1] Parl. paper, c. 6701, 92.

She has not attempted to compete with the military operations of her neighbour.' The despatch further notes that one feature was originally common to all the West African possessions of both countries, 'their frontiers were open in the rear.' Only of late years have international difficulties arisen in the interior.

Of all European nations the French have, during the present century, been most consistently and most continuously active in West Africa. While the British government was struggling to carry out the recommendations of the Committee of 1865, to restrict the number and the area of its West African dependencies, and to confine British responsibilities within the narrow compass of the coast stations, the French people and the French government were ever looking inland, up the course of their own special river the Senegal. The route from the Senegal to the Niger was prospected as early as 1863; but years followed when troubles in Europe caused comparative inaction in Africa. From 1876 we may date the new advance. In 1879, a comprehensive scheme for the development of the French power in Senegambia, for the building of forts, and the construction of railways, was laid before the Chamber of Deputies and partially adopted; and, in the years 1880-3, a line of stations was carried from the Senegal to the Upper Niger, reaching the latter river in 12½ degrees North latitude. Elsewhere, but as part of the same policy—a policy of making the whole of the Western Sudan a great dependency of France—equal energy was displayed. On the Rivers of the South, as the French term them, the estuaries and coast-line between the Gambia and Sierra Leone, the area of French territory and French influence was widened; newborn German claims were eliminated by a convention of 1885; and an agreement with Portugal, in 1886, adjusted the frontier between the possessions of the two countries, the Portuguese government recognising a French Protectorate

CHAPTER VI.

Recent advance of the French.

SECTION II.

over the inland district of Footah Jallon. As in Senegambia, so also on the Guinea Coast. Here the old French dependency of Assinee was revived, and its boundary extended, until the whole shore-line between the British Gold Coast colony on the east and the Republic of Liberia on the west has now been secured by France. Further to the east again, Porto Novo and other stations on what was once the Slave Coast are in French occupation, and from them they have carried their arms into the Kingdom of Dahomey.

Even on the Lower Niger, for a short time, between the years 1880 and 1885, the French competed with the English; and, had they established themselves firmly in the river, it would have gone hard with British trade in West Africa; but the National African company proved too strong for foreign rivals, and, after the Berlin conference of 1884-5, the French withdrew.

German annexation in West Africa.

In 1884 began the career of Germany in Africa. In July of that year the German flag was set up at Togo at the eastern end of the Gold Coast, and at the Cameroons hard by the Oil Rivers and the Niger Delta.

The position in 1884.

Thus, whereas in 1874 the power of Great Britain in West Africa was almost unchallenged, ten years later it was confronted at nearly every point with claims on the part of France or Germany. The French were gradually encircling the West Coast dependencies of the Gambia and Sierra Leone, and barred at Assinee any extension of the Gold Coast colony to the west; while the Germans closed the Gold Coast in on the eastern side, and threatened British trade at the mouth of the Niger. British policy in West Africa was and is complicated by various considerations. The French wished to retrieve losses by making gains. The Germans had nothing to lose and all to gain. The English, on the other hand, had enough and more than enough already in West Africa. They would advance only if driven to do so by necessity, and not because aggression and annexation suited the views either of the Government or of the nation. Further, their interests in South and East Africa were far greater than those of either France or Germany. Beyond other nations, they were obliged, in their dealings in West Africa, to have reference also to Central, Southern, and Eastern Africa; to hold the balance with a view to Africa as a whole, and, if need were, to yield in one direction in order to add strength in another. Above all, the keys of the position in West Africa were already in great measure in their hands, and therefore, within limits, their strength was to sit still.

CHAPTER VI.

In 1870, and again in 1876, negotiations took place between Great Britain and France, with a view to marking out a definite sphere in West Africa for either country, and thereby reducing to a minimum the possibility of future complications. In the latter year, an arrangement was suggested, by which the Gambia should be ceded to France in return for any positions held by the French between the Pongas river, to the north of Sierra Leone, and the Equator. This exchange had much to recommend it. It would have given the French undisputed control of the rivers of Senegambia, while from Sierra Leone to the Niger Delta the English would have had a free hand. But the proposal was unpopular in this country, as involving the cession of British territory, the giving up of a river which had long been regarded as specially belonging to Great Britain, and the handing over to a Roman Catholic power a considerable body of native Wesleyans. The negotiations accordingly fell through; and, while on the Gambia and at Sierra Leone the English were content with little more than holding their ground, the French, partly by force of arms and partly by a succession of treaties, gradually secured ascendency over the tribes of the interior.

Negotiations and conventions between France and Great Britain.

At length, in 1882, an Anglo-French convention was signed, which drew a line of demarcation between the two

152 HISTORICAL GEOGRAPHY OF THE COLONIES.

SECTION II.

powers in the neighbourhood of Sierra Leone, the basin of the Scarcies river being assigned to Great Britain, and that of the Mellicourie to France. But the arrangement was a purely local one, and, even in the district to which it referred, left outstanding points of difference to be subjects for further dispute and for future conventions. An arrangement of wider scope, including the Guinea Coast as well as Senegambia, was subsequently signed by representatives of the two countries at Paris on August 10, 1889; and in it provision was made for the appointment of special Commissioners, to trace out on the spot the lines of demarcation, which had been laid down in the articles of agreement.

The English on the Niger.

In these two conventions Great Britain and France were alone concerned, and in neither of them did any question arise as to national or international rights on the Niger. Here, and here alone in West Africa, Great Britain kept pace with present or prospective rivals, for here and here alone was a motive force given by a strong combination of British merchants. Between 1879 and 1884, the National African company made a succession of treaties with the various native states on the Lower Niger; and, in the summer of 1884, urged on by German intervention at the Cameroons, the British government endorsed the action of the company, and extended British protection to the east along the coast-line of the Niger Delta and the Oil Rivers.

The Berlin conference on West Africa.

At the end of the same year and the beginning of 1885, the Powers of Europe met in conference at Berlin, and sat in judgement on West Africa. They met, in view of the scramble for Africa, to draw up rules of the game. They laid down uniform conditions under which future occupations should take place. They renewed declarations against the slave trade, and they secured free navigation of the Congo and the Niger. By implication, they recognised that Great Britain was the paramount power on the Lower Niger, while similar recognition was given to French authority over the Upper waters of the same river.

When the conference was over, it still remained to fix the line between the British and French spheres inland on the Niger, and between the British and German spheres in the region of the Cameroons. It remained too for the British government to give more tangible form to their somewhat indefinite rights over the lands and coasts at the head of the Gulf of Guinea. In April, May, and June, 1885, correspondence passed between the British and German governments, which resulted in fixing the boundary between the spheres of the two countries at the right bank of the Rio del Rey, a creek to the east of the Old Calabar river. By a supplementary agreement in the following year, the line of demarcation was carried inland, in a northerly and north-easterly direction, to a point near Yola on the Benue river; and one more difficulty was removed in March 1887, when the Baptist mission station at Victoria on Ambas Bay in the Cameroon district, which had been annexed by Great Britain in 1884 and held in reserve pending purchase by Germany of the rights of the Missionary Society, was finally placed under German sovereignty. Subsequently, the famous Anglo-German Agreement of 1890, relating to Africa and Heligoland, restated and revised the boundary between the two Powers in the Niger regions, and also marked a line between the German Protectorate of Togo and the British Gold Coast colony.

Following up immediately their preliminary arrangement with Germany, the British government, in the London Gazette of June 5, 1885, proclaimed to the world a formal Protectorate over the Niger districts; on the coast, from Lagos to the Rio del Rey; inland, over both banks of the Niger from its confluence with the Benue river to the sea, together with the territories watered by the latter river up to a point named Ibi. In the next year, 1886, on

CHAPTER VI.

Demarcation of the Anglo-German frontier at the head of the Gulf of Guinea.

The British Niger Protectorate, the Royal Niger company, and the Niger Coast Protectorate.

SECTION II.
July 10, the National African company received a charter from the Crown; and, taking the title of the Royal Niger company, was duly authorised to administer the territories over which it had acquired rights by treaties and acts of cession. The range of these treaties extended beyond the limits of the Protectorate as recently proclaimed, and accordingly the Gazette of October 18, 1887, contained an amended Proclamation, by which the British Protectorate of the Niger districts was declared to comprise, in addition to the coast-line as agreed upon with Germany, 'all territories in the basin of the Niger and its affluents, which are or may be for the time being subject to the government of the National African company, now called the Royal Niger company.' Far-reaching as is the scope of the company's control, it does not include the whole area of British influence on the Lower Niger. The coast-line and part of the interior from the Benin to the Forcados, and from the Nun mouth of the Niger to the Rio del Rey, including the Calabar estuaries, is excepted from its jurisdiction, and forms a separate consular district, now bearing the name of the Niger Coast Protectorate.

Latest Anglo-French conventions.

On the coast, the English have had to settle with the Germans. Inland, the Niger company is face to face with the French also. The Berlin conference recognised French authority on the Upper, British authority on the Lower Niger; but no line was drawn, until an Anglo-French convention was signed on August 5, 1890. The second article of that convention embodied a recognition by Great Britain of the Sphere of influence of France to the south of her Mediterranean possessions, 'up to a line from Say on the Niger to Barruwa on Lake Chad, drawn in such a manner as to comprise in the Sphere of action of the Niger company all that fairly belongs to the kingdom of Sokoto, the line to be determined by the Commissioners to be appointed.' The same Commissioners were charged with determining the French and English spheres to the west and south of the Middle and Upper Niger under the articles of the previous arrangement of 1889, the general lines of delimitation being sketched out in a supplementary convention, dated June 26, 1891.

So matters stand at the present day. In some districts, as on the Gambia, the frontiers have been actually surveyed and accurately delimited on the spot; but, for the most part, West Africa has been parcelled out in advance of geographical knowledge. Maps have to be corrected, mountains to be verified, courses of rivers to be ascertained. Arrangements on paper have to be squared with actual facts, before conflicting European claims can be adjusted with any approach to finality. Meanwhile, in this great region, which of all parts of the world is perhaps the least suited to Europeans in climate or in conditions of life, the stream of European competition continues to run fast and strong; and, with a curious mixture of reason and unreason, of political calculation and vague uncertain quest, one nation and another still as of old seems irresistibly drawn to the unhealthy coasts, the strange, wild lands of West Africa.

BOOKS AND PUBLICATIONS RELATING TO THE SUBJECT
OF THE PRECEDING CHAPTERS.

Among numerous Blue Books and Parliamentary Reports, special mention should be made of The Report of the Lords of the Committee of Council, appointed for the consideration of all matters relating to Trade and Foreign Plantations, on Trade to Africa and Trade in Slaves [1789]. This report with its Appendices is a mine of information respecting the Slave Trade and the African companies.

On the subject of the Slave Trade, reference should also be made to
 BRYAN EDWARDS' *History of the West Indies*, Book IV. Chap. II. [4th Ed. 1807], and
 BANDINEL'S *Account of the Trade in Slaves from Africa as connected with Europe and America* [1842].

SECTION II.

The following are books of authority on the past history of Europeans in West Africa.

A Description of the Coasts of North and South Guinea, by JOHN BARBOT, agent-general of the Royal Company of Africa and Islands of America at Paris. The bulk of the book was originally written in 1682, but there are later supplements. It is contained in CHURCHILL's *Collection of Voyages*, vol. v. [1746 ed.].

A New and Accurate Description of the Coast of Guinea, written originally in Dutch, by WILLIAM BOSMAN, chief factor for the Dutch at the castle of St. George D'Elmina [English Translation, 2nd Ed. 1721].

MEREDITH's *Account of the Gold Coast of Africa, with a brief history of the African Company* [1812].

Among very recent books—

Mr. Scott Keltie's valuable work, *The Partition of Africa* [1893], should most certainly be consulted.

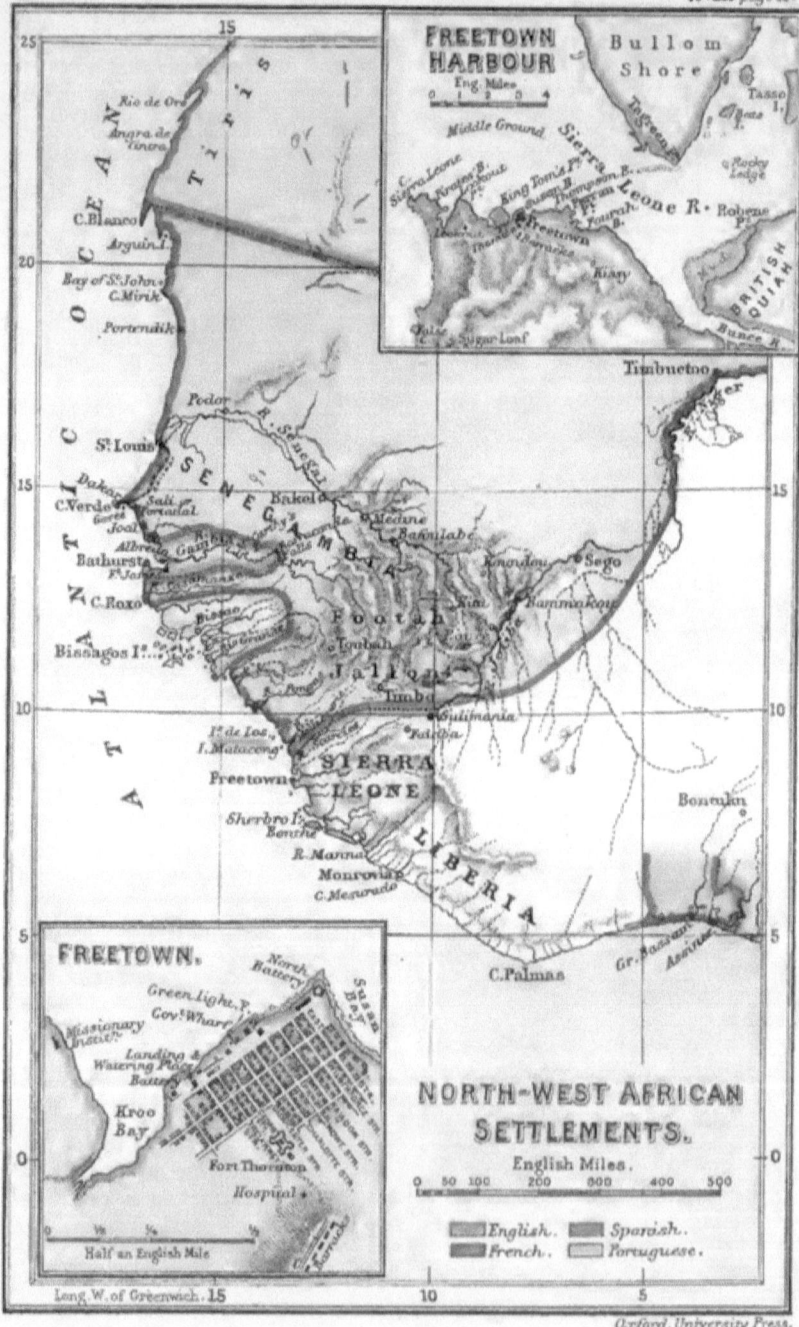

CHAPTER VII.

THE GAMBIA.

THE present British colony, or rather dependency, of the Gambia dates from 1816. In that year, British traders who had been forced to leave the Senegal, when the settlements upon that river were finally restored to France, established themselves on St. Mary's island at the mouth of the Gambia, close to its southern shore, the island being subsequently ceded to Great Britain by the native King of Combo. The new settlement, which was named Bathurst, was left for a short time without any regular administration, and without any definite recognition from or protection by the British government. In 1819, however, some West Indian troops were sent there; and in 1821, by the Act of Parliament which abolished the African company, it was included with all the other British possessions in West Africa in the colony of the West Africa settlements, and placed under the central government of Sierra Leone. By degrees the limits of the dependency were extended. In 1823, McCarthy's island, called after Sir Charles McCarthy, the first ill-fated Governor-in-Chief of British West Africa, was purchased from its native King. This island is situated in the river, about 150 miles from Bathurst, marking the limits of navigation on the Lower Gambia for vessels of large size, and it was bought in order to serve as a depôt for produce, and as an advanced post for the protection of trade. In 1826, the Ceded mile, a narrow strip of territory on the northern bank of the river, over against Bathurst, one mile in breadth by 35 to 40 miles in length, was acquired from

CHAPTER VII.

History of the present colony of the Gambia.

SECTION II.

the King of Barra, to whom in return the sum of £100 was paid annually. The acquisition was made in order to forestall any possible occupation by the French, to facilitate the collection of customs duties, and to keep the native tribes at arm's length from Bathurst. For similar reasons, combined with sanitary considerations, Cape St. Mary, on the southern bank of the mouth of the river, which is separated from Bathurst by Oyster Creek, and which forms part of what is now called British Combo, was annexed in 1827 and 1840. It is high ground as compared with the neighbouring coast, and is therefore considered to be comparatively healthy. A little later, the rest of British Combo, a mainland district adjoining Cape St. Mary, was taken, to put an end to the constant interference of the native chiefs with the dwellers in the British settlement; and pensioners from the black West India regiments, together with some Liberated Africans, were placed there, to serve as a living barrier between the colony and its warlike neighbours. Thus the English obtained command of both sides of the estuary of the Gambia, and their possession was more fully assured when the French factory at Albreda was finally withdrawn in 1857 [1].

Importance of the Gambia river.

It will be noticed that this British dependency is always known not as 'Gambia' but as 'the Gambia [2],' pointing to the fact that it is the river itself and its banks, rather than any great stretch of territory, which belong to and are valued by great Britain. It is true that here, as elsewhere in West Africa, British influence has been indirectly exercised among the native tribes of the district; but there has been no continuous growth of Protectorate, no constantly widening area of British rule. What British governments have been

---

[1] See above, p. 110.
[2] According to old accounts, however, 'Gambra' or 'Gambia' was the name given by the natives to the country, not to the river. The natives now apply the name more especially to Bathurst itself.

concerned with is the waterway itself; and, until the Anglo-French frontier was recently defined, only a few square miles of shore-line or islets were owned by Great Britain. It is the river which is spoken of in treaties. By the treaty of Versailles, in 1783, the French government guaranteed to the English the possession of 'Fort James and of the River Gambia'; and the treaty with the native King of Barra in 1826, which added to the colony the 'Ceded mile,' proclaimed the transfer to the British Crown of the 'full, entire, free, and unlimited right, title, sovereignty, and possession of the River Gambia, with all the branches, creeks, inlets, and waters of the same, as they have been held and possessed by the Kings of Barra from time immemorial.'

While the English thus confined themselves closely to the river, disposed rather to contract than to extend their frontier, while the Parliamentary Committee of 1865 recommended the withdrawal of the outpost at McCarthy's island, and a few years later negotiations were opened for ceding the Gambia to the French, the latter nation have of late been perpetually advancing both north and south of the Gambia, confining their rivals within the narrow limits which they had voluntarily prescribed to themselves. Eventually, the Agreement of Aug. 10, 1889, laid down a line of demarcation between the English and French Protectorates, in accordance with which the frontier was delimited in 1891. *Delimitation of the British and French frontiers.*

On the coast, the northern line starts from the Jinnak creek, in about 13° 36′ North latitude, some seven miles to the north of Barra point at the mouth of the Gambia; while the southern line starts from the mouth of the San Pedro or Allahi river, in about 13° 3′ North latitude, and about 35 miles by the coast to the south of Cape St. Mary and the opening of the Gambia estuary. The former line follows the parallel of 13° 36′, until it reaches a point 10 kilometres distant from the Gambia, opposite what is known as the Sarmi creek, in about 15° 27′ West longitude. The

Section II.

latter—the southern line—follows the Allahi river as far as 13° 10′ North latitude, and is then carried along that parallel as far as about 15° 46′ West longitude, where it runs due north to a point 10 kilometres distant from the Gambia. From these two points, either line follows the course of the river at 10 kilometres distance, until a native town called Yarbutenda is reached, which is 243 miles by river from Bathurst, and 14 miles by river from the Barraconda rapid. At Yarbutenda, the frontier line is drawn at a radius of 10 kilometres from the centre of the town, carrying the British frontier nearly up to the rapid. The net result of the demarcation is that, for 250 miles from the sea, the Gambia, with a strip of land 10 kilometres or rather more than 6 miles deep on either side, together with a somewhat larger area near the coast, has been recognised as subordinate to Great Britain, whereas all the territory outside this frontier, together with the river itself from Barraconda upwards, has been assigned to the French.

Constitutional changes.

In 1843 the government of the West Africa Settlements was broken up, and the Gambia was constituted a separate colony; but in 1866 all the settlements were again combined under one Governor-in-Chief, though each continued to have its own Legislative Council. When, in 1874, the Gold Coast and Lagos were united into the Gold Coast Colony, the Gambia still remained attached to Sierra Leone, and the name West Africa Settlements was in official documents somewhat inconveniently and inaccurately confined to these two dependencies, the Governor-in-Chief residing at Sierra Leone, and the Administrator of the Gambia being subordinate to him. Since 1888, the Gambia has been once more independent of Sierra Leone, and is a separate Crown Colony, with a Governor, who is still styled Administrator,

Present Constitution.

an Executive and a Legislative Council. The Executive Council at present consists of three official members in addition to the Administrator, viz. the Treasurer, the Chief

Magistrate, and the Collector of Customs, together with one nominated unofficial member. The composition of the Legislative Council is, so far as regards the official element, the same as that of the Executive Council, but it contains two nominated unofficial members.

Chapter VII.

The law of the Gambia is the Common law of England, together with such Statutes of general application as were in force in England on January 1, 1880, supplemented and modified by local ordinances[1]. The Chief Magistrate is the only judicial officer of the colony; and one remaining bond between the Gambia and Sierra Leone is that the Supreme Court of Sierra Leone is the Court of Appeal for the Gambia.

Law and Justice.

Prior to the recent demarcation of the Anglo-French frontier, the total area of the Gambia Settlements, including St. Mary's island, British Combo, the Ceded mile, McCarthy's island, and other islets in the river, was taken to be not more than 69 square miles, being rather less than half the size of the Isle of Wight, and rather larger than Jersey and Guernsey combined. Outside the settlements, the Sphere of British influence was wholly undefined. Since the frontier has been delimited, the territory owned by or under the protection or influence of Great Britain has been found to amount to 3,550 square miles, being a little less than twice the size of Lancashire.

Area and Geography.

The geography of the Gambia colony is the geography of the Gambia river up to the Barraconda fall or rapid. This rapid, 257 miles distant from Bathurst, divides the Gambia into the Upper and Lower river. It is formed by a ledge of rock extending across the whole width of the stream, over which there is but little depth of water in the dry season; and consequently, at the present time, it makes a complete break in the navigation of the river. Taking the river below the

---

[1] See the Sierra Leone Act, No. 9 of 1881, passed while the Gambia still formed part of the same colony (clause xix).

rapid, navigation is simple as far as McCarthy's island; vessels drawing 10 feet of water can at all seasons reach a point one mile above Yarbutenda, or 244 miles from Bathurst; and vessels drawing 5 feet of water can, even in the dry season, ascend the whole way to the rapid. Thus the Gambia furnishes a navigable waterway for more than 250 miles from the sea, which is under exclusive British control. Its value is further greatly enhanced by the fact that there is always sufficient depth of water on the bar at its mouth to admit of the passage of vessels of the largest size, in which respect it has the advantage of the Senegal and indeed of all the other large rivers of West Africa. At low tide there is a depth of 26 feet on the bar, whereas the average depth on the bar of the Senegal is only 10 feet. Hence, while large ocean-going ships can come to Bathurst, St. Louis, which is the capital of the French possessions in West Africa, and which is situated on an island just within the mouth of the Senegal, is accessible only to small vessels, and has for its seaport Dakar[1] at a distance of 125 miles to the south.

The banks of the Gambia, for some distance from the sea, are fringed with mangrove swamps, behind which are plains densely covered with grass, growing to a height of 10 feet and interspersed with clumps of timber. The country is open, as compared with the forest-belt of West Africa, which begins between 60 and 70 miles lower down the coast at the river Casamanze and extends as far as Accra on the Gold Coast. At a distance of 100 miles from the sea the water of the Gambia is fresh, and the swamps and mangroves gradually give way to steep banks covered with trees, the valley of the river from McCarthy's island to Barraconda being enclosed by low rocky hills of volcanic formation from 50 to 100 feet high, and the surrounding country being park-like in its character.

[1] Dakar is connected with St. Louis by rail.

CHAPTER VII.

The entrance of the Gambia, between Bathurst on the south, and Barra point on the north, is only two miles in width, but immediately above the town the river widens out to a breadth of nearly seven miles. St. Mary's island, on which Bathurst stands, has an area of four and a half square miles; it is little more than a mixture of swamp and sandbank, lying so low that it is liable to inundation in times of floods and high tides. The little town of Bathurst, the principal settlement in the colony, with a population of some 6,000 inhabitants, is built at the extreme eastern end of the island, on a promontory stretching out into the river, its position being such as to command all the trade passing into or out of the Gambia. It is less than 100 miles distant from the French settlement of Goree, which lies to the north, and 500 miles from the British settlement of Freetown in Sierra Leone, which lies to the south. It is connected with Europe and with other places in West Africa by submarine cable. Eighteen miles up the river from Bathurst is the tiny islet, on which stand the deserted ruins of Fort James, once so prominent a landmark in the history of the English in West Africa; while far away up stream a small settlement is still maintained on McCarthy's island, low-lying, swampy, and unhealthy, slightly larger in size than the island of St. Mary.

St. Mary's Island and Bathurst.

Fort James.

McCarthy's Island.

All parts of the coast of West Africa are unhealthy, but the climate of the Gambia, at any rate in the dry months, is superior to that of the other West African dependencies of Great Britain. The year is very clearly divided into a wet and dry season, the wet months being from June to October inclusive, while the other seven months are months of drought. The most oppressive and sickly months are July and October. The dry north-east wind, known as the Harmattan, cold in the morning, hot in the middle of the day, blows intermittently from December to April; and the rainy season usually begins and ends with tornadoes. The rain is heavy in the wet months, but the total annual

Climate.

SECTION II. rainfall only averages 48 inches; nor is the heat excessive, the mean temperature at Bathurst, as taken in the shade at noon, varying from 72 to 82 degrees[1]. Beyond the reach of the sea-breeze, the temperature is 20 degrees higher than at Bathurst.

Products. Subject as it is to long periods of drought, and having a light and sandy soil, the Gambia colony is not particularly rich from the point of view of agriculture; nor is the country sufficiently opened up, or the native population sufficiently skilled, for cultivation of the soil to have made much progress. Consequently, though a considerable amount of corn and rice is grown, it is not enough fully to supply the local market. Ground nuts (Arachis hypogaea) are the staple product, the 'commercial idol' of the Gambia, as they are styled in a Blue Book report, accounting for more than four-fifths in value of the total exports of the colony. They are mainly exported to Marseilles, where they are converted into an oil which is sold as olive-oil. The trade is of comparatively recent origin, and latterly has shown a tendency to decline. In 1845 the value of the nuts exported was only £199; in 1858 it was £188,000; in the five years 1880-4 it averaged £154,000; and in 1892 it was £150,000. Next to ground nuts, the most important product is India-rubber, the export of which quadrupled in the three years ending with 1891. Bees-wax and hides are also exported in small quantities. Gum, which from time immemorial has been one of the staple products of the Senegal region, hardly finds a place in the list of exports from the Gambia; and the same may be said of timber, of which there is notwithstanding a considerable variety and which was at one time to be found in European markets. Shortly after the settlement of Bathurst was founded, a certain amount of gold was brought down from the interior for export; but, from the year 1824, the trade died away, having been, it is said, diverted at that time to Sierra Leone.

[1] The readings, however, taken at 3 p.m. are considerably higher.

Animal life, it need hardly be said, is plentiful on the Gambia. The natives have their cattle, sheep, and goats; there is a variety of antelopes; and the river, from McCarthy's island upwards, abounds in hippopotami.

Chapter VII

Financially, the Gambia is at present, in a small way, a flourishing colony, the annual income covering the annual expenditure and leaving a balance. There is, however, an element of unsoundness in the account, in that the prosperity of the settlement depends entirely upon a single industry; nor is there as yet much to show in the way of developement of the district by roads and buildings, the bridge, which spans Oyster Creek and leads from Bathurst to British Combo, being the principal public work of great utility. Five-sixths of the revenue are derived from customs, including an export duty on ground nuts; and the next most important item is licences. In 1892, the revenue amounted to £31,000, the highest sum yet realised in any year, except 1891. The imports, which come principally from Great Britain or the colonies, and the exports which are sent chiefly to foreign countries— France being, as already stated, the great market for ground nuts—have varied very greatly in different years, the exports usually but not always exceeding the imports. In 1882, the imports were valued at £174,000, and the exports at £255,000; in 1886, the value was returned only at £69,000 and £79,000 respectively; and in 1892 at £170,000 and £172,000.

Revenue and Trade.

British sterling is the standard of the currency; but the French gold twenty-franc piece, and the silver five-franc piece of the Latin Union, are also legal tender at fixed rates. It is estimated that about 80 per cent. of the coin in circulation consists of five-franc pieces, the remainder being chiefly British silver. There is little or no gold in circulation.

Currency.

At the 1891 census, the population of the 69 or 70 square miles which comprise the settlements was returned at 14,266. These numbers must be taken as approximate only, and

Population.

166 *HISTORICAL GEOGRAPHY OF THE COLONIES.*

SECTION II.

they are exclusive of the inhabitants of the far larger extent of territory which has been assigned to Great Britain by the recent delimitation of frontier. The parallel returns in 1881 amounted to 14,150, so that the population of the settlements remained stationary during the ten years, any increase being fully counterbalanced by a very large emigration from the district of British Combo. The inhabitants are nearly all Africans, and the large majority are indigenous to the soil, though some are colonists or the descendants of colonists brought in by the Government, viz. Liberated Africans, and pensioners from the West India regiments. The European element in the population is most insignificant, amounting to not more than fifty or sixty, of whom there are rather more French than English.

Religion and Education.

The native Christians in the settlements, whose numbers cannot be accurately estimated, are divided between the Church of England, the Wesleyans, and the Roman Catholics. The schools, such as they are, are all mission schools, to which grants in aid are allowed by the Government; but their number has tended of late years to diminish rather than to increase, and education on the Gambia is at present in a sadly backward condition.

The native races.

The origin and variety of the native races in the valley of the Gambia is an interesting subject, but one too large to receive more than a passing reference in this book. It is dealt with at some length in the valuable Blue Book report for 1885[1] by Mr. (now Sir) G. T. Carter, who was then acting as Administrator. There are two main races in West Africa, the negroes and the Fulahs, the latter being distinguished from the former by a much lighter complexion. The Fulahs are met with on the Upper Gambia, but the valley of the Lower river, with which the English are concerned, is almost entirely inhabited by negroes. The negro race

---

[1] Parl. paper, c. 5071, 87.

includes various distinct tribes or subdivisions, and of these the Mandingoes are the most numerous and the strongest people on the Lower Gambia. Their original home and headquarters is in the mountains from which the Gambia and the Niger alike take their source, from whence they have spread westward to the sea, bringing with them the Mohammedan religion, to which most of them belong. The trade of the river below the Barraconda falls is said to be principally in their hands, and they grow the bulk of the ground nuts which the colony exports, and the cotton from which the native cloth is woven. Of the other tribes, the most important are the Mohammedan Jolofs, whose home is to the north of the Gambia, between that river and the Senegal; and the Jolas, a primitive pagan race, who dwell to the south of the river, between Combo and the Casamanze. These latter are a brave, independent people, strongly hostile to the Mohammedans; and their country produces the India-rubber, which has of late figured prominently in the trade returns of Bathurst, though the export fell off in 1892.

General Summary.

It is not easy to form a true estimate of the Gambia colony, or to determine what place should be assigned to it in the long list of multifarious possessions which make up the British empire. From most points of view, it is of very little importance. It is in no true sense a colony of Great Britain, for, though it is called a British settlement, the English are conspicuous by their absence. It has no large volume of trade. It is not and is never likely to be a great naval station. It has never, like Sierra Leone, been connected with a great philanthropic movement. It has never, like the Gold Coast, had a rich sounding name. It has more than once been all but given up by the English; and yet, from the very earliest days, the English have kept their hold upon it. Of its historic interest there is no doubt. Fort James on the Gambia is one of the central points in the story of British trade and settlement in West Africa; it could no more be

SECTION II.

left out of the narrative than Cape Coast Castle itself; and it cannot be doubted that sentiment for the past has had much to do with the retention of the dependency in later times.

But sentiment alone would not have prevailed to keep the Gambia, unless the river had been of actual or prospective value to English merchants and the English government. Nearer home than Sierra Leone or the Gold Coast, deeper and easier of access than any other water-way in West Africa, it gives for 250 miles facilities for traffic in the coast districts, which are not to be found elsewhere; and from the Barraconda rapid the land route to the Niger has been said to be shorter and easier than that from the Senegal. In old days, the Gambia was a favourite starting-point for those who wished to make their way into Central Africa; and, down to the last few years, hopes were entertained of opening up by the line of this river British trade with the Niger Basin and the States of the Western Sudan. There is, however, a mountain barrier between the sources of the Gambia and those of the Niger. The Upper river above Barraconda has been reported to be difficult of navigation, 'being in the dry season not navigable for vessels of over a few feet draught, and in the rains hardly navigable on account of the rapidly running stream which must pour down its channel'[1]; the inland route from Sierra Leone has been given the preference; and the recent delimitation of boundary has confined the English to the lower reaches of the river. At the present time the Gambia settlement is an isolated British dependency in the midst of what has become a great French province of Senegambia, surrounded on all sides by French territory, wholly cut off from the other British possessions on the West Coast, dealing mainly with France, using mainly French coins, and counting rather more Frenchmen than Englishmen in its handful of white residents.

[1] See Correspondence relating to Dr. Gouldsbury's expedition to the Upper Gambia, in 1881 [Parl. paper, c. 3065, 81].

From an economic point of view, the Gambia has the drawback of depending upon a single industry, and that industry again depends in great measure upon friendly relations with the savage tribes of a savage region. The picture, truth to say, is not a cheering one. Here is one of the earliest scenes of British commercial enterprise; here the English have been coming and going for the better part of three centuries; yet progress and developement are far to seek, education makes little or no way, Mohammedanism grows faster than Christianity, trade consists in dealing with barbarous races and procuring primitive products, and the uses to which a fine river may possibly be put are still all in the future.

CHAPTER VII.

BOOKS AND PUBLICATIONS RELATING TO THE GAMBIA.

The older history of the Gambia will be found in books relating to West Africa generally. The later history must be gathered from official publications. There are two valuable Blue Book reports on the settlements, one for the year 1884 by Administrator Moloney [Parl. paper, c. 4842, 86], the other for the year 1885 by Administrator Carter [Parl. paper, c. 5071, 87]. For an account of the river above Barraconda see *Correspondence relating to the recent expedition to the Upper Gambia under Administrator V. S. Gouldsbury, M.D., C.M.G.* [Parl. paper, c. 3065, 81].

CHAPTER VIII.

SIERRA LEONE.

Section II.

Origin of the Name.

VARIOUS explanations have been given of the name Sierra Leone, 'mountain of lions,' or more correctly 'mountain of the lioness' (Serra da Leôa). The shape of one of the mountains upon the far-famed peninsula, supposed to resemble a recumbent and maneless lion, the actual existence of lions or rather leopards among the hills, the roaring of the waves upon the shore, have all been given as the origin of the name; but, from Cadamosto's narrative of its first discovery, we learn that it was the noise of the thunder upon the cloud-capped mountain-top which led the Portuguese voyagers to give to this African promontory the high-sounding title, which is now so familiar to English ears.

Early notices of Sierra Leone.

Though the history of Sierra Leone as a British colony dates only from the year 1787, constant notices of the place occur in the records of earlier times. With its fine natural harbour and its ample water-supply, it could not but have been a favourite point of call for the traders and adventurers, who sailed to and by the West Coast of Africa. Exactly 100 years after it had been, in 1461 or 1462, first sighted by Pedro de Cintra[1], John Hawkins[2] came there, and carried off negroes to the West Indies. Thus the place, where in after-times were seen the first outward and visible signs in Africa of English determination to abolish the slave trade, was strangely enough the identical spot where Englishmen first began to take part in the traffic.

[1] See above, p. 21. [2] Above, p. 54.

Before the sixteenth century ended, many other British sailors touched at Sierra Leone, among them Sir Francis Drake. William Finch, who sailed with Keeling and William Hawkins to the East Indies in the years 1607-8, tells how on their way the ships put into the river of Sierra Leone; and there, at the watering-place 'of excellent water continually running,' he and his companions found on the rocks 'the names of divers Englishmen which had been there, amongst the rest Sir Francis Drake which had been there seven and twenty years before,' Thomas Cavendish, and others[1]. Finch's account and the chronicles of other voyages give some interesting particulars of Sierra Leone and its inhabitants in these old days. The Portuguese had found out its commercial value, and they traded there for gold and for elephants' teeth, both of which commodities were brought from the interior, the ivory being of a finer quality than could be procured elsewhere in West Africa. Their missionaries too had been at work, they had made native converts and built a chapel; and apparently the white men had taught the negroes among other lessons the use of tobacco, for smoking was universally prevalent, and the tobacco-plant was largely grown in the neighbourhood.

Passing on to the later years of the seventeenth century, we read in Barbot[2] that 'this river of Sierra Leona has been long frequented by all European nations, but more by the English and French than any other, either for trade or to take in refreshment on their way to the Gold Coast and Whydah'; for Sierra Leone had always a twofold value, it was at once a depôt for trade with the interior, and a safe

---

[1] See Purchas' Pilgrims, bk. iv. chap. iv. sec. 1. vol. i, pp. 414-16 [1625 ed.], containing Finch's Remembrances touching Sierra Leona in August, 1607, and the Calendar of State Papers, East Indies, 1513-1616, No. 412. See also the account of Fenton's Voyage to Brazil in 1582, in Hakluyt (1811 ed.), vol. iv. p. 263, and Calendar of State Papers as before, No. 206.

[2] Bk. ii. chap. ii.

SECTION II.

and convenient harbour, where ships going further south could refit and take in water and supplies, 'so convenient for wooding and watering,' says a rather later writer[1], 'that it occasions many of our trading ships, especially those of Bristol, to call in there.'

English slave traders and pirates at Sierra Leone in the seventeenth and eighteenth centuries.

From about the year 1660[2] onwards, there appears always to have been an English factory or depôt for slaves at Sierra Leone, on one or other of the little islands which lie in the estuary higher up than Freetown. One of these factories, on Tasso island, was broken up by De Ruyter, and it was subsequently rebuilt on Bance or Bense island, about fifteen miles above Freetown. There it stood at the end of the seventeenth century, and its barracoons were still full of slaves waiting to be shipped to the West Indies, when a hundred years later English abolitionists painfully founded their free colony on the neighbouring peninsula[3]. The Bance island factory was for many years kept up by the Royal African company; and, while it was in their hands, it was, on July 17, 1704, taken and pillaged by two small French men-of-war. But the company had at least as much to fear from their own countrymen as from foreigners, inasmuch as in the early days of the eighteenth century Sierra Leone was a noted rendezvous for pirates, one of the bays on the coast close to Cape Sierra Leone being still known as 'Pirates' bay.'

The exploits of one of these scoundrels, a certain Captain Roberts, who came to Sierra Leone in the year 1721, are recounted in Johnson's history of the Pirates, which was

---

[1] Johnson's History of the Pirates, 1724, p. 250.
[2] In a memorandum furnished to the Select Committee of 1842 (vol. i. p. 570), Macgregor Laird stated: 'The harbour of Sierra Leone has been in virtual possession of Great Britain since the commencement of the sixteenth century'; but 'sixteenth' must be a clerical error; 'eighteenth' would be nearer the truth.
[3] See Mrs. Falconbridge's letters published in 1794, and giving an account of two voyages to Sierra Leone in 1791, 2-3; she also mentions a French factory close by on an islet called Gambia island.

published three years later, in 1724; and from his narrative it appears that there was a regular pirate settlement here at this time. 'Sierra Leon river,' he says, 'disgorges with a large mouth, the starboard side of which draughts into little bays safe and convenient for cleaning and watering; what still made it preferable to the pirates is that the traders settled there are naturally their friends.' He goes on to state that there were some thirty Englishmen, ex-buccaneers, living on the highland of the peninsula, who welcomed men of their own type, and interfered with the trade of the Royal African company. Under such circumstances, it is not surprising that the company, in 1728, gave up their depôt on Bance island, which passed into the hands of private traders; and, in the Act of 1752, which finally dissolved the company, a special clause was inserted, ensuring to these traders, who were at the time three London merchants, quiet possession of the island [1].

The founding of the colony of Sierra Leone.

In the eighteenth century, when rich planters from the American and West Indian colonies came over to England, they used in the ordinary course to bring with them some of their domestic slaves, who in many cases absconded when they reached this country. If found, the negroes were forcibly reclaimed; but slavery, as the planters understood it, was alien to the soil of England [2], and the capture of runaway slaves was little to the taste of the English public. Especially was this the case, if a slave had been baptized, for there was a very general impression that a negro who became a Christian could no longer be kept in a state of slavery. To strengthen their hands, the slave owners, in 1729, obtained an opinion from the Law Officers of the Crown to the effect that slaves by coming to Great Britain and Ireland did not become free,

Runaway slaves in England in the eighteenth century.

---

[1] 25 Geo. II. cap. 40. sec. 3.
[2] It may be noted, however, that there were serfs in Scotland down to the year 1779. See the interesting note on this point in Dr. Birkbeck Hill's edition of Boswell's Life of Johnson, vol. iii. p. 202.

that baptism did not confer liberty upon them, and that they could be compelled by their masters to return to the plantations. Thus fortified, they openly advertised for the runaways, and seized them in the streets; while kidnappers set up false claims, and carried off into new bondage negroes who had never belonged to them.

These proceedings called forth the protests of right-thinking men, and gave an impetus to the growing movement against slavery and the slave trade. Foremost among the champions of the black men was Granville Sharp, who on one count or another compassed the release of various slaves, and finally, in 1772, secured, in the case of James Somerset, the ever-memorable judgement of Lord Mansfield that a slave by setting foot in England became free.

Granville Sharp.

Lord Mansfield's decision in the Somerset case.

The grounds assigned for this decision were as important as, perhaps more important than, its immediate results. The Judge laid down that slavery is so odious in its nature, that nothing can support it except positive law; whence it followed that the slave system could in future be regarded as no more than an artificial creation of acts and ordinances, the bad handiwork of man, the contradiction not the complement of natural law. Lord Mansfield gave utterance to these views in answer to the argument that public inconvenience would be caused, if all the negro slaves in England at the time were set free, the number being estimated at 14,000. He replied with the maxim 'Fiat justitia ruat cælum,' and the outcome of his judgement was that a considerable number of black servants were turned adrift into the streets of London.

Its results.

Destitute negroes in London.

The number of these destitutes was swelled by negroes who had served on the British side by sea or land in the American war, and who, when the peace of 1783 was signed, were taken, some to Nova Scotia, some to the Bahamas, and some to London, where they joined the ranks of the unemployed. To meet this growing evil, a voluntary 'committee for relieving the black poor' was formed, the chairman of which

The committee for relieving

was Jonas Hanway, and which numbered Samuel Hoare and the Messrs. Thornton among its members. These active philanthropists adopted a scheme for sending out a certain number of the negroes to form a colony on the West Coast of Africa. The scheme originated with a Dr. Smeathman, who had spent some four years in West Africa, and it also secured the powerful advocacy of Granville Sharp, while the Government consented to pay the expenses of transport, glad to take this method of ridding the country of some of the superfluous poor.

CHAPTER VIII.

The black poor.

Their scheme for a free colony in West Africa.

Unfortunately the project, like so many other plans of emigration before and since, was marred by the character of the intended colonists. Many of the blacks, as might be expected, were merely worthless loafers; and, by an extraordinary error in judgement, the promoters sent out in their company a number of white women of loose character, so that both physically and morally the constituents of the new colony were ill-chosen. There was also long delay in starting, which led to sickness and loss of life. Some of the emigrants were embarked in the Thames before Christmas, 1786, but the ships did not reach Portsmouth till towards the end of the following February; and, before they finally set sail from Plymouth on April 9, fifty of the passengers had died. In the end, Captain Thompson of H.M.S. Nautilus, who had charge of the expedition, left England with over 400 negroes and 60 whites in three vessels; and, after again losing 34 by death at sea, reached Sierra Leone with the survivors on May 9, 1787.

The first settlement at Sierra Leone, 1787, and the causes of its failure.

From Naimbana the king of the country, and from the chief in the immediate neighbourhood known as King Tom, he procured a grant of land for the settlers; and the cession was formally confirmed by a treaty signed rather more than a year later, on August 22, 1788, when King Naimbana swore allegiance to the King of England, indicating that the grant was made to the Crown with a view to the establishment

SECTION II.

upon it of a free community of British subjects. The area of land ceded was about 20 miles square, and it included the site of Freetown, where the settlers began to build their new homes. Misfortunes pursued the colony from the first; the rains set in, bringing sickness and death; many of the survivors preferred idleness to steady work, and went off into the bush; slave factories, English and French, were close at hand, bad neighbours for a struggling settlement, the design of which was directly counter to their own objects; and eventually, in 1790, the town was burnt, and its remaining inhabitants driven out by a native chief, in revenge for the destruction of his village by the crew of a British vessel, to whom two of the colonists had acted as guides.

The St. George's Bay Association, which becomes

In the meantime, Granville Sharp and his friends, in February 1790, formed themselves into a company under the name of the St. George's Bay association, 'for the purpose of opening and establishing a trade in the natural productions of Africa to the Free settlement in St. George's harbour,' St. George's Bay being a part of Freetown harbour[1];

The Sierra Leone company.

and in the following year, 1791, the company was incorporated by Act of Parliament[2] under the new title of the Sierra Leone company. The object of the company was stated in the preamble of the Act to be 'general trade and commerce from these kingdoms to and with the coasts of Africa, and from thence to and with the several interior kingdoms and countries of that continent,' for its promoters saw that the true way to abolish the slave trade was to encourage general commerce, and to open up the interior of Africa, which the slave traders and their factories had kept closed in a ring fence. 'The general object of the founders' of the company, says the report of the Directors in 1804, ' was the introduction of

---

[1] The treaty with Naimbana of August 22, 1788, specified the grant of land as extending from 'the bay commonly called Frenchman's bay, but by these presents changed to that of St. George's bay.'

[2] 31 Geo. III. cap. 55.

civilisation into Africa. The principal means proposed for effecting this end was the establishment of a secure factory at Sierra Leone, with the view to a new trade in produce, chiefly with the interior.' The Act of incorporation also spoke of the ceded ground at Sierra Leone as being vested in the Crown, so that here, if nowhere else in West Africa at this time, there was British territory in the fullest sense.

Chapter VIII.

The company sent out, in 1791, an agent, Mr. Falconbridge, who collected together the scattered remnant of the original band of colonists, and planted them at a village about two miles to the east of the former settlement, naming it Granvilletown in honour of Granville Sharp; and, in 1792, the colony was greatly strengthened in numbers by the introduction of negroes from Nova Scotia. It has been seen[1] that, at the close of the American war, some of the slaves, who had gained their freedom by taking the British side in the war, were settled in Nova Scotia. Finding the climate too rigorous for them, and discontented at the non-fulfilment of the terms which they alleged to have been promised, they sent a delegate to England and asked to be removed to Sierra Leone. The Directors of the Sierra Leone company consented to receive them, and the Government consented to pay the cost of transport. Accordingly, they arrived in West Africa to the number of 1,131; and, upon their arrival, the original settlement was revived and received for the first time the name of Freetown. Although the undertaking on the whole now thrived better than before, the newcomers caused constant trouble by their turbulence and insubordination; sickness was terribly prevalent; and to other difficulties was added attack by a foreign foe. In Sir George Trevelyan's life of Lord Macaulay will be found an account of the looting and burning of the town in September, 1794, by a French republican squadron, the members of which, while

The colony re-established in 1791.

Negroes introduced from Nova Scotia.

The settlement named Freetown.

The town plundered by French republicans.

---

[1] Above, p. 174.

Section II.

Zachary Macaulay.

professing the creed of liberty, equality, and fraternity, played the game of the slave dealers in bringing destruction and ruin upon the newborn home of freedom. The company's governor at the time was Zachary Macaulay, father of the great historian; and to him the Sierra Leone colony owed more than to any other man in the first troubled years of its existence. Macaulay had gone out to West Africa in 1793; and, returning to England after the French inroad, to recruit his health and strength, he went back to Sierra Leone in 1796, and stayed there till 1799. Before he finally left, the colony had made solid progress; and in 1798 Freetown was a town of some 300 houses and 1,200 inhabitants, the centre of a considerable trade with the natives.

Beginning of trade with the interior.

In 1794, before the French burnt down the town, the first attempt was made to open up trade with the interior. Two of the company's officers were sent to Timbo, the capital of the Fulah kingdom, about 300 miles inland; and in turn a deputation from the king of Timbo came to Sierra Leone, with a view to establishing commercial relations between the two places. There were however two great obstacles to the realisation of this and similar schemes of commerce. The first was that the coming and going of natives was perpetually intercepted by slave catchers. The root of the second difficulty was in the colony itself. The elements of which it was composed were too numerous, too various, and too unmanageable to permit of its developement on the lines of a trading factory. The Nova Scotians required to be governed, and the machinery of government was wholly inadequate. To remedy this evil, the company obtained from the Government, in the year 1800, a Charter of Justice. By this Charter the lands which had been ceded by the negro chiefs to the Crown were made over in full right to the company, subject to a nominal rent to the king of England of 10 shillings per annum. The Directors were also empowered to purchase the other parts of the peninsula which

The Charter of Justice of 1800.

were still in possession of their native owners[1]; and the whole was constituted 'one independent and separate colony by the name of the colony of Sierra Leone.' Authority was given to the company to appoint a Governor and Council, and to legislate for the colony, either directly or through the Council, subject to the restriction that the laws so made were not to be repugnant to the law of England. Provision was also made for the appointment of a mayor and aldermen, and for the administration of criminal and civil justice. Thus Sierra Leone was given a colonial constitution, the supreme power being placed in the hands of the company to whom the settlement owed its existence; and grants in aid were made by Parliament at once for defence purposes and for the maintenance of the civil establishment.

Coming of the Maroons

In this same year, 1800, yet another strain was added to the mixed population of the colony. A body of Jamaica Maroons, who had rebelled against the island government in 1795, was in 1796 transported to Nova Scotia; and, suffering from the cold of the climate, like the band of negroes already mentioned, they were carried over the sea from Halifax to Sierra Leone. They numbered about 550 in all; they and their forefathers for many generations had jealously maintained their freedom in the mountains of Jamaica[2]; and thus they contributed a strong and healthy element to the Sierra Leone community. Almost immediately after their arrival, in October 1800, their fighting qualities were called into play, for the imposition of a quit-rent led to an outbreak among the Nova Scotians, who contended with some show of reason that the grants of land, which the Directors of the company had promised them, were to be free of all taxation.

---

[1] The boundaries of the peninsula were defined in the charter. It was stated to be 'bounded on the north by the river Sierra Leone, on the south by the river Caramanca, on the east by the river Bunce, and on the west by the sea.'

[2] For an account of the Maroons in Jamaica, see vol. ii. of this work, pp. 101-5.

Section II. It was owing to the support which the authorities received from the Maroons, that they were able to quell this dangerous outbreak. Years afterwards, when slave emancipation was an accomplished fact, the survivors of these Maroon settlers and their descendants returned once more to their old homes in Jamaica.

Equipped with full powers of government, and subsidised by Parliament, the Directors of the Sierra Leone company had yet great difficulties to contend with. Though the settlement had outgrown the dimensions of a factory, the slave trade was a perpetual obstacle to the extension of commerce; while the progress of the community as an agricultural settlement within the bounds of the peninsula was hindered by the character of the colonists. The discontented Nova Scotians made little use of their plots of ground, the Maroons thrived in trade or as mechanics, but in hardly a single case as agriculturists; and the field work of the colony was mainly carried on by hired native labourers, known as grumettas[1]. Eventually, in 1807, the year of the abolition of the slave trade, an Act of Parliament was passed, by which the Crown took back the colony from January 1, 1808; and the Sierra Leone company resolved itself into the African Institution, the members of which, as voluntary advisers of the Government, continued to promote the interests of Sierra Leone, and to follow up the good work of stamping out the remains of the African slave trade.

The colony taken over by the Crown.

Sierra Leone as a Crown Colony.

As a Crown Colony, Sierra Leone became the head-quarters of the British power on the West Coast of Africa; and when, on the dissolution of the African company in 1821, all the British forts and dependencies in West Africa were combined into a single colony under the name of the West Africa Settlements, at Sierra Leone, and not at the Gambia or on the Gold Coast, was placed the seat of

---

[1] See above, p. 103, n. 3.

Government. Its central position and natural advantages, no less than its association with the cause of freedom and progress, marked it out to be the leading settlement; and its population was continually being recruited from the slave ships, whose living cargoes were rescued by British vessels and landed at Freetown. It was estimated that, up to the end of the year 1825, nearly 18,000 Liberated Africans were brought into the colony: and, among other settlers, there came, in 1817-8, 1,200 pensioners from the black West India regiments, and, in 1819, 85 Barbadian negroes, brought over in consequence of a slave rebellion in that island. Thus there has been a medley of races in Sierra Leone, to an extent unknown in any other British dependency in West Africa. It has, beyond all the other settlements, been a colony in the true sense, though a colony of negroes, not of Europeans, and not derived from one stock only, but from many.

CHAPTER VIII.

The Liberated Africans.

While Freetown was thus being made a receptacle for all sorts and conditions of black men, the boundaries of the colony were continually enlarged by a series of cessions obtained from the natives. In 1818, the Isles de Los, at a considerable distance to the north of Freetown, were ceded to the Crown. In 1819, the eastern limit of the colony was widened by the acquisition of territory on the banks of the Bunce river; and, in 1824, British sovereignty was carried across the Sierra Leone estuary to its northern bank, covering a strip of coast one mile deep inland, together with the islands in the river which had been in older days the scenes of slave factories. This last annexation was caused by the developement of the timber trade, which, beginning in the year 1816, led to the establishment of European depôts upon the northern bank of the river. In 1825, territorial rights were acquired in the Sherbro district to the south of Sierra Leone, and the name of Turner's Peninsula, which is still borne by

Additions to the area of the colony.

182   *HISTORICAL GEOGRAPHY OF THE COLONIES.*

SECTION II.

a narrow tract of coast-land below the island of Sherbro, commemorates the governor to whom the acquisition was due. In that same year, and in 1827, important annexations were made in the north, including the coast-line from the Sierra Leone estuary to the Little Scarcies river. Years went on; various treaties were made, gradually extending the area of British influence; and, in 1861, two districts were annexed, which added materially to the area and possibly to the strength of the colony. The first of these was the mainland district of Quiah, immediately to the east of the peninsula of Sierra Leone; the second was the island of Sherbro, commanding a network of estuaries and lagoons, rich with promise of future trade. Then came a lull in the onward movement, under the restraining influence of the report issued by the Parliamentary Committee of 1865, until, about the year 1876, annexations began again, and cessions obtained in that year and in 1877, in the neighbourhood of the Great Scarcies river, carried the northern boundary of the colony up to a point, where it has been met by the counter claims of the French advancing south.

The boundary between the colony and the Liberian Republic on the south.

In the year 1863, efforts were made to fix the limits of the Liberian Republic towards the north, and thereby to determine the line to which the British colony or Protectorate of Sierra Leone might fairly extend in a southerly direction. These efforts were renewed in 1879, without any definite result being achieved; and, as it was important that no foreign power should gain a foothold on the coast between the colony and the republic, a treaty was, in 1882, negotiated by the governor of Sierra Leone with the native chiefs concerned, by which the coast-line of what is now the southernmost part of the colony, reaching as far south as the Manna river, and extending inland for half a mile from high-water mark, was ceded to the Crown. In the following year, the strip thus ceded was declared to be

British territory; and, in 1886, the Manna river was accepted by the Liberian Republic as the boundary line. Thus on the south a definite frontier was at length secured.

The Anglo-French boundary on the north and east of the colony.

In the case of Sierra Leone, as in that of the Gambia, the chief difficulties which have arisen of late years have been due to the want of a fixed boundary between the English and the French Protectorates. An Anglo-French convention of 1882, which, though not formally ratified, was accepted as binding by both powers, established a basis for the delimitation of the frontier, providing that the line should be drawn between the basins of the Scarcies and the Mellicourie rivers, so as to give full control of the former to Great Britain and of the latter to France. This convention was supplemented by two subsequent agreements, in 1889 and 1891. The line starts from a point a little to the north of the Mahela creek, between the Scarcies and the Mellicourie rivers; and all the coast-line and islands, including Yellaboi island, from this point southward, as far as the frontier of the Liberian Republic, are assigned to Great Britain; while the coast-line and islands to the north, as far as the Rio Nunez, including the island of Matacong, but excluding the Isles de Los, are assigned to France. The Isles de Los, though geographically within the French Sphere, remain in British possession. Inland, the boundary-line runs from the coast in a north-easterly direction between the Scarcies and the Mellicourie, up to the 10th degree of North latitude; and it follows that degree as far as the crest of the hills bordering on the sources of the Niger, the upper waters of which here flow from south to north. Both banks of this section of the Niger shall, it is expressly provided, be henceforth included in the French Sphere, the boundary being 10 kilometres from the left bank. This delimitation gives to Great Britain, as against other European powers, a large tract of hinterland, including the districts of Sulimania and Falaba;

184 HISTORICAL GEOGRAPHY OF THE COLONIES.

SECTION II.

but extension to the Niger and to the great interior plateau is for the present barred by the concessions which have been made to France.

Government and Administration.

Twice, in 1821 and again in 1866, has Sierra Leone been made the seat of Government for all the West African dependencies of Great Britain; but in neither case did the union last long, and, since the separation of the Gambia in 1888, the authority of the Governor of Sierra Leone has been confined to the limits of his own colony. Like the other West Africa settlements, Sierra Leone is a Crown Colony, with the usual Executive and Legislative Councils. The Executive Council now consists of seven members, all officers of the Government, viz. the Governor, the Chief Justice, the Officer commanding the troops, the Colonial Secretary, the Colonial Treasurer, the Queen's Advocate, and the present head of the Medical department. The Legislative Council is composed of the above-named officials, together with three nominated unofficial members.

Law and Justice.

The law of the colony is the Common law of England, and the Statutes of general application which were in force in England on January 1, 1880, supplemented by local ordinances. There is a Supreme Court consisting of a Chief Justice; and minor cases are tried by the police magistrate of Freetown, and by the District Commissioners of Sherbro, the Eastern, and the Western district.

Area and Boundaries.

Letters patent, under date of November 28, 1888, define the colony of Sierra Leone as comprising all places, settlements, and territories, which may at any time belong to the Queen in Western Africa, between the fifth and twelfth degrees of North latitude, and lying to the westward of the tenth degree of West longitude. As a matter of fact, the northern limit of the colony on the coast, where the English and French frontiers meet each other, is in about 9·3 degrees of North latitude (though the Isles de Los lie much further to the north); and its southern limit is in about 6.55 degrees of North latitude, where the creek of the Manna river forms the boundary with the Liberian Republic—a state, it may be noted, whose origin was similar to that of Sierra Leone itself, though the founders of it were not English but American philanthropists. Freetown is in 8.30 degrees of North latitude, about 35 miles by coast from the northern boundary of the colony, and about 190 miles from its southern boundary. The length of the coast-line of the colony is therefore about 220 miles. The inland limits have not yet been finally defined; but, as already stated, the British Sphere may be taken to extend as far as the hills bordering on the rivers which form the sources of the Niger, its greatest breadth nowhere reaching 200 miles in a direct line from the sea. In the absence of accepted frontiers, of accurate maps, and of fuller knowledge of the various districts concerned, it is impossible to give more than a very rough estimate of the area which has been, or rather is being, assigned to Great Britain, but 24,000 square miles may be taken as approximate to the truth, representing an extent of territory equal in size to three-fourths of Ireland. This province comprises some districts which have been formally ceded to the Crown, and others which are more or less definitely under British protection, but to which, owing to geographical difficulties and to political reasons, the advantages of direct British administration have not yet been extended.

The part, which is actually British territory, adjoins the sea; and, outside the mountainous peninsula of Sierra Leone, is, as it has been described in the Blue Book Report of 1891, a network of rivers and creeks. The country behind, over which British influence extends, includes the low-lying alluvial lands of the West African coast region, watered by rivers which rise on the outer edge of the great African plateau, with a background of hills and valleys, gradually rising in level, until, at an average distance of from 80 to 100 miles from the sea, the mountains are reached, on the other side of which is the rich basin of the Niger and its tributary streams.

The colony proper.

The colony itself, the territory, that is to say, which is owned by Great Britain, is estimated to cover nearly 4,000 square miles. In other words its area is double that of Lancashire.

The Isles de Los.

Separated from the main body of the dependency, at a distance of nearly 70 miles north of Freetown, the Isles de Los, the isles of Idols (*dos Idolos*), lie over against a mainland promontory, known as Tumbo Point. The group consists of three islands and reefs. The largest and westernmost is Tamara island; the easternmost and next in size is Factory island; and in the centre, encircled by the others, is Crawford island, the smallest of the three, once used for a short time as a military station.

Throughout the greater part of its length the colony consists merely of a narrow strip of coast-line, generally not more than half a mile in breadth, the sovereignty of which has been acquired solely in order that goods may not be carried into the interior without first paying customs duties on landing.

Districts of the colony.

There are only two districts of any considerable size, viz. the peninsula of Sierra Leone proper with the adjacent territory of British Quiah, and the island of Sherbro, between 70 and 100 miles south of Freetown, with a portion of the adjoining mainland. The Sierra Leone peninsula and British Quiah are, for police and magisterial purposes, divided into three districts—the district of Freetown, which takes in the northern part of the peninsula; the Western district, including its southern part; and the Eastern district, comprising most of British Quiah. A fourth district has been constituted at Sherbro.

The peninsula of Sierra Leone.

The peninsula of Sierra Leone is about 25 miles in length, and from 10 to 12 miles in breadth at its widest point. It has an area of 300 square miles, and is therefore twice as large as the Isle of Wight. It is one of the few points on the West African coast where there is high land near to the sea. It is formed by a range of volcanic mountains, running parallel to the sea from NNW. to SSE., the summits of which, in the Sugar Loaf and Leicester mountains, rise in conical form to a height of from 2,000 to 3,000 feet. The mountains are composed principally of granite, and are thickly wooded. They are intersected by ravines and small valleys; and there are considerable tracts of level ground, especially on the eastern side of the peninsula, where it sinks towards the mainland.

On the north and north-east is the estuary of the Sierra Leone river, which has an average breadth of five miles. Here, under the shelter of the peninsula, there is good and commodious anchorage for vessels of all sizes, the main entrance being on the southern side, by a deep channel which is everywhere more than a mile in breadth. It is to the harbour thus formed that the colony owes its importance. There is no other harbour, worthy of the name, between the French naval station of Dakar and the island of Fernando Po; and its strategical importance is increased by the fact that it is half-way between England and the Cape of Good Hope.

What is called, as an arm of the sea, the Sierra Leone river, is higher up known as the Rokell river, which is navigable for steamers for about 15 miles above Freetown, and for small boats for 40 miles. The peninsula stretches out into the ocean in Cape Sierra Leone, four miles from which up the estuary is Freetown, the capital of the colony. The town stands on sloping ground, at the foot of the hills which fringe the northern shore of the peninsula. It faces the harbour, and looks to the north and north-west. It is well laid out, with broad streets and an exceptionally good water-supply; but its position is unhealthy, as the hills cut it off from the south-westerly sea-breezes. At the last census

188 HISTORICAL GEOGRAPHY OF THE COLONIES.

SECTION II.

the town and suburbs had a population of 30,000. It is one of the Imperial coaling stations, and as such is fortified and garrisoned; it is the headquarters of the West India regiments on the West Coast of Africa; and it is in telegraphic communication with all parts of the world. It is about 500 miles from Bathurst, about 1,050 from Cape Coast Castle, and 1,150 from the island of Ascension; and, in round numbers, its distance from England on the north and from the Cape on the south is, in either case, over 3,000 miles.

Freetown is the only town in the colony, for the villages in the peninsula, many of which were originally settlements of Liberated Africans, are all of small size, Waterloo being the largest; and, outside the peninsula, the only place deserving special mention is Bonthe on Sherbro island, on the side nearest the mainland, which is the administrative centre of the Sherbro district.

Sherbro Island.

This last-named district is a very important part of the colony, contributing a large proportion of the revenue. Sherbro island itself is about 33 miles in extreme length, and 17 in extreme breadth, and it comprises an area of rather less than 250 square miles. It is of triangular shape, its northern end being over 70 miles distant from Freetown. Low-lying and unhealthy, the centre of what is little more than a large swamp, its position, like that of Lagos, is admirably suited to control the trade of an extensive district, for it lies over against a section of the mainland, at which rivers, creeks, and lagoons converge, forming a series of waterways which carry down to the sea the produce of the coast region, to be exchanged for imported European commodities.

Climate.

The climate of Sierra Leone has a bad name; from the date of the first settlement it has dealt ill with Europeans; and the title, which has been given to the colony, of the White Man's Grave illustrates the common, if somewhat exaggerated, impression which has been formed of its unhealthiness. The mean annual temperature is over 80 degrees, and the rainfall is much heavier than at the Gambia, averaging at Freetown over 150 inches in the year. The amount of moisture at Freetown, and in consequence its unhealthiness, is increased by the large number of trees in the neighbourhood. The year is divided into a wet and dry season, the former lasting from May till October, the latter from November to April, the temperature being somewhat lower in the rainy than in the dry months. The most sickly time of the year is at the beginning and at the end of the wet months, when sun and rain combine to breed fever and pestilence. The colony is within the range of the Harmattan wind, which blows over the Sahara in the early months of the year; and here, as at the Gambia, tornadoes are one of the meteorological phenomena.

CHAPTER VIII.

Sierra Leone is essentially a place of transit, and only a small proportion of the exports represents the produce of the colony itself. It is estimated that one-sixth of the resident population in British territory are traders, and agriculture has made little way, though considerable efforts have been made by enterprising members of the community to stimulate the cultivation of tropical products. The people grow vegetables for local consumption, and some ginger, rice, and cassada is produced; but the palm kernels, the rubber, the kola nuts, and other staple exports come in the main from districts outside direct British jurisdiction, where labour is no doubt in great measure still performed by slaves. The tribes to the north and east cultivate ground nuts, beniseed, and rice; while those on the south make palm oil and shell palm kernels for the market. On the north, trade is mainly carried on in the dry season; but on the south, it is when the rains have made the small rivers navigable, that the natives are able to bring down their produce to the merchants on the coast. The products enumerated above are chiefly products of the coast region, though not so much of the

Products.

SECTION II.

narrow strip which is under British sovereignty; but Sierra Leone has also parties and caravans of visitors from the more distant interior, from Sego, Bouré, and elsewhere, who bring down hides and a little ivory and gold to be exchanged for firearms, cotton cloth, and salt. This more distant traffic is seriously threatened by the political arrangements, under which the French are encircling the colony and cutting it off from the Niger. Early in the present century, the gold trade of Sierra Leone was of some importance. It is said to have begun about the year 1822, growing at the expense of a similar trade on the Gambia; and the report on Sierra Leone and its dependencies, which was presented to Parliament in 1827, stated that it was then chiefly in the hands of the firm of Macaulay and Babington. The amount of gold, however, now brought down from the interior is quite insignificant, and Sierra Leone is not likely to grow rich from gold-dust or from the developement of any mineral resources either within or without the bounds of the colony. It depends in the main, like other West African dependencies, upon forest produce, upon the nuts and gums of trees and plants, which grow and give their fruit and sap without any systematic cultivation. In 1891, the chief exports of the colony were, in order of importance, palm kernels, rubber, kola nuts, palm oil, gum copal, rice, and hides; palm kernels representing one-third in value of the total exports of the year. The oil palm (Elæis Guineensis) gives both the palm oil, and the palm kernels from which on arrival in Europe further supplies of oil are extracted. The oil is exported principally to the United Kingdom, the kernels to the United Kingdom, France, and Germany; and both the one and the other are utilised in the manufacture of soap and candles, and as grease for lubricating machinery[1]. India-rubber, which comes next to the oil palm among the products of Sierra Leone, is exported principally to Great Britain, and the same

Chief Exports.

Palm oil and kernels.

India-rubber.

---

[1] See below, Appendix, p. 243.

may be said of gum copal. The hides are sent to American markets; and the kola nuts mainly to other parts of West Africa, such as the Gambia and the Senegal. These nuts are much prized by the Mohammedan tribes, partly for superstitious reasons, and partly because of their peculiar power to stay the pangs of hunger—a property which in times of fast is of no small value.

Chapter VIII.

Kola nuts.

The trade statistics of the colony in 1891 showed a great increase on previous years, the value of the imports and exports in the three years 1889-91 being returned as follows :—

Trade Returns.

	Imports.	Exports.
1889	£278,000	£320,000
1890	£390,000	£349,000
1891	£453,000	£478,000

It is satisfactory to not that a large proportion of the trade is with the United Kingdom, which sends about three-fourths in value of the imports into the colony, cotton goods being the principal article, and takes nearly half of the ports.

As more than three-quarters of the colonial revenue are derived from customs duties, the finances of Sierra Leone have improved *pari passu* with the growth of imports. The total revenue in 1891 amounted to nearly £90,000, the average annual receipts for the five years 1887-91 being about £72,000. There is a small Public Debt of less than £50,000, but the sinking fund for its redemption will shortly cover the whole amount, and the colony may be considered as practically free from liabilities.

Revenue.

The standard of the colonial currency is British sterling, but there is no limit on the tender of silver. Some foreign coins are rated for concurrent circulation, among them the French gold twenty-franc piece, and the silver five-franc piece of the Latin Union. This last coin divides the circulation with British silver.

Currency.

Any statistics of the population of a West African de-

Population.

SECTION II.

pendency at the present time must from the nature of things be partial and inaccurate. In Sierra Leone, the 1891 census did not include even the whole of what is actually British territory, but only the more organised districts, the population of which was returned at 74,835, against 60,546 for the same area in 1881. Of these, 58,000 were residents in the peninsula and the adjoining districts, 13,000 in Sherbro, and under 1,600 in the Isles de Los. There was a large increase in the numbers of Freetown and the neighbourhood, and a falling off in the population of Quiah. The number of inhabitants in the unenumerated parts of the colony is estimated at about 50,000; so that for a total area of 4,000 square miles there is supposed to be a population of between 120,000 and 130,000. The Europeans, chiefly Englishmen, are but a handful, a little more than 200 in all, including the Government officers; and of the black population, about a half consists of Liberated Africans and their descendants, the balance being composed of members of the neighbouring tribes. As the former class represents slaves carried off from all parts of Africa, there is the most extraordinary variety of races in the colony, but the majority of the Liberated Africans are said to be either Akus, whose original home was near Lagos, or Eboes from the banks of the Niger. The other—the more indigenous section of the population—contains almost as great a diversity of elements as is to be found among the Liberated Africans. They include Timmanehs, the original inhabitants of the Sierra Leone peninsula, Mendis from behind the Sherbro district, Sherbros, Mandingoes, Soosoos, Kroomen, and many others, no less than sixty languages, it is said, being spoken in the streets of Freetown.

Occupations and condition of the population.

There are, as already stated, no manufactures, no mines, and little agriculture beyond market gardening in the colony. From the first, from the days of the Sierra Leone company, all attempts to make Sierra Leone an agricultural, a planting colony, after the type of the West Indian islands, have failed.

The place is designed by its situation to be a trading emporium, through which goods are carried from the sea to the interior and from the interior to the sea; and the mixture of races, and perpetual incoming of new settlers, not constrained by slave laws to work, has proved an obstacle to agriculture. In the West Indies, it was the slave system which made the West African a tiller of the soil; he is not by nature an agriculturist; and, when he is trained to work, fruit-growing and gardening are more to his taste than cultivation of the field. In his own home, on the West Coast of Africa, he has never known the plantation system, nor learnt to grow more than enough for domestic use; the jungle is hard by, giving produce for export which needs little or no tilling; and where, as at Sierra Leone, nature has formed a trading station, the favourite occupation of the people is to traffic and barter, rather than to raise crops and to develope an agricultural community. The Sierra Leone negro is a born trader, and is to be found at all the commercial centres in West Africa.

CHAPTER VIII.

In religion, as in race and language, there is great diversity at Sierra Leone. Christians of various sects, Mohammedans, and Pagans are all well represented. Mohammedanism is said to be growing faster than Christianity, but, at the 1891 census, some 41,000 were returned as professing Christians. The Church of England, which alone receives any state aid, has the largest number of adherents; and the next most important denominations are the Wesleyans and the Free Church Methodists. The Roman Catholics are very few in number.

Religion.

The present system of education in the colony dates from 1882, when an ordinance was passed, establishing a Board of education, and providing at once for purely Government schools and for grants-in-aid to private schools. As a matter of fact private schools, subsidised by or wholly independent of the Government, do the whole or nearly the whole of the work

Education.

SECTION II. of elementary education; and, to judge from the decrease in the number of pupils at the grant-in-aid schools in the three years 1889-91, no progress whatever is being made. More advanced education is given at High Schools in Freetown, and at the Training College of the Church Missionary Society at Fourah Bay which is affiliated to Durham University.

General summary. There are four stages in the history of Sierra Leone. At first it appears to have been the scene of more or less honest trade. Next it was given over, like all other parts of the West African coast, to slave trading, with a special local accompaniment of piracy. Then it became the headquarters in Africa of the Abolition movement, and its name will ever be hallowed by association with the memory of the men who set the negroes free. Lastly, when their work was done, it entered upon the fourth, the present stage, in which it takes rank as a commercial emporium and as a coaling station of the empire. It has in fact come back to some extent to its original position. In old days sailors and traders, as we have seen, went there to refit and water their ships, or to traffic with the natives of the interior. They come there still for much the same reason; but the ships are steamers, requiring coal; and, instead of ivory and gold, the exports are palm oil and palm kernels. As a fine harbour on the way to the South, unrivalled for very many miles of coast, Sierra Leone must always be of value to any trading European power, most of all to the power which owns the Cape, India, and Australia. As a place at which to focus the commerce of a large province of West Africa, it is or ought to be great, in that the coast-line is honeycombed with water-ways, while inland the trade-routes from the headwaters of the Niger lead naturally to Freetown. Unfortunately, as these routes are cut by the French boundary, trade with the Upper Niger will, if present arrangements continue, henceforth largely be measured by the goodwill of France; and, even if the competition of rival European nations does not prevent the commerce of this region from flowing down to the sea in the channels marked out by nature, the prosperity of the colony will still depend on maintaining peace among the savage tribes who dwell afar and near, on keeping roads open by force of arms or by subsidies, and on giving some security to property and life. For it must be realised that, though Sierra Leone has been in its origin and in its developement more of a settlement, more of a colony than the other West African dependencies of Great Britain, though there has been more evidence here than elsewhere on the coast of British sovereignty and British ownership of soil, though Freetown has twice been made the centre of government and administration for British West Africa, and its harbour is recognised as having an Imperial as well as a local value, yet its background is still that of African savagery, and its surroundings are little different from those which existed centuries ago. The coast tribes still, as in the days of the slave trade, and as in the days before the slave trade, play the part of middlemen, jealously interposing themselves between the Europeans and the natives of the interior, while the latter in their turn levy black mail on each other, wage intertribal wars, and barter the results of slave labour for what Europe can send them. Lightly taxed in British territory, the Liberated African contributes little or nothing to the developement of that territory, or to the peace, freedom, and prosperity of those who live outside its limits, and who really pay the customs duties from which the revenue of the colony is derived. The forest gives the produce, the native bargains and palavers, but civilisation and cultivation of soil or of human beings is far to seek; and the settlement, which is christened after Freedom and which cherishes the traditions of emancipation, year after year draws its wealth from a region where slavery and barbarism are rife. It is impossible not to feel that something more might have been

SECTION II.

done, and might still be done by the English, than to stop by the sea-shore, and that a little leaven of French forwardness, lavish as it seems to be, would not be unwholesome. Roads and railways mean light and life in savage lands. There are few roads and no railways in British West Africa.

BOOKS AND PUBLICATIONS RELATING TO SIERRA LEONE.

The early history of the colonisation of Sierra Leone is well given in *An Essay on Colonisation particularly applied to the Western Coast of Africa*, by C. B. WADSTRÖM [1794].

Reference should also be made to the report of the Court of Directors of the Sierra Leone Company in 1804.

For later information, in addition to official reports and the evidence taken by Parliamentary Committees, see the excellent address to the Colonial Institute (December 13, 1881) on *Sierra Leone, Past, Present, and Future*, by Mr. RISELY GRIFFITH, then Colonial Secretary of the colony. [Proceedings of the Royal Colonial Institute, vol. xiii.]

See also Colonial Reports, Miscellaneous, No. 3, Sierra Leone. *Reports on Botany and Geology*, by G. F. SCOTT ELLIOT, Esq., and Miss CATHARINE A. RAISIN, 1893, c. 6998.

Various books have been written giving a description of the colony, but they hardly require special mention.

CHAPTER IX.

THE GOLD COAST[1].

The Dutch and English merchants of the seventeenth century named each section of the Guinea Coast after its principal product. But, though the Grain or Pepper Coast, the Ivory Coast, the Gold Coast, and the Slave Coast, may still be found marked on modern maps, these names with one exception are no longer in common use. The Grain Coast is comprised within the Republic of Liberia; the elephants have long since disappeared from the Ivory Coast; slaves are no longer exported either from the district to the east of the Gold Coast, which was once known pre-eminently as the Slave Coast, or from any other part of the West Coast of Africa; and the one exception is the Gold Coast itself, from which gold is still shipped in considerable quantities to Europe, and which therefore still retains and deserves to retain its golden name.

The Gold Coast of the geographers extends from Assinee, or perhaps from Grand Bassam, upon the west to the mouth of the Volta river upon the east. The Guinea Coast, between Cape Palmas and the Cameroons, forms a great bay—the Gulf of Guinea, but the curve is broken by two projections, which are geologically interesting, as having come into being in different ways. The more easterly of the two projections is the Delta of the Niger, formed by the great quantities of alluvial matter, which the river has

Natural and political boundaries of the Gold Coast.

---

[1] The History of the Gold Coast has been given at such length in previous chapters, that little or no further reference will be made to it in this place.

SECTION II.

brought down and poured out into the sea. The other, in the middle of the bay, owes its existence to the fact that the gold-bearing rocks, of which it consists, are harder than the coast on either side and therefore have not been so much worn away by the waves.

The geographical and geological limits of the Gold Coast are thus clearly marked upon the map; but the political boundaries do not entirely coincide with them, and here, as at Sierra Leone, have been much debated. On the west the English have the French for their neighbours; on the east they have the Germans. Under the Anglo-French arrangements of August 1889, June 1891, and July 1893, the frontier line between the French at Assinee and the English on the Gold Coast starts from the sea at Newtown in about 3 degrees of West longitude, and takes a straight line due north to the Tendo lagoon; it follows that lagoon, the Ahy lagoon, and the Tendo or Tanoe river as far as a place called Nougoua, and is carried thence up to the ninth degree of North latitude, in a direction determined by the treaties which either nation has made with the native tribes. Five miles east of Nougoua, the line runs successively north, west, and north-west to nearly 6·50 degrees of North latitude, from which point it runs north-east and north, until it strikes the western branch of the Volta in about 8·40 degrees of North latitude. It then follows the course of that river up to the ninth parallel.

The Anglo-French frontier.

The Anglo-German frontier.

On the other side, the boundary between the Gold Coast and the German Protectorate of Togoland is laid down general terms in the fourth article of the Anglo-German agreement of July 1890—the agreement which ceded Heligoland to Germany. The line leaves the sea-coast at Afflao in about 1·14 degrees East longitude; and, after running due north as far as 6·10 degrees of North latitude, it takes a course west and north, until it reaches the Volta in about 6·40 degrees North latitude. Thence it follows that river up to its confluence with the river Dakka in about 8·8 degrees North latitude. Here a Neutral Zone has been established, extending between 8·8 and 10 degrees North latitude, and between 1·32 West and 0·16 East longitude, within which both nations have bound themselves not to acquire Protectorates.

Such are the limits of the British Sphere of influence in this part of West Africa, so far as any limits have hitherto been determined; but the bounds of what is more definitely known as the Gold Coast Colony and Protectorate are, it need hardly be said, very much more circumscribed.

In tracing the history of European trade and settlement in West Africa, stress was laid upon the fact that, down to the present century, European nations, with the exception perhaps of the Portuguese, did not, as a general rule, exercise sovereignty or enjoy territorial ownership on the West African coast [1]. They had forts and trading establishments, for which they paid ground-rents to the natives; but their authority as rulers did not in most cases extend beyond the lines of the forts and the walls of the factories. On the Gold Coast this system—a system which implied trade and nothing more—was most fully developed. To judge from the old maps, a row of isolated forts and factories lined the water's edge, but they had no territory or territorial rights attached to them. These forts, which originally were built by and belonged to different European peoples, having all been formally ceded to Great Britain, and the ground-rents having been forfeited or having lapsed in course of time, the soil on which they stand is British territory; but outside them, the large area of country, which is commonly included under the name of the Gold Coast, and which for all practical purposes is in the position of a British dependency, is, strictly

The Gold Coast Protectorate.

---

[1] See above, pp. 105-6.

SECTION II.

speaking, not a **colony** but a Protectorate. Except in the case of small strips of seaboard, most of the treaties, **which have been** made with native **chiefs and** have been ratified by the Home Government, have been treaties involving British protection and jurisdiction, but not actual **cession** of territory. The natives recognise the authority of the Queen of England and her representative the Governor of the Gold Coast, but as being their guardian and referee rather than as the owner of their lands. There **is** one exception to this general statement. On the eastern side of the Gold Coast, in the Volta districts, the Danes appear in past times, though the evidence is not clear, to have claimed and possibly exercised sovereign rights to a fuller and wider extent than was the case with other Europeans on the Gulf of Guinea; and therefore the English, having inherited whatever powers their predecessors possessed, may be held to be entitled to regard these districts as actually belonging to the British Crown. **The** point however is one of little moment, of historical **or legal interest** rather than of political importance. For practical purposes it matters little where the colony ends and the Protectorate begins, for in colony and Protectorate alike British authority, so far as it can as a matter of fact be exercised, is undisputed and supreme.

Origin and growth of the Protectorate.

We have seen how the Protectorate began and was developed, mainly through the energy and sagacity of Governor Maclean[1]. It was based on sufferance, on usage, on voluntary submission by the natives to British control, on their voluntary acceptance of British jurisdiction, which was the keystone of the system. They consented to give up certain savage customs, to be amenable in criminal matters to the general principles of British law; and, in 1844, the Fantee chiefs signed an agreement, known as the **Bond,** which contained a formal recognition of the authority

[1] See above, p. 121.

to which they had already tacitly assented. In 1874, after the Ashantee war, a further step was taken towards giving a legal sanction to existing facts, and an Order in Council was passed, which defined the powers exercised by the British Crown in the Protectorate as being exercised under the Foreign Jurisdiction Act, and delegated to the Legislature of the Gold Coast colony whatever powers the Crown possessed. This Order in Council was immediately followed by the enactment of two local ordinances, which abolished slave-dealing and slavery throughout the Protected Territories.

CHAPTER IX.

The Gold Coast colony and Protectorate is in many respects similar to the colony of the Straits Settlements with the adjoining protected States of the Malay peninsula, some account of which has been given in a preceding volume of this book[1]. The actual colony of the Straits Settlements is small in area, consisting of the islands of Singapore, Penang, and Pangkor, and the mainland districts of Malacca, Province Wellesley, and the Dindings. These islands and districts, separated one from another, are British soil, and outside them is a much larger extent of protected territory, consisting of the Native States of Perak, Selangor, and others, which stretch in a continuous line along the peninsula. Similarly, the Gold Coast colony consists of a number of settlements, detached from each other, or, if connected, connected only by a narrow line of coast, while outside the colony is an extensive and continuous area of protected territory. The Protected States of the Malay peninsula are governed by their native rulers, who are however advised by British Residents and assisted by a staff of European officers; and in like manner the administration of the Gold Coast Protectorate is mainly conducted through the native chiefs, and the inhabitants are not, technically speaking, British subjects. But, in the case of the Malay states, though they are for all practical purposes under British

Comparison of the Gold Coast Protectorate and the Protected States of the Malay peninsula.

[1] See vol. i. pp. 95–126.

202 HISTORICAL GEOGRAPHY OF THE COLONIES.

SECTION II.

control, and though the Residents take their instructions from the Governor of the Straits Settlements, there is a distinct line between the colony and the Protected States, and the Legislature of the former exercises no authority over the latter. This difference does not exist on the Gold Coast. The Crown, and through the Crown, by direct delegation, the Colonial Government and Legislature, has by usage acquired the right of exercising, and in the Coast districts does actually exercise, all the powers of a Sovereign ruler, in regard to the preservation of the public peace, the collection of revenue, and the administration of civil and criminal justice; and the nature and extent of British authority is measured, not by well-defined limits, but by geographical possibilities and political convenience.

Government.

The Gold Coast is a Crown Colony, and the government consists of a Governor, an Executive Council, and a Legislative Council. The members of the Executive Council are the Governor, the Colonial Secretary, the Queen's Advocate, the Treasurer, and the Inspector-General of police. The Legislative Council consists of the same officials with the addition of the Chief Justice, and of two nominated unofficial members.

Law and Justice.

The Supreme Court consists of a Chief Justice and three puisne Judges. The law which is administered is, in addition to the ordinances of the local legislature and native laws and customs, 'the Common law, the doctrines of Equity, and the Statutes of general application which were in force in England at the date when the colony obtained a local legislature, that is to say, on the 24th day of July 1874,' together with all Imperial laws declared to extend or apply to the colony and the territories over which the Court has jurisdiction, so far as they are applicable under local circumstances[1]. The chief magisterial

---

[1] See ord. 4 of 1876, sects. 14, 17, 19.

and administrative officers are the District Commissioners, and order is maintained by a strong police force called the Gold Coast Constabulary. This force includes both a military and a civil police, the former branch being recruited mainly from the Houssas who are brought down from the interior, the latter from the Fantees of the Gold Coast. A colonial ordinance[1], it may be added, gives validity to the authority of the native chiefs in the Protectorate, empowering them to make by-laws on certain subjects, the breaches of which, together with other minor cases, both civil and criminal, are tried by native tribunals.

It has been seen that the Gold Coast colony and Protectorate extends along the coast from about 3 degrees West longitude to about 1·14 degrees East longitude, the length of the coast-line being about 350 miles. Inland the breadth of the Protectorate varies very greatly at different points, and new districts are from time to time brought within its limits; but at present it nowhere extends into the interior for much more than 150 miles in a direct line from the sea, and the average breadth is very much less— not more than 50 miles.

The total area of the colony and Protectorate together may be taken in round numbers at 40,000 square miles, being rather more than two-thirds of the size of England and Wales. The coast of this British dependency begins with lagoons on the west on the Assinee frontier, and ends in lagoons on the east in the Volta district. Between these two lagoon regions is the Gold Coast proper, with shores of harder formation, though running out here and there into sandy spits and peninsulas. Hills of small size along the sea, in the Apollonia district—the westernmost district of the colony, are succeeded by a low-lying coast, which in turn gives way, between Cape Coast Castle and Accra, to higher hills, rising at intervals in cliffs above the sea. Beyond Accra the coast sinks again,

---

[1] The Native Jurisdiction ordinance, 5 of 83.

and the colony ends on the east in a dead level of sandy shore. The Gold Coast is difficult of access; it has no harbours; bars of sand block the mouths of the rivers; there is no point at which vessels of any size can come close to the shore, and boats land with difficulty their passengers and cargoes amid surf and breakers. The best landing-places are said to be at Axim, Elmina, and Dixcove. On the edge of this harbourless coast, facing the angry sea, stand the various settlements, most of them the scenes of old forts and stations in days gone by. Taking them from west to east, the first place of any importance is Beyin or Apollonia, east of which, at a distance of about 25 miles by sea, is Axim, near the mouth of the Ancobra river, the port of the gold mines of Wassaw and the outlet of a large timber trade. About 30 miles by sea from Axim, round Cape Three Points, the cape where the Brandenburghers once established themselves, is Dixcove; and 40 miles further to the east, passing by Secondee, Chama at the mouth of the Prah, and Commendah, we come to Elmina, oldest of all the stations on the coast, the stronghold first of the Portuguese and then of the Dutch, with the old castle of St. George still standing by the sea. Elmina, which is a town of over 11,000 inhabitants, was in Dutch times the port of Ashantee; but, since the war of 1873, when a forest road was constructed to Prahsue and Coomassie from Cape Coast Castle, the Ashantee trade has come down rather to this latter town. Cape Coast Castle, the old English capital on the coast, is only eight miles to the east of its neighbour and historic rival Elmina, the mouth of the Sweet river lying between them. Though no longer the seat of government, it is still a flourishing town with a considerable trade, and a population of nearly 12,000, the chief settlement in the western division of the Gold Coast, as Accra is in the eastern. The castle, which gives it its name, is built on a rock fronting the sea, with the town lying behind it to the north. Some 15 miles from Cape Coast, past Annamaboe and Cormantine, is Saltpond, one of the chief commercial centres of the colony, especially in connexion with the palm-oil industry. From Saltpond to Winnebah is a distance of 35 miles, and from Winnebah to Accra over 30. Accra is now the most important and most populous settlement on the coast. It has a large trade, a population of 20,000, including the villages of Victoriaborg and Christiansborg, and it is the political and administrative centre of the colony and Protectorate, the governor's residence being at the old Danish castle of Christtiansborg, about three miles east of the town.

Saltpond.
Accra.

From Accra to Addah at the mouth of the Volta is a distance of 60 miles, the station of Pram Pram intervening; and beyond the Volta, 35 miles from Addah, is town of Quittah, situated on a sandy isthmus between a lagoon and the open sea. The neighbourhood of the muddy lagoon makes Quittah a most unhealthy settlement, but it has a very large import trade, and it is the easternmost station of any size in the Protectorate.

Addah.
Quittah.

As the Gold Coast is difficult of access from the sea, so the interior is difficult of access from the coast. The country to the west of Accra is in the forest belt of Africa. For about five miles from the sea-shore the timber has been cleared and has been replaced by a dense growth of scrub or jungle, behind which the forest stretches away over low rolling hills far into the continent. At Accra a range of higher hills, rising to 2,000 feet, runs down to the sea in a south-westerly direction from the Volta. They are known as the Aquapim or Acropong hills or mountains, and are the healthiest tract on the Gold Coast. Here, at Aburi, 1,400 feet above sea-level, the Government have established a sanatorium for their officers, as well as a botanical station for exploiting and developing the vegetable resources of the Colony. To the west of these hills, within the forest zone, are the hills of Akim or Quahoo; to the east is the basin of the Volta, where the forest disappears and is succeeded by open plains covered

The interior.

206 *HISTORICAL GEOGRAPHY OF THE COLONIES.*

SECTION II.

with coarse grass. Accra marks the dividing line on the coast between these two very distinct belts of vegetation.

Rivers.

The rivers of the Gold Coast are many in number, and some of them are of considerable size, but as water-ways to and from the interior they are of little use. Their mouths are barred; they have rocks and rapids in their channels; and their volume and current varies greatly at the different seasons of the year. Some of them, notably the Volta and the Ancobra, are for a considerable distance navigable in native canoes, or even in light steam launches, and they are valuable for floating timber down to the sea; but, as means of regular communication, as routes of commerce, they compare most unfavourably with rivers of the same size and length in other parts of the world. The finest is the Volta, which rises far inland near the water-parting of the Niger basin, and comes down to the sea in the eastern district of the colony. The most useless of all, though perhaps the best known, is the Prah, whose upper waters form the frontier between Ashantee territory and the Protectorate, Prahsue being the border station. Its course has been described in an official report as 'one succession of rapids with projecting rocks[1].' The Ancobra in the west is perhaps the most available river from a commercial point of view, and has the advantage of flowing through a rich timber district. The fourth large river, the Tanoe or Tendo, forms for part of its course the western boundary of the Protectorate[2].

Climate.

The Gold Coast has, under present conditions, a very unhealthy climate, especially in the moist forest zone and near the coast. In the more open country, and on the hill country behind Accra, the conditions are more favourable to health.

---

[1] Geological report in Parl. Paper, c. 3064–81, pp. 184–7.

[2] The Protectorate is divided on the maps into districts or provinces, representing old native kingdoms or groups of kindred tribes, such as Wassaw, Denkera, Akim, and others. The divisions however are not sufficiently definite geographically or politically to make it desirable to give an exhaustive list.

It is the damp atmosphere, rather than excess of heat, which injures European constitutions, and the wet seasons with lower temperature are more unhealthy than the dryer and hotter times of the year. The thermometer ranges from 70° to 90° Fahr. throughout the year, the mean shade temperature being about 80°. The rainfall at Accra is small, not averaging more than 30 inches in the year. At other places, however, especially in the western districts, the fall is much greater, and the amount of moisture in the air cannot be measured by the statistics of the rain-gauge. There are two wet seasons, the first from April to July, the second in October and November. From December to March dry weather prevails, with its accompaniment of the Harmattan wind, and the end of the dry season and beginning of the wet is marked by tornadoes.

Among the products of the Gold Coast, gold deserves the first mention. Not that it is by any means the most important product, for, as an article of export, it ranks far below palm oil and rubber. But it is gold which has given the country its name, and which from the earliest Portuguese times has been the speciality of this particular section of the coast region of West Africa. The statistics of the amount of gold brought to Europe from the Gold Coast in former days are most uncertain; and it is doubtful whether the export was ever very large, even before the discovery of gold fields in other parts of the world[1]. In the report of the Committee of the Privy Council on the African trade in 1789, gold does not appear in the list of exports from West Africa to Great Britain; and the evidence was to the effect that 'gold is purchased so dear on the coast that it is not worth buying.' It was sold at £4 sterling to the ounce[2], 'and is therefore seldom carried off except by the Dutch.' The Dutch, it will

---

[1] Some information on the subject will be found in the Appendix to Burton and Cameron's To the Gold Coast for Gold, but the figures which are given require verification.

[2] At the present time £4 sterling are about equal to an ounce (Troy) in weight.

208   *HISTORICAL GEOGRAPHY OF THE COLONIES.*

SECTION II.

be remembered, held Elmina, whose name bore witness to the mineral wealth of the coast, and which, being the receptacle of the Ashantee trade, no doubt exported some of the gold of that kingdom. In 1891, the export of gold was valued at £88,000, and the average of the six years 1886-91 was nearly the same, being valued at £87,500. The returns for 1892 were considerably higher, viz. £99,000. This represents not nuggets so much as gold dust—alluvial gold. Gold dust is so abundant that it used to be the common currency of the country: it is found between the hills, in the beds of the rivers, and on the sea-shore. There are also regular gold mines, notably at Tarquah in the Wassaw district; but no Johannesberg has as yet sprung up upon the Gold Coast, if only because the mining industry is sadly hampered by want of roads and of facilities for transport. It is difficult to carry machinery up from the coast, it is difficult to carry the gold down to the coast; and, over and above these difficulties, there is the unhealthy climate, a perpetual bar to steady European enterprise. Next to Wassaw, the richest gold regions within the Protectorate appear to be the districts of Akim and Quahoo lying to the north-east, in the direction of the Volta basin. In fact the gold-bearing stratum runs diagonally across the Protectorate in a north-easterly and south-westerly direction, and extends beyond its borders into the kingdom of Ashantee.

Vegetable products and agriculture.

On the sea-coast, and along the banks of the rivers, a large proportion of the population are fishermen, and at the principal towns and settlements there is of course a number of traders. Elsewhere the people are mainly agriculturists; but on the Gold Coast, as at Sierra Leone and on the Gambia, agriculture is in a most primitive condition; and the Gold Coast suffers more than any other of the West African dependencies from want of adequate means of communication by land or water. The very richness of the soil is a bar to the developement of agriculture, by producing a dense growth of jungle and forest; the villages stand in isolated clearings; the roads are but forest paths; the rivers are most indifferent highways; and, in the words of a late report on the subject, 'the only available beast of burden is man, the weakest and most costly of all [1].'

Land, as a rule, is held in common by families, though there is individual ownership within limits in the results of cultivation; and it is a constant practice to mortgage the right of cultivating to native money-lenders. Under this semi-communistic system, patches of ground are cleared and planted in the rudest way with maize, plantains, yams, cassava, and, in the Axim and Quittah districts, with rice. No agricultural science is needed to produce abundant crops, and land is so plentiful that ground which has been planted in one year is left untilled for the next three or five years, new plots being cleared and grubbed up in the meantime.

The grain and fruit thus grown supply the natives' own wants, while the requirements of commerce are met by nature without the slightest assistance from the hand of man. The district behind Saltpond, in the centre of the coast, and the districts of Aquapim and Croboe, more to the east, with their ports at Accra and Addah, are pre-eminent on the Gold Coast for palm oil and palm kernels. Rubber is shipped from Cape Coast, Accra, and Quittah. Timber, mainly mahogany, is exported in increasing amount from Axim, Dixcove, Chama, and Secondee. Cocoa-nut palms line the coast, but the export of nuts or of copra is very small. Kola nuts grow abundantly in the interior, notably in the Akim and Assin districts; and among other products are ground nuts, dyes, especially camwood, and gum copal. Cotton grows wild in the Protectorate, but has only been cultivated to a small extent, in the Volta district; tobacco also grows wild; and a little coffee is raised on the Aquapim hills under the guidance of the Basel missionaries.

[1] Report on Economic Agriculture on the Gold Coast (1889), printed for Parliament in Colonial Reports, No. 110 [1890].

VOL. III. P

210 HISTORICAL GEOGRAPHY OF THE COLONIES.

SECTION II.

It would seem that there is hardly any tropical fruit or plant which could not be successfully cultivated on the Gold Coast; but so much comes to hand without any effort at all, that there is little inducement to cultivate; and it would be useless to lay out time and money on plantations, in the absence of roads or railways to the markets and the sea. Among articles of export, other than gold or vegetable produce, are monkey skins, brought down chiefly from Ashantee, and a small quantity of ivory.

Exports and Imports.

The trade of the Gold Coast has latterly made great strides. The average annual value of the exports in the years 1886–1891 was £477,000; in 1892 the value was £665,000, nearly three-fourths of which represented articles sent to the United Kingdom.

The United Kingdom also contributes two-thirds of the imports, the total value of which, in 1892, was £597,000. The commerce of the colony with foreign countries is in great measure in the hands of German traders, of whom there is a considerable number in the eastern districts adjoining the German Protectorate. The exports to foreign countries, in 1892, went principally to Germany, France, and the United States. The imports from foreign countries in the same year were contributed by the United States, Germany, France, and Holland.

In 1892, palm oil and kernels represented over 42 per cent. in value of the total exports of the colony, rubber 25 per cent., and gold dust nearly 15 per cent. Cotton goods head the list of imports, far exceeding any other article; and it is not satisfactory to find that the import which takes the second place is rum, imported mainly from the United States.

Revenue and Currency.

The revenue for 1892 amounted to £183,000, as against £186,000 received in 1891 and an average for the six years 1886–91 of £132,000. Nearly 90 per cent. was derived from customs duties. On the expenditure side of the account, the Gold Coast Constabulary is a prominent item, having cost in 1892 over £35,000. The colony has no Public Debt. The coins in circulation are principally British gold and silver, but Spanish and South-American doubloons, and American and French gold, are also legal tender. A few United States silver half-dollars are current among the native traders at 2s. It is interesting to notice that gold dust and nuggets were not demonetised till 1889, and that cowries are still used by the natives.

CHAPTER IX.

The population of the colony and Protectorate, according to the last returns, is estimated in round numbers at 1,500,000, only about 200 of whom are Europeans. There are many different tribes of natives, speaking various languages or dialects, but all are members of the negro race. The tribes of the Fantee confederation, who line the coast from Elmina to Accra, perhaps deserve special mention, as having been from time immemorial brought into close contact with the English. Of the natives who are not indigenous to the Protectorate, the most important are the Mohammedan Houssas from the Niger districts of the interior, who man the ranks of the military police, and the Kroomen from the coast to the west, in the neighbourhood of Cape Palmas, who make the best sailors of any natives in West Africa.

Population.

The great bulk of the population are Pagans, gradually modifying, under European influence, their fetish worship and savage rites. The number of Christians is returned at 37,500, the largest proportion being at the old European settlements of Cape Coast and Elmina. The Wesleyans have the greatest number of adherents. They began their work on the coast in 1837, their headquarters are at Cape Coast, and their chief field of missionary enterprise is in the western districts of the colony. Next to the Wesleyans in numerical returns comes the Basel mission, whose headquarters are at Accra, and whose stations are in the east of the colony, especially in the Acropong district. The first

Religions.

SECTION II. Basel missionaries came to the Gold Coast in 1828, and were the pioneers of Christian enterprise in these lands. Over and above their purely religious work, they deserve all praise for their efforts to promote technical education, industry, and agriculture, as well as for the medical relief which they have given to the sick poor of their districts. Among other religious sects are the Roman Catholics, who established themselves at Elmina in 1881, the Bremen mission, an off-shoot of the Basel mission, and the Church of England, which has two chaplains, at Accra and Cape Coast, in receipt of salaries from the Colonial Government. The Anglican bishop of Sierra Leone is also bishop of the Gold Coast, the Gambia, and Lagos, receiving a small stipend from each government.

The Mohammedans on the Gold Coast are, with the exception of the Houssas, mainly traders; and are to be found in the larger settlements on the coast and along the trade routes to the interior. They traffic in kola nuts, exporting them to Lagos for the benefit of their co-religionists, and they bring down live stock from Salaga and other countries to the north of the Protectorate.

Education. Education is backward on the Gold Coast, but still some good work has been and is being done. The present system dates from 1887, when an Education Act was passed and a Board of Education established. The Government supports elementary schools at Accra and Cape Coast, in addition to a special school for the children of the Houssa police; and it gives grants-in-aid to the various mission schools. No provision is made for higher education, unless the government botanical station at Aburi, whose object is to improve agricultural methods and promote agricultural science, can be considered in this light.

Distances. In the statistics of distances Cape Coast Castle is usually given as the central point of the colony. It is about 3,500 miles distant from Plymouth, 1,050 from Freetown, 300 from

Lagos, under 700 from the island of Fernando Po, 1,340 from Ascension, and under 1,200 from the Congo.

From the southern boundary of Sierra Leone to the western boundary of the Gold Coast is about 700 miles. From the easternmost point of the Gold Coast to the westernmost point of Lagos is under 100 miles.

There is ample steam and telegraphic communication with Europe, and with other British and foreign settlements in Africa. On land, there are over 260 miles of telegraph open, from Axim on the west to Quittah on the east, with a branch line of 26 miles to Aburi; and the wires are still being carried forward. The want of roads has already been commented upon. The best track is from Cape Coast to Prahsue, a distance of 75 miles, dating from the time of the last Ashantee war, and from Accra to Aburi. Elsewhere the paths through the bush, which do duty for roads, are kept up by a system of subsidies to the native chiefs, in return for which a space is kept clear up to a minimum breadth of twelve feet.

Of the four Crown Colonies of Great Britain upon the West Coast of Africa, viz. the Gambia, Sierra Leone, the Gold Coast, and Lagos, the Gold Coast is much the largest; and it shares with the Gambia the honour of being the oldest dependency. What is its real value, if any, to Great Britain? What reasons are there for keeping it, based on the past, the present, or the future? The British connexion with it is of long standing, nearly three centuries old, but old ties and traditions did not prevent other nations, the Dutch and the Danes, from voluntarily leaving the coast for ever. The English, it will be answered, are not as the Dutch and Danes. They have thrown in their lot for good or evil with Africa. Their withdrawal from any part of Africa would have more than merely local results; it would break a link in a long chain; it would alter the balance of power now so difficult to adjust; it would invite and suggest further withdrawals; it would lead to new complications, new misgivings, and new

General Summary.

SECTION II.

unrest. It is difficult no doubt to break with the past: and, with French and Germans pressing onward on either side, the natural instinct is to hold fast. But arguments from the past must be supplemented by arguments from the present, and the shadows of general considerations by the substance of existing facts. What are the facts? The disadvantages of the Gold Coast are that it has no river like the Gambia, no harbour like Sierra Leone, no geographical attraction to a people wanting to find their way into and out of the land: while life after life is sacrificed year by year in keeping up British administration along a deadly coast. Its advantages, on the other hand, are its undoubtedly great mineral wealth, and its rich prolific soil. It has more variety of resources than perhaps any other part of West Africa. The French on the west, the Germans on the east, are hemming in the English, and trying to secure the trade routes and divert the traffic. But, apart from Hinterland and trade routes, the Gold Coast Protectorate, within its present limits alone, is a rich natural sphere of production, with hill country and plain country, with wealth above and below ground. Even at the present time, when its developement is as yet no more than the native agriculture, a scratch upon the surface, it has a flowing revenue and a most thriving trade, it costs nothing to the United Kingdom except—an important exception, it is true—the health and lives of English officers; and, on the other hand, it sends yearly a large amount of produce to the Liverpool merchants, taking in return cargoes of cotton goods. There is substantial gain at the present, and, what is more, there is good hope for the future. It may be difficult ever to create a suitable harbour, or to do more than reduce in some small degree the difficulties of landing. The cost of making the rivers navigable to any considerable extent may be prohibitive. The climate no doubt always will be unfavourable to Europeans. But much may yet be done for trade and for health. Swamps may be drained and

jungles cleared; with the developement of roads and light
railways the seat of Government may be moved to the hills;
and the various stations, whether on high or low ground, need
not be so unhealthy in themselves nor so isolated from each
other as they now are. As an organised colony, the Gold
Coast is in its childhood. The resources of civilisation have
here not only not been exhausted, they have hardly been
used at all. It will be time to discuss whether the Gold
Coast is worth keeping, when modern appliances have really
been tried and really been found wanting. There are other
considerations too besides merely striking the balance of
present and future advantages and disadvantages. The
Africans have to be borne in mind as well as the English.
It cannot seriously be doubted that of late years British rule
and protection has done something towards mitigating
savagery, and introducing more human and more humane
customs and modes of life. It is the case that the Christian
religion has not made much progress yet; and quite possibly
it will not make much progress for years to come, until
generations grow up, to whom fetish worship is a mere name.
But the law and justice of a Christian people has its effect
among West African natives, and the English would not be
justified in withdrawing that law and justice, or in transferring
to some other less qualified and less trained European nation
the burden which history has given them to bear.

CHAPTER IX.

Books, Publications, etc. relating to the Gold Coast.

Among official publications, a great deal of information as to the present condition of the Gold Coast is given in the report on the Census for 1891, and in two reports which have been given to Parliament on *Economic Agriculture on the Gold Coast*. Colonial Series, No. 110, 1890, and Colonial Series, Miscellaneous, No. 1, 1891.

SECTION II.

The names of some of the old books relating to the Gold Coast have been given on p. 156. Among later books may be mentioned:—

WINWOOD READE'S *African Sketch Book* (1873), and *Story of the Ashantee Campaign* (1874); MAJOR ELLIS' *West African Sketches* (1881), and *The Land of Fetish* (1883); C. A. GORDON'S *Life on the Gold Coast* (1881); and Sir C. A. MOLONEY'S *West African Fisheries, with particular reference to the Gold Coast Colony* (published for the International Fisheries Exhibition, 1883), and *Sketch of the Forestry of West Africa* (1887).

CHAPTER X.

LAGOS.

LAGOS is the youngest of the four British Crown Colonies upon the West Coast of Africa, having only been annexed in 1861. It owes its name to the Portuguese, and the river and channel of Lagos is mentioned in old books and marked on old maps. The island, however, played no part in the early history of European trade and settlement in West Africa, and it is not known to have been inhabited before a hundred and fifty years ago.

It seems that, in the eighteenth century, some Yoruba settlers from the mainland established themselves in the little island of Iddo close to Lagos, and from thence went over to the sister island to farm and cultivate the ground. The first settlement of Lagos therefore was for agricultural purposes. Towards the end of the eighteenth century, some new native colonists arrived at Lagos from Benin, and the Yorubas and Benins continued to hold the island in joint occupation. Lagos grew and Iddo declined in importance, until their relative positions were reversed, and Iddo became a dependency of Lagos. By this time Lagos had grown to be a kingdom, the king being a member of the Yoruba royal family, but paying tribute to the king of Benin as his suzerain. About the year 1830, the king of Lagos became strong enough to refuse to pay tribute to Benin, and thenceforward the relations between these two savage states were similar to the relations between a Greek colony and its mother city, implying hereditary friendship rather than feudal dependence.

What gave Lagos strength and riches was the slave trade.

SECTION II.

The island is so situated, as to command a wide area of traffic; and from the year 1815 onward, when the slave traders had been driven from their old haunts, they here found for a while a new and thriving centre. The slaves were supplied from the Yorubas and Egbas of the mainland, whose countries were desolated by long-continued wars; and an exiled chief of Lagos, Kosoko by name, having learnt the ways of the slave trade at Whydah, the port of Dahomey, returned in time to his old home, where he became king, and, in league with the kings of Dahomey and Porto Novo and with Portuguese slave-dealers, gave every encouragement to the export of slaves. At the end of 1851 the English interfered. They stormed and took the town of Lagos, ejected the usurper Kosoko, and reinstated a former king who was bound over by treaty to prohibit the slave trade; a British consular agent was appointed to reside on the spot; and the Church Missionary Society established a mission in the island. The intrigues of the slave-traders, however, soon made mischief again, and fresh civil war broke out in 1853. Peace was restored, but progress was not assured, until in August 1861, with the declared object of putting an end once for all to the slave traffic, the reigning King Docemo ceded the port and island and territories of Lagos to Great Britain, receiving a pension for life of £1000 per annum. The territories of Lagos included, or were supposed to include, the native towns and districts of Palma and Leckie, lying to the eastward. These places were at the time of the cession held by Kosoko, who had been throughout the mainstay of the slave-traders and the enemy of the English. In 1863, however, he too formally relinquished his claims, returning to Lagos as a pensioner of the British Government; and Palma and Leckie became and have remained an integral part of the colony. In the same year Badagry[1], to the west of

---

[1] Badagry will be remembered in connexion with the Niger discoveries. See above, p. 141.

Lagos, the sovereignty of which had been in dispute between the kings of Lagos and Porto Novo, was also ceded by treaty to the British Crown, and British protection was claimed over the native states of Addo, Pocra, and Okeodan. Thus, with the exception of the easternmost district of the colony—the territory of Mahin, which was not definitely ceded to Great Britain till 1885—the limits of Lagos along the coast, at the end of 1863, were much the same as they are at the present day.

Government. When Lagos was first annexed, it was constituted a separate colony, the Governor being also the consul for the neighbouring districts. In 1866, after the report of the select Parliamentary Committee on West Africa, it was, with the other West Africa settlements, placed under the Governor-in-chief at Sierra Leone, though it retained a separate Legislative Council and Lieutenant-Governor. When the Central government was broken up in 1874, Lagos was incorporated with the Gold Coast; and it was not until 1886 that it became again a separate Crown colony. The Executive Council at present consists of the Governor, the Colonial Secretary, the Treasurer, and the Queen's Advocate. The same four officers and the Chief Justice constitute the official element in the Legislative Council, the unofficial members being five in number.

Law and Justice. By a local ordinance of 1863, it was enacted that all laws and statutes, which were in force in England on January 1, 1863, and which were not inconsistent with any ordinance passed by the colonial legislature, should be in force in the colony of Lagos, and be applied so far as local circumstances permitted. Subsequently Lagos, having been in 1874 included in the colony of the Gold Coast, came within the application of the Gold Coast ordinance of 1876, which has been quoted above on page 202. English law, therefore, under these limitations and colonial ordinances, constitutes the legal system of the colony. The law is administered by a Chief Justice,

220 HISTORICAL GEOGRAPHY OF THE COLONIES.

SECTION II.

and by District Commissioners, of whom there are three, one for Lagos, one for Badagry, and one for Palma and Leckie.

Boundaries.

Lagos is more fortunate than Sierra Leone or the Gold Coast in having its boundaries comparatively well defined, and in being therefore less likely to be involved in international difficulties. On the east it ends, in 5·10 degrees East longitude, at the Benin river, on the other side of which are the British Niger Protectorates. On the west the frontier marches with the French settlements and Protectorate in the Porto Novo district. The French connexion with Porto Novo began in 1863, shortly after the British annexation of Lagos; and, though it was abandoned in the course of a year, it was revived in 1883. The necessary consequence was a series of frontier disputes, which were adjusted by the Anglo-French agreement of 1889. Under the terms of this agreement, the boundary between the two Protectorates has been taken to be the middle of the channel of the Ajera river, so far as it separates the two states of Porto Novo and Pocra, leaving Porto Novo to the French and Pocra to the English. From the point where the river flows into the Porto Novo lagoon, the meridian of its centre is carried south to the sea-coast, in 2·45° East longitude. From the point where it ceases to separate Porto Novo from Pocra, the meridian of its centre, in 2·46° East longitude, is followed north as far as the ninth parallel of North latitude. Beyond this parallel is the British Niger Protectorate and the sphere of the Royal Niger company.

Thus Lagos is bounded on the south by the sea, on the west by a French Protectorate, and on the north and east by British Protectorates. At the same time it must be remembered that the dependency, as defined by treaties of cession and protection, does not extend to the ninth parallel, although the intervening territory is all within the British Sphere of protection. On the contrary, the colony and Protectorate has but little depth inland, not extending at any point to more than from 20 to 30 miles from the sea-coast, although treaties of friendship have been made with more distant tribes, with the Egbas of Abbeokuta, the Yorubas of Oyo, the Jebus and others [1].

Area and Geography.

The area of the colony and Protectorate is given at about 1,100 square miles, being rather smaller than the area of Staffordshire. The length of the coast-line is about 170 miles. Inside the coast, and parallel with it for the whole length of the dependency, is a series of lagoons, extending on the east as far as the Benin river, on the west to the Porto Novo lagoon and the lake known as Denham waters, and inland far into the kingdom of Dahomey. The one outlet to the sea of this curious and almost unparalleled series of water-ways is at the island of Lagos, which thus holds a unique position for purposes of trade with the French Protectorate as well as with the territory under British rule or protection. It is no wonder that the Portuguese gave to the island, the native title of which is Eko, the generic name of Lagos ('lakes' or 'lagoons [2]'). Its position may be compared to that of the island of British Sherbro [3] in the colony of Sierra Leone; but it commands a larger area, and the natural canals, which converge to it, lead further afield.

The island, town, and harbour of Lagos.

The island has an extreme length of about 3¼ miles, an extreme breadth of about 1½, and an area of about 4 square miles. It is a low-lying island of sand and swamp, cultivated in some places, but for the most part covered with coarse

---

[1] In 1891 the area of the Lagos Protectorate was increased by the definite and final addition of the kingdoms of Pocra, Addo, Ilaro, and Igbessa to the north-west of Lagos; and in 1892 a small strip of Jebu territory to the north-east of Lagos was annexed to the colony.

[2] Lagos, however, was in old times rather the name of the channel than of the island. Eko or Oko means a farm, the island having been cultivated by the inhabitants of Iddo. See above, p. 217.

[3] See above, p. 188.

SECTION II.

grass, which is under water in the rainy season. The town stands at its western extremity, looking to the south-west and facing the main channel to the sea. The open sea is nearly 7 miles below the town, but the entrance to the main channel, about half a mile in width, is only between 4 and 5 miles distant. Beyond it is a dangerous bar, over which there breaks a heavy surf, caused by the meeting of a strong current of fresh water from the lagoons with the waves of the Gulf of Guinea. The dangers of this bar were well known in old times, for we read in Barbot[1] that the 'river Lagos has a bar at the entrance into the Lagos channel, which is scarce navigable for boats because of the mighty surges that render it very difficult.' The bar cannot be crossed by steamers drawing more than 12 feet of water; and large ships lie in the outside anchorage, leaving small tenders to communicate with the town. Inside the channel, there is smooth and comparatively deep water close to the shore, and lines of wharves form the frontage to the town of Lagos. The population of the town and harbour of Lagos at the 1891 census was returned at 32,500. The town is well built, busy, and prosperous, the most flourishing commercial centre in British West Africa. Its distance from Liverpool is 4,300 miles, from Freetown (Sierra Leone) about 1,200, from Cape Coast about 300, from Benin about 120, and from Brass at the mouth of the Niger about 230. It is connected by submarine cable with the Gold Coast and Europe in one direction, and with the Niger, Congo, and South Africa in another. Outside the island of Lagos, the main divisions of the colony are the Western district, of which Badagry is the centre; the Eastern district, in which Palma and Leckie are the chief places; and the Northern district, including the old native town of Ebute Metta, and a strip of territory to the north of the main

Distances.

The Districts.

---

[1] Bk. iv. chap. 5.

line of lagoons, to which a small addition has lately been CHAPTER X.
made, cut out of the Jebu country.

The geographical features are much the same in all the districts. Both between the lagoons and the sea, and on the northern side of the lagoons for some little distance inland, there are long stretches of alluvial flats, interspersed with swamps. Further inland there comes a belt of forest, which is in turn succeeded by more open country rising towards the watershed of the Niger. *Geography of the colony and Protectorate.*

The largest river is the Ogun, which flows into the lagoon due north of Lagos; and on it, at a distance of from 60 to 70 miles from Lagos by the direct route, is situated Abbeokuta, the capital of the Egbas, a walled African city of considerable size and population, which has always been an important factor in the relations of Lagos to the native communities of the interior. *Abbeokuta.*

The meteorology of Lagos is much the same as that of the Gold Coast. The mean annual temperature in the shade is 81°; the average annual rainfall is about 60 inches, the chief rainy season being from April to the end of July, which is supplemented by later rains from September to the middle of November. Unhealthy as the climate is, it is on the whole not so injurious to Europeans as is the climate of the Gold Coast; or perhaps it would be more correct to say that there are fewer isolated out-stations, and the officers are therefore more within reach of the social and sanitary advantages which are available at headquarters. *Climate.*

Lagos is superior to the Gold Coast in means of communication, and in the character of the native inhabitants of the colony, the Protectorate, and the neighbouring territories. Its lagoons are so many miles of canal, and they all lead to one market, to one outlet to the sea. There is therefore no difficulty in transport; and native canoes bring down to the port the produce of many miles from north, east, and west. The Yoruba tribes too of the mainland take

SECTION II.

more kindly to cultivation of the soil, and approximate more nearly to agricultural communities, than is the case with the natives of the Gold Coast. The country and its inhabitants, therefore, have on the whole a more definite and more settled character than is to be found elsewhere in British West Africa.

Products. Palm oil and kernels.

The one great product, however, overshadowing all others, is the oil palm, which requires and receives little or no culture by the hand of man. Lagos palm oil has the reputation of being the finest of any which comes from West Africa, this result being due partly to natural causes, partly to greater skill in and to improved methods of preparation. Within the colony and Protectorate the chief oil-producing districts are the Western and Northern; but the bulk of the oil and kernels, which are shipped from Lagos to Europe, is brought from beyond the limits of the immediate Protectorate, from the territory of which Abbeokuta is the centre, and, now that communication is open, from the Jebu country and from central Yoruba.

Minor products.

Among minor products, which the Colonial government is at pains to encourage, are grain, vegetables, and fruits of various kinds, cassava which grows in the sandy soil of the sea-coast, sweet potatoes, yams, maize, beans, bananas, and cocoa nuts. Beniseed appears in the list of exports; a little cocoa and coffee is being grown: and in the Yoruba country a large amount of cotton is cultivated, mainly for home manufacture, but to some extent for export also. Most of these products, like the palm oil, come more from without than from within the limits of what is more strictly known as the Lagos colony and Protectorate.

Occupations of the inhabitants.

Judging from the statistics of the late census, the native population of the colony proper, so far as it has been classified, is mainly occupied in trading, and in farming and gardening; the townsmen of Lagos, as of Sierra Leone, being traders, while the farmers and gardeners are to be found mainly in the Central district, near the town, and in the

Western or Badagry district. There is also a number of fishermen, and the manufacture of palm oil employs a good many workmen.

The imports and exports for the year 1891 were valued at £608,000 and 718,000, respectively, being the largest in either case in any one year except 1877. The United Kingdom sent more than two-thirds of the imports, cotton goods being the principal item; and it took two-fifths of the exports, mainly in the form of palm oil. The exports to Germany slightly exceeded those to the United Kingdom, and consisted chiefly of palm kernels. Palm oil and palm kernels together represented nearly 83 per cent. in value of the total exports. Of the imports, cotton goods were far the most important article, spirits and silver coming next. The revenue for 1891 amounted to £79,000, and was the largest ever collected in the colony, 85 per cent. being derived from customs duties. The largest item of expenditure here, as on the Gold Coast, is the Houssa Constabulary and the Civil police. Lagos has no Public Debt. British sterling is the standard currency of the colony; but Spanish, American, and French gold are also legal tender. No foreign silver is recognised; and the circulation therefore consists of a certain amount of gold, and of British silver, mainly in small coins. British bronze coins are also current at a discount of 10 per cent. Cowries are still in common use at 6*d*. per 'head' of 2,000 cowries, but the large import of silver indicates that money is taking the place among the natives of this cumbrous substitute for coinage, and that the primitive system of barter is dying out. It is noted in this connexion that the French firms, which once did the largest business at Lagos, and whose dealings were on the barter system, have now removed elsewhere.

According to the census of 1891, the population of the colony and Protectorate of Lagos was 85,607; but these figures are very incomplete, no account being taken in them

SECTION II.
of some of the newly-acquired portions of the Protectorate, nor of the easternmost district between Odi and the Benin river. Even where the enumeration took place, there were of necessity many omissions. The town and harbour of Lagos contributed 32,500 to the total; the Central district, exclusive of Lagos, about 22,000; the Western district, including Pocra, about 22,000; and the Eastern district, about 9,000. The number of Europeans was not more than 150. The natives included some 20,000 of the Ekos or Lagos tribe, 16,000 Egbas, 13,000 Popos, 11,000 Yorubas, and others. The Yoruba race, covering in its wider sense the Egbas and Jebus, is the leading native race in and near Lagos; but the Popos in the west are a different stock, akin to the people of Dahomey; and in the east a third race, the Benins, are to be found, who, as has been seen, took part in the original settlement of Lagos island. There is a considerable number of Houssas and Kroomen at Lagos as in other West African colonies; and a valuable element in the community consists of ex-slaves or their descendants, mainly of Yoruba origin, who, having been carried years ago to Brazil, have been re-patriated, bringing back with them habits of industry, and knowledge of agriculture, or training as mechanics, and who have indirectly promoted trade between Lagos and Brazil.

Religion.   The number of Christians was returned at 10,000, of Mohammedans at 21,000, and of Pagans at 54,000. The Christian denominations are the Church of England, Wesleyans, and Roman Catholics, the number of children on the registers of the Church of England schools exceeding those of the Wesleyans and Roman Catholics put together.

Education.   Education in the colony is almost entirely denominational, the missionary schools being subsidised by a system of grants-in-aid from the Government, which are administered by a Board of Education. The number of schools under Government Inspection in 1891 was thirty, and the total amount given for grants-in-aid was larger than in any previous year. It would seem therefore that education, though very backward, is making some progress; but special difficulty is found in attracting the Mohammedan children to school, and little has as yet been done in the way of industrial and technical education.

CHAPTER X.

On the whole Lagos is perhaps the most satisfactory of the British settlements in West Africa. It is not hampered by evil traditions of past centuries, having only been for a few years the centre of an unauthorised slave trade, which was summarily extinguished. Nor is its developement as a British dependency endangered by the encroachments of other European nations; its frontiers are fixed; and there is no fear of French or Germans cutting off the trade of the interior. It is again singularly concentrated, for every district is connected with one and the same port. Thus administration is facilitated, revenue is easily collected, and commerce thrives, because there is constant and steady circulation between the heart of the colony and its extremities. Financially, Lagos is most successful at the present time; and there is every indication that prosperity will continue, inasmuch as the tribes of the interior are at once more inclined to agricultural industry, and more within reach than the peoples who live at the back of the Gold Coast or of Sierra Leone. On the Gold Coast or at Sierra Leone there can be no assured progress without large outlay on roads, but roads are little wanted at Lagos, the water communication being so admirable. In short, taking West Africa as it is, Lagos, but for its climate, and but for the fact that it depends upon a single industry, is a prosperous and promising nook in the British empire. But no one can rest satisfied with the present conditions of West Africa. A community may flourish by sending palm oil and kernels to Europe, but it flourishes after all as an uncivilised community, gaining wealth from sources which give little or no impetus to con-

General Summary.

SECTION II.

tinuous and systematic effort, no such training as converts a savage into a civilised race.

It is one thing, and it is a great thing, to prohibit barbarous practices; this the English have done. It is another and a more difficult task to make new habits and better modes of life and thought take root downwards and bear fruit upwards, to raise the African economically and socially to a higher level. This has not yet been done to any appreciable extent. It may well be that in time the good will come. Lagos in particular is quite in its youth as a British settlement, and more could hardly have been expected than has been achieved already. But it is useless to ignore the fact that the work of the English in West Africa has hitherto been little more than undoing to some extent the evil of the past. For positive good, for constructive policy, we must look to the future.

Information about Lagos must be gathered from official reports and from notices in books dealing with West Africa generally. There is no book on the colony which deserves special mention.

CHAPTER XI.

THE NIGER PROTECTORATES.

In the foregoing pages some account has been given of the four British Crown Colonies upon the West Coast of Africa, with the adjoining Protectorates. It remains to notice very shortly the latest and the largest British dependency in West Africa, viz. the Niger Protectorates, no part of which is under a colonial government.

The notification published by the Foreign Office in the London Gazette of October 18, 1887, announced that 'the British Protectorate of the Niger Districts comprises the territories on the line of coast between the British Protectorate of Lagos and the right or western river bank of the mouth of the Rio del Rey. It further comprises all territories in the basin of the Niger and its affluents, which are or may be for the time being subject to the government of the National African company limited (now called the Royal Niger company) in accordance with the provisions of the Charter of the said company, dated July 10, 1886.'

On the coast, the Benin river is the western boundary of this great sphere of British trade, as it is also the eastern boundary of the Lagos Protectorate; while the creek of the Rio del Rey is its eastern limit, separating it from the German dependency of the Cameroons. Inland, its northern boundary is, under the Anglo-French agreement of 1890, a line drawn from Say on the Niger to Barruwa on Lake Chad, leaving to the British Niger company 'all

Boundaries of and between the Protectorates.

SECTION II.

that fairly belongs to the Kingdom of Sokoto.' Its eastern boundary, as far as the Benue river, is provisionally fixed by agreements with Germany in 1885, 1886, 1890, and 1893. The line follows the right bank of the Rio del Rey creek, and is carried from its head direct to a point marked on the British Admiralty map in about 9.8 degrees of East longitude, whence it takes a north-easterly course, until it strikes the Benue river at a point to the east of and close to the town of Yola. Its western boundary is the Lagos Protectorate and Sphere of influence as far as the ninth degree of North latitude, beyond which the treaties of the Niger company extend to the west behind Yoruba, Dahomey, and Togoland, including the state of Borgu, just as on the opposite side the same company have extended their sphere to the north and east of Yola into the Sultanate of Bornu.

The territory within these limits includes the Niger Delta with the adjoining creeks and rivers, and the basin of the Lower Niger and the Benue. A great part of the coast-line of the Delta is under consular jurisdiction, and forms the Niger Coast Protectorate; while part of the coast and most of the interior, with the channels of the Lower Niger and the Benue and their affluents, is under the control of the Royal Niger company, subject only to the principles of freedom and navigation for the merchant ships of all nations, which were laid down at the International Berlin conference of 1885.

The boundary between the territories of the Royal Niger company and the Niger Coast Protectorate has been roughly demarcated as follows. East of the Nun, the main mouth of the Niger, which is situated in about 6.5 degrees of East longitude, the line of delimitation is carried from the coast, at a point midway between the Nun and the Brass rivers, straight to the town of Idu, the company being secured in any case a strip of land,

not less than three miles in width, along the eastern bank
of the Nun. Between this line and the Rio del Rey, the
whole of the coast region is included in the Niger Coast
Protectorate.

West of the Nun, the Delta, as far as the Forcados
river, is assigned to the company. The Forcados river,
which connects with the Niger at the head of the Delta,
flows in its lower course nearly due east and west.
The line of demarcation is carried up the middle of its
channel, giving the southern bank to the company and
the northern to the Niger Coast Protectorate, until a point
is reached somewhat above the creek on which stands,
within consular jurisdiction, the trading station of Wari.
Here it turns north-east for ten miles, and then due
north for thirty, leaving in the company's sphere both banks
of the upper waters of the channel between the Forcados
and the main Niger. All the country north and west of
the Forcados, up to and including the Benin river, belongs
to the Niger Coast Protectorate.

THE ROYAL NIGER COMPANY AND ITS TERRITORIES.

To the men who created the Royal Niger company, and
who have directed its operations, more especially to Sir George
Taubman-Goldie, Great Britain owes her present strong
position in West Africa. In this instance, as in many others,
private British enterprise successfully competed with the
state-directed efforts of foreign nations. The company has
a twofold character. In its private capacity, it trades and
owns land. In its public capacity, it is responsible for the
administration of an immense extent of territory, the area

The company and its administrations.

of which may be estimated at some 500,000 square miles. The Directors procured their charter in July 1886; and, by that charter, they are empowered to exercise to the full all rights obtained by treaties, 'with the kings, chiefs, and peoples of various territories in the basin of the river Niger in Africa,' subject only to international obligations, and to general provisions against monopoly of trade, against slavery, and against ill-treatment of the natives. They are authorised to govern, to administer justice, and to levy customs duties on goods landed in their territories, though not (by the terms of the Berlin conference) on goods which are merely in process of transit on the river. In a word, they are recognised as responsible rulers and protectors of life and property.

The policy and working of the company is controlled by the London council, but in Africa there is the usual machinery of local government, judges, executive officers, and a military force of about 1,000 men; while a fleet of river steamers keeps up communication along many hundred miles of the Niger and its tributaries. The revenue for administrative purposes is mainly derived from export duties on palm oil and kernels, shea butter, ivory, and other native produce. The import duties are few in number, being levied only on guns, powder, salt, spirits, and tobacco. The duties on spirits are very heavy, and the importation is entirely prohibited to the north of the seventh degree of North latitude. No rifles, breech-loading guns, or cartridges are allowed to be imported into any part of the territories.

The Niger Territories are a continental possession.

The British Crown Colonies in West Africa are, in the main, coast colonies. The Gambia, it is true, is in a sense a river settlement; and Sierra Leone, the Gold Coast, and Lagos have behind them inland areas, which, it is hoped, will in due course be opened up. But the Gambia colony is little more than Bathurst at the mouth of the estuary; Sierra Leone centres in Freetown and British Sherbro; the Gold Coast is a series of seaside stations; and Lagos has length with little breadth, it is essentially at present a strip of coast-line.

<small>CHAPTER XI.</small>

Widely different is the case of the Niger company. It has been formed to open up not a seaboard but the line of a great river, or rather of two great rivers. Its avowed sphere is not so much the coast as the continent. In the words of the preamble of the charter, it is engaged in developing the resources of the regions in the Basin of the Niger 'and in extending trade further into the interior.' Herein lies the importance of the company and its work. It is the pioneer, on the British side, of the new movement in West Africa. It represents what may be called the continental policy, as opposed to the old system of coast settlements. Its local centre of administration is not at the mouth of the Niger, but at Asaba 160 miles higher up the river; and its military headquarters are still further inland, at Lukoja, where the Niger and the Benue meet, 300 miles by river from the sea. Its ports and custom-houses are at Akasa, 2 miles within the mouth of the main channel of the Niger, and at Gana Gana about 30 miles up the Forcados river. In all there are about 50 trading stations, extending up to Bussa on the Niger, about 720 miles by river from the sea, and to Ribago on the Benue, about 750 miles by river from the sea and only about 200 miles distant from Lake Chad. which, geographers tell us, is the goal of European enterprise in Central Africa. *Stations of the Niger company.*

The Niger territories may be divided into three sections, the Delta, the country between the head of the Delta and Idda, and the country to the north of Idda. The Delta is a land of swamp, low lying, hot, moist, and unhealthy. Some little way above the head of the delta are the first signs of low hills, the original fringe of the continent, before the Niger threw out into the sea a peninsula of sand and mud. This lowland district extends for over 120 miles, still within the forest zone of Africa, until Idda is reached. Here the uplands of Africa begin, the Niger runs *Geography of the Niger Territories.*

Section II.

through mountainous scenery, and the country becomes more open and park-like, developing above the confluence of the Niger and the Benue into the plateau of the Western Sudan, dry, fresh, and salubrious as compared with the regions of the coast.

Products.

The chief products, which are brought down the Niger to the sea at the present time, are rubber, ivory, gum, and palm oil and kernels. The oil palm is especially associated with the Delta and the lands near the sea, but it is not confined to the coast districts, being found also far into the interior.

There is no sharply drawn line between the Delta and the mainland, or between the low country and the great plateau of the Sudan, but the transition from one region to another is very gradual.

Races.

The same may be said of the races and the religions in this part of Africa. Above the confluence of the Niger and the Benue are large Mohammedan states, such as Sokoto, Gandu, and Bornu[1]. Below it are Pagan negroes, the Idzoes of the coast, the Iboes at the head of the Delta, the Igaras, and others. As, however, the forest zone begins to shade off into the higher and more open country some way south of the Benue, so, before that river is reached from the south, there is a borderland where Islamism and Fetishism meet. Here, as in other parts of Africa, the Mohammedans of the interior, stronger races from healthier lands, with a crusading religion, and a natural affinity for the slave trade and the wars which the slave trade involves, have been pressing towards the coast, but they are met on the Niger by the counter efforts of Christian missionaries, belonging mainly to the Church Missionary Society, who have done something to redeem the negroes from their more inhuman practices, and who find a more

---

[1] Borgu, however, to the west of the Niger and to the north of the confluence, is a great Pagan kingdom.

hopeful sphere of work among Pagans, than among those races which have embraced Mohammedanism as a political as well as a religious creed.

The Niger river.

Though the Niger is navigated by the light steamers of the company at all seasons of the year, it is in many respects but an indifferent water-way, and the malarious climate of its lower reaches is not the only disadvantage with which traders have to contend. Its mouths are rendered dangerous by bars, the deepest entrance being that of the Forcados river. Its volume of water, as it draws near to the sea, is dissipated through various shallow channels. Higher up, where it flows in a single stream, rocks and rapids constantly impede navigation; and the depth varies very greatly with the season of the year, the river below the meeting with the Benue being lowest in March or April and highest in September. The Nun mouth is over a mile in breadth, but the river, drained by outlets on either side, soon narrows to a very inconsiderable channel, until Abo, just above the head of the delta, is reached, about 112 miles from the sea. Above this point is the undivided Niger, flowing from Lukoja nearly due north and south. Between 40 and 50 miles above Abo is the town and mission station of Onitsha on the eastern bank of the river, with Asaba, the centre of the company's administration, almost directly opposite, the breadth of the river at this point being about 1,200 yards. Higher up, 240 miles from the sea, is Idda, a large native town, built on the slope of a hill, which here forms the eastern bank of the river; and some 60 miles to the north of Idda, up a rocky channel and against a strong current, the steamers reach Lukoja, 300 miles from the sea, finely situated on the western bank of the Niger, directly over against the mouth of the Benue. From a point a little way above Lukoja the course of the Niger is from northwest to south-east. It flows through Nupeh, a province

SECTION II. of the Mohammedan Sultanate of Gandu, and past the town of Egga, 420 miles from the sea, where the company have an important trading station. Up to Bussa is a further distance of about 300 miles.

The Benue river. At Lukoja the Benue flows from the north-east and east into the Niger. It is a great river with many tributaries, its three main affluents from the south being the Katsena, the Donga, and the Teraba. It has a rapid rise and fall, and is very shallow in the dry season. The company's headquarters upon it are 250 miles above the confluence, and 550 miles by river from the sea, at Ibi on the southern bank, perhaps the finest of all the trading stations. About 150 miles above Ibi is Yola, capital of the Mohammedan state of Adamawa, whose ruler is a vassal of the Sultan of Sokoto; and a little to the east of Yola is the northern end of the Anglo-German boundary, Ribago, the most distant of the company's stations, being yet another 50 miles higher up the river.

General Summary. It would be idle to attempt to forecast the future of the Niger territories, and of the vigorous company which has undertaken to develope and administer them. The difficulties of climate are great, the water communication—which is the only kind of communication—is in many respects defective, there are trading jealousies to be appeased, and thorny international questions are still outstanding. But it is not too soon to register the value of the pioneer work which has been done; and, seeing that in the face of great difficulties the company has prospered financially, seeing that it has more than held its own against foreign rivals, that it was originally constituted on sound principles, and that any grave abuse of its powers is safeguarded by the terms of its charter, the future may be looked to with reasonable confidence. In any case it deserves well of those who believe in British influence as a civilising factor in barbarous regions, for it is due to the Royal Niger company that the great Basin of the Lower Niger has been secured to Great Britain, instead of falling to the lot of France or Germany.

Books on the Niger.

Up the Niger, by CAPTAIN MOCKLER FERRYMAN (1892), is the latest and most valuable book on the subject.

THE NIGER COAST PROTECTORATE.

THE Niger Coast Protectorate, known till lately as the Oil Rivers Protectorate, originated with a series of treaties made, in 1884, by Consul Hewett, the British representative in the Bight of Benin, in consequence of the German annexation of the Cameroons district. The estuaries, to which the name of Oil Rivers has been given, were well known to English merchants as early as the sixteenth century, although the fact that many of them form part of the Niger Delta was not discovered till the nineteenth. The Benin river especially was much frequented by traders in old times. Windham and Pinteado sailed thus far in 1553 [1]. Hakluyt [2] gives an account of 'a voyage to Benin beyond the country of Guinea' in the year of the Armada, 1588, which resulted in bringing back to England 'oil of palm,' Guinea pepper, and 'elephants teeth'; and in Barbot's [3] later narrative a full description is given of this coast, including the Benin river, which 'is very pleasant,

---

[1] See above, p. 52.
[2] 'A voyage to Benin beyond the country of Guinea, set forth by Master Bird and Master Newton, merchants of London . . . written by James Walsh who was chief master of the said voyage begun in the year 1588' (Hakluyt, 1810 ed., vol. ii. pp. 613-7), also a second voyage by the same, in 1590 (pp. 618-21).
[3] Bk. iv. chap. v.

SECTION II.

for which reason the Portuguese gave it the name of Fermoso, but very unwholesome, as most of the rivers of Guinea are'; the kingdom of Ouwere or Oveiro, which 'lies along Rio Forcado,' and which is now known as Wari; and Old and New Calabar.

The Coast of the Niger Protectorates.

From the Benin river to the Rio del Rey, the coast-line of the Niger Protectorates extends for a distance of about 330 miles. For some 140 miles, from Benin to the Nun mouth of the Niger, the coast runs south-east. From Cape Formoso, about six miles east of the Nun, which is the southernmost headland in the Delta, and the dividing point between the Bight of Benin on the west and the Bight of Biafra on the east, the direction of the coast-line as far as the Cameroons is nearly due east. Taking the coast from west to east, from the Benin to the Escravos (slaves) river, is a distance of 15 miles. From the Escravos to the Forcados is a distance of 13 miles. Between the Forcados and the Nun, under the control of the Niger company, are some 110 miles of coast broken by various creeks, such as the Ramos and Middleton rivers. The Brass river is rather over 10 miles east of the Nun, and between 40 and 50 miles from Brass is the Sombrero river, adjoining which on the east are the New Calabar and Bonny river, the estuaries of these three rivers forming the outlets of the New Calabar district. The distance from Brass to Bonny is about 70 miles. About 35 miles east of the Bonny estuary is the Opobo river, where King Ja Ja built his town. The next estuary to the east, 30 miles from the Opobo, is the Kwa Ibo river; and about 25 miles beyond the last-mentioned river is the beginning of the easternmost, the largest, and the most important of the Oil Rivers, the Old Calabar estuary, into which the great Cross river discharges itself, after a course, it is supposed, of 400 to 500 miles.

Main features of the district.

Behind the actual coast, the geography of the district which is watered by the Oil Rivers is at present but little known. Its great feature is the extraordinary intersection of creeks and rivers which continue the lagoons of the Lagos Protectorate. The Benin river is supposed to have an independent source from the Niger; but, as it is connected on the west with the Lagos water-ways, by a creek known as the Lagos creek, so on the east it is connected, by the Agara and Wari creeks, with the Escravos and Forcados rivers, the Forcados being in its turn connected with the Niger. Most of the rivers between the Forcados and the Kwa Ibo are little more than mouths of the Niger, the rivers of the New Calabar estuary and the Opobo flowing, it would seem, from a small lake named Oguta, which is held to be a receptacle of the overflow of the Niger. The Kwa Ibo, though connected by creeks with the Opobo, is an independent river from the Niger, while the Cross river and the smaller streams which feed the Old Calabar estuary are quite separate from the Delta. In spite of bars at their mouths, the rivers and creeks are navigable in all directions for light steamers. On the west of the main Niger the most accessible estuary is the Forcados. Its mouth is between two and three miles wide, and the bar is deeper and safer than that of any of the other estuaries. For this reason, when the channels of the Niger are full, it is a valuable water-way to the head of the Delta, in addition to being the outlet of the Wari district. East of the Nun the best harbours are at Bonny and Old Calabar.

The European factories on the Oil Rivers are usually at some little distance from the native towns, and in some cases they consist merely of hulks moored at the mouths of the rivers. West of the main Niger, the chief stations for traffic are on the Benin, the Forcados, and the Wari creek. East of it, the trading centres are more numerous, including Brass, Bonny, Opobo, and Old Calabar. The last-named town, well situated on the Old Calabar river, prosperous but very hot and unhealthy, is the headquarters of the British consular administration, and commercially the most important point in the Protectorate. It is formed out of a collection of native villages, and has a population of some 15,000. Near it is Creek Town, also a place of some importance; and at both places, as well as at Bonny and Brass and elsewhere, British missionaries and British traders have taken up their residence. Away from the coast are native cities, hardly known to Europeans, strongholds of barbarism and fetish worship, such as Benin city, and Bende and Aron in the Opobo and Kwa Ibo districts.

Various steamship companies keep up communication between Europe and the Oil Rivers; and the submarine cable touches at Brass and Bonny.

Climate and Products.

The climate of the Niger Delta is on a par with that of the rest of the West African coast. It has the reputation of being peculiarly deadly to Europeans, but the loss of life is on the whole not above the average in West Africa. The temperature is equable, usually ranging from 75 to 90 degrees, and the great feature of the climate is the heavy rainfall, there being on the coast no marked difference between the wet and dry seasons.

The rich alluvial soil of the Delta is most prolific in vegetation. From a commercial point of view the oil palm overshadows all other products, but nearly all the West African trees and plants are to be found, including kola nuts, rubbers, gums, silk cotton, the seeds which give the 'shea butter,' and, in the Cross River district, ebony. According to the trade returns for the year ending July 31, 1892, palm oil and kernels represented about 94 per cent. in value of the total exports of the Protectorate, rubber being the only other item deserving special mention.

Administration of the Protectorate.

The Oil Rivers Protectorate, as it was then called, was constituted a 'local jurisdiction' under the Africa Order in Council of 1889. That is to say, under the powers conferred by the Foreign Jurisdiction Acts, a consular jurisdiction, primarily for British subjects, was established in these districts, with a right of appeal to the Supreme Court of the colony of Lagos (now also to that of the Gold Coast or of Sierra Leone). Administrative powers have also by sufferance and consent come into being; and, from August 1, 1891, a scale of import duties was fixed and proclaimed 'to provide for the expenses of the administration of the British Protectorate of the Oil Rivers.' These expenses include the salaries of the Imperial Commissioner and consul-general, of the vice-consuls and consular agents, of medical officers, of customs officers and clerks, and of a small body of police. The Imperial Commissioner takes his instructions from the Foreign Office, not from the Colonial Office, and the original object of the Consular establishment was the control of European traders and of their dealings with the natives and with one another, the authority of the native chiefs over their own people not being interfered with. As a matter of fact, however, it is becoming difficult to distinguish for practical purposes between this Protectorate and a Crown Colony; and, at the places where British representatives are stationed, the consular officer is rather a District Commissioner, responsible for security of life and property, than a diplomatic agent in the ordinary sense of the word.

Trade of the Protectorate.

The trade of the Oil Rivers is mainly with Liverpool, and most of the traders belong to the African association of that city. There is also a considerable traffic with Havre and with Hamburg, but carried mainly in British ships. In the year ended July 31, 1892, the imports and exports of the Protectorate were valued at £748,000 and £780,000, respectively. The United Kingdom sent 77 per cent. of the imports, cotton goods being the largest item, and took nearly 55 per cent. of the exports, absorbing therefore about two-thirds of the total trade. In the list of importing countries Holland stood second, sending gin and guns, and Germany stood third; while among the receivers of exports France held the second place, and Germany the third. It is noteworthy that France sent no imports, and Holland took

SECTION II. no exports. Of the Oil River ports, Old Calabar, including Kwa Ibo, contributed 28 per cent. of the total import and export trade, Bonny and New Calabar 24 per cent., and Opobo 23 per cent. The remainder was credited to Benin, Wari, and Brass in the order given. The amount of customs duties collected during the year was £88,000, levied almost entirely on spirits and tobacco.

General Summary. There is little to be said of the Niger Coast Protectorate at present, except that it is being rapidly and skilfully organised by Sir Claude MacDonald and his officers without any expense to the British taxpayer, and that it is the scene of a large and growing trade. The climate is bad, but so is the climate of West Africa generally; and, if the commercial wealth consists almost entirely of palm oil, the same drawback has been shown to attach to the flourishing Crown colony of Lagos. Missionary enterprise and British supervision have done a good deal to humanise the natives; and, in view of what the future may bring forth, it is well that the control of this important section of the West African coast should be vested in Great Britain.

APPENDIX.

OIL NUTS AND SEEDS OF BRITISH WEST AFRICA.

VEGETABLE oil, in one form or another, is so pre-eminently the export from British West Africa, and indeed from West Africa generally, that it may be useful to group together a few very simple facts on the subject, without any pretension to give such scientific information as can only be furnished by a botanical expert.

Oil, and the vegetable products from which it is produced, represented, according to the latest returns to hand:—

(1) 87 per cent. in value of the exports of the Gambia.
(2) Nearly 38 per cent. ,, ,, ,, Sierra Leone.
(3) 42 per cent. . ,, ,, ,, Gold Coast.
(4) 83 per cent. . ,, ,, ,, Lagos.
(5) ? per cent. . ,, ,, ,, Niger Territories.
(6) More than 90 per cent. ,, ,, Niger Coast Protectorate.

It has only one rival, in certain parts, i.e. rubber.

The chief European ports into which oil and oil nuts and seeds are imported from British West Africa, are, Liverpool for the United Kingdom; Marseilles for France; Hamburg for Germany.

The trees or plants, which give the oil are:—

(1) The Oil palm [*Elæis Guineensis*].
(2) The Ground nut [*Arachis hypogæa*].
(3) Various less important plants.

SECTION II.

None of these products, except the ground nut, have been as yet to any extent systematically cultivated on the West Coast. They are not grown in regular plantations, like the sugar-cane in the West Indies, cotton in Louisiana, or tea in Ceylon. They are for the most part a natural growth of the jungle, and the export does not represent the result of tilling of the soil.

The export of palm oil from British West Africa is at least a century old[1], that of ground nuts and palm kernels has existed for the last fifty years.

1. The oil palm has practically no place at the Gambia. It grows at Sierra Leone, especially in the southern—the Sherbro—district; it is still more prominent on the Gold Coast; and it is all-important at Lagos, and in the Niger Delta.

The tree bears best in a moist soil, 'flourishing in the warm damp valleys, where it grows in extensive forests.' From it are sent to Europe (a) palm oil, (b) palm kernels. From the latter a further supply of oil is subsequently extracted by European machinery.

(a) The palm oil is derived from the husk which covers the nut, and which is separated from it by boiling and pounding. The best oil, known as 'soft' oil, is obtained when the nuts are fresh; but, as a rule, the nuts, when gathered, are thrown into a hole in the ground, where a certain amount of fermentation takes place, the result being 'hard' oil, thicker and coarser in proportion to the time during which the nuts have been left covered up.

(b) After the oily husk has been removed, the nuts are dried, and the kernels are taken out and shipped to Europe, where the oil extracted from each kernel averages 30 per cent. of its weight.

[1] In the list of imports from Africa into Great Britain, printed in the Report of the Privy Council on Trade to Africa and the Slave Trade (1789), 1,091 cwt. of palm oil are given for the year 1783, valued apparently at £1 per cwt.

Palm oil, whether from the fibre or from the kernel, is used, the pure 'soft' quality in making soap, the coarser in making candles. It is also used for lubricating machinery, e.g. as grease on the axles of the wheels of railway carriages, in the manufacture of tin plate, and for various other purposes. The residue of the kernels, after the oil has been extracted, is still valuable as oil cake.

The purest oil, which fetches the highest price, comes from Lagos; the most adulterated oil comes from Saltpond, Appam, and Winnebah, in the central districts of the Gold Coast. The price of palm oil has varied very greatly in consequence both of local causes and of the discovery of mineral oils. In the Blue Book Report of Lagos for 1891, it is stated that 'in the early sixties' Lagos palm oil fetched £52 a ton, in May 1887 only £18 10s., in July 1891 £25.

2. The ground nut grows chiefly in Senegambia, as the oil palm grows chiefly in Lower Guinea. The two products meet in Sierra Leone, the northern districts of which colony produce ground nuts and the southern districts palm oil. At the Gambia, ground nuts constitute more than four-fifths in value of the exports. On the Gold Coast these nuts are to be found, having been, it is said, introduced from Brazil by the Portuguese; but here they are very poor in quality, and of no commercial value.

The ground nut takes its botanical name of Arachis hypogæa from the fact that, when the plant has flowered, it matures its fruit buried under the surface of the ground. The seeds are exported to Europe, especially to Marseilles, and the oil extracted from them is largely used as a substitute for olive oil: it is also used in the manufacture of butterine, pomades, soap, &c., as well as for purposes of lighting.

3. In addition to the oil palm and ground nut, various trees and plants in West Africa produce oil of one kind or another. Of these, beniseed (Sesamum Indicum), which is exported from Sierra Leone and from Lagos, is probably

SECTION II.

the most important. Its oil, like that of the ground nut, is used, among other purposes, as a substitute for olive oil. The cocoa-nut palm grows freely on the Gold Coast and at Lagos, but as yet it is little used for commercial purposes.

Reference should be made to Sir A. Moloney's *Sketch of the Forestry of West Africa*, 1887, which contains a 'list of economic plants of Western Africa,' by Mr. Hillier of the Royal Gardens, Kew; to the *Report on Economic Agriculture on the Gold Coast*, 1889; Colonial Series of Parliamentary Reports, No. 110, 1890; and to the *Kew Bulletin* (Eyre and Spottiswoode), 1887-1893.

SECTION III.

THE ISLANDS IN THE SOUTH ATLANTIC.

ASCENSION.

THE island of Ascension was first discovered by the Portuguese sailor De Nova on Lady Day 1501, and was named by him Conception. Two years later it was sighted by Albuquerque on Ascension Day, May 20, 1503. Hence its present name. The island is mentioned by Linschoten and other old travellers; and, according to one account[1], 'malefactors' were left there by passing ships, just as sick men were landed at St. Helena.

Section III. Discovery and early notices of the island.

Dampier was wrecked on its shores in 1701, and was detained from February 23, to March 8, when he was picked up by an English ship. During his stay he found traces of former visitors in the figures 1642 carved on a tree, and made the more important discovery of fresh water in the island, which, as he tells us overrating the distance, was eight miles from the landing-place. What is now known as Dampier's spring is on the north side of Green mountain, rather more than four miles from Georgetown. In the eighteenth century, turtle-catching at Ascension attracted fishing vessels from the American colonies; and Cook, who visited the island in 1775, speaks of ships coming there from New York and the Bermudas,

---

[1] From the Account of Roggeveen's Voyage, 1721-3, in Harris' Collection.

248 *HISTORICAL GEOGRAPHY OF THE COLONIES.*

SECTION III.

which supplemented their fishing [1] by illicit trade with the East India company's merchant-men.

British occupation.

In 1815, in view of the detention of Napoleon at St. Helena, the British government thought fit to occupy and garrison Ascension; and, after his death, the island was retained by the Admiralty as a naval station. At one time it was the headquarters of the West African squadron, but of late years it has been used mainly as a sanatorium.

System of administration.

In his narrative of the Voyage of the Beagle, Darwin says of Ascension, that 'the whole island may be compared to a huge ship kept in first rate order.' This description well applies to the administrative arrangements at the present day. With the exception of the Channel islands and the Isle of Man, whose dealings are with the Home Office, Ascension is the only fully organised British dependency, which is not subordinate either to the Colonial Office or to the India Office [2]. It is under the rule of the Admiralty; it is garrisoned by marines; its expenses are defrayed from naval funds; and it is rated as a ship of war.

Geography, position, area, &c.

Ascension island is situated in 7° 56′ South latitude and 14° 20′ West longitude. It is in nearly the same latitude as St. Paul de Loanda in West Africa, which is a little south of the mouth of the Congo, and as Pernambuco in Brazil. It is 800 statute miles north-west of St. Helena, 1,340 miles from Cape Coast, 1,150 from Sierra Leone, 1,880 from the Congo, 2,850 from the Cape, and 2,280 from Rio Janeiro.

In shape it is an irregular oval, slightly pointed towards the east. It is about 8 miles in length from east to west, 6½ in breadth from north to south, and 22 miles in circumference. In size it is midway between Jersey and Guernsey, its area being 34 square miles. Its shores are steep at nearly

---

[1] See Cook's voyage of 1775 to the South Pole and Round the World, 1784 ed., vol. ii. chap. x. pp. 272-3.
[2] The Protectorates subordinate to the Foreign Office are not British territory in the strict sense.

every point except on the north-west, which is the lee side of the island. Here is the anchorage at Clarence Bay, and the little settlement of Georgetown.

The whole island is, in the words of the Narrative of the Challenger expedition, 'a series of extinct volcanic cones[1].' It is entirely bare of vegetation except on Green mountain, towards the south-east of the island, which is the highest point, rising to 2,820 feet. Linschoten writes that Ascension 'in show seemeth as great as the island of St. Helena but not so high. It is full of hills and dales.... There is not any fresh water in the island nor one green leaf or branch. It hath many hills of a reddish colour[2].' Cook's description is that 'it shows a surface composed of barren hills and vallies,' and that it had evidently been destroyed by a volcano, a mountain at the south-eastern end being left in its original condition.' Other accounts are all to much the same effect. Since, however, the Admiralty have been in possession, a great deal has been done to make the island more habitable. A road has been constructed for six miles from the top of Green mountain to the landing-place. The scanty water supply has been collected in tanks, and is carried in pipes from the mountain to Georgetown. Plants and shrubs have been introduced, mainly from Australia, and the belt of vegetation on Green mountain has been gradually extended, the castor-oil plant among others thriving very well. There is a farm on the mountain, where fruits and vegetables of various kinds are grown, and cows and sheep are pastured.

Fish are very plentiful at Ascension; turtle have always been a speciality of the place, being kept when taken in turtle ponds; and edible birds' eggs—the eggs of the 'wideawake'—are taken in very large quantities at the times when the birds congregate to the island. Among imported or indigenous nuisances are or were wild goats and cats, rats, and landcrabs.

Products.

---

[1] Vol. i. part ii. p. 929.
[2] Vol. ii. chap. xcv. Hakluyt Series.

250 HISTORICAL GEOGRAPHY OF THE COLONIES.

SECTION III.

Climate.

The climate of Ascension is extremely healthy, although the island is so near the Equator. Its healthiness is due to the prevalence of the south-east trade winds and to the entire absence of anything like marshy ground. The average annual rainfall is very small, the rainy months being March and April. There is however much more rain and mist on Green mountain than on the lower ground, and the temperature by day at a height of 2,500 feet averages 75° as against 85° at the landing-place.

Residents.

The normal number of residents in Ascension is about 160, consisting of sailors, marines, and Kroomen from the Liberian coast. With the exception of the station on Green mountain, the only settlement is the little town at the anchorage, which was officially christened Georgetown in 1830. It is built on ashes, at the end of a valley which gradually leads up to Green mountain; it is defended by guns; and it contains a church, hospitals, and barracks in addition to dwelling-houses.

General Summary.

In barrenness and scarcity of water Ascension resembles Aden, and it possesses a further drawback in the rollers which constantly make landing on the island difficult and dangerous. On the other hand, its healthy climate is a great point in its favour, considering its comparative nearness to the coast of West Africa, and there seems reason to hope that, if the island continues to be inhabited, future generations may see a considerably larger area of cultivated or cultivable soil. Originally occupied for a special purpose, it is not a possession of much value to Great Britain; but, as a coaling station in the hands of a foreign power, it might be a menace to British trade. If the island were now uninhabited and unowned, it would probably not be worth while for the English to take it, but, having been taken, it is sufficiently useful to be kept.

Books, etc. relating to Ascension.

SECTION III.

Good accounts of Ascension will be found in the *Africa Pilot*, part ii. (1884); in the reports of the *Challenger*; in Sir C. Wyville Thompson's *Voyage of the Challenger—The Atlantic* (1877); and in Mr. Moseley's *Notes by a Naturalist on the Challenger* (1879). The above publications should also be consulted for information about Tristan da Cunha.

See also *Six Months in Ascension*, by Mrs. Gill (1880).

St. Helena.

The island of St. Helena was first discovered on May 21, 1502[1]. The discoverer was De Nova, commander of the third Portuguese expedition to the East. On the way out, in 1501, he first sighted Ascension. On the way home, in 1502, he came to St. Helena. According to some accounts he lost one of his ships there, and from the timbers of the wreck built a chapel, which gave the name of Chapel Valley to the ravine in which Jamestown now stands. Thus Europeans came to know this little distant island, 'standing as it were in the midst of the sea between the mainland of Africa and the main of Brazilia and the coast of Guinea[2].'

Discovery of St. Helena.

It was by no mere chance that St. Helena was first found from the south, not from the north. It is situated in the heart of the south-east trade winds, as easy for sailing ships to reach from the Cape, as it is difficult, indeed impossible, for them to make direct from Europe. 'When we were under sail,' wrote an old traveller returning from the East round the Cape in the year 1649[3], 'the mariners cried out

Its position as regards the trade wind.

---

[1] In the modern Roman Catholic calendar, St. Helena's Day is August 18; but in the calendar of the Greek Church May 21 is dedicated to Helena and Constantine. Helena was the mother of Constantine the Great.

[2] From Cavendish's voyage in Hakluyt.

[3] Tavernier, taken from Harris' Collection of Voyages.

SECTION III.

they would sleep till they came into St. Helen's Road, for the wind is very constant and carries you in sixteen or eighteen days to the road of the island.' On the other hand, a sailing ship bound from Europe to St. Helena would have to beat out towards the South American coast, and come up with the wind by a circular course from the South.

Its connexion with the Cape and the East, and its value to the Portuguese.

Owing mainly to the trade wind, St. Helena has never had any connexion with the West Coast of Africa. It has been connected rather with the Cape and with the East. To the Portuguese, the earliest of European navigators in these seas, the island was specially valuable. The ships of their day were small and ill-found, requiring many places of call; and on the voyage home there was naturally more need to replenish stores of food and water than on the way out from Europe. It is true that St. Helena was not so many days sail from the Cape; but the Portuguese made little use of the Cape, for one reason because the natives there were troublesome to deal with, whereas St. Helena was uninhabited. Nor was the island only on the direct route from the East to Portugal; it was also on the way from the Indies to Brazil, and the same kindly wind, which was blowing towards home, would carry the ships across the Atlantic, to the South American land which was so profitable a dependency of the Portuguese nation. St. Helena, then, was an important link in the chain which held together the great empire of the Portuguese; and it is perhaps surprising that they did not make a settlement there, build a fort, and keep the island garrisoned. They did not do so, probably because, with the many calls upon their resources, they did not wish to spend men and money on an island where there were no natives to hold in check, which was only wanted for passing ships, and which, as long as they commanded the sea, was securely in their power. They dealt with it as they dealt with Mauritius[1],

[1] The Portuguese custom of placing live stock on islands (e. g. according to one account even on Sable Island in North America) had the

importing live stock, sowing fruits and vegetables, keeping up the chapel with a few adjoining houses, and leaving the sick there to be picked up, if still alive, in the following year.

Old notices of St. Helena.

Very excellent things were spoken of St. Helena by old writers. In Purchas we read, 'It seems God had planted it in convenient place for the long and dangerous Indian navigations': in Hakluyt, 'This island is a great succour to the shipping which return for Portugal': and in the account left by Linschoten, who visited the island in 1589, 'It is an earthly Paradise for the Portingall ships.' In truth St. Helena had in abundance all that sailors or other men could want; a healthy climate, a plentiful supply of water, fresh meat, fish, salt, and fruits of the earth. So ship after ship came up from the south-east, sailing before the wind; and, rounding the northern end of the island, anchored on the leeward or western side, where James Valley, then Chapel Valley, runs down between steep cliffs to the sea.

The earliest inhabitant.

St. Helena, in the sixteenth century, had its Robinson Crusoe. Perhaps it would be more correct to say, judging from the accounts, that it had a succession of Crusoes. The name of one, however, has been specially recorded. He was Fernando Lopez, who had turned traitor to the Portuguese in India, and, on being handed over to Albuquerque with the condition that his life should be spared, had been barbarously mutilated, his nose, ears, and right hand being cut off. On the way back to Europe, in 1513, maimed and disgraced, he left the ship at St. Helena, and lived there unmolested by his countrymen. After some years he paid a visit to Portugal

---

result, if not the intention, of a very public spirited policy. Tavernier (in Harris' Collection) says of St. Helena: 'There are great store of citrons and some oranges which the Portuguese had formerly planted there: for that nation have that virtue that, wherever they come, they make the place better for those that come after them, whereas the Dutch endeavour to destroy all things, wherever they set footing.' He wrote, however, with great animus against the Dutch.

SECTION III.

at the King's command, but returned to and died in the island in the year 1546[1].

It is stated that the Portuguese tried to keep the situation of St. Helena a secret from other nations. However that may be, for many years Portuguese ships alone sailed the southern seas; and, whether known or not, the island was not visited by Dutch or English sailors. It is mentioned *Cavendish's visit.* in English state papers about the year 1582; and in June, 1588, an Englishman, Thomas Cavendish, touched there, returning from his voyage round the world. He landed at the 'marvellous fair valley,' where were standing the chapel and other 'divers handsome buildings and houses'; he found three or four slaves living on the island; and he bore testimony, like others, to the goodness of the place and to the abundance of beasts, birds, and fruits. It must be added that he ill-requited the hospitality of the island, for it appears from the narrative of Linschoten, who visited St. Helena in the following year, that he and his men beat down the altar and cross which stood in the church.

Before Cavendish visited St. Helena, the Portuguese had fallen from their high estate and become, in 1580, subjects of the Spanish King. In the very year in which he came to the island, the defeat of the Great Armada broke the naval power of Spain. Henceforward, therefore, other peoples besides Portuguese or Spaniards began to make a show in the South Atlantic.

Lancaster's visits. In 1591, three English ships, under captains Kendall, Raymond, and Lancaster, set sail for the East Indies. On reaching the Cape, with their crews stricken by scurvy, one of them, 'The Royal Merchant,' turned home again, taking the sick men. The ship touched at St. Helena and deposited a sailor, John Legar by name, on the chance of saving his

---

[1] See the Commentaries of Afonso D'Alboquerque in the Hakluyt Series, vol. iii. Introduction, pp. 35–9.

life; and there he was found by Lancaster in 1593, when he touched at the island on his way back from the East. Unhappily, the castaway was so excited at seeing friends again, that he took, we are told, no natural sleep for eight days, and died in consequence. Lancaster came again to St. Helena in 1603, on his return from a memorable voyage to the Indies —the first voyage designed and equipped by the English East India company. With the history of that company the history of St. Helena was bound up for the better part of two centuries.

Occupation of St. Helena by the East India Company.

From the beginning of the seventeenth century, the Portuguese deserted the island altogether, and in 1645 the Dutch are said to have taken possession of it. If they did so, however, their occupation was little more than a name, and ceased in 1651, the year before they established their settlement at the Cape. Thereupon St. Helena passed into the hands of the English, being appropriated by homeward-bound ships of the East India company, and ten years later the company were confirmed in their possession by a clause in the charter which they received from Charles II on April 3, 1661. The clause in question empowered the Directors to fortify and garrison the island; and accordingly a fort was built, and named James Fort in honour of the Duke of York, afterwards James II. When war broke out between Great Britain and the Netherlands—the war in which De Ruyter did so much damage on the West Coast of Africa[1]—the Dutch, in 1665, took St. Helena, but were driven out in the same year. A few years later, in January 1673[2], they again attacked the island. After one unsuccessful attempt, they effected a landing by night near Bennett's point on the west coast, through the treachery, it was said, of one of the planters, and climbing up Swanley Valley gained after a fight the heights of Ladder Hill overlooking

Dutch attacks.

---

[1] See above, p. 98.   [2] 1672 Old Style.

SECTION III.

Jamestown. Unable to hold out against a superior force, the English governor and his people evacuated the settlement, and, embarking on ships in the harbour, sailed off to Brazil, leaving the Dutch masters of the island. The latter only enjoyed their conquest for a few months. Off the coast of Brazil the fugitives fell in with a British squadron commanded by Captain Munden, who took prompt measures to retrieve the disaster. He arrived at St. Helena on May 14, and on the next day landed a party in the north-east corner of the island, at a spot since known as Prosperous Bay. Scaling the cliffs above the bay [1], the soldiers marched overland to Rupert's Hill on the eastern side of James Valley, while Munden and his ships threatened the town in front. The result was an immediate surrender, and thenceforward down to the present day the English have held undisputed possession of St. Helena.

The island finally secured to the English.

The island had been recovered by the forces of the Crown, and therefore the legal ownership of it had passed away from the company and become vested in the Crown by right of conquest. But there was no wish to deprive the company of their station, 'very necessary and commodious for our loving subjects the said governor and company of merchants trading into the East Indies for refreshing of their servants and people in their returns homewards [2]';

The Charter of 1673.

and accordingly, by a new charter dated December 16, 1673, they were declared to be in the fullest extent 'the true and absolute lords and proprietors' of St. Helena. The charter was in most respects similar to those which were issued in the case of the American colonies belonging to proprietors or to chartered companies. The royal sovereignty over the inhabitants was maintained, and they were guaranteed all the rights of British citizens; but the ownership of the soil, and all legislative, administrative, and

---

[1] The rock is still known as Holdfast Tom.
[2] From the preamble to the new charter.

judicial powers, were vested in the company. On receiving their charter, the Directors appointed a governor of the island, a deputy-governor, and three lieutenants of the garrison, to form a Council. There never was in St. Helena any vestige of an elected local legislature. The laws were made by the company at home, and were administered on the spot by the governor and council, all of whom were nominated by the Court of Directors in Leadenhall Street. Moreover, by a clause in a subsequent charter issued in August 1683, the company were authorised to govern any of their possessions, if they thought fit, under martial law— a provision sufficient of itself to preclude any idea of local self-government.

St. Helena under the East India Company.

The records of the East India company's rule in St. Helena contain little of general interest. The island community consisted of three classes; the company's employés and the garrison; the settlers, who were given grants of land on specified conditions, one of which was liability to military service; and the black slaves. The introduction of negroes appears to have been almost coincident with the first English settlement of the island; and, by the end of the first quarter of the eighteenth century, the slaves were more numerous than the whites, the numbers in 1723 being 610 blacks, against 500 whites including the garrison. The policy of the Directors with regard to the introduction of negroes varied. In 1679 the importation was restricted, but a few years later every ship from Madagascar which touched at the island was obliged to leave one negro for work on the company's plantations. At no time, however, did the slaves largely outnumber the whites. In 1780 they were under 1,200, as against more than 900 Europeans; and in 1817, the year before the first step was taken towards emancipation, they numbered 1,540 out of a total population of 6,150, against a white population, exclusive of naval and

Negro slavery in the island.

SECTION III.

military forces, of 821. In this year the garrison was very large owing to Napoleon's detention on the island, and the labouring class was swelled by 500 free blacks, and also by more than 600 Chinese, the importation of whom from the East India company's factory at Canton had begun in 1810.

Although the slave population in St. Helena was never so large in proportion to the whites, as it was in Jamaica and other West Indian islands, there were the same scares from time to time of negro rebellions; the slave laws were as barbarous as they were in the West Indies; and the treatment of the slaves by their proprietors almost more inhuman. At length, in 1792, the Court of Directors passed a new code of regulations for the protection of the slaves, the result of which was a diminution of the death-rate. Before these rules were passed, it was estimated that the planters lost on an average 10 per cent. of their negroes annually[1], whereas afterwards, though the importation of any fresh slaves was strictly prohibited, the numbers increased.

The Act for the abolition of slavery in the British colonies which was passed in 1833, to take effect from August, 1834, did not apply to the territories under the jurisdiction of the East India company. They were separately dealt with by the new Charter Act[2], also passed

---

[1] See Sir G. Staunton's Authentic Account of Lord Macartney's mission to China, written in 1797, vol. ii. chap. viii. The writer visited St. Helena on the return voyage in 1794.

[2] 3 and 4 Will. IV. cap. lxxxv: 'An Act for effecting an arrangement with the East India company and for the better government of His Majesty's Indian territories.' Sec. 88 referred to the slavery question, and sect. 112 provided that the island of St. Helena 'shall be vested in His Majesty' and be governed by 'such orders as His Majesty in Council shall from time to time issue in that behalf.' Inasmuch as, for the reasons given above, there was no general law against slavery which included St. Helena, a special ordinance was passed, after the transfer to the Crown, declaring slavery to be illegal in the colony (ord. 24 of 1839).

in 1833, a section in which provided that slavery should be mitigated at once and should be extinguished as soon as possible. But neither did this latter act cover the case of St. Helena, for it contained another clause transferring the island from the company to the Crown. As a matter of fact slavery was abolished in the island under instructions from the Directors, and with the consent of the proprietors of the negroes, without waiting for any legislation on the part of the Imperial government. Owing in great measure to the influence of the governor, Sir Hudson Lowe, it was, on August 24, 1818, resolved at a general meeting of the inhabitants, that all children born of slaves, from and after the following Christmas Day, should be free; and a proclamation issued on the same day endorsed the resolution and declared it to be a law of the island[1]. The existing slaves still remained to be dealt with, and, at the end of 1826, the Directors wrote out declaring their 'deliberate conviction' that 'so soon as a slave understands and appreciates the nature and blessings of freedom, that boon should, if possible, be conferred.' With that end in view they not only pressed on the education of the negroes, but also authorised the issue of loans to enable deserving slaves to purchase their freedom; and in the next three or four years a considerable number obtained their liberty in this way. Finally, in 1832, a valuation was made of all the remaining slaves; and it was decided that one-fifth should be liberated every year, the purchase money in each case being treated as a loan to the slave. Thus every slave in the island was set free by May 1, 1836.

[1] The Proclamation began as follows: 'Whereas by the universal concurrence of the inhabitants and slave proprietors on this island, it was resolved at a meeting held this day that from and after the 25th day of December next, being the anniversary of the birth of our Blessed Saviour, Jesus Christ, all children born of slaves shall be free.' See Sir G. Birdwood's Report on the Old Records of the India Office, p. 98.

SECTION III.

The account of slave emancipation in St. Helena is interesting, as showing the way in which a private company solved, though on a very small scale, this difficult problem. They took their measures, as far as can be judged, prudently and well. They proceeded on the principles that the proprietors should be fully compensated, that the slaves should be enabled to work out their own salvation, and that the change of system should be gradually effected. Hence slavery died out, it would seem, without any appreciable friction, and without disturbing the social economy of the little community.

Records of St. Helena. Apart from the negro question, and the episode of the detention of Napoleon, there is little to be said of St. Helena history. From the date when the island was last re-taken from the Dutch, it has never been attacked by a foreign foe, though on one occasion, in 1706, two of the company's ships, which were anchored off Jamestown, were carried off by the French. A very small and isolated society always spends a great deal of its time in petty quarrels, and St. Helena was no exception to the rule. There seems to have been at one time a series of truculent and disreputable chaplains, who, having the right to sit at the governor's table, enjoyed considerable facilities for annoyance; and among more serious difficulties were occasional mutinies in the garrison, in one of which, in the year 1693, the governor of the time was taken and shot. Of the men whom the Directors sent out to govern the island, the most active appears to have been Governor Roberts, who ruled from 1708 to 1711; while his predecessor, Governor Poirier, deserves mention as having been one of the Huguenot refugees who were driven out from France by the Revocation of the Edict of Nantes, and as having attempted with indifferent success to introduce into St. Helena the vine-growing of his native land. Another and later governor, in 1741, was Robert Jenkins, whose ears had lately helped on a war with Spain[1]. Dampier came twice to the island, in 1691 and 1701, and left a short but interesting account of the earlier visit; and in 1676-8 the astronomer Halley, the first of various scientific men who have been attracted to St. Helena, studied the stars from a ridge which has since borne the name of Halley's Mount.

Section III.

In October 1815, the greatest man who ever set foot in the island was brought there to end his life; and the house at Longwood was fitted up to be Napoleon's residence, until he died in May 1821. During the years which he spent at St. Helena, it was strongly garrisoned by the King's troops; the Governor, Sir Hudson Lowe, was nominated by the Crown, though receiving his commission from the Directors; and the island, while still owned by the company, was practically treated as an Imperial fortress[2]. These special arrangements were at once discontinued upon Napoleon's death, and the old order of things was restored, until the Act of 1833 finally vested the island in the Crown from and after April 22, 1834[3].

The detention and death of Napoleon.

Since St. Helena has been a Crown Colony, its prosperity and its importance have sadly declined. For awhile it profited by being made a centre for putting down the African slave trade and for the disposal of the Liberated Africans. But of late years this source of employment of men and money, like others, has disappeared. Sailing ships, larger and better equipped than of old, no longer need constantly to put to land for water and supplies. The strength of steam can nowadays afford to despise small halfway halting-places in the ocean; and, since the Suez Canal has been opened, the

St. Helena as a Crown Colony.

---

[1] The story of Jenkins' ears is too familiar to require explanation.
[2] See the Act of 1816, 56 Geo. III. cap. 23 : 'An Act for regulating the intercourse with the island of Saint Helena during the time Napoleon Buonaparte shall be detained there.' The Act greatly restricted communication with the island, while safeguarding the rights of the East India company over it.
[3] The company, as a matter of fact, continued by arrangement to administer the island till the spring of 1836.

262 HISTORICAL GEOGRAPHY OF THE COLONIES.

SECTION III.

traffic from the East no longer comes round the Cape. Thus the causes which led to the settlement of St. Helena have ceased to operate; and, in spite of the fact that it is still fortified and garrisoned as an Imperial coaling-station, the island seems doomed to droop and decay.

Government, Law and Justice, &c.

St. Helena is a Crown Colony; but, unlike most Crown Colonies, though like Gibraltar, it has no Legislative Council, the local legislative power being vested in the Governor alone. He is advised by an Executive Council, consisting at present of four members besides himself, viz. the Officer Commanding the troops, and three of the principal residents, one of whom at the present time is the Bishop. The Crown has retained power to make laws for the island by Order in Council. Municipal instituitons are represented by a Poor Relief Board, the members of which are elected annually by the rate-payers; by a Public Market Committee; and by a Board of Health. The Governor acts as Chief Justice, and minor cases are decided by the Police Magistrate. The law of the colony is the law of England for the time being, so far as it is applicable to local circumstances, modified by such by-laws of the East India company as still remain in force, by local ordinances, and Orders in Council.

Situation, Area, and Geography.

The island is situated in the South Atlantic Ocean, in 15° 55′ South latitude, and 5° 42′ West longitude. It is nearly due west of Benguela in West Africa, and nearly due east of Bahia in Brazil. It is about 1,200 statute miles distant from the nearest point in West Africa, and more than 2,000 miles from the nearest point in South America. It is 800 miles south-east of Ascension, nearly 1,500 miles distant from the Congo, 2,000 miles from the Cape, and 2,500 from Rio de Janeiro. In shape it is between an oval and a rectangle, with the line of length running north-east and south-west. It is 10½ miles in length and 6½ in breadth. Its area is 47 square miles. In other words, it is a little larger than Jersey.

The island is of volcanic formation. The main feature

in its structure is a semicircular ridge of mountains, open towards the south-east and south, and enclosing the Sandy Bay district. This is in fact the edge of a crater, submerged on the south-eastern—the windward—side, while outside its rim in the opposite direction volcanic deposits have gradually heaped up the land. In this ridge are the highest points in the island, the loftiest, Diana's Peak, rising to 2,704 feet. The largest extent of level ground is to be found towards the north-east, where are Deadwood and Longwood plains, over 1,700 feet above the sea. Elsewhere the surface of the land is a constant succession of hills and valleys, or rather an inclined plain broken by perpetual gullies.

Section III.

In his account of the Voyage of the Beagle, Darwin speaks of St. Helena as rising abruptly 'like a huge black castle from the ocean.' It is surrounded by high cliffs, intersected by steep and narrow ravines, and there are very few points at which it is possible to land. James Bay, an open roadstead, is on the lee side, in the north-west of the island; and the narrow triangular valley which here runs inland for a mile and a half is, and always has been, the only practicable entrance into St. Helena. Fronting the sea is the Castle, which is the seat of government, though the Governor's home is elsewhere, at Plantation House on the high ground in the interior; and behind the Castle, Jamestown, the only town in the island, stretches up the length of the valley. The ridge on the east is Rupert's Hill; that on the west is Ladder Hill, with barracks on its summit. On either side of the valley carefully engineered carriage roads lead up the mountain sides to the highlands beyond, and a ladder is carried for 600 feet straight up the face of Ladder Hill, whose steepness recalls an old saying of St. Helena that 'a man may choose whether he will break his heart in going up or his neck in coming down'[1]. From the top of these hills the ground still

James Bay and Jamestown.

---

[1] Quoted in Pinkerton's Collection of Voyages, vol. ii: A voyage to Borneo, by Captain D. Beeckman, 1714.

264 HISTORICAL GEOGRAPHY OF THE COLONIES.

SECTION III.

rises towards the south-east, culminating in the volcanic semicircle which has been already described.

Climate.   Though St. Helena lies well within the tropics, it has a climate which is almost proverbial for healthiness. Far removed from any other land, kept cool by the south-east trade wind which blows throughout the year, and by the cold waters of the South Atlantic current, its temperature is uniform, and on the higher levels is never, even at midsummer, oppressive to Europeans. The thermometer at Jamestown stands on an average throughout the year from 9 to 10 degrees higher than it does at Plantation or Longwood, where the mean annual temperature is stated to be about 61 degrees. The rainfall, which varies considerably from year to year, is very much larger on the highlands than at Jamestown. The mean annual fall in the upper parts of the island is about 30 inches; but on Diana's Peak and the neighbouring ridge the average must be higher, the mountain tops being usually enveloped in cloud and mist. St. Helena is a land of many springs, but, owing to the small size and the configuration of the island, it has no rivers.

Vegetation.   There are three zones of vegetation in St. Helena: the coast zone, which extends inland for a mile to a mile and a half, including the greater part of the surface of the island; the middle zone, which has a depth of three-quarters of a mile from the limit of the coast zone; and the central zone, which for a certain distance comprises either side of the high mountain ridge, being about three miles in length but little more than one in breadth. The island is reputed to have been at one time covered with green to a greater extent than at present, but the goats which were brought in by the early settlers destroyed the shrubs and young trees, and the soil in consequence disappeared. The coast zone is now hardly more than an expanse of bare rock, having, except in a few of the valleys, little or no vegetation beyond prickly pears. The middle zone, in which Plantation House, Longwood, and Deadwood are situated, includes most of the grass-land of the colony. Having a cooler temperature than that of the coast-line, and a less rocky soil, it has become the home of plants and trees imported from temperate climates, from the Cape, from England, from Australia, and from America; and here oaks, pines, and gorse have almost entirely supplanted the native vegetation, driving it back to the mountain ridge in the third or central zone, where, in a rich soil and a cool moist climate, the indigenous flora of St. Helena, including cabbage trees, ferns, and smaller plants, is mostly to be found.

It is estimated that less than one-third of the island is now suitable for cultivation, though the tendency of the trees is to spread down the valleys into the barren zone towards the sea. In the fruitful districts too, as at Deadwood and Longwood, much that was once forest is now open grass. The ebony trees have wholly disappeared; the gumwoods[1] are only found here and there; but there are still over sixty species of plants which are native to the island. The existence of this indigenous vegetation side by side with English trees, and the combination of the products of the tropics with those of temperate regions, has given to St. Helena a peculiar interest in the eyes of botanists, and has endowed it with a variety of trees, fruits, and vegetables, out of all proportion to its restricted area.

Farm and garden produce constitutes the whole wealth of St. Helena, and its entire trade consists, as it always has consisted, in supplying fresh provisions to the garrison and to the ships which call at the island. Live stock are pastured on the grassy uplands, potatoes are grown in large quantities, maize is cultivated but more for forage than for food, nearly every English fruit and vegetable flourishes except strawberries, and in the warmer spots bananas and other tropical or

---

[1] Conyza gummifera, not to be confounded with the Eucalyptus.

266 HISTORICAL GEOGRAPHY OF THE COLONIES.

SECTION III.

subtropical fruits grow well. Coffee, cinchona, and cotton cultivation has been or is being tried; fibre cultivation from aloes and flax has been contemplated; sericulture has lately been revived; but these products and industries have in no case passed beyond the experimental stage. Fish is very plentiful at the island, and, with imported rice, forms the staple food of the bulk of the inhabitants. It may be added that some of the islanders find employment on the American ships engaged in the South Sea Whale Fishery.

Finances. The financial outlook of St. Helena is a very gloomy one. The annual revenue, which in 1892 realised £7,691, is only about one-third of the amount received a quarter of a century ago. Customs duties are the chief item of revenue, and in 1892 contributed 56 per cent. of the total. Among other items may be mentioned licences, rents of Government property, and postal receipts. In the three years prior to 1869, the year in which the Suez canal was opened for traffic, the customs duties produced on an average nearly £16,000 per annum; in 1892 the receipts from this source were only £4,352. The colony has a small Debt, due to the mother country and not likely under existing circumstances to be repaid; and the expense of the mail service, of the main roads, and, in part, of the inland telegraphs, is borne by the Imperial government.

Trade Statistics. The imports were valued in 1891 at a little more than £27,000, nearly 62 per cent. of the total being credited to the United Kingdom. The value of the exports in the same year was slightly over £3,000; but two-thirds of this small amount consisted of specie, and St. Helena as a matter of fact has no export trade.

Currency. The currency of the island is British sterling, and only the gold, silver, and bronze coins of the United Kingdom are legal tender in St. Helena. No foreign coins are in circulation, except a very few American quarter-dollars which pass as shillings.

The population statistics tell the same tale as the revenue and trade returns. The resident population in 1891 showed a decrease of 14 per cent. on the numbers of 1881, and the 1881 returns were smaller than those of 1871 by nearly 23 per cent., the diminution being caused by emigration to the Cape. The civil population in 1891 numbered 3,877, of whom 2,000 lived in Jamestown. Including the garrison and shipping, the total was 4,116. *Section III. Population.*

The inhabitants of St. Helena are mostly coloured, and, as might be expected, of very mixed origin, Europeans, Africans, and East Indians having all contributed to the population. Possibly the East Indian element predominates, in consequence of the island having from time immemorial been so closely connected with the East.

The Church of England, which no longer receives aid from the Government, is the leading religious denomination, but the Baptists and the Salvation Army have each a considerable following. *Religion.*

Ample provision is made for elementary education, which is by law compulsory, but not free for those who can afford to pay fees. There are undenominational Government schools, and there are also charity schools connected with the Church of England. Three of these latter schools are maintained from the funds of the Hussey Charity [1], and one is supported by the Benevolent Society of the island. *Education.*

The central fact in the story of St. Helena is that it has always been connected with the Cape and the East Indies rather than with West Africa. In old days the Western side of Africa was within the sphere of West India companies, or of African companies whose dealings were with America. St. Helena, on the contrary, was first known to Europeans as a landmark and a halting-place for ships coming back by *General Summary.*

---

[1] Under the will of Miss Rebecca Hussey, the Hussey charity was founded in 1865, to provide for the education of emancipated slaves in Lagos and St. Helena.

SECTION III.

the Cape from the East. It was settled and definitely occupied by the British East India company, and in the possession of that company it remained till less than 60 years ago. Its population is in great measure of East Indian extraction, and the overflow is almost invariably to the Cape. It is only since the abolition of the slave trade that the island has had any connexion with West Africa, through having been for some years a depôt for Liberated Africans, and owing to the advantages which it offers as a sanatorium for the West African squadron. It is not far from West Africa, but has never been of it. It has rather been from first to last an isolated outpost of the East Indies.

The importance of St. Helena has now died away, and, even if the Suez canal were closed, the colony would never recover the trade which came to it perforce in the times of slow, small, sailing ships. No British dependency has passed more decisively from prosperity to decay; none has been so completely an index to the changes wrought by modern science; yet hardly any other has such great and such abiding scientific and historical interest. It has still 'the wonderfully healthy climate, neither too hot nor too cold; the beautiful scenery; the mixture of tropical and temperate vegetation; the rare indigenous plants; the clearly marked geological structure[1].' Here the old Roman punishment of 'deportatio in insulam' was carried out upon a man of Roman type, but who surpassed all Roman emperors in greatness; and, like Napoleon in exile, the little island to which he was banished, and in which he died, seems to have had its day and to be living mainly in the past.

[1] From the Blue Book Report of 1889, by R. L. Antrobus, acting Governor.

Books and Publications relating to St. Helena.

SECTION III.

BROOKE'S *History of St. Helena* (1808) is a standard history of the island down to the year 1806.

MELLISS' *St. Helena* (1875) is the fullest and most complete work on the island from a scientific as well as a historical point of view.

Extracts from the St. Helena Records, from 1673 to 1835, have been published in the island [1885], compiled by a late governor, Mr. H. R. JANISCH, and form a most valuable record of the colony under the rule of the East India company.

A good historical account of the island is given in Mr. DANVERS' *Report on the Records of the India Office* (1887), vol. i. part i. *The African Pilot*, part ii, should be consulted. For information respecting the Botany of the island, reference should be made to MELLISS' *St. Helena*, already mentioned; to Mr. HEMSLEY'S *Report on the Botany of the Atlantic Islands*, in the *Reports of the Challenger Expedition*, Botany, part i. pp. 49-122; and to a *Report upon the Present Position and Prospects of the Agricultural Resources of the Island of St. Helena*, by Mr. D. MORRIS, now Assistant Director of Kew Gardens (printed for the Colonial Office in 1884).

Tristan da Cunha and Gough Island.

Early notices of the islands.

THE three islands, which are collectively known by the name of Tristan da Cunha, were first sighted by the Portuguese admiral whose name they bear. He was in charge of a fleet bound for India in the year 1506, in company with Albuquerque, when 'they came in sight of land very extensive and very beautiful [1].' This land, which is certainly not extensive, and wild rather than beautiful, was the main island of the group. The islands were known to the Dutch in the seventeenth century, and the French landed on them in the year 1767.

Lying to the west of and in slightly lower latitudes than the Cape, the Tristan da Cunha group are nearly in the circuitous track of vessels sailing from Europe to the East.

---

[1] From the Commentaries of Afonso D'Alboquerque (Hakluyt Series, 1875, vol. i. p. 24).

270 HISTORICAL GEOGRAPHY OF THE COLONIES.

SECTION III.

Hence, even before the seventeenth century ended, it was contemplated by the East India company to establish a station there for outgoing ships, such as existed at St. Helena for the homeward bound[1]. No step of the kind, however, was actually taken; and down to the present century the islands were left without any permanent inhabitants. About 1810 three Americans settled at Tristan for a while, attracted by the sealing; and, when a British ship took possession of the island in 1816, there were two men upon it, one of whom had been there since 1810, and the other since 1814.

Their occupation by Great Britain, and origin of the present colony.

On August 14, 1816, Tristan da Cunha was annexed by H.M.S. 'Falmouth,' the object being, as in the case of Ascension, to prevent the islands from being made a base of operations for rescuing Napoleon from St. Helena. A small garrison was placed in the main island; but the occupation was very short, for in November 1817 the troops were again removed. When the removal took place, William Glass, a corporal of the Royal Artillery, obtained permission to remain behind with his wife and two children, and with two other single men. This was the beginning of the little community as it exists at the present day. Other settlers joined from time to time, chiefly from whaling ships; in 1852 the total number of men, women, and children amounted to 85; and in 1880, to 109. Since that date the population has decreased, and in March 1893 was only 52. The wives of the early settlers were coloured women from the Cape and St. Helena; and the majority of the present colonists are of mixed extraction, though to all intents and purposes English. They are of fine physique, strong, and healthy. They regard themselves as living directly under the charge of the British government, and they are members of the Church of England.

An organised system of law and government has never

---

[1] See Brooke's History of St. Helena, pp. 114-6, and Sir G. Staunton's Account of Lord Macartney's mission to China, vol. i. chap. vi.

been required, and the tiny commonwealth has been carried on under a patriarchal system. Glass was by common consent and force of character governor and head of the community, until he died in 1853. Subsequently Mr. Taylor, a clergyman sent out in 1851 for five years by the Society for the Propagation of the Gospel, was the chief man on the island, until in 1857 he left for the Cape, taking with him forty-five of the islanders. Since his departure Peter Green, one of the oldest residents, has held the first place.

Section III.

The two smaller islands, Inaccessible and Nightingale, have no inhabitants, though two Germans, brothers, lived for two years on Inaccessible island, before they were taken off by the Challenger.

The Tristan da Cunha group are in 37° South latitude and 12° West longitude. They are due south of Ascension, and south-west of St. Helena, from which latter island they are over 1,500 miles distant. They are about 2,000 miles due west of the Cape of Good Hope, and double that distance from Cape Horn. A line drawn between the two Capes would pass close to them. The main island, Tristan island, is the northernmost of the group; Inaccessible island is the westernmost, lying south-west from Tristan at a distance of about 23 miles; and Nightingale island is the southernmost, being 20 miles from Tristan a little to the west of south, and about 12 miles south-east of Inaccessible.

Geography of the group.

Like Ascension and St. Helena, the Tristan da Cunha islands are volcanic, but the cone in Tristan island rises to a much greater height than any mountain in Ascension or St. Helena, being 7,640 feet high[1], and usually capped with snow. Tristan island is nearly circular in shape, having this volcanic dome in the centre. The diameter

Tristan island.

---

[1] Mr. Moseley in his Notes by a Naturalist on the Challenger, gives the mountain a still greater height, 8,326 feet.

SECTION III. of the island is about 7 miles, and the area in square miles is 16. Its size therefore is about half that of Ascension. The island is surrounded by precipitous cliffs from 1,000 to 2,000 feet high, except in the north-west, where a strip of low grassy land, 2½ miles in length and half a mile in breadth, projects in front of the cliffs, about 100 feet above the level of the sea. At the northern end of this tongue of land, and nearly due north of the island, is the tiny settlement, consisting of about a dozen houses, and bearing the name of Edinburgh in honour of the Duke of Edinburgh's visit in 1867. The bay on which it stands is called Falmouth Bay after the ship which brought the British troops to the island in 1816.

Inaccessible. The shores of Inaccessible island, like those of Tristan, are very precipitous, but the highest point does not rise to more than 1,840 feet. The island is quadrilateral in shape, each side being about 2 miles long. The greatest length at any point is from 3 to 4 miles, and the area is about 4 square miles.

Nightingale. Nightingale island, which has two islets adjoining to it, is rather over a mile in length by three-quarters of a mile in breadth, and its area is not more than one square mile. Its shores are not so continuously precipitous as those of the other islands, and its highest point is only 1,100 feet.

Climate, Products, &c. Judged by the range of temperature, Tristan da Cunha has a mild climate, the average temperature in summer being 68°, and in winter 55°, occasionally falling to 40°. The climate, however, is very rainy and very windy, the prevailing winds being from the west. The strength of the gales may be gauged by the solidity of the walls of some of the buildings, which consist of enormous blocks of stone; and the uncertain weather, combined with the danger of the anchorage, makes communication with the land difficult and dangerous, though the landing is helped by a strong belt of seaweed. Whatever may be the drawbacks of the climate, however, it is beyond all question **exceedingly** healthy, **the islanders being** singularly free from ailments of all kinds.

There is only one kind of stunted native tree on the islands, and the vegetation consists principally of brushwood, fern, and long coarse grass. The matted tufts of grass, known as tussock, form, especially on the two smaller islands, an almost impenetrable jungle, amongst which innumerable penguins have formed their 'rookeries.' The settlers grow potatoes and other vegetables, with a few apples and peaches, and they have fowls and geese, cattle, and sheep, the sheep supplying them with wool for the island-made spinning-wheels. Flour, tea, sugar, and other articles are obtained by barter from the few whaling vessels which visit the islands in the course of the season or from Her Majesty's ships. There is abundance of fish and of sea-birds' eggs; and wild goats and rabbits were at one time to be found on Tristan island, but are now said to be extinct. A few years ago the loss at sea of most of the able-bodied men, and a plague of rats, threatened the islanders with starvation; but recent reports show that they are living in comparative comfort and content. They till their gardens and tend their live stock, they fish and pay occasional visits to the smaller islands in search of seals. They are visited by four or five whalers a year, and by an American sealing schooner which is commanded by a native islander; and one or other of the Queen's ships is periodically sent to enquire into their condition. Thus, though the younger and more enterprising members of the community generally emigrate to the Cape or take to a seafaring life, though any idea of making Tristan da Cunha a place of call belongs to the distant past, and though the seals are no longer plentiful as they once were, there seems to be no reason why the colony should entirely die out, or why Tristan da Cunha in the South Atlantic, like Pitcairn island in the Pacific, should not continue to be the home of a select few, contented to live under British

SECTION III.

SECTION III. protection in this remote island, and ready to give relief to and receive relief from such vessels as come to or are driven to their shores.

Gough Island.

Gough island or Diego Alvarez lies to the south of Tristan da Cunha in 40 degrees South latitude and 9 degrees West longitude. It was probably discovered by the Portuguese, but is now called after Captain Gough, the commander of an English ship who sighted the island in 1731. It is stated in the Admiralty Pilot to be about four miles in length, precipitous, and having a summit over 4,000 feet high. The island used to be visited by sealers.

For books, &c. relating to Tristan da Cunha see under Ascension. Various accounts have been given from time to time of the islands and the islanders; and, in 1887, a Blue Book on the subject was given to Parliament [c. 4959]. The Admiralty receive periodical reports from the commanders of H. M. ships who are sent to visit the islands.

INDEX

ABBEOKUTA, pp. 221, 223-4.
Abo, 235.
Abolition Act, 87, 91-94.
Aburi, 205, 212-3.
Accra, 12 *n.*, 49 *n.*, 67, 100, 105-6, 109 and *n.*, 117, 119-20, 129, 162, 203-7, 211-3.
Acropong, District and Mountains, 205, 209, 211.
Adamawa, 236.
Addah, 205, 209.
Addo, 219, 221 *n.*
Afflao, 198.
Agara Creek, 239.
Ahy Lagoon, 198.
Ajera River, 35, 220.
Akasa, 233.
Akim, 126, 133, 205-9.
Akus, The, 192.
Albreda, 102, 104-5, 110, 158.
Albuquerque, 45, 247, 253, 269.
Alfonso, King, 21-2.
Alfonso de Payva, 24.
Algeria, 144.
Algoa Bay, 23.
Allahi River, 159-60.
Ambas Bay, 153.
Amis des Noirs, Society of, 92.
Amoaful, 135.
Ancobra River, 204, 206.
Angola, 39, 48-50, 56, 100.
Annamaboe, 100, 117-8, 204.
Anne d'Arfet, 16.
Annobon, 21 and *n.*, 39.
Apollonia, 110, 122, 203-4.
Aquapim. *See* Acropong.
Arabia and Arabs, 12 *n.*, 13, 14 and *n.*, 18.

Arguin Bay and Island, 19, 21, 69, 77, 101 *n.*, 109.
Aron, 240.
Asaba, 233, 235.
Ascension, Island of, 4, 6, 188, 213, 247-51, 262.
Ashantee and the Ashantees, 106, 118-21, 130, 133 *n.*, 206, 208, 210, 213.
Ashantee War, 132-7.
Assiento contract, 84-5, 87, 106.
Assin District, 209.
Assinee, 103, 124, 150, 197-8, 203.
Axim, 65, 68, 98, 204, 209, 213.
Azores, The, 18, 43.

Badagry, 141, 218 and *n.*, 220, 222.
Bahamas, The, 174.
Bahia, 262.
Bance Island, 172-3.
Baptists, The, 267.
Barbados, 59, 75, 80, 81 and *n.*, 88, 98.
Barbary, 52, 109.
Barra, King of, 105, 158-9.
Barra Point, 159, 163.
Barraconda Rapid, 59, 160-2, 167-8.
Barruwa, 154, 229.
Barth, Dr., 142.
Basel mission, 209, 211-2.
Bassam, Grand, 197.
Basutoland, 4.
Bathurst, 59, 117, 123, 157-8, 160-5, 167, 188, 232.
Baxter, Richard, 92.
Bechuanaland Protectorate, 4.

Belem, 25.
Belgians, King of, 147.
Bende, 240.
Benguela, 262.
Benin, Conntry and River, 35, 52, 154, 217, 220-2, 226, 229, 231, 237-40, 242.
Benins, The, 217, 226.
Bennett's Point, 255.
Benue River, 34, 142, 153, 230, 232-6.
Berlin conference, 148, 152.
Bermudas, The, 59, 247.
Bethencourt, Jean de, 16.
Beyin, 204.
Bight of Benin, 127-8, 141, 237-8.
  „   Biafra, 238.
Bissos or Bissagos Islands, 102.
Blanco, Cape, 34, 69, 101.
Bojador, Cape, 19, 25 n., 34 and n.
Bonny, 238-40, 242.
Bonthe, 188.
Borgu, 230, 234 n.
Bornu, 141, 230, 234.
Bouré, 58, 190.
Brandenburghers, 66, 68 n., 69, 105, 132, 140 n., 145, 204.
Brass, 222, 230, 238-40, 242.
Brazil, 39, 44-52, 56, 61, 64-5, 79, 80, 226, 248, 251-2, 256.
Breda, Peace of, 99 and n.
Bremen mission, 212.
Bristol, 16, 87-8, 172.
British Bechuanaland, 4.
British Central Africa Protectorate, 4.
British Combo, 127, 158, 161, 165-7.
British East Africa Company, 4, 6, 146.
British North Borneo Company, 60.
British South Africa Company, 4, 6, 146.
Brue, André, 112.
Bunce, River, 179 n., 181.
Bussa, 141, 233, 236.

Cabo Corso. *See* Cape Coast Castle.
Cabot, 50-1.
Cabral, 46-7.
Cadamosto, 20 and n., 170.
Cajet, River, 35.

Calabar, 153-4, 238-42.
Calicut, 24, 26.
Cameroons. The, 31, 35, 150, 152, 197, 229, 237-8.
Cananore, 24.
Canary Islands, 11 and n., 15-6, 43, 60.
Cape, The, 2, 3, 17, 23-6, 39, 48, 64, 82, 101, 187, 248, 252, 262, 267, 271.
Cape Coast Castle, 64, 67-8, 96, 99, 100, 103-7, 117-20, 131, 135, 168, 188, 203-4, 209, 211-2, 222, 248.
Cape Colony, 4, 23.
Carthage and Carthaginians, 5, 10-12, 14, 25 n.
Cartier, Jacques, 60.
Casamanze, River, 162, 167.
Cavendish, Thomas, 171, 254.
'Ceded mile,' The, 157, 159, 161.
Cerda, Luis de la, 16.
Ceuta, 17.
Chad, Lake, 141, 154, 229, 233.
Chama, 204, 209.
Chancellor, 52.
Chapel Valley, 251, 253.
Charles I, 59.
  „   II, 32 n., 82, 97, 255.
  „   V, 78-9.
China and Chinese, 15, 105, 258.
Christian IV of Denmark, 67.
Christiansborg, 67-8, 126, 205.
Church Missionary Society, 194, 218, 234.
Church of England, 92, 166, 193, 212, 226, 267, 270.
Cintra, Pedro de, 21, 170.
Clapperton, 141-2.
Clarence Bay, 249.
Clarkson, 92.
Colbert, 100-1.
Coligny, 61.
Columbus, 18 and n., 26, 28.
Combo, King of, 157.
Commendah, 100, 106, 109, 131, 204.
Conception, 247.
Condorcet, 92.
Congo, The, 22-3, 35-6, 47-8, 113, 141, 147-8, 213, 262.
Congo Free State, 2, 147-8.

INDEX.

Cook, Captain, 247, 249.
Coomassie, 118, 133, 135-6, 204.
Corisco Island, 35.
Cormantine, 31, 58, 96, 99, 204.
Corrientes, Cape, 25 n.
Courlanders, 66.
Covilham, Pedro de, 24.
Crawford Island, 186.
Creek Town, 240.
Croboe District, 209.
Cromwell, 81-2.
Cross River, 238, 240.
Cuba, 130.
Cumming, 107.
Curaçoa, 68.
Cyprus, 5.
Cyrene, 12.

Dahomey, 35, 77, 128, 150, 218, 221, 226, 230.
Dakar, 101, 109, 162 and n., 187.
Dakka, River, 199.
Dampier, 247, 261.
Danes, The, 33, 38, 66-8, 91, 116-7, 126, 200, 205.
Danish East India Company, 67.
  „ Mount, 67.
  „ West India Company, 67.
Darwin, 248, 263.
Deadwood Plain, 263, 265.
De Kersaint, 107 and n.
Denham Waters, 221.
Denkera, 133-4, 206.
Denmark, King of, 93.
De Nova, 247, 251.
De Ruyter, Admiral, 98-9, 101, 132, 172, 255.
D'Estrées, Admiral, 101.
Diana's Peak, 263-4.
Diaz, Bartholomew, 23-4.
Diaz, Dinis, 19, 23 n.
Dieppe, 16, 61-2, 100.
Diogo Cam, 22.
Dioscorides, Island of, 11.
Dixcove, 100, 106, 117, 131, 204, 209.
Docemo, King, 128, 218.
Dolben, Sir W., 93.
Donga River, 236.
Drake, Sir Francis, 53, 171.
Dupuis, Mr., 118.
Dutch, The, 32-3, 38-9, 45-9, 54, 63-9, 75, 80-3, 88, 91, 96-110, 116-9, 126, 129-35, 139, 145, 204, 254-6, 269, &c.
Dutch East India Company, 65.
Dutch West India Company, 39, 63-5, 100, 110.

East India Company, 255-61, 268, 270.
Eboes, The, 192.
Ebute Metta, 222.
Edinburgh, 272.
Edrisi, 58.
Edward III, 16.
  „ IV, 51.
Egbas, The, 218, 221, 223, 226.
Egga, 236.
Eko and the Ekos, 221 and n., 226.
Elmina, 15, 22, 38-9, 47-8, 50, 53, 64-5, 68, 97-8, 100, 109, 131-6, 204, 208, 211-2.
Erichs, Bernard, 63.
Escobar, Pedro de, 22.
Escravos River, 238-9.
Exeter, 55.

Factory Island, 186.
Falaba, 183.
Falconbridge, Mr., 177.
Falmouth Bay, 272.
Fantees, The, 118-9, 132, 135, 200, 203, 211.
Ferdinand, King, 78.
Fernando Po, 21 and n., 39, 187, 213.
Festing, Colonel, 135.
Finch, William, 171.
Fish River, 23.
Florida, 61.
Fommana, 136.
Footah Jallon, 33, 150.
Forcados River, 154, 231, 233, 235, 238-9.
Foreign Jurisdiction Acts, 124, 240.
Formosa. *See* Fernando Po.
Formoso, Cape, 238.
Fort Fredericksborg, (Danish) 67.
Fort Fredericksburg, (Brandenburgher), 68-9.
Fort Hollandia. *See* Fort Fredericksburg.

278 INDEX.

Fort James, 31 n., 58 n., 98, 102–106, 109–10, 117, 159, 163, 167.
Fort Nassau, 65.
Fort Royal. *See* Fort Frederichsborg.
Fort St. Anthony, 65 and n.
Fort St. Francis, 101.
Fortunate Islands, 11 n., 16.
Fourah Bay, 194.
Frederick III, of Denmark, 67.
„ William, Elector, 68.
Free Church Methodists, 193.
Freetown, 163, 172, 176–8, 181, 186–9, 192, 194–5, 212, 222, 232.
French, The, 15, 34–6, 38–9, 52–3, 55, 57, 60–4, 80–5, 91, 100–10, 124, 137–40, 144–5, 148–55, 158–60, 168, 177–8, 183–4, 194, 198, 220, 269, &c.
French Revolution, 91, 93.
French West African Company, 62, 102, 112.
French West India Company, 39, 62, 100, 102.
Fulahs, The, 166.

Gabun River, 35, 36 n.
Gades, City of, 11.
Galam, 108.
Gambia, The, 3, 6, 12, 20–1, 30–1, 33–7, 48, 55–60, 62, 90, 96, 98, 101, 106, 112–3, 117, 123, 137, 141, 157–69, 232, 243, 245.
Gana Gana, 233.
Gandu, 234, 236.
Georgetown, 247, 249–50.
Germans, The, 140–5, 150–4, 198, 210, 230, &c.
Gibraltar, 5, 10, 13.
Glass, William, 270–1.
Glover, Sir John, 135–6.
Godwin, 91.
Gold, 19, 21, 24, 32, 37, 40, 44, 53, 58, 71, 136, 164, 190, 207–8.
Gold Coast, 3, 6, 21–2, 30, 33, 35–7, 126, 197–216, 232, 241, &c.
Gold Coast Constabulary, 203.
Gold Coast Protectorate, 121, 125–7 n., 200–2.

Gomez, 21–2.
Goree, 63, 98, 101, 104–5, 108, 110, 117, 163.
Gough Island, 274.
Gourgues, Domenic de, 61.
Gouritz River, 23.
Grain Coast, 21, 54, 197.
Grand Popo, 35.
Granvilletown, 177.
Green, Peter, 271.
Green Mountain, 247, 249–50.
Gregory, Mr. T., 57.
Grenville, Lord, 93–4.
'Gromettoes,' 103 and n., 180.
Ground nuts, 164–5, 167, 189, 209, 243–6.
Guiana, 81, 98.
Guinea, 18, 31–9, 47–51, 61–4, 98, 142, 144, 150, 251, &c.
Guinea, coin, 32 and n.
Guinea 'grains,' or pepper, 53 and n., 54, 237.
Guinea, Gulf of, 6, 9, 21, 31, 32–6, 62, 96, 128, 141, 197, &c.
Gums, 107, 164, 190–1, 209, 234, 265.
Gustavus Adolphus, 66.

Halley, 261.
Hamburg, 241, 243.
Hanno, 11, 12 n.
Hanway, Jonas, 175.
Harmattan wind, The, 163, 189, 207.
Havre, 241.
Hawkins, Sir **John**, 51, 54, 59, 75, 78, 170.
Hawkins, Mr. William, 51, 171.
Henry VIII, 51.
Herodotus, 10, 12 and n.
Hewett, Consul, 237.
Hispaniola, 54, 71, 78, 80.
Hoare, Samuel, 175.
Holmes, Captain, 98, 103.
Horn, Cape, 271.
Houssas, 136, 203, 211–2, 225–6.
Hudson, 64.
„ Bay Company, 146.
„ River, 98–9.
Huguenots, The, 60–1, 260.
Hussey Charity, 267 and n.

INDEX.

Ibi, 236.
Iboes, The, 234.
Idda, 233, 235.
Iddo, Island of, 217, 221 *n.*
Idu, 230.
Idzoes, The, 234.
Igaras, The, 234.
Igbessa, 221 *n.*
Ilaro, 221 *n.*
'Ile aux Anglois,' 103.
Inaccessible Island, 271-2.
India, 15, 18, 24, 26, 44.
India Rubber, 164, 167, 190, 209, 234, 240, 243.
Isles de Los, 181, 183, 186, 192.
Isola de la Legname, 11 *n.*
Italy, 140.
Ivory Coast, 21, 197.

Ja Ja, King, 238.
Jamaica, 80-1, 84, 179.
James Bay, 263.
  ,, I, 57.
  ,, II, 82, 255.
Jamestown, 251, 255, 260, 263-4, 267.
James Valley, 253, 256.
Jebus, The, 221, 223-4, 226.
Jenkins, Governor, 260, 261 *n.*
Jersey, 161, 248, 262.
Jesuits, 49.
Jews, 49.
Joala, 56 and *n.*
Jobson, Captain R., 59.
John I, of Portugal, 17.
  ,, II, 22, 24-5, 50.
  ,, of Gaunt, 17.
Jolas, 167.
Jolofs, 167.
Juba, 11 *n.*

Kalahari Desert, 32.
Kassan, 58.
Katsena, 236.
Keeling, Captain, 171.
Kendall, Captain, 254.
Keppel, Commodore, 107.
Kola nuts, 189-91, 209, 212, 240.
Kosoko, 218.
Kotonou, 35.
Kroomen, The, 192, 211, 226, 250.
Kwa Ibo, 238-42.

Ladder Hill, 255, 263.
Lafayette, 92.
Lagos, 3, 6, 30-1, 33, 35, 37, 127-129, 135, 137, 153, 160, 188, 212, 217-30, 239, 241.
Lagos [Portuguese town], 18-9.
Laing, 142.
Laird, Macgregor, 142.
La Mina. *See* Gold Coast.
Lancaster, Captain, 254-5.
Lander, 141-2.
Lanzarote, 16, 19.
Las Casas, 74.
Leckie, 218, 220, 222.
Leicester Mountain, 187.
Leo Africanus, 58.
Leo X, 77.
Liberated Africans, 166, 188, 192, 268.
Liberia, 21, 34-5, 54, 150, 182-3, 185, 197, 250.
Libya, 10.
Linschoten, 247, 249, 253-4.
Lisbon, 25, 46, 79.
Liverpool, 87-8, 93, 222.
Livingstone, 140.
Loanda. *See* San Paulo.
Lok, Captain, 53.
London, 55, 87, 88, 93.
Longwood Plain, 263-5.
Lopez, Fernando, 253.
Louis XIV, 100.
Lowe, Sir Hudson, 259, 261.
Lukoja, 233, 235-6.

Macaulay, Zachary, 178.
McCarthy, Sir C., 119, 157.
McCarthy's Island, 123, 129, 157, 159, 161-5.
MacDonald, Sir Claude, 242.
Machin, Robert, 16, 17 *n.*
Maclean, Governor, 121-3, 125, 129, 200.
Madagascar, 24, 25 *n.*, 257.
Madden, Dr., 122.
Madeira, 11 and *n.*, 16, 18.
Madrabumba, 57.
Mahé, 6.
Mahela Creek, 183.
Mahin, 219.
Malay Peninsula, 201.
Malta, 5.

Mandingoes, The, 167, 192.
Manna River, 182-3, 185.
Mansfield, Lord, 92, 174.
Manuel, King, 25.
Marco Polo, 15.
Maroons, The, 179 and *n.*, 180.
Mashonaland, 6.
Matacong, Island of, 183.
Mauritius, 4, 6, 252.
Médine, 112.
Melinde, 26.
Mellicourie River, 152, 183.
Mendis, The, 192.
Menendez, 61.
Mesurado, Cape, 21.
Middleton River, 238.
Miquelon, Island of, 108.
Mohammedans, 13, 72, 73, 167, 169, 191, 193, 212, 226, 234.
Mombasa, 6, 26.
Monk, General, 98.
Montesquieu, 92.
Moors, The, 17, 19, 24, 72, 77.
Morocco, 5, 17-8, 34, 58.
Mouree, 65, 96, 105.
Mozambique, 26, 48, 50.
Munden, Captain, 256.
Mungo Park, 113, 115, 140-1.

Naimbana, King, 175, 176 *n.*
Nantes, Edict of, 260.
Napoleon, 248, 258, 260, 261 and *n.*, 268, 270.
Nassau, Count Maurice of, 65.
Nassau Fort, 98, 101.
Natal, 4, 26.
National African Company, 142, 150, 152, 154, 229. *See* also Royal Niger Company.
Navigation Acts, 82.
Negro, Cape, 32.
Negro Slavery, in St. Helena, 257-260.
Netherlands. *See* Dutch.
New Amsterdam, 64.
New Calabar. *See* Calabar.
Newfoundland, 50, 51, 60, 89, 108-9.
Newhaven, 61.
New Netherlands, 98-9.
Newtown, 198.
New York, 64, 99, 247.

Niger, The, 12, 33-4, 36-7, 44, 58, 112-3, 128, 140-2, 150-5, 168, 183, 197, 229-42, &c.
Niger Coast Protectorate, 3, 30-1, 154, 229-31, 237-42.
Niger Protectorates, 6, 35, 152-4, 220, 229-42.
Nightingale Island, 272.
Nile, The, 9, 10, 142.
Nimeguen, Peace of, 101.
Nivaria, 11 *n.*
Non, Cape, 18.
North American Indians, 62, 71.
Nougoua, 198.
Nova Scotia, 174, 177, 179.
Nun River, 154, 230-1, 235, 238-9.
Nunez River, 57, 141.
Nuño Tristam, 20.
Nupeh, Province of, 235.
Nyassaland, 6.

Odi, 226.
Ogowe River, 35.
Ogun River, 223.
Oguta, Lake, 239.
Oil Rivers, 128, 141, 150, 152, 237-42.
Okeodan, 219.
Old Calabar. *See* Calabar.
Onitsha, 235.
Ophir, 11.
Opobo, 238-42.
Orange River, 6, 23.
Ordasa, 135.
Ouwere. *See* Wari.
Oveiro. *See* Wari.
Oyo, 221.
Oyster Creek, 158, 165.

Palm oil, 37, 40, 190, 209-10, 224-5, 234, 237, 240, 242-5.
Palma, 218, 220, 222.
Palmas, Cape, 21, 54, 197, 211.
Paris, Peace of, 109.
Pemba, 4.
Perestrello, 18 and *n.*
Perim, 5, 11.
Pernambuco, 248.
Philip II, 46, 55, 139.
Philippa, 17.
Philippine Islands, 39, 46.
Phœnicians, The, 10-1, 14, 25 *n*

INDEX.

Pillars of Hercules, 11, 13, 17.
Pinteado, 52, **237**.
Pitcairn Island, 273.
Plantation House, 263-4.
Plate, River, 85 *n*.
Plymouth, 52, **175**, **212**.
Poera, 219-21, **226**.
Podor, 108.
Poirier, Governor, **260**.
Pongas River, 151.
Popos, The, 226.
Port Louis, 6.
Portendik, 109-10.
Porto d'Ally, 56.
Porto Novo, 35, 150, 218-21.
Porto Santo, 18 and *n*.
Portugal, Prince Henry of, 12, 16-21, 25-9, 33, 35, 74, 77-8.
Portugal and Portuguese, 15-29, 31-3, **35**, 38-9, 42-69, 74, 78-81, **104-5**, 117, 132, 139, 144, 252 and *n*., &c.
Prah, The, 119, **135-6**, 204, 206.
Prahsue, 204, **206**, **213**.
Pram Pram, 205.
Prester John, 22 and *n*., 23.
Prosperous Bay, 256.
Prussia, Duchy of, 68.
Pungwe River, 6.

Quahoo, 205, **208**.
Quakers, 92, 107.
Queen Elizabeth, 54-5, **57**.
Quiah, **127**, 182, 186, 192.
Quittah, **67**, **205**, **209**, **213**.

Rainolds, Richard, 56, 61.
Ramos River, 238.
Raymond, Captain, **254**.
Red Sea, The, 2, 24, 44.
Ribago, 233, 236.
Ribault, 61.
Rich, Sir R., **57**.
Richelieu, 62.
Rio del Rey, 35, **153-4**, **229-31**, 238.
Rio Grande, 20, 35, 102, 112.
Rio Janeiro, 61, 248, 262.
Rio Nunez, 142, 183.
Roberts, Governor, **260**.
Rochelle, 16.
Rokell River, 187.

Roman Catholics, 151, 166, 193, 212, 226.
Romans, The, **12**.
Rouen, 62, 100.
Roxo or Rouge, Cape, 35, 109.
Royal Adventurers, Company of, 82, 96-9.
Royal African Company, 82-3, 87, 99, 103, 106.
Royal Niger Company, 3, 30-1, 146-7, 154, 220, **229-37**.
Ryswick, Peace of, 104.

Sable Island, 252 *n*.
Sagres, 18.
Sahara, The, **9**, **12**, 19, **32**, 36 *n*., 144, 189.
St. Catherine, Cape, 22.
St. Eustatius, 68.
St. George's Bay, **176** and *n*.
St. Helena, 4, 6, **247-9**, **251-69**, 270-1.
St. John, River, 109.
St. Kitts, 50, 59, 62.
St. Louis, 104, 107-12, **162**.
St. Mary, Cape, 158-9.
St. Mary's Island, 117, 157, 161, 163.
St. Pierre, Island of, 108.
St. Thomas, Island of, 21 and *n*.
,, ,, [West Indies], 67-8.
Salaga, 212.
Sallee, 82.
Saltpond, 205, **209**.
Salvation Army, 267.
Sama, 22.
Sandy Bay District, 263.
San Jorge de Mina. *See* Elmina.
San Juan, Cape, 35.
San Paulo de Loanda, 48-9 and *n*., 248.
San Pedro River. *See* Allahi River.
Santa Cruz, **23**.
Santarem, Joao de, **22**.
Saracens, 13, 72.
Sarmi Creek, **159**.
Say, 154, **229**.
Scarcies Rivers, 152, 182-3.
Secondee, **100**, 106, 204, 209.
Sego, 190.
Senegal, The, **12**, 18-20, 31-4, 56 and *n*., 61, 62 and *n*., 101-9, 117, 125, 149, 157, 162, 167-8.

INDEX

Senegambia, 39, 56, 61-2, 102-4, 141, 144, 149-51, 168.
Sestos, River of, 51-2, 54.
Seven Years' War, 106-7.
Seychelles Islands, 4, 6.
Sharp, Granville, 92, 174-7.
Sherbro, 127, 181-2, 186, 188, 192, 221, 232.
Sherbros, The, 192.
Shirley, Captain, 109 *n*.
Sierra Leone, 3, 6, 12, 21, 30-7, 54, 57, 93, 100, 110, 112-20, 129-30, 150-2, 170-96, 232, 241, 248; meaning of name, 21, 170.
Slave Coast, 21, 100, 150, 197.
Slave Trade and Traders, 19, 41-2, 47, 49, 54, 59, 66, 70-95, 218, &c.
Smeathman, Dr., 175
Socotra, 4 *n*., 11 and *n*.
Sofala, 24, 48.
Sokoto, 141, 154, 230, 234, 236.
Somali Protectorate, 5.
Sombrero River, 238.
Somerset, James, 174.
Soosoos, The, 192.
Sordwana Point, 6.
Spain and Spaniards, 13, 16, 27, 34-9, 42-50, 54-6, 61, 74-5, 80, 85.
Spanish America, 78, 84-5.
Stanley, 140, 147.
Straits Settlements, 201.
Sudan, 9, 19, 33, 142.
Suez Canal, 3, 26, 261, 268.
Sugar Loaf Mountain, 187.
Sulimania, 183.
Surinam, 99.
Swanley Valley, 255.
Swedes, The, 66-7.
Sweet River, 131, 204.

Tamara Island, 186.
Tangier, 5.
Tanoe. *See* Tendo.
Tantumquerry, 106.
Tarquah, 208.
Tasso Island, 172.
Taubman-Goldie, Sir G., 231.
Taunton, 57.
Tenda, 59.
Tendo River, 198, 206.

Teraba River, 236.
Thompson, G., 58.
  ,, Captain, 175.
Thornton, Messrs., 175.
Three Points, Cape, 68, 204.
Timbo, 178.
Timbuctoo, 34, 58-9, 142.
Timmanehs, The, 192.
Tobago, 66, 101.
Togoland, 35, 150, 153, 198, 230.
Tom, King, 175.
Towrson, W., 53.
Tristan da Cunha, 4, 269-74.
Tuckey, Lieutenant, 141.
Tumbo Point, 186.

Utrecht, Peace of, 84-5 *n*., 91, 104, 106.

Varthema, Ludovico di, 24.
Vasco da Gama, 25-6, 28, 45, 47.
Verde, Cape, 19, 20 *n*., 31-2, 34, 48, 63, 98, 101, 103, 109.
Vermandois. *See* Fort St. Francis.
Versailles, Peace of, 109-10, 159.
Victoria, 153.
Victoriaborg, 205.
Villegagnon, 61.
Virginia, 59, 75, 92.
Vleesch Bay, 23.
Volta River and District, 35, 67, 126, 197-200, 205-6, 209.
Voltas, Cape, 23.

Walfisch Bay, 6.
Warburton, Bishop, 92.
Wari, 238-9, 242.
Wassaw, 204, 208.
Waterloo, Settlement of, 188.
Wesleyans, 92, 122, 151, 166, 193, 211, 226.
West Africa Settlements, 118-9, 124, 160, &c.
West Coast of Africa, 33, &c.
West Indies, 39, 50, 64, 94, &c.
Western Sudan, 141, 144, 149, 168, 234.
Westminister, Peace of, 99 *n*.
Whydah, 100, 106, 117, 122, 171, 218.
Wilberforce, 92-3, 113.
William III, 83.

Willoughby, 52.
Windham, Captain, 52, 237.
Winnebah, 100, 106, 118, 122, 205.
Wolseley, Sir G., 135-6.

Ximenes, Cardinal, 77.

Yarbutenda, 160, 162.
Yarrow, Vale of, 113.

Yellaboi Island, 183.
Yola, 153, 230, 236.
York, Duke of, 82, 255.
Yoruba and the Yorubas, 217-8, 221, 224, 226, 230.

Zambesi River, 6, 142.
Zanzibar, 4 and *n.*, 6.
Zululand, 4.

THE END

Clarendon Press, Oxford.

I. LITERATURE AND PHILOLOGY.

SECTION I.
DICTIONARIES, GRAMMARS, &c.

ANGLO-SAXON. An Anglo-Saxon Dictionary, based on the MS. Collections of the late JOSEPH BOSWORTH, D.D., Professor of Anglo-Saxon, Oxford. Edited and enlarged by Prof. T. N. TOLLER, M.A. Parts I–III. A—SAR. 4to, 15s. each. Part IV. Sect. I. SÁR–SWÍÐRIAN. 8s. 6d.

ARABIC. A Practical Arabic Grammar. Compiled by A. O. GREEN, Brigade Major, Royal Engineers.
    Part I. *Third Edition. Enlarged.* Crown 8vo, 7s. 6d.
    Part II. *Third Edition, Enlarged and Revised.* 10s. 6d.

BENGALI. Grammar of the Bengali Language; Literary and Colloquial. By JOHN BEAMES. Crown 8vo, cloth, 7s. 6d.

CELTIC. Ancient Cornish Drama. Edited and translated by E. NORRIS, with a Sketch of Cornish Grammar, an Ancient Cornish Vocabulary, &c. 2 vols. 8vo, 1l. 1s.
    The Sketch of Cornish Grammar separately, stitched, 2s. 6d.

CHINESE. A Handbook of the Chinese Language. By JAMES SUMMERS. 8vo, half-bound, 1l. 8s.

ENGLISH. A New English Dictionary, on Historical Principles: founded mainly on the materials collected by the Philological Society. Vol. I. A and B, and Vol. II. C. Imperial 4to, half-morocco, *each* 2l. 12s. 6d.
    Part VIII. Section I. CROUCHMAS—CZECH. End of Vol. II, 4s.
  Edited by JAMES A. H. MURRAY, LL.D.
    Vol. III. D and E.
        D. Edited by Dr. MURRAY. [*In the Press.*]
        E—EVERY. Edited by H. BRADLEY, M.A. 12s. 6d. [*Published.*]

Oxford: Clarendon Press. London: HENRY FROWDE, Amen Corner, E.C.

I. Literature and Philology.

ENGLISH (*continued*).

ENGLISH. An Etymological Dictionary of the English Language. By W. W. SKEAT, Litt.D. *Second Edition.* 4to, 2*l.* 4*s.*

—— A Concise Etymological Dictionary of the English Language. By W. W. SKEAT, Litt.D. *Fourth Edition.* Crown 8vo, 5*s.* 6*d.*

—— A Concise Dictionary of Middle English, from A.D. 1150 to 1580. By A. L. MAYHEW, M.A., and W. W. SKEAT, Litt. D. Crown 8vo, half-roan, 7*s.* 6*d.*

—— A Middle English Dictionary. By FRANCIS HENRY STRATMANN. *A New Edition*, Re-arranged, Revised, and Enlarged by HENRY BRADLEY, M.A. Small 4to, 1*l.* 11*s.* 6*d.*

—— A Primer of Spoken English. By HENRY SWEET, M.A., Ph.D. Extra fcap. 8vo, 3*s.* 6*d.*

—— A New English Grammar, Logical and Historical. By HENRY SWEET, M.A., Ph.D. Part I. Introduction, Phonology, and Accidence. Crown 8vo, 10*s.* 6*d.*

—— A Short Historical English Grammar. By HENRY SWEET, M.A., Ph.D. Extra fcap. 8vo, 4*s.* 6*d.*

—— A Primer of Historical English Grammar. Extra fcap. 8vo, 2*s.*

—— A Primer of Phonetics. By HENRY SWEET, M.A., Ph.D. Extra fcap. 8vo, 3*s.* 6*d.*

—— Elementarbuch des Gesprochenen Englisch. Grammatik. Texte und Glossar. By HENRY SWEET, M.A., Ph.D. *Third Edition.* Extra fcap. 8vo, stiff covers, 2*s.* 6*d.*

FINNISH. A Finnish Grammar. By C. N. E. ELIOT, M.A. Crown 8vo, roan, 10*s.* 6*d.*

GOTHIC. A Primer of the Gothic Language; with Grammar, Notes, and Glossary. By JOSEPH WRIGHT, Ph.D. Extra fcap. 8vo, cloth, 4*s.* 6*d.*

GREEK. A Greek-English Lexicon, by H. G. LIDDELL, D.D., and ROBERT SCOTT, D.D. *Seventh Edition, Revised and Augmented throughout.* 4to, 1*l.* 16*s.*

—— An Intermediate Greek-English Lexicon, founded upon the Seventh Edition of the above. Small 4to, 12*s.* 6*d.*

—— A Greek-English Lexicon, abridged from Liddell and Scott's 4to edition, chiefly for the use of Schools. *Twenty-fifth Edition.* Square 12mo, 7*s.* 6*d.*

Dictionaries, Grammars, &c.

GREEK. A Concordance to the Septuagint and the other Greek Versions of the **Old Testament** (including the **Apocryphal Books**). By the late EDWIN HATCH, M.A., and HENRY REDPATH, M.A. Parts I and II. A–ΈΠΑΙΝΟΣ. Imperial 4to, *each* 21s. Part III. *In the Press.*

☞ *To be completed in Six Parts,* at 1l. 1s. *per Part; or to Subscribers at* 4l. 4s. *for the whole work.*

—— A copious Greek-English Vocabulary, compiled from the best authorities. 24mo, 3s.

—— Etymologicon Magnum. Ad Codd. mss. recensuit et notis variorum instruxit T. GAISFORD, S.T.P. 1848. fol. 1l. 12s.

—— Suidae **Lexicon.** Ad Codd. mss. recensuit T. GAISFORD, S.T.P. Tomi III. 1834. fol. 2l. 2s.

HEBREW. A Hebrew and English Lexicon of the Old Testament, with an Appendix containing the Biblical Aramaic, based on the Thesaurus and Lexicon of GESENIUS, by FRANCIS BROWN, D.D., S. R. DRIVER, D.D., and C. A. BRIGGS, D.D. Parts I and II. Small 4to, 2s. 6d. *each.*

—— The Book of Hebrew Roots, by ABU 'L-WALÎD MARWÂN IBN JANÂH, otherwise called RABBÎ YÔNÂH. Now first edited, with an Appendix, by AD. NEUBAUER. 4to, 2l. 7s. 6d.

—— A Treatise on the use of the Tenses in Hebrew. By S. R. DRIVER, D.D. *Third Edition.* Crown 8vo, 7s. 6d.

ICELANDIC. An Icelandic-English Dictionary, based on the MS. collections of the late RICHARD CLEASBY. Enlarged and completed by G. VIGFÚSSON, M.A. 4to, 3l. 7s.

—— A List of English Words the Etymology of which is illustrated by comparison with Icelandic. Prepared in the form of an Appendix to the above. By W. W. SKEAT, Litt.D. Stitched, 2s.

—— An Icelandic Primer, with Grammar, Notes, and Glossary. By HENRY SWEET, M.A., Ph.D. Extra fcap. 8vo, 3s. 6d.

——An Icelandic Prose Reader, with Notes, Grammar, and Glossary, by Dr. GUÐBRAND VIGFÚSSON and F. YORK POWELL, M.A. Extra fcap. 8vo, 10s. 6d.

LATIN. A Latin Dictionary, founded on Andrews' edition of Freund's **Latin** Dictionary, revised, enlarged, and **in great part** rewritten by CHARLTON T. LEWIS, Ph.D., and CHARLES SHORT, LL.D. 4to, 1l. 5s.

—— A School Latin Dictionary. By CHARLTON T. LEWIS, Ph.D. Small 4to, 18s.

—— An Elementary Latin Dictionary. By CHARLTON T. LEWIS, Ph.D. Square 8vo, 7s. 6d.

I. Literature and Philology.

LATIN. Scheller's Dictionary of the Latin Language, revised and translated into English by J. E. RIDDLE, M.A. 1835. fol. 1*l.* 1*s.*

—— Contributions to Latin Lexicography. By HENRY NETTLESHIP, M.A. 8vo, 21*s.*

MELANESIAN. The Melanesian Languages. By ROBERT H. CODRINGTON, D.D., of the Melanesian Mission. 8vo, 18*s.*

RUSSIAN. A Grammar of the Russian Language. By W. R. MORFILL, M.A. Crown 8vo, 6*s.*

SANSKRIT. A Practical Grammar of the Sanskrit Language, arranged with reference to the Classical Languages of Europe, for the use of English Students, by Sir M. MONIER-WILLIAMS, D.C.L. *Fourth Edition.* 8vo, 15*s.*

—— A Sanskrit-English Dictionary, Etymologically and Philologically arranged, with special reference to Greek, Latin, German, Anglo-Saxon, English, and other cognate Indo-European Languages. By Sir M. MONIER-WILLIAMS, D.C.L. 4to, 4*l.* 14*s.* 6*d.*

—— Nalopákhyánam. Story of Nala, an Episode of the Mahá-Bhárata: the Sanskrit text, with a copious Vocabulary, and an improved version of Dean MILMAN'S Translation, by Sir M. MONIER-WILLIAMS, D.C.L. *Second Edition, Revised and Improved.* 8vo, 15*s.*

—— Sakuntalá. A Sanskrit Drama, in Seven Acts. Edited by Sir M. MONIER-WILLIAMS, D.C.L. *Second Edition.* 8vo, 21*s.*

SYRIAC. Thesaurus Syriacus: collegerunt Quatremère, Bernstein, Lorsbach, Arnoldi, Agrell, Field, Roediger: edidit R. PAYNE SMITH, S.T.P. Vol. I, containing Fasc. I–V, sm. fol. 5*l.* 5*s.*

Fasc. VI, 1*l.* 1*s.*; VII, 1*l.* 11*s.* 6*d.*; VIII, 1*l.* 16*s.*; IX, 1*l.* 5*s.*

TAMIL. First Lessons in Tamil. By G. U. POPE, D.D. *Fifth Edition.* Crown 8vo, 7*s.* 6*d.*

BIBLIOGRAPHICAL DICTIONARIES.

Cotton's Typographical Gazetteer. 1831. 8vo, 12*s.* 6*d.*

—— Typographical Gazetteer. Second Series. 1866. 8vo, 12*s.* 6*d.*

Dowling (J. G.). Notitia Scriptorum SS. Patrum aliorumque vet. Eccles. Mon. quae in Collectionibus Anecdotorum post annum Christi MDCC. in lucem editis continentur. 8vo, 4*s.* 6*d.*

Ebert's Bibliographical Dictionary, translated from the German. 4 vols. 1837. 8vo, 1*l.* 10*s.*

SECTION II.

ANGLO-SAXON AND ENGLISH.

HELPS TO THE STUDY OF THE LANGUAGE AND LITERATURE.

A NEW ENGLISH DICTIONARY on Historical Principles, founded mainly on the materials collected by the Philological Society. Vol. I. A and B, and Vol. II. C. Imperial 4to, half-morocco, *each* 2*l.* 12*s.* 6*d.*

    Part VIII. Section I. CROUCHMAS—CZECH. End of Vol. II, 4*s.*

Edited by JAMES A. H. MURRAY, LL.D.

    Vol. III. D and E.

        D. Edited by Dr. MURRAY. [*In the Press.*]

        E—EVERY. Edited by H. BRADLEY, M.A. 12*s.* 6*d.* [*Published.*]

Bosworth and **Toller.** An Anglo-Saxon Dictionary, based on the MS. collections of the late JOSEPH BOSWORTH, D.D. Edited and enlarged by Prof. T. N. TOLLER, M.A. Parts I–III. A—SAR. 4to, stiff covers, 15*s.* each. Part IV. Sect. I. SÁR–SWÍÐRIAN. 8*s.* 6*d.*

Earle. A Book for the Beginner in Anglo-Saxon. By JOHN EARLE, M.A. *Third Edition.* Extra fcap. 8vo, 2*s.* 6*d.*

—— The Philology of the English Tongue. *Fifth Edition*, *Newly Revised.* Extra fcap. 8vo, 8*s.* 6*d.*

Mayhew. Synopsis of Old English Phonology. By A. L. MAYHEW, M.A. Extra fcap. 8vo, bevelled boards, 8*s.* 6*d.*

Mayhew and **Skeat.** A Concise Dictionary of Middle English, from A.D. 1150 to 1580. By A. L. MAYHEW, M.A., and W. W. SKEAT, Litt.D. Crown 8vo, half-roan, 7*s.* 6*d.*

I. Literature and Philology.

Skeat. An Etymological Dictionary of the English Language, arranged on an Historical Basis. By W. W. SKEAT, Litt.D. *Second Edition.* 4to, 2*l*. 4*s*.

    A Supplement to the First Edition of the above. 4to, 2*s*. 6*d*.

—— A Concise Etymological Dictionary of the English Language. *Fourth Edition.* Crown 8vo, 5*s*. 6*d*.

—— Principles of English Etymology. First Series. *The Native Element. Second Edition.* Crown 8vo, 10*s*. 6*d*.

—— Principles of English Etymology. Second Series. *The Foreign Element.* Crown 8vo, 10*s*. 6*d*.

—— A Primer of English Etymology. Extra fcap. 8vo, stiff covers, 1*s*. 6*d*.

—— Twelve Facsimiles of Old English Manuscripts, with Transcriptions and an Introduction. 4to, paper covers, 7*s*. 6*d*.

Stratmann. A Middle English Dictionary, containing Words used by English Writers from the Twelfth to the Fifteenth Century. By FRANCIS HENRY STRATMANN. *A New Edition*, Re-arranged, Revised, and Enlarged by HENRY BRADLEY, M.A. Small 4to, half-morocco, 1*l*. 11*s*. 6*d*.

Sweet. A New English Grammar, Logical and Historical. Part I. Introduction, Phonology, and Accidence. Crown 8vo, 10*s*. 6*d*.

—— A Short Historical English Grammar. Extra fcap. 8vo. 4*s*. 6*d*.

—— A Primer of Historical English Grammar. Extra fcap. 8vo, 2*s*.

—— History of English Sounds from the Earliest Period. With full Word-Lists. 8vo, 14*s*.

—— An Anglo-Saxon Primer, with Grammar, Notes, and Glossary. *Seventh Edition.* Extra fcap. 8vo, 2*s*. 6*d*.

—— An Anglo-Saxon Reader. In Prose and Verse. With Grammatical Introduction, Notes, and Glossary. *Sixth Edition, Revised and Enlarged.* Extra fcap. 8vo, 8*s*. 6*d*.

—— A Second Anglo-Saxon Reader. Extra fcap. 8vo, 4*s*. 6*d*.

—— Old English Reading Primers:

    I. Selected Homilies of Ælfric. Stiff covers, 1*s*. 6*d*.
    II. Extracts from Alfred's Orosius. *Second Edition*, 2*s*.

Sweet (*continued*). **First Middle English Primer**, with Grammar and Glossary. *Second Edition.* Extra fcap, 8vo, 2s.

—— Second Middle English **Primer. Extracts from Chaucer**, with Grammar and Glossary. *Second Edition.* Extra fcap. 8vo, 2s. 6d.

—— Elementarbuch des Gesprochenen Englisch. **Grammatik**, Texte und Glossar. *Third Edition.* Extra fcap. 8vo, stiff covers, 2s. 6d.

—— **A Primer of** Spoken English. Extra fcap. 8vo, 3s. 6d.

—— An Icelandic **Primer, with Grammar, Notes** and Glossary. Extra fcap. 8vo, 3s. 6d.

—— A Primer of Phonetics. Extra fcap. 8vo, 3s. 6d.

—— **A Manual of Current Shorthand, Orthographic and** Phonetic. Crown 8vo, 4s. 6d.

Tancock. An Elementary English Grammar and Exercise Book. By O. W. TANCOCK, M.A. *Third Edition.* Extra fcap. 8vo, 1s. 6d.

—— **An English Grammar and Reading Book, for Lower** Forms in Classical Schools. *Fourth Edition.* Extra fcap. 8vo, 3s. 6d.

Saxon Chronicles. Two of the Saxon Chronicles Parallel; with Supplementary Extracts from the others. A Revised Text. Edited, with Introduction, Notes, Appendices, and Glossary. By C. PLUMMER, M.A., and J. EARLE, M.A. Vol. I. Text, Appendices, and Glossary. 10s. 6d.

—— —— (787–1001 A.D.) Crown 8vo, stiff covers, 3s.

Specimens of Early English. A New and Revised Edition. With Introduction, Notes, and Glossarial Index.

Part I. From Old English Homilies to King Horn (A.D. 1150 to A.D. 1300). By R. MORRIS, LL.D. *Second Edition.* Extra fcap. 8vo, 9s.

Part II. From Robert of Gloucester to Gower (A.D. 1298 to A.D. 1393). By R. MORRIS, LL.D., and W. W. SKEAT, Litt. D. *Second Edition.* Extra fcap. 8vo, 7s. 6d.

Specimens of English Literature, from the 'Ploughman's Crede' to the 'Shepheardes Calender' (A.D. 1394 to A.D. 1579). With Introduction, Notes, and Glossarial Index. By W. W. SKEAT, Litt.D. *Fifth Edition.* Extra fcap. 8vo, 7s. 6d.

Typical Selections from the best English Writers, with Introductory Notices. In 2 vols. *Second Edition.* Extra fcap. 8vo, 3s. 6d. each.

Vol. I. Latimer to Berkeley.   Vol. II. Pope to Macaulay.

I. Literature and Philology.

A SERIES OF ENGLISH CLASSICS.

The Deeds of Beowulf. An English Epic of the Eighth Century done into Modern Prose. With an Introduction and Notes, by JOHN EARLE, M.A. Crown 8vo, 8s. 6d.

The Gospel of St. Luke in Anglo-Saxon. Edited from the MSS. With Introduction, Notes, and Glossary. By JAMES W. BRIGHT, Ph.D. Extra fcap. 8vo, 5s.

The Ormulum, with the Notes and Glossary of Dr. R. M. WHITE. Edited by R. HOLT, M.A. 2 vols. Extra fcap. 8vo, 1l. 1s.

CHAUCER.

I. **The Prologue to the Canterbury Tales.** (School Edition.) Edited by W. W. SKEAT, Litt.D. Extra fcap. 8vo, 1s.

II. **The Prologue, the Knightes** Tale, The Nonne Preestes Tale; from the Canterbury Tales. Edited by R. MORRIS, LL.D. A New Edition, with Collations and Additional Notes by W. W. SKEAT, Litt.D. Extra fcap. 8vo, 2s. 6d.

III. **The Prioresses Tale; Sir Thopas; The Monkes Tale;** The Clerkes Tale; The Squieres Tale, &c. Edited by W. W. SKEAT, Litt.D. *Fifth Edition.* Extra fcap. 8vo, 4s. 6d.

IV. **The Tale of the Man of Lawe; The Pardoneres** Tale; The Second Nonnes Tale; The Chanouns Yemannes Tale. By W. W. SKEAT, Litt.D. *New Edition.* Extra fcap. 8vo, 4s. 6d.

V. **Minor Poems.** Edited by W. W. SKEAT, Litt.D. Crown 8vo, 10s. 6d.

VI. **The Legend of Good Women.** Edited by W. W. SKEAT, Litt.D. Crown 8vo, 6s.

Langland, W. The Vision of William concerning Piers the Plowman, in three Parallel Texts; together with Richard the Redeless. By WILLIAM LANGLAND (about 1362–1399 A.D.). Edited from numerous Manuscripts, with Preface, Notes, and a Glossary, by W. W. SKEAT, Litt.D. 2 vols. 8vo, 1l. 11s. 6d.

—— **The Vision** of William concerning Piers the Plowman, by WILLIAM LANGLAND. Edited, with Notes, by W. W. SKEAT, Litt.D. *Sixth Edition.* Extra fcap. 8vo, 4s. 6d.

Gamelyn, The Tale of. Edited, with Notes, Glossary, &c., by W. W. SKEAT, Litt.D. Extra fcap. 8vo, stiff covers, 1s. 6d.

Oxford: Clarendon Press.

WYCLIFFE.

    I. The Books of Job, Psalms, Proverbs, Ecclesiastes, and the Song of Solomon: according to the Wycliffite Version made by NICHOLAS DE HEREFORD, about A.D. 1381, and Revised by JOHN PURVEY, about A.D. 1388. With Introduction and Glossary by W. W. SKEAT, Litt.D. Extra fcap. 8vo, 3*s.* 6*d.*

    II. The New Testament in English, according to the Version by JOHN WYCLIFFE, about A.D. 1380, and Revised by JOHN PURVEY, about A.D. 1388. With Introduction and Glossary by W. W. SKEAT, Litt.D. Extra fcap. 8vo, 6*s.*

Minot (Laurence). Poems. Edited, with Introduction and Notes, by JOSEPH HALL, M.A., Head Master of the Hulme Grammar School, Manchester. Extra fcap. 8vo, 4*s.* 6*d.*

Spenser's Faery Queene. Books I and II. Designed chiefly for the use of Schools. With Introduction and Notes by G. W. KITCHIN, D.D., and Glossary by A. L. MAYHEW, M.A. Extra fcap. 8vo, 2*s.* 6*d.* each.

Hooker. Ecclesiastical Polity, Book I. Edited by R. W. CHURCH, M.A. Extra fcap. 8vo, 2*s.* [See also p. 53.]

OLD ENGLISH DRAMA.

    I. York Plays. The Plays performed by the Crafts or Mysteries of York, on the day of Corpus Christi, in the 14th, 15th, and 16th centuries; now first printed from the unique manuscript in the library of Lord Ashburnham. Edited, with Introduction and Glossary, by LUCY TOULMIN SMITH. 8vo, 1*l.* 1*s.*

    II. English Miracle Plays, Moralities, and Interludes. Specimens of the Pre-Elizabethan Drama. Edited, with an Introduction, Notes, and Glossary, by ALFRED W. POLLARD, M.A. Crown 8vo, 7*s.* 6*d.*

    III. The Pilgrimage to Parnassus, with the Two Parts of the Return from Parnassus. Three Comedies performed in St. John's College, Cambridge, A.D. MDXCVII–MDCI. Edited from MSS. by W. D. MACRAY, M.A., F.S.A. Medium 8vo, bevelled boards, gilt top, 8*s.* 6*d.*

    IV. Marlowe's Edward II. With Introduction, Notes, &c. By O. W. TANCOCK, M.A. *Second Edition.* Extra fcap. 8vo, stiff covers, 2*s.*; cloth, 3*s.*

    V. Marlowe and Greene. Marlowe's Tragical History of Dr. Faustus, and Greene's Honourable History of Friar Bacon and Friar Bungay. Edited by A. W. WARD, Litt.D. *New and enlarged Edition.* Crown 8vo, 6*s.* 6*d.*

SHAKESPEARE. Select Plays. Extra fcap. 8vo, stiff covers.

Edited by W. G. CLARK, M.A., and W. ALDIS WRIGHT, D.C.L.

The Merchant of Venice. 1s.   Macbeth. 1s. 6d.
Richard the Second. 1s. 6d.   Hamlet. 2s.

Edited by W. ALDIS WRIGHT, D.C.L.

The Tempest. 1s. 6d.   Midsummer Night's Dream. 1s. 6d.
As You Like It. 1s. 6d.   Coriolanus. 2s. 6d.
Julius Caesar. 2s.   Henry the Fifth. 2s.
Richard the Third. 2s. 6d.   Twelfth Night. 1s. 6d.
King Lear. 1s. 6d.   King John. 1s. 6d.
Henry the Eighth. 2s.

Shakespeare as a Dramatic Artist; a popular Illustration of the Principles of Scientific Criticism. By R. G. MOULTON, M.A. *Third Edition, Enlarged.* Crown 8vo, 7s. 6d.

Bacon.

I. Advancement of Learning. Edited by W. ALDIS WRIGHT, D.C.L. *Third Edition.* Extra fcap. 8vo, 4s. 6d.

II. The Essays. Edited, with Introduction and Illustrative Notes, by S. H. REYNOLDS, M.A. 8vo, half-bound, 12s. 6d.

MILTON.

I. Areopagitica. With Introduction and Notes. By JOHN W. HALES, M.A. *Third Edition.* Extra fcap. 8vo, 3s.

II. Poems. Edited by R. C. BROWNE, M.A. In two Volumes. *New Edition, Revised.* Extra fcap. 8vo, 6s. 6d.

Sold separately, Vol. I, 4s.; Vol. II, 3s.

In paper covers:

Lycidas, 3d.   L'Allegro, 3d.   Comus, 6d.

Edited with Notes, by O. ELTON, B.A.

Lycidas, 6d.   L'Allegro, 4d.   Il Penseroso, 4d.   Comus, 1s.

III. Paradise Lost. Book I. Edited by H. C. BEECHING, M.A. Extra fcap. 8vo, stiff covers, 1s. 6d.; in Parchment, 3s. 6d.

IV. Paradise Lost. Book II. Edited by E. K. CHAMBERS, B.A. Extra fcap. 8vo, 1s. 6d.

Books I and II combined, 2s. 6d.

V. Samson Agonistes. Edited, with Introduction and Notes, by J. CHURTON COLLINS, M.A. Extra fcap. 8vo, stiff covers, 1s.

Milton's Prosody. By ROBERT BRIDGES. Small 4to, 8s. 6d. *net.*

Bunyan.
    I. The Pilgrim's Progress, Grace Abounding, Relation of the Imprisonment of Mr. JOHN BUNYAN Edited, with Biographical Introduction and Notes, by E. VENABLES, M.A. Extra fcap. 8vo, cloth, 3s. 6d.; in Parchment, 4s. 6d.
    II. The Holy War, and The Heavenly Footman. Edited by MABEL PEACOCK. Extra fcap. 8vo, 3s. 6d.

Fuller. Wise Words and Quaint Counsels of Thomas Fuller. Selected by AUGUSTUS JESSOPP, D.D. Crown 8vo, 6s.

Clarendon.
    I. History of the Rebellion. Book VI. Edited by T. ARNOLD, M.A. Extra fcap. 8vo, 4s. 6d.
    II. Characters and Episodes of the Great Rebellion. Selections from Clarendon. Edited by G. BOYLE, M.A., Dean of Salisbury. Crown 8vo, gilt top, 7s. 6d. [See also p. 55.]

Dryden. Select Poems. (Stanzas on the Death of Oliver Cromwell; Astraea Redux; Annus Mirabilis; Absalom and Achitophel; Religio Laici; The Hind and the Panther.) Edited by W. D. CHRISTIE, M.A. *Fifth Edition.* Revised by C. H. FIRTH, M.A. Extra fcap. 8vo, 3s. 6d.

—— An Essay of Dramatic Poesy. Edited, with Notes, by THOMAS ARNOLD, M.A. Extra fcap. 8vo, 3s. 6d.

Locke. Conduct of the Understanding. Edited, with Introduction, Notes, &c., by T. FOWLER, D.D. *Third Edition.* Extra fcap. 8vo, 2s. 6d.

Addison. Selections from Papers in the Spectator. With Notes. By T. ARNOLD, M.A. Extra fcap. 8vo, 4s. 6d.; in Parchment, 6s.

Steele. Selections from the Tatler, Spectator, and Guardian. Edited by AUSTIN DOBSON. Extra fcap. 8vo, 5s.; in Parchment, 7s. 6d.

Swift. Selections from his Works. Edited, with Life, Introductions, and Notes, by HENRY CRAIK. Two Vols. Crown 8vo, cloth extra, 15s.

Each volume may be had separately, price 7s. 6d.

Pope. Select Works. With Introduction and Notes. By MARK PATTISON, B.D.
    I. Essay on Man. *Sixth Edition.* Extra fcap. 8vo, 1s. 6d.
    II. Satires and Epistles. *Fourth Edition.* Extra fcap. 8vo, 2s.

Parnell. The Hermit. Paper covers, 2d.

Thomson. The Seasons, and The Castle of Indolence. Edited by J. LOGIE ROBERTSON, M.A. Extra fcap. 8vo, 4s. 6d.

—— The Castle of Indolence. By the same Editor. Extra fcap. 8vo, 1s. 6d.

I. Literature and Philology.

Gray. Selected Poems. Edited by EDMUND GOSSE, M.A. Extra fcap. 8vo. In Parchment, 3s.
—— *The same*, together with **Supplementary Notes for** Schools, by FOSTER WATSON, M.A. Stiff covers, 1s. 6d.
—— **Elegy**, and Ode on Eton College. Paper covers, 2d.

Chesterfield. Lord Chesterfield's Worldly Wisdom. Selections from his Letters and Characters. Edited by G. BIRKBECK HILL, D.C.L. Crown 8vo, 6s.

Goldsmith.
    I. Selected Poems. Edited with Introduction and Notes, by AUSTIN DOBSON. Extra fcap. 8vo, 3s. 6d.; in Parchment, 4s. 6d.
    II. **The** Traveller. Edited by G. BIRKBECK HILL, D.C.L. Stiff covers, 1s.
    III. The Deserted Village. Paper covers, 2d.

JOHNSON.
    I. Rasselas. Edited, with Introduction and Notes, by G. BIRKBECK HILL, D.C.L. Extra fcap. 8vo, bevelled boards, 3s. 6d.; in Parchment, 4s. 6d.
    II. **Rasselas;** Lives of Dryden and Pope. Edited by ALFRED MILNES, M.A. (London). Extra fcap. 8vo, 4s. 6d.; or Lives of DRYDEN and POPE only, stiff **covers,** 2s. 6d.
    III. **Life** of Milton. Edited by **C. H.** FIRTH, M.A. Extra fcap. 8vo, cloth, 2s. 6d.; **stiff covers,** 1s. 6d.
    IV. Wit and Wisdom of Samuel Johnson. Edited by G. BIRKBECK HILL, D.C.L. Crown 8vo, 7s. 6d.
    V. Vanity of Human Wishes. With Notes, by E. J. PAYNE, M.A. Paper covers, 4d.
    VI. Letters of Samuel Johnson, LL.D. Collected and Edited by G. BIRKBECK HILL, D.C.L. 2 vols. Medium 8vo, half-roan, 28s.

BOSWELL.
    Boswell's **Life of Johnson.** With the Journal of a **Tour** to the Hebrides. Edited by G. BIRKBECK HILL, D.C.L., **Pem**broke College. 6 vols. Medium 8vo, half-bound, 3l. 3s.

Cowper. Edited, with Life, Introductions, and Notes, by H. T. GRIFFITH, B.A.
    I. The Didactic Poems of 1782, with Selections from the Minor Pieces, A.D. 1779-1783. Extra fcap. 8vo, 3s.
    II. The Task, with Tirocinium, and Selections from the Minor Poems, A.D. 1784-1799. *Second Edition.* Extra fcap. 8vo, 3s.

Oxford: Clarendon Press.

Burke. Select Works. Edited, with Introduction and Notes, by E. J. PAYNE, M.A.

    I. Thoughts on the Present Discontents; the two Speeches on America. *Second Edition.* Extra fcap. 8vo, 4s. 6d.

    II. Reflections on the French Revolution. *Second Edition.* Extra fcap. 8vo, 5s.

    III. Four Letters on the Proposals for Peace with the Regicide Directory of France. *Second Edition.* Extra fcap. 8vo, 5s.

Burns. Selected Poems. Edited, with Introduction, Notes, and a Glossary, by J. LOGIE ROBERTSON, M.A. Crown 8vo, 6s.

Keats. Hyperion, Book I. With Notes by W. T. ARNOLD, B.A. Paper covers, 4d.

Byron. Childe Harold. With Introduction and Notes, by H. F. TOZER, M.A. *Second Edition.* Extra fcap. 8vo, 3s. 6d.; in Parchment, 5s.

Scott. Lady of the Lake. Edited, with Preface and Notes, by W. MINTO, M.A. Extra fcap. 8vo, 3s. 6d.

—— Lay of the Last Minstrel. By the same Editor. With Map. *Second Edition.* Extra fcap. 8vo, 2s.; in parchment, 3s. 6d.

—— Lay of the Last Minstrel. Introduction and Canto I, with Preface and Notes, by the same Editor. 6d.

—— Lord of the Isles. Edited, with Introduction and Notes, by THOMAS BAYNE. Extra fcap. 8vo, 3s. 6d.

—— Marmion. Edited, with Introduction and Notes, by T. BAYNE. Extra fcap. 8vo, 3s. 6d.

Shelley. Adonais. Edited, with Introduction and Notes, by W. M. ROSSETTI. Crown 8vo, 5s.

Campbell. Gertrude of Wyoming. Edited, with Introduction and Notes, by H. MACAULAY FITZGIBBON, M.A. *Second Edition.* Extra fcap. 8vo, 1s.

Wordsworth. The White Doe of Rylstone, &c. Edited by WILLIAM KNIGHT, LL.D. Extra fcap. 8vo, 2s. 6d.

Shairp. Aspects of Poetry; being Lectures delivered at Oxford, by J. C. SHAIRP, LL.D. Crown 8vo, 10s. 6d.

Palgrave. The Treasury of Sacred Song. With Notes Explanatory and Biographical. By F. T. PALGRAVE, M.A. *Thirteenth Thousand.* Extra fcap. 8vo, 4s. 6d.

SECTION III.

EUROPEAN LANGUAGES, MEDIAEVAL AND MODERN.

(1) FRENCH AND ITALIAN.

Brachet's Etymological Dictionary of the French Language. Translated by G. W. KITCHIN, D.D. *Third Edition.* Crown 8vo, 7s. 6d.

—— Historical Grammar of the French Language. Translated by G. W. KITCHIN, D.D. *Seventh Edition.* Extra fcap. 8vo, 3s. 6d.

Saintsbury. Primer of French Literature. By GEORGE SAINTSBURY, M.A. *Third Edition, Revised.* Extra fcap. 8vo, 2s.

—— Short History of French Literature. *Fourth Edition.* Crown 8vo, 10s. 6d.

—— Specimens of French Literature, from Villon to Hugo. *Second Edition.* Crown 8vo, 9s.

Song of Dermot and the Earl. An Old French Poem. Edited, with Translation, Notes, &c., by G. H. ORPEN. Extra fcap. 8vo, 8s. 6d.

Toynbee. Specimens of Old French (IX–XV centuries). With Introduction, Notes, and Glossary. By PAGET TOYNBEE, M.A. Crown 8vo, 16s.

Beaumarchais' Le Barbier de Séville. Edited, with Introduction and Notes, by AUSTIN DOBSON. Extra fcap. 8vo, 2s. 6d.

Corneille's Horace. Edited, with Introduction and Notes, by GEORGE SAINTSBURY, M.A. Extra fcap. 8vo, 2s. 6d.

Molière's Les Précieuses Ridicules. Edited, with Introduction and Notes, by ANDREW LANG, M.A. *Second Edition.* Extra fcap. 8vo, 1s. 6d.

Musset's On ne badine pas avec l'Amour, and Fantasio. Edited, with Prolegomena, Notes, &c., by W. H. POLLOCK. Extra fcap. 8vo, 2s.

Oxford: Clarendon Press.

Racine's Esther. Edited, with Introduction and Notes, by GEORGE SAINTSBURY, M.A. Extra fcap. 8vo, 2s.

Voltaire's Mérope. Edited, with Introduction and Notes, by GEORGE SAINTSBURY, M.A. Extra fcap. 8vo, 2s.

*** *The above six Plays may be had in ornamental case, and bound in Imitation Parchment, price* 12s. 6d.

Molière. Le Misanthrope. Edited by H. W. G. MARKHEIM, M.A. Extra fcap. 8vo, 3s. 6d.

MASSON'S FRENCH CLASSICS.

Edited by Gustave Masson, B.A.

Corneille's Cinna. With Notes, Glossary, &c. Extra fcap. 8vo, 2s.; stiff covers, 1s. 6d.

Louis XIV and his Contemporaries; as described in Extracts from the best Memoirs of the Seventeenth Century. With English Notes, Genealogical Tables, &c. Extra fcap. 8vo, 2s. 6d.

Maistre, Xavier de, &c. Voyage autour de ma Chambre, by XAVIER DE MAISTRE; Ourika, by MADAME DE DURAS; Le Vieux Tailleur, by MM. ERCKMANN-CHATRIAN; La Veillée de Vincennes, by ALFRED DE VIGNY; Les Jumeaux de l'Hôtel Corneille, by EDMOND ABOUT; Mésaventures d'un Écolier, by RODOLPHE TÖPFFER. *Third Edition, Revised.* Extra fcap. 8vo, 2s. 6d.

—— Voyage autour de ma Chambre. Limp, 1s. 6d.

Molière's Les Fourberies de Scapin, and **Racine's** Athalie. With Voltaire's Life of Molière. Extra fcap. 8vo, 2s. 6d.

—— Les Fourberies de Scapin. With Voltaire's Life of Molière. Extra fcap. 8vo, stiff covers, 1s. 6d.

—— Les Femmes Savantes. With Notes, Glossary, &c. Extra fcap. 8vo, cloth, 2s.; stiff covers, 1s. 6d.

Racine's Andromaque, and **Corneille's** Le Menteur. With LOUIS RACINE'S Life of his Father. Extra fcap. 8vo, 2s. 6d.

Regnard's Le Joueur, and **Brueys and Palaprat's** Le Grondeur. Extra fcap. 8vo, 2s. 6d.

Sévigné, Madame de, and her chief Contemporaries. Selections from their Correspondence. Extra fcap. 8vo, 3s.

Blouët. L'Éloquence de la Chaire et de la Tribune Françaises.
Edited by PAUL BLOUËT, B.A. Vol. I. Sacred Oratory. Extra fcap. 8vo, 2s. 6d.

Gautier, Théophile. Scenes of Travel. Selected and Edited
by GEORGE SAINTSBURY, **M.A.** *Second Edition.* Extra fcap. 8vo, 2s.

Perrault's Popular Tales. **Edited** from the Original Editions,
with Introduction, &c., by A. LANG, M.A. **Extra fcap.** 8vo, 5s. 6d.

Quinet's Lettres à sa Mère. Selected and Edited **by GEORGE**
SAINTSBURY, M.A. Extra fcap. 8vo, **2s.**

Sainte-Beuve. Selections from the Causeries du Lundi.
Edited by GEORGE SAINTSBURY, M.A. Extra fcap. 8vo, 2s.

A Primer of Italian Literature. By F. J. SNELL, M.A.
Extra fcap. 8vo, 3s. 6d.

Dante. Selections from the Inferno. With Introduction
and Notes. By H. B. COTTERILL, B.A. **Extra fcap.** 8vo, 4s. 6d.

Tasso. La Gerusalemme Liberata. Cantos i, ii. With Introduction and Notes. By the same Editor. Extra fcap. 8vo, 2s. 6d.

(2) GERMAN AND GOTHIC.

Max Müller. The German Classics, from the **Fourth to the**
Nineteenth Century. **With** Biographical Notices, Translations **into**
Modern German, **and Notes.** By F. MAX MÜLLER, M.A. A New
Edition, Revised, **Enlarged, and** Adapted to WILHELM SCHERER'S
'History of German **Literature,' by** F. LICHTENSTEIN. 2 vols. Crown
8vo, 21s.

Scherer. A History of German Literature by WILHELM
SCHERER. Translated from the Third German **Edition by Mrs.** F.
C. CONYBEARE. Edited by F. MAX MÜLLER. 2 vols. 8vo, 21s.
Or, separately, 10s. 6d. each volume.

—— **A** History of German Literature, from the Accession of
Frederick the Great to the Death of Goethe. By the same. Crown 8vo, 5s.

Skeat. The Gospel of St. Mark in Gothic. By W. W.
SKEAT, Litt.D. Extra fcap. 8vo, cloth, 4s.

Wright. An Old High **German** Primer. With Grammar,
Notes, and Glossary. By JOSEPH WRIGHT, Ph.D. Extra fcap. 8vo, 3s. 6d.

—— A Middle High German Primer. With Grammar,
Notes, and **Glossary.** By the same Author. **Extra fcap.** 8vo, 3s. 6d.

—— A Primer of the Gothic Language. With Grammar,
Notes, and Glossary. **By the** same Author. Extra fcap. 8vo, 4s. 6d.

Oxford: Clarendon Press.

LANGE'S GERMAN COURSE.

By HERMANN LANGE, *Lecturer on French and German at the Manchester Technical School, and Lecturer on German at the Manchester Athenaeum.*

I. Germans at Home; a Practical Introduction to German Conversation, with an Appendix containing the Essentials of German Grammar. *Third Edition.* 8vo, 2s. 6d.

II. German Manual; a German **Grammar,** Reading Book, and a Handbook of German Conversation. *Second Edition.* 8vo, 7s. 6d.

III. Grammar of the German Language. 8vo, 3s. 6d.

IV. German Composition; A Theoretical and Practical Guide to the Art of Translating English Prose into German. *Third Edition.* 8vo, 4s. 6d.

*** *A Key to the above*, price 5s. net.

German Spelling; A Synopsis of the Changes which it has undergone through the Government Regulations of 1880. 6d.

BUCHHEIM'S GERMAN CLASSICS.

Edited, with Biographical, Historical, and Critical Introductions, Arguments (to the Dramas), and Complete Commentaries, by C. A. BUCHHEIM, *Phil. Doc., Professor in King's College, London.*

Becker (the Historian). Friedrich der Grosse. Edited, with Notes, an Historical Introduction, and a Map. *Second Edition.* 3s. 6d.

Goethe:
- (*a*) Egmont. **A Tragedy.** *Fourth Edition.* 3s.
- (*b*) Iphigenie auf Tauris. A Drama. *Third Edition.* 3s.

Heine:
- (*a*) Prosa: being Selections from his Prose Writings. *Second Edition.* 4s. 6d.
- (*b*) Harzreise. *Second Edition.* 2s. 6d.

Lessing:
- (*a*) Nathan der Weise. A Dramatic Poem. *Second Edition.* 4s. 6d.
- (*b*) Minna von Barnhelm. A Comedy. *Fifth Edition.* 3s. 6d.

Schiller:
- (*a*) Wilhelm Tell. **A Drama.** Large Edition. With Map. *Seventh Edition.* 3s. 6d.
- (*b*) Wilhelm Tell. School Edition. With Map. *Fourth Edition.* 2s.
- (*c*) Historische Skizzen. With Map. *Fifth Edition.* 2s. 6d.
- (*d*) Jungfrau von Orleans. 4s. 6d.
- (*e*) Maria Stuart. [*Immediately.*]

Modern German Reader. A Graduated Collection of Extracts from Modern German Authors:—
    Part I. Prose Extracts. With English Notes, a Grammatical Appendix, and a complete Vocabulary. *Seventh Edition.* 2s. 6d.
    Part II. Extracts in Prose and Poetry. With English Notes and an Index. *Second Edition.* 2s. 6d.

German Poetry for Beginners. Edited with English Notes and a complete Vocabulary, by EMMA S. BUCHHEIM. Extra fcap. 8vo, 2s.

Elementary German Prose Composition. With Notes, Vocabulary, &c. By the same Editor. Cloth, 2s.; stiff covers, 1s. 6d.

Chamisso. Peter Schlemihl's Wundersame Geschichte. Edited with Notes and a complete Vocabulary, by EMMA S. BUCHHEIM. *Fourth Thousand.* Extra fcap. 8vo, 2s.

Lessing. The Laokoon; with English Notes by A. HAMANN, Phil. Doc., M.A. Revised, with an Introduction, by L. E. UPCOTT, M.A. Extra fcap. 8vo, 4s. 6d.

Niebuhr: Griechische Heroen-Geschichten (Tales of Greek Heroes). With English Notes and Vocabulary, by EMMA S. BUCHHEIM. Second Revised Edition. Extra fcap. 8vo, cloth, 2s.; stiff covers, 1s. 6d. Edition A. *Text in German Type.* Edition B. *Text in Roman Type.*

Riehl's Seines Vaters Sohn *and* **Gespensterkampf.** Edited with Notes by H. T. GERRANS. Extra fcap. 8vo, 2s.

Schiller's Wilhelm Tell. Translated into English Verse by E. MASSIE, M.A. Extra fcap. 8vo, 5s.

(3) SCANDINAVIAN.

Cleasby and Vigfússon. An Icelandic-English Dictionary, based on the MS. collections of the late RICHARD CLEASBY. Enlarged and completed by G. VIGFÚSSON, M.A. With an Introduction, and Life of Richard Cleasby, by G. WEBBE DASENT, D.C.L. 4to, 3l. 7s.

Sargent. Grammar of the Dano-Norwegian Language. By J. Y. SARGENT, M.A. Crown 8vo, 7s. 6d.

Sweet. Icelandic Primer, with Grammar, Notes, and Glossary. By HENRY SWEET, M.A. Extra fcap. 8vo, 3s. 6d.

Vigfússon. Sturlunga Saga, including the Islendinga Saga of Lawman STURLA THORDSSON and other works. Edited by GUDBRAND VIGFÚSSON, M.A. In 2 vols. 8vo, 2l. 2s.

Vigfússon and Powell. Icelandic Prose Reader, with Notes, Grammar, and Glossary. By G. VIGFÚSSON, M.A., and F. YORK POWELL, M.A. Extra fcap. 8vo, 10s. 6d.

—— Corpvs Poeticvm Boreale. The Poetry of the Old Northern Tongue, from the Earliest Times to the Thirteenth Century. Edited, classified, and translated, with Introduction, Excursus, and Notes, by GUDBRAND VIGFÚSSON, M.A., and F. YORK POWELL, M.A. 2 vols. 8vo, 2l. 2s.

SECTION IV.
CLASSICAL LANGUAGES.
(1) LATIN.
STANDARD WORKS AND EDITIONS.

King and **Cookson.** The Principles of Sound and Inflexion, as illustrated in the Greek and Latin Languages. By J. E. KING, M.A., and CHRISTOPHER COOKSON, M.A. 8vo, 18s.

Lewis and **Short.** A Latin Dictionary, founded on Andrews' edition of Freund's Latin Dictionary, revised, enlarged, **and** in great part rewritten by CHARLTON T. LEWIS, Ph.D., and CHARLES SHORT, LL.D. 4to, 1l. 5s.

Merry. Selected Fragments of Roman Poetry. Edited with Introduction and Notes by W. W. MERRY, D.D. Crown 8vo, 6s. 6d.

Nettleship. Contributions to Latin Lexicography. By HENRY NETTLESHIP, M.A. 8vo, 21s.

—— Lectures and Essays on Subjects connected with Latin Scholarship and Literature. Crown 8vo, 7s. 6d.

—— The Roman Satura. 8vo, sewed, 1s.

—— Ancient Lives of Vergil. 8vo, sewed, 2s.

Papillon. Manual of Comparative Philology. By T. L. PAPILLON, M.A. Third Edition. Crown 8vo, 6s.

Pinder. Selections from the less known Latin Poets. By NORTH PINDER, M.A. 8vo, 15s.

Rushforth. Latin Historical Inscriptions, illustrating the History of the Early Empire. By G. McN. RUSHFORTH, M.A. 8vo, 10s. net.

Sellar. Roman Poets of the Republic. By W. Y. SELLAR, M.A. Third Edition. Crown 8vo, 10s.

—— Roman Poets of the Augustan Age. VIRGIL. Second Edition. Crown 8vo, 9s.

—— —— HORACE and the ELEGIAC POETS. With a Memoir of the Author by ANDREW LANG, M.A., and a Portrait. 8vo, cloth, 14s.

Wordsworth. Fragments and Specimens of Early Latin. With Introductions and Notes. By J. WORDSWORTH, D.D. 8vo, 18s.

I. Literature and Philology.

Avianus. The Fables. Edited, with Prolegomena, Critical Apparatus, Commentary, &c., by R. ELLIS, M.A., LL.D. 8vo, 8s. 6d.

Catulli Veronensis Liber. Iterum recognovit, apparatum criticum prolegomena appendices addidit, ROBINSON ELLIS, A.M. 8vo, 16s.

Catullus, a Commentary on. By ROBINSON ELLIS, M.A. *Second Edition.* 8vo, 18s.

Cicero. De Oratore Libri Tres. With Introduction and Notes. By A. S. WILKINS, Litt.D. 8vo, 18s.

Also separately:—
Book I, *Second Edition.* 7s. 6d. Book II, *Second Edition.* 5s. Book III, 6s.

—— Philippic Orations. With Notes. By J. R. KING, M.A. *Second Edition.* 8vo, 10s. 6d.

—— Select Letters. With English Introductions, Notes, and Appendices. By ALBERT WATSON, M.A. *Fourth Edition.* 8vo, 18s.

Horace. With a Commentary. Vol. I. The Odes, Carmen Seculare, and Epodes. By E. C. WICKHAM, M.A. *Second Edition.* 8vo, 12s.

—— Vol. II. The Satires, Epistles, and De Arte Poetica. By the same Editor. 8vo, 12s.

Livy, Book I. With Introduction, Historical Examination, and Notes. By J. R. SEELEY, M.A. *Third Edition.* 8vo, 6s.

Manilius. Noctes Manilianae; sive Dissertationes in Astronomica Manilii. Accedvnt Coniectvrae in Germanici Aratea. Scripsit R. ELLIS. Crown 8vo, 6s.

Ovid. P. Ovidii Nasonis Ibis. Ex Novis Codicibus edidit, Scholia Vetera Commentarium cum Prolegomenis Appendice Indice addidit, R. ELLIS, A.M. 8vo, 10s. 6d.

—— P. Ovidi Nasonis Tristium Libri V. Recensuit S. G. OWEN, A.M. 8vo, 16s.

Persius. The Satires. With a Translation and Commentary. By JOHN CONINGTON, M.A. Edited by HENRY NETTLESHIP, M.A. *Third Edition.* 8vo, 8s. 6d.

Plautus. Rudens. Edited, with Critical and Explanatory Notes, by E. A. SONNENSCHEIN, M.A. 8vo, 8s. 6d.

—— Bentley's Plautine Emendations. From his copy of Gronovius. By E. A. SONNENSCHEIN, M.A. (Anecdota Oxon.) 2s. 6d.

Quintilian. Institutionis Oratoriae Liber X. Edited by W. PETERSON, M.A. 8vo, 12s. 6d.

Scriptores Latini rei Metricae. Ed. T. GAISFORD, S.T.P. 8vo, 5s.

Tacitus. **The Annals.** Books I–VI. Edited, with Introduction and Notes, by H. FURNEAUX, M.A. 8vo, 18*s*.

—— Books XI–XVI. By the same Editor. 8vo, 20*s*.

—— **Dialogus De Oratoribus.** A Revised Text, with Introductory Essays and Critical and Explanatory Notes. By W. PETERSON, M.A., LL.D. 8vo, 10*s*. 6*d*.

LATIN EDUCATIONAL WORKS.

GRAMMARS, EXERCISE BOOKS, &C.

ALLEN.
Rudimenta Latina. Comprising Accidence, and Exercises of a very Elementary Character, for the use of Beginners. By JOHN BARROW ALLEN, M.A. Extra fcap. 8vo, 2*s*.

An Elementary Latin Grammar. By the same Author. *Ninety-Seventh Thousand.* Extra fcap. 8vo, 2*s*. 6*d*.

A First Latin Exercise Book. By the same Author. *Seventh Edition.* Extra fcap. 8vo, 2*s*. 6*d*.

A Second Latin Exercise Book. By the same Author. *Second Edition.* Extra fcap. 8vo, 3*s*. 6*d*.

*** A Key to First and Second Latin Exercise Books, in one volume, price 5*s*. *net*. Supplied *to Teachers only*, on application to the Secretary, Clarendon Press.

An Introduction to Latin Syntax. By W. S. GIBSON, M.A. Extra fcap. 8vo, 2*s*.

First Latin Reader. By T. J. NUNNS, M.A. *Third Edition.* Extra fcap. 8vo, 2*s*.

A Latin Prose Primer. By J. Y. SARGENT, M.A. Extra fcap. 8vo, 2*s*. 6*d*.

Passages for Translation into Latin. Selected by J. Y. SARGENT, M.A. *Seventh Edition.* Extra fcap. 8vo, 2*s*. 6*d*.

*** A Key to the above, price 5*s*. *net*. Supplied *to Teachers only*, on application to the Secretary, Clarendon Press.

Latin Prose Composition. By G. G. RAMSAY, M.A., LL.D. *Third Edition.* Extra fcap. 8vo.

Vol. I. *Syntax,* **Exercises** with **Notes,** *&c.* 4*s*. 6*d*.

Vol. II. *Passages of Graduated Difficulty for Translation into Latin, together with an Introduction on Continuous Prose.* 4*s*. 6*d*.

*** A Key to Vol. I of the above, price 5*s*. *net*. Supplied *to Teachers only*, on application to the Secretary, Clarendon Press.

I. Literature and Philology.

Hints and Helps for Latin Elegiacs. By H. LEE-WARNER, M.A. Extra fcap. 8vo, 3s. 6d.

∗ A Key to the above, price 4s. 6d. *net.* Supplied *to Teachers only,* on application to the Secretary, Clarendon Press.

Reddenda Minora; or, Easy Passages, Latin and Greek, for Unseen Translation. For the use of Lower Forms. Composed and selected by C. S. JERRAM, M.A. *Third Edition.* Extra fcap. 8vo, 1s. 6d.

Anglice Reddenda; or, Extracts, Latin and Greek, for Unseen Translation. By C. S. JERRAM, M.A. *Fourth Edition.* Extra fcap. 8vo, 2s. 6d.

—— *Second Series.* By the same Editor. 3s.

Models and Exercises in Unseen Translation. By H. F. FOX, M.A., and T. M. BROMLEY, M.A. *Revised Edition.* Extra fcap. 8vo, 5s. 6d.

∗ A Key to Passages quoted in the above, price 6d. Supplied *to Teachers only,* on application to the Secretary, Clarendon Press.

An Elementary Latin Dictionary. By CHARLTON T. LEWIS, Ph.D. Square 8vo, 7s. 6d.

A School Latin Dictionary. By CHARLTON T. LEWIS, Ph.D. Small 4to, 18s.

An Introduction to the Comparative Grammar of Greek and Latin. By J. E. KING, M.A., and C. COOKSON, M.A. Extra fcap. 8vo, 5s. 6d.

LATIN CLASSICS FOR SCHOOLS.

Caesar. The Commentaries (for Schools). With Notes and Maps. By CHARLES E. MOBERLY, M.A.

The Gallic War. *Second Edition.* Extra fcap. 8vo.

—— Books I and II, 2s.; III–V, 2s. 6d.; VI–VIII, 3s. 6d.

—— Books I–III, *stiff cover,* 2s.

The Civil War. Extra fcap. 8vo, 3s. 6d.

Catulli Veronensis Carmina Selecta, secundum recognitionem ROBINSON ELLIS, A.M. Extra fcap. 8vo, 3s. 6d.

CICERO. Selection of Interesting and Descriptive Passages. With Notes. By HENRY WALFORD, M.A. In three Parts. *Third Edition.* Extra fcap. 8vo, 4s. 6d.

Each Part separately, limp, 1s. 6d.

Part I. Anecdotes from Grecian and Roman History.
Part II. Omens and Dreams: Beauties of Nature.
Part III. Rome's Rule of her Provinces.

Latin: Educational Works.

Cicero. De Amicitia. With Introduction and Notes. By St. George Stock, M.A. Extra fcap. 8vo, 3s.

—— De Senectute. Edited, with Introduction and Notes, by L. Huxley, M.A. Extra fcap. 8vo, 2s.

—— pro Cluentio. With Introduction and Notes. By W. Ramsay, M.A. Edited by G. G. Ramsay, M.A. Second Edition. Extra fcap. 8vo, 3s. 6d.

—— pro Marcello, pro Ligario, pro Rege Deiotaro. With Introduction and Notes. By W. Y. Fausset, M.A. Extra fcap. 8vo, 2s. 6d.

—— pro Milone. With Notes, &c. By A. B. Poynton, M.A. Extra fcap. 8vo, 2s. 6d.

—— pro Roscio. With Notes. By St. George Stock, M.A. Extra fcap. 8vo, 3s. 6d.

—— Select Orations (for Schools). In Verrem Actio Prima. De Imperio Gn. Pompeii. Pro Archia. Philippica IX. With Introduction and Notes by J. R. King, M.A. Second Edition. Extra fcap. 8vo, 2s. 6d.

—— In Q. Caecilium Divinatio, and In C. Verrem Actio Prima. With Introduction and Notes, by J. R. King, M.A. Extra fcap. 8vo, limp, 1s. 6d.

—— Speeches against Catilina. With Introduction and Notes, by E. A. Upcott, M.A. Second Edition. Extra fcap. 8vo, 2s. 6d.

—— Selected Letters (for Schools). With Notes. By the late C. E. Prichard, M.A., and E. R. Bernard, M.A. Second Edition. Extra fcap. 8vo, 3s.

—— Select Letters. Text. By Albert Watson, M.A. Second Edition. Extra fcap. 8vo, 4s.

Cornelius Nepos. With Notes. By Oscar Browning, M.A. Third Edition. Revised by W. R. Inge, M.A. Extra fcap. 8vo, 3s.

Horace. With a Commentary. (In a size suitable for the use of Schools.) Vol. I. The Odes, Carmen Seculare, and Epodes. By E. C. Wickham, M.A. Second Edition. Extra fcap. 8vo, 6s.

—— Odes, Book I. By the same Editor. Extra fcap. 8vo, 2s.

—— Selected Odes. With Notes for the use of a Fifth Form. By E. C. Wickham, M.A. Extra fcap. 8vo, 2s.

London: Henry Frowde, Amen Corner, E.C.

I. Literature and Philology.

Juvenal. Thirteen Satires. Edited, with Introduction and Notes, by C. H. PEARSON, M.A., and HERBERT A. STRONG, M.A., LL.D. *Second Edition.* Crown 8vo, 9s.

Livy. Books V–VII. With Introduction and Notes. By A. R. CLUER, B.A. *Second Edition.* Revised by P. E. MATHESON, M.A. Extra fcap. 8vo, 5s.

—— Book V. By the same Editors. Extra fcap. 8vo, 2s. 6d.

—— Book VII. By the same Editors. Extra fcap. 8vo, 2s.

—— Books XXI–XXIII. With Introduction and Notes. By M. T. TATHAM, M.A. *Second Edition, Enlarged.* Extra fcap. 8vo, 5s.

—— Book XXI. By the same Editor. Extra fcap. 8vo, 2s. 6d.

—— Book XXII. With Introduction, Notes, and Maps. By the same Editor. Extra fcap. 8vo, 2s. 6d.

—— Selections (for Schools). With Notes and Maps. By H. LEE-WARNER, M.A. Extra fcap. 8vo. In Parts, limp, each 1s. 6d.

    Part I. The Caudine Disaster.
    Part II. Hannibal's Campaign in Italy.
    Part III. The Macedonian War.

Ovid. Selections for the use of Schools. With Introductions and Notes, and an Appendix on the Roman Calendar. By W. RAMSAY, M.A. Edited by G. G. RAMSAY, M.A. *Third Edition.* Extra fcap. 8vo, 5s. 6d.

—— Tristia. Book I. The Text revised, with an Introduction and Notes. By S. G. OWEN, B.A. *Second Edition.* Extra fcap. 8vo, 3s. 6d.

—— Tristia. Book III. With Introduction and Notes. By the same Editor. Extra fcap. 8vo, 2s.

Plautus. Captivi. Edited by WALLACE M. LINDSAY, M.A. Extra fcap. 8vo, 2s. 6d.

—— Trinummus. With Notes and Introductions. (Intended for the Higher Forms of Public Schools.) By C. E. FREEMAN, M.A., and A. SLOMAN, M.A. Extra fcap. 8vo, 3s.

Pliny. Selected Letters (for Schools). With Notes. By C. E. PRICHARD, M.A., and E. R. BERNARD, M.A. *Third Edition.* Extra fcap. 8vo, 3s.

Quintilian. Institutionis Oratoriae. Liber X. By W. PETERSON, M.A. Extra fcap. 8vo, 3s. 6d.

Sallust. With Introduction and Notes. By W. W. CAPES, M.A. *Second Edition.* Extra fcap. 8vo, 4s. 6d.

Tacitus. The Annals. Books I–IV. Edited, with Introduction and Notes (for the use of Schools and Junior Students), by H. Furneaux, M.A. Extra fcap. 8vo, 5*s*.

—— The Annals. Book I. With Introduction and Notes, by the same Editor. Extra fcap. 8vo, limp, 2*s*.

Terence. Andria. With Notes and Introductions. By C. E. Freeman, M.A., and A. Sloman, M.A. Extra fcap. 8vo, 3*s*.

—— Adelphi. With Notes and Introductions. (Intended for the Higher Forms of Public Schools.) By A. Sloman, M.A. Extra fcap. 8vo, 3*s*.

—— Phormio. With Notes and Introductions. By A. Sloman, M.A. Extra fcap. 8vo, 3*s*.

Tibullus and Propertius. Selections. Edited by G. G. Ramsay, M.A. (In one or two parts.) Extra fcap. 8vo, 6*s*.

Virgil. With an Introduction and Notes. By T. L. Papillon, M.A., and A. E. Haigh, M.A. 2 vols. Crown 8vo, 12*s*.

—— Aeneid. By the same Editors. *In Four Parts.* Crown 8vo, 3*s*. each.

—— Bucolics and Georgics. By the same Editors. Crown 8vo, 3*s*. 6*d*.

—— Bucolics. Edited by C. S. Jerram, M.A. Extra fcap. 8vo, 2*s*. 6*d*.

—— Georgics, Books I, II. By the same Editor. Extra fcap. 8vo, 2*s*. 6*d*.

—— Georgics, Books III, IV. By the same Editor. Extra fcap. 8vo, 2*s*. 6*d*.

—— Aeneid I. With Introduction and Notes. By the same Editor. Extra fcap. 8vo, limp, 1*s*. 6*d*.

—— Aeneid IX. Edited, with Introduction and Notes, by A. E. Haigh, M.A. Extra fcap. 8vo, limp, 1*s*. 6*d*. In two Parts, 2*s*.

(2) GREEK.

STANDARD WORKS AND EDITIONS.

Allen. Notes on Abbreviations in Greek Manuscripts. By T. W. Allen, M.A., Queen's College, Oxford. Royal 8vo, 5*s*.

Chandler. A Practical Introduction to Greek Accentuation, by H. W. Chandler, M.A. *Second Edition.* 10*s*. 6*d*.

I. Literature and Philology.

Haigh. The Attic Theatre. A Description of the Stage and Theatre of the Athenians, and of the Dramatic Performances at Athens. By A. E. HAIGH, M.A. 8vo, 12s. 6d.

Head. Historia Numorum : A Manual of Greek Numismatics. By BARCLAY V. HEAD, D.C.L. Royal 8vo, half-bound, 2l. 2s.

Hicks. A Manual of Greek Historical Inscriptions. By E. L. HICKS, M.A. 8vo, 10s. 6d.

King and Cookson. The Principles of Sound and Inflexion, as illustrated in the Greek and Latin Languages. By J. E. KING, M.A., and CHRISTOPHER COOKSON, M.A. 8vo, 18s.

Liddell and Scott. A Greek-English Lexicon, by H. G. LIDDELL, D.D., and ROBERT SCOTT, D.D. *Seventh Edition, Revised and Augmented throughout.* 4to, 1l. 16s.

Papillon. Manual of Comparative Philology. By T. L. PAPILLON, M.A. *Third Edition.* Crown 8vo, 6s.

Paton and Hicks. The Inscriptions of Cos. By W. R. PATON and E. L. HICKS. Royal 8vo, linen, with Map, 28s.

Veitch. Greek Verbs, Irregular and Defective. By W. VEITCH, LL.D. *Fourth Edition.* Crown 8vo, 10s. 6d.

Vocabulary, a copious Greek-English, compiled from the best authorities. 24mo, 3s.

Aeschinem et Isocratem, Scholia Graeca in. Edidit G. DINDORFIUS. 1852. 8vo, 4s.

Aeschines. See under Oratores Attici, and Demosthenes.

Aeschyli quae supersunt in Codice Laurentiano quoad effici potuit et ad cognitionem necesse est visum typis descripta edidit R. MERKEL. Small folio, 1l. 1s.

Aeschylus: Tragoediae et Fragmenta, ex recensione GUIL. DINDORFII. *Second Edition.* 1851. 8vo, 5s. 6d.

—— Annotationes GUIL. DINDORFII. Partes II. 1841. 8vo, 10s.

Anecdota Graeca Oxoniensia. Edidit J. A. CRAMER, S.T.P. Tomi IV. 1835. 8vo, 1l. 2s.

—— Graeca e Codd. MSS. Bibliothecae Regiae Parisiensis. Edidit J. A. CRAMER, S.T.P. Tomi IV. 1839. 8vo, 1l. 2s.

Apsinis et **Longini** Rhetorica. E Codicibus MSS. recensuit JOH. BAKIUS. 1849. 8vo, 3s.

Aristophanes. A Complete Concordance to the Comedies and Fragments. By Henry Dunbar, M.D. 4to, 1*l*. 1*s*.

—— J. Caravellae Index in Aristophanem. 8vo, 3*s*.

—— Comoediae et Fragmenta, ex recensione Guil. Dindorfii. Tomi II. 1835. 8vo, 11*s*.

—— Annotationes Guil. Dindorfii. Partes II. 8vo, 11*s*.

—— Scholia Graeca ex Codicibus aucta et emendata a Guil. Dindorfio. Partes III. 1838. 8vo, 1*l*.

ARISTOTLE.

—— Ex recensione Immanuelis Bekkeri. Accedunt Indices Sylburgiani. Tomi XI. 1837. 8vo, 2*l*. 10*s*.

The volumes (except vols. I and IX) may be had separately, price 5*s*. 6*d*. each.

—— **Ethica Nicomachea**, recognovit brevique Adnotatione critica instruxit I. Bywater. 8vo, 6*s*.

—— The same, on 4to paper, for Marginal Notes, 10*s*. 6*d*.

—— Contributions to the Textual Criticism of Aristotle's Nicomachean Ethics. By Ingram Bywater. Stiff cover, 2*s*. 6*d*.

—— Notes on the Nicomachean Ethics of Aristotle. By J. A. Stewart, M.A. 2 vols. 8vo, 32*s*.

—— The Politics, with Introductions, Notes, &c., by W. L. Newman, M.A., Fellow of Balliol College, Oxford. Vols. I and II. Medium 8vo, 28*s*.

—— **The Politics**, translated into English, with Introduction, Marginal Analysis, Notes, and Indices, by B. Jowett, M.A. Medium 8vo. 2 vols. 21*s*.

—— **Aristotelian** Studies. I. On the Structure of the Seventh Book of the Nicomachean Ethics. By J. C. Wilson, M.A. 8vo, stiff covers, 5*s*.

—— The English Manuscripts of the Nicomachean Ethics, described in relation to Bekker's Manuscripts and other Sources. By J. A. Stewart, M.A. (Anecdota Oxon.) Small 4to, 3*s*. 6*d*.

—— On the History of the process by which the Aristotelian Writings arrived at their present form. By R. Shute, M.A. 8vo, 7*s*. 6*d*.

—— **Physics.** Book VII. Collation of various MSS.; with Introduction by R. Shute, M.A. (Anecdota Oxon.) Small 4to, 2*s*.

I. Literature and Philology.

Choerobosci Dictata in Theodosii Canones, necnon Epimerismi in Psalmos. E Codicibus MSS. edidit THOMAS GAISFORD, S.T.P. Tomi III. 8vo, 15s.

Demosthenes. Ex recensione GUIL. DINDORFII. Tomi IX. 8vo, 2l. 6s.
Separately:—
Textus, 1l. 1s.   Annotationes, 15s.   Scholia, 10s.

Demosthenes and Aeschines. The Orations of Demosthenes and Aeschines on the Crown. With Introductory Essays and Notes. By G. A. SIMCOX, M.A., and W. H. SIMCOX, M.A. 8vo, 12s.

Euripides. Tragoediae et Fragmenta, ex recensione GUIL. DINDORFII. Tomi II. 1833. 8vo, 10s.

—— Annotationes GUIL. DINDORFII. Partes II. 8vo, 10s.

—— Scholia Graeca, ex Codicibus aucta et emendata a GUIL. DINDORFIO. Tomi IV. 8vo, 1l. 16s.

—— Alcestis, ex recensione G. DINDORFII. 8vo, 2s. 6d.

Harpocrationis Lexicon. Ex recensione G. DINDORFII. Tomi II. 8vo, 10s. 6d.

Hephaestionis Enchiridion, **Terentianus Maurus, Proclus, &c.** Edidit T. GAISFORD, S.T.P. Tomi II. 10s.

Heracliti Ephesii Reliquiae. Recensuit I. BYWATER, M.A. Appendicis loco additae sunt Diogenis Laertii Vita Heracliti, Particulae Hippocratei De Diaeta Lib. I, Epistolae Heracliteae. 8vo, 6s.

Herodotus. Books V and VI. Terpsichore and Erato. Edited, with Notes and Appendices, by EVELYN ABBOTT, M.A., LL.D. 8vo, with two Maps, 10s. 6d.

HOMER.

—— A Complete Concordance to the Odyssey and Hymns of Homer; to which is added a Concordance to the Parallel Passages in the Iliad, Odyssey, and Hymns. By HENRY DUNBAR, M.D. 4to, 1l. 1s.

—— Seberi Index in Homerum. 1780. 8vo, 6s. 6d.

—— A Grammar of the Homeric Dialect. By D. B. MONRO, M.A. *Second Edition.* 8vo, 14s.

—— Ilias, cum brevi Annotatione C. G. HEYNII. Accedunt Scholia minora. Tomi II. 8vo, 15s.

Greek: Standard Works.

HOMER (*continued*).

—— Ilias, ex rec. GUIL. DINDORFII. 8vo, 5s. 6d.

—— Scholia Graeca in Iliadem. Edited by W. DINDORF, after a new collation of the Venetian MSS. by D. B. MONRO, M.A., Provost of Oriel College. 4 vols. 8vo, 2l. 10s.

—— Scholia Graeca in Iliadem Townleyana. Recensuit ERNESTUS MAASS. 2 vols. 8vo, 1l. 16s.

—— Odyssea, ex rec. G. DINDORFII. 8vo, 5s. 6d.

—— Scholia Graeca in Odysseam. Edidit GUIL. DINDORFIUS. Tomi II. 8vo, 15s. 6d.

—— Odyssey. Books I–XII. Edited with English Notes, Appendices, &c. By W. W. MERRY, D.D., and the late JAMES RIDDELL, M.A. *Second Edition.* 8vo, 16s.

—— **Hymni Homerici.** Codicibus denuo collatis recensuit ALFREDUS GOODWIN. Small folio. With four Plates. 21s. net.

Oratores Attici, ex recensione BEKKERI:
   I. Antiphon, Andocides, et Lysias. 8vo, 7s.
   II. Isocrates. 8vo, 7s.
   III. Isaeus, Aeschines, Lycurgus, Dinarchus, &c. 8vo, 7s.

Paroemiographi Graeci, quorum pars nunc primum ex Codd. MSS. vulgatur. Edidit T. GAISFORD, S.T.P. 8vo, 5s. 6d.

PLATO.

—— **Apology**, with a revised Text and English Notes, and a Digest of Platonic Idioms, by JAMES RIDDELL, M.A. 8vo, 8s. 6d.

—— **Philebus**, with a revised Text and English Notes, by EDWARD POSTE, M.A. 8vo, 7s. 6d.

—— **Sophistes and Politicus**, with a revised Text and English Notes, by L. CAMPBELL, M.A. 8vo, 18s.

—— **Theaetetus**, with a revised Text and English Notes, by L. CAMPBELL, M.A. *Second Edition.* 8vo, 10s. 6d.

—— **The Dialogues**, translated into English, with Analyses and Introductions, by B. JOWETT, M.A. *Third Edition.* 5 vols. medium 8vo, 4l. 4s. In half-morocco, 5l.

—— **The Republic**, translated into English, with Analysis and Introduction, by B. JOWETT, M.A. *Third Edition.* Medium 8vo, 12s. 6d.; half-roan, 14s.

—— **Index** to Plato. Compiled for Prof. Jowett's Translation of the Dialogues. By EVELYN ABBOTT, M.A. 8vo, paper covers, 2s. 6d.

I. Literature and Philology.

Plotinus. Edidit F. Creuzer. Tomi III. 4to, 1*l*. 8*s*.

Plutarchi **Moralia**, id est, Opera, exceptis Vitis, reliqua. Edidit Daniel Wyttenbach. Accedit Index Graecitatis. Tomi VIII. Partes XV. 1795–1830. 8vo, cloth, 3*l*. 10*s*.

Polybius. Selections. Edited by J. L. Strachan-Davidson, M.A. With Maps. Medium 8vo, buckram, 21*s*.

SOPHOCLES.

—— The Plays and Fragments. With English Notes and Introductions, by Lewis Campbell, M.A. 2 vols.

    Vol. I. Oedipus Tyrannus. Oedipus Coloneus. Antigone. 8vo, 16*s*.

    Vol. II. Ajax. Electra. Trachiniae. Philoctetes. Fragments. 8vo, 16*s*.

—— Tragoediae et Fragmenta, ex recensione et cum commentariis Guil. Dindorfii. *Third Edition.* 2 vols. Fcap. 8vo, 1*l*. 1*s*.

    Each Play separately, limp, 2*s*. 6*d*.

—— Tragoediae et Fragmenta cum Annotationibus Guil. Dindorfii. Tomi II. 8vo, 10*s*.

    The Text, Vol. I, 5*s*. 6*d*. The Notes, Vol. II, 4*s*. 6*d*.

Stobaei Florilegium. Ad mss. fidem emendavit et supplevit T. Gaisford, S.T.P. Tomi IV. 8vo, 1*l*.

—— Eclogarum Physicarum et Ethicarum libri duo. Accedit Hieroclis Commentarius in aurea carmina Pythagoreorum. Ad mss. Codd. recensuit T. Gaisford, S.T.P. Tomi II. 8vo, 11*s*.

STRABO, Selections from. With an Introduction on Strabo's Life and Works. By H. F. Tozer, M.A., F.R.G.S. With Maps and Plans. 8vo, cloth, 12*s*.

Thucydides. Translated into English, with Introduction, Marginal Analysis, Notes, and Indices. By B. Jowett, M.A., Regius Professor of Greek. 2 vols. Medium 8vo, 1*l*. 12*s*.

XENOPHON. Ex rec. et cum annotatt. L. Dindorfii.

    I. Historia Graeca. *Second Edition.* 8vo, 10*s*. 6*d*.

    II. Expeditio Cyri. *Second Edition.* 8vo, 10*s*. 6*d*.

    III. Institutio Cyri. 8vo, 10*s*. 6*d*.

    IV. Memorabilia Socratis. 8vo, 7*s*. 6*d*.

    V. Opuscula Politica Equestria et **Venatica cum** Arriani Libello de Venatione. 8vo, 10*s*. 6*d*.

Oxford: Clarendon Press.

GREEK EDUCATIONAL WORKS.

Grammars, Exercise Books, &c.

Chandler. The Elements of Greek Accentuation: abridged from his larger work by H. W. CHANDLER, M.A. Extra fcap. 8vo, 2s. 6d.

King and Cookson. An Introduction to the Comparative Grammar of Greek and Latin. By J. E. KING, M.A., and C. COOKSON, M.A. Extra fcap. 8vo, 5s. 6d.

Liddell and Scott. An Intermediate Greek-English Lexicon, founded upon the Seventh Edition of LIDDELL and SCOTT'S Greek Lexicon. Small 4to, 12s. 6d.

Liddell and Scott. A Greek-English Lexicon, abridged from LIDDELL and SCOTT'S 4to edition. Square 12mo, 7s. 6d.

Miller. A Greek Testament Primer. An Easy Grammar and Reading Book for the use of Students beginning Greek. By the Rev. E. MILLER, M.A. *Second Edition.* Extra fcap. 8vo, 3s. 6d.

Moulton. The Ancient Classical Drama. A Study in Literary Evolution. Intended for Readers in English and in the Original. By R. G. MOULTON, M.A. Crown 8vo, 8s. 6d.

Wordsworth. A Greek Primer, for the use of beginners in that Language. By the Right Rev. CHARLES WORDSWORTH, D.C.L. *Seventy-seventh Thousand.* Extra fcap. 8vo, 1s. 6d.

—— Graecae Grammaticae Rudimenta in usum Scholarum. Auctore CAROLO WORDSWORTH, D.C.L. *Nineteenth Edition.* 12mo, 4s.

A Primer of Greek Prose Composition. By J. Y. SARGENT, M.A. Extra fcap. 8vo, 3s. 6d.

*** A Key to the above, price 5s. *net*. Supplied *to Teachers only*, on application to the Secretary, Clarendon Press.

Passages for Translation into Greek Prose. By J. YOUNG SARGENT, M.A. Extra fcap. 8vo, 3s.

Exemplaria Graeca. Being Greek Renderings of Selected 'Passages for Translation into Greek Prose.' By the same Author. Extra fcap. 8vo, 3s.

I. Literature and Philology.

Models and Materials for Greek Iambic Verse. By J. Y. SARGENT, M.A. Extra fcap. 8vo, 4s. 6d.

Graece Reddenda. By C. S. JERRAM, M.A. Extra fcap. 8vo, 2s. 6d.

Reddenda Minora; or, Easy Passages, Latin and Greek, for Unseen Translation. By C. S. JERRAM, M.A. *Third Edition.* Extra fcap. 8vo, 1s. 6d.

Anglice Reddenda; or, Extracts, Latin and Greek, for Unseen Translation. By C. S. JERRAM, M.A. Extra fcap. 8vo, 2s. 6d.

Anglice Reddenda. *Second Series.* By the same Author. Extra fcap. 8vo, 3s.

Models and Exercises in Unseen Translation. By H. F. FOX, M.A., and T. M. BROMLEY, M.A. Extra fcap. 8vo, 5s. 6d.

*** A Key to Passages quoted in the above, price 6d. Supplied to *Teachers* only, on application to the Secretary, Clarendon Press.

Golden Treasury of Ancient Greek Poetry. By R. S. WRIGHT, M.A. *Second Edition.* Revised by EVELYN ABBOTT, M.A., LL.D. Extra fcap. 8vo, 10s. 6d.

Golden Treasury of Greek Prose, being a Collection of the finest passages in the principal Greek Prose Writers, with Introductory Notices and Notes. By R. S. WRIGHT, M.A., and J. E. L. SHADWELL, M.A. Extra fcap. 8vo, 4s. 6d.

GREEK READERS.

Easy Greek Reader. By EVELYN ABBOTT, M.A. In one or two Parts. Extra fcap. 8vo, 3s.

First Greek Reader. By W. G. RUSHBROOKE, M.L. *Third Edition.* Extra fcap. 8vo, 2s. 6d.

Second Greek Reader. By A. M. BELL, M.A. *Second Edition.* Extra fcap. 8vo, 3s.

Specimens of Greek Dialects; being a Fourth Greek Reader. With Introductions, &c. By W. W. MERRY, D.D. Extra fcap. 8vo, 4s. 6d.

Selections from Homer and the Greek Dramatists; being a Fifth Greek Reader. With Explanatory Notes and Introductions to the Study of Greek Epic and Dramatic Poetry. By EVELYN ABBOTT, M.A. Extra fcap. 8vo, 4s. 6d.

Greek: Educational Works.

GREEK CLASSICS FOR SCHOOLS.

Aeschylus. In Single Plays. Extra fcap. 8vo.
  I. Agamemnon. With Introduction and Notes, by ARTHUR SIDGWICK, M.A. *Fourth Edition.* 3s.
  II. Choephoroi. By the same Editor. 3s.
  III. Eumenides. By the same Editor. *New Edition.* 3s.
  IV. Prometheus Bound. With Introduction and Notes, by A. O. PRICKARD, M.A. *Second Edition.* 2s.

Aristophanes. In Single Plays. Edited, with English Notes, Introductions, &c., by W. W. MERRY, D.D. Extra fcap. 8vo.
  I. The Acharnians. *Third Edition,* 3s.
  II. The Clouds. *Third Edition,* 3s.
  III. The Frogs. *Third Edition,* 3s.
  IV. The Knights. *Second Edition,* 3s.
  V. The Birds. 3s. 6d.
  VI. The Wasps. 3s. 6d.

Cebes. Tabula. With Introduction and Notes. By C. S. JERRAM, M.A. Extra fcap. 8vo, 2s. 6d.

Demosthenes. Orations against Philip. With Introduction and Notes, by EVELYN ABBOTT, M.A., and P. E. MATHESON, M.A.
  Vol. I. Philippic I. Olynthiacs I–III. *Third Edition.* Extra fcap. 8vo, 3s.
  Vol. II. De Pace, Philippic II, De Chersoneso, Philippic III. Extra fcap. 8vo, 4s. 6d.

Euripides. In Single Plays. Edited with Introduction and Notes. Extra fcap. 8vo.
  I. Alcestis. By C. S. JERRAM, M.A. *Third Edition.* 2s. 6d.
  II. Cyclops. By W. E. LONG, M.A. 2s. 6d.
  III. Hecuba. By C. H. RUSSELL, M.A. 2s. 6d.
  IV. Helena. By C. S. JERRAM, M.A. 3s.
  V. Heracleidae. By C. S. JERRAM, M.A. 3s.
  VI. Iphigenia in Tauris. By the same Editor. 3s.
  VII. Medea. By C. B. HEBERDEN, M.A. *Second Edition.* 2s.
  VIII. Bacchae. By A. H. CRUICKSHANK, M.A. 3s. 6d.

Herodotus. Book IX. Edited, with Notes, by EVELYN ABBOTT, M.A. Extra fcap. 8vo, 3s.

—— Selections. Edited, with Introduction and Notes, by W. W. MERRY, D.D. Extra fcap. 8vo, 2s. 6d.

Homer.
- I. For Beginners. Iliad, Book III. By M. T. TATHAM, M.A. Extra fcap. 8vo, 1s. 6d.
- II. Iliad, Books I–XII. With an Introduction and a brief Homeric Grammar, and Notes. By D. B. MONRO, M.A. *Third Edition.* Extra fcap. 8vo, 6s.
- III. Iliad, Books XIII–XXIV. With Notes. By the same Editor. *Second Edition.* Extra fcap. 8vo, 6s.
- IV. Iliad, Book I. By the same Editor. *Second Edition.* Extra fcap. 8vo, 2s.
- V. Iliad, Book XXI. With Introduction and Notes. By HERBERT HAILSTONE, M.A. Extra fcap. 8vo, 1s. 6d.
- VI. Odyssey, Books I–XII. By W. W. MERRY, D.D. *Fiftieth Thousand.* Extra fcap. 8vo, 5s.
  - Books I and II, separately, each 1s. 6d.
  - Books VI and VII. Extra fcap. 8vo, 1s. 6d.
- VII. Odyssey, Books VII–XII. By the same Editor. Extra fcap. 8vo, 3s.
- VIII. Odyssey, Books XIII–XXIV. By the same Editor. *Thirteenth Thousand.* Extra fcap. 8vo, 5s.

Lucian. Vera Historia. By C. S. JERRAM, M.A. *Second Edition.* Extra fcap. 8vo, 1s. 6d.

Lysias. Epitaphios. Edited, with Introduction and Notes, by F. J. SNELL, B.A. Extra fcap. 8vo, 2s.

Plato. With Introduction and Notes. By ST. GEORGE STOCK, M.A. Extra fcap. 8vo.
- The Apology. *Second Edition.* 2s. 6d. Crito, 2s.
- Meno. *Second Edition.* 2s. 6d.

—— Selections. With Introductions and Notes. By JOHN PURVES, M.A., and Preface by B. JOWETT, M.A. *Second Edition.* Extra fcap. 8vo, 5s.

Plutarch. Lives of the Gracchi. Edited, with Introduction, Notes, and Indices, by G. E. UNDERHILL, M.A. Crown 8vo. 4s. 6d.

Sophocles. Edited, with Introductions and English Notes, by LEWIS CAMPBELL, M.A., and EVELYN ABBOTT, M.A. *New Edition.* 2 vols. Extra fcap. 8vo, **10s. 6d.**

Sold separately: Vol. I, Text, 4s. 6d.; Vol. II, **Explanatory Notes, 6s.**

Or in single Plays:—

Oedipus Coloneus, Antigone, 1s. 9d. each; Oedipus **Tyrannus,** Ajax, Electra, Trachiniae, Philoctetes, 2s. each.

—— Oedipus Rex: Dindorf's Text, with Notes by the present Bishop of St. David's. Extra fcap. 8vo, limp, 1s. 6d.

Theocritus (for Schools). With English Notes. By H. KYNASTON, **D.D.** (late SNOW). *Fifth Edition.* Extra fcap. 8vo, 4s. **6d.**

XENOPHON. Easy Selections (for Junior Classes). With a Vocabulary, Notes, and Map. By J. S. **PHILLPOTTS,** B.C.L., and C. S. JERRAM, M.A. *Third Edition.* Extra fcap. **8vo, 3s. 6d.**

—— **Selections** (for **Schools).** With Notes and Maps. By J. S. PHILLPOTTS, B.C.L. *Fourth Edition.* Extra fcap. **8vo, 3s. 6d.**

—— Anabasis, Book **I.** Edited for the use of Junior **Classes** and Private Students. With Introduction, Notes, &c. By J. MARSHALL, **M.A.** Extra fcap. 8vo, 2s. 6d.

—— Anabasis, Book II. With Notes and Map. **By C. S.** JERRAM, M.A. Extra fcap. 8vo, 2s.

—— Anabasis, **Book III.** With Introduction, **Analysis,** Notes, &c. By J. **MARSHALL,** M.A. Extra fcap. 8vo, 2s. **6d.**

—— Anabasis, Book **IV.** By J. MARSHALL, M.A. Extra fcap. 8vo, 2s.

—— Vocabulary to the Anabasis. By J. MARSHALL, M.A. Extra fcap. 8vo, 1s. 6d.

—— Cyropaedia, Book I. With Introduction and Notes. By C. BIGG, D.D. **Extra fcap. 8vo,** 2s.

—— Cyropaedia, Books IV and V. With Introduction and Notes. By **C.** BIGG, D.D. Extra fcap. 8vo, 2s. 6d.

—— Hellenica, Books I, II. With Introduction and Notes. By G. E. UNDERHILL, M.A. Extra fcap. 8vo, **3s.**

—— **Mem**orabilia. Edited with Introduction and Notes, &c., by J. MARSHALL, M.A. Extra fcap. 8vo, 4s. 6d.

SECTION V.
ORIENTAL LANGUAGES*.
THE SACRED BOOKS OF THE EAST.

Translated by various Oriental Scholars, and edited by
F. Max Müller.

First Series, Vols. I—XXIV. Demy 8vo, cloth.

Vol. I. The Upanishads. Translated by F. Max Müller. Part I. 10s. 6d.

Vol. II. The Sacred Laws of the Âryas, as taught in the Schools of Âpastamba, Gautama, Vâsishtha, and Baudhâyana. Translated by Prof. Georg Bühler. Part I. 10s. 6d.

Vol. III. The Sacred Books of China. The Texts of Confucianism. Translated by James Legge. Part I. 12s. 6d.

Vol. IV. The Zend-Avesta. Part I. The Vendîdâd. Translated by James Darmesteter. 10s. 6d.

Vol. V. The Pahlavi Texts. Translated by E. W. West. Part I. 12s. 6d.

Vols. VI and IX. The Qur'ân. Translated by E. H. Palmer. 21s.

Vol. VII. The Institutes of Vishnu. Translated by Julius Jolly. 10s. 6d.

Vol. VIII. The Bhagavadgîtâ, with The Sanatsugâtîya, and The Anugîtâ. Translated by Kâshinâth Trimbak Telang. 10s. 6d.

Vol. X. The Dhammapada, translated from Pâli by F. Max Müller; and The Sutta-Nipâta, translated from Pâli by V. Fausböll; being Canonical Books of the Buddhists. 10s. 6d.

Vol. XI. Buddhist Suttas. Translated from Pâli by T. W. Rhys Davids. 10s. 6d.

Vol. XII. The Satapatha-Brâhmana, according to the Text of the Mâdhyandina School. Translated by Julius Eggeling. Part I. Books I and II. 12s. 6d.

Vol. XIII. Vinaya Texts. Translated from the Pâli by T. W. Rhys Davids and Hermann Oldenberg. Part I. 10s. 6d.

---

* See also Anecdota Oxon., Series II, III, pp. 41-42, below.

The Sacred Books of the East (*continued*).

Vol. XIV. The Sacred Laws of the Âryas, as taught in the Schools of Âpastamba, Gautama, Vâsish*tha* and Baudhâyana. Translated by GEORG BÜHLER. Part II. 10s. 6d.

Vol. XV. The Upanishads. Translated by F. MAX MÜLLER. Part II. 10s. 6d.

Vol. XVI. The Sacred Books of China. The Texts of Confucianism. Translated by JAMES LEGGE. Part II. 10s. 6d.

Vol. XVII. Vinaya Texts. Translated from the Pâli by T. W. RHYS DAVIDS and HERMANN OLDENBERG. Part II. 10s. 6d.

Vol. XVIII. Pahlavi Texts. Translated by E. W. WEST. Part II. 12s. 6d.

Vol. XIX. The Fo-sho-hing-tsan-king. A Life of Buddha by Asvaghosha Bodhisattva, translated from Sanskrit into Chinese by Dharmaraksha, A.D. 420, and from Chinese into English by SAMUEL BEAL. 10s. 6d.

Vol. XX. Vinaya Texts. Translated from the Pâli by T. W. RHYS DAVIDS and HERMANN OLDENBERG. Part III. 10s. 6d.

Vol. XXI. The Saddharma-pu*nd*arika; or, the Lotus of the True Law. Translated by H. KERN. 12s. 6d.

Vol. XXII. Gaina-Sûtras. Translated from Prâkrit by HERMANN JACOBI. Part I. 10s. 6d.

Vol. XXIII. The Zend-Avesta. Part II. Translated by JAMES DARMESTETER. 10s. 6d.

Vol. XXIV. Pahlavi Texts. Translated by E. W. WEST. Part III. 10s. 6d.

Second Series.

Vol. XXV. Manu. Translated by GEORG BÜHLER. 21s.

Vol. XXVI. The *S*atapatha-Brâhma*n*a. Translated by JULIUS EGGELING. Part II. 12s. 6d.

Vols. XXVII and XXVIII. The Sacred Books of China. The Texts of Confucianism. Translated by JAMES LEGGE. Parts III and IV. 25s.

Vols. XXIX and XXX. The Grihya-Sûtras, Rules of Vedic Domestic Ceremonies. Translated by HERMANN OLDENBERG.

Part I (Vol. XXIX). 12s. 6d.
Part II (Vol. XXX). 12s. 6d.

I. Literature and Philology.

The Sacred Books of the East (*continued*).

Vol. XXXI. The Zend-Avesta. Part III. Translated by L. H. MILLS. 12s. 6d.

Vol. XXXII. Vedic Hymns. Translated by F. MAX MÜLLER. Part I. 18s. 6d.

Vol. XXXIII. Nârada, and some Minor Law-books. Translated by JULIUS JOLLY. 10s. 6d.

Vol. XXXIV. The Vedânta-Sûtras, with Sankara's Commentary. Translated by G. THIBAUT. 12s. 6d.

Vol. XXXV. The Questions of King Milinda. Part I. Translated from the Pâli by T. W. RHYS DAVIDS. 10s. 6d.

Vols. XXXIX and XL. The Sacred Books of China. The Texts of Tâoism. Translated by JAMES LEGGE. 21s.

Vol. XXXVII. The Contents of the Nasks, as stated in the Eighth and Ninth Books of the Dînkard. Part I. Translated by E. W. WEST. 15s.

Vol. XLI. Satapatha-Brâhmana. Part III. Translated by JULIUS EGGELING. 12s. 6d.

In the Press:—

Vol. XXXVI. The Questions of King Milinda. Part II. Translated by T. W. RHYS DAVIDS.

Vol. XXXVIII. The Vedânta-Sûtras. Part II.

Vol. XLII. The Buddha-karita. Translated by E. B. COWELL. The Sukhâvatî-vyûha. Translated by F. MAX MÜLLER.

ARABIC. A Practical Arabic Grammar. Compiled by A. O. GREEN, Brigade Major, Royal Engineers.
Part I. *Third Edition.* Revised and Enlarged. Crown 8vo, 7s. 6d.
Part II. *Third Edition.* Revised and Enlarged. 10s. 6d.

BENGALI. Grammar of the Bengali Language; Literary and Colloquial. By JOHN BEAMES. Crown 8vo, cloth, 4s. 6d.

CHINESE. The Chinese Classics: with a Translation, Critical and Exegetical Notes, Prolegomena, and Copious Indexes. By JAMES LEGGE, D.D., LL.D. In Eight Volumes. Royal 8vo.

Vol. I. Confucian Analects, &c. *New Edition.* 1l. 10s.

Vol. II. The Works of Mencius. 1l. 10s.

Vol. III. The Shoo-King; or, The Book of Historical Documents. In two Parts. 1l. 10s. each.

Vol. IV. The She-King; or, The Book of Poetry. In two Parts. 1l. 10s. each.

Vol. V. The Ch'un Ts'ew, with the Tso Chuen. In two Parts. 1l. 10s. each.

Oxford: Clarendon Press.

CHINESE. The Nestorian Monument of Hsî-an Fû in Shen-hsî, China, relating to the Diffusion of Christianity in China in the Seventh and Eighth Centuries. By JAMES LEGGE, D.D. 2s. 6d.

—— Record of Buddhistic Kingdoms; being an Account by the Chinese Monk FÂ-HIEN of his travels in India and Ceylon (A.D. 399–414). Translated and annotated, with a Corean recension of the Chinese Text, by JAMES LEGGE, D.D. Crown 4to, boards, 10s. 6d.

—— Catalogue of the Chinese Translation of the Buddhist Tripitaka, the Sacred Canon of the Buddhists in China and Japan. Compiled by BUNYIU NANJIO. 4to, 1l. 12s. 6d.

—— Handbook of the Chinese Language. Parts I and II. Grammar and Chrestomathy. By JAMES SUMMERS. 8vo, 1l. 8s.

CHALDEE. Book of Tobit. A Chaldee Text, from a unique MS. in the Bodleian Library. Edited by AD. NEUBAUER, M.A. Crown 8vo, 6s.

COPTIC. Libri Prophetarum Majorum, cum Lamentationibus Jeremiae, in Dialecto Linguae Aegyptiacae Memphitica seu Coptica. Edidit cum Versione Latina H. TATTAM, S.T.P. Tomi II. 8vo, 17s.

—— Libri duodecim Prophetarum Minorum in Ling. Aegypt. vulgo Coptica. Edidit H. TATTAM, A.M. 8vo, 8s. 6d.

—— Novum Testamentum Coptice, cura D. WILKINS. 12s. 6d.

HEBREW. Psalms in Hebrew (without points). Cr. 8vo, 2s.

  Driver. Notes on the Hebrew Text of the Books of Samuel. By S. R. DRIVER, D.D. 8vo, 14s.

  —— Treatise on the use of the Tenses in Hebrew. By S. R. DRIVER, D.D. *Third Edition*. Crown 8vo, 7s. 6d.

  —— Commentary on the Book of Proverbs. Attributed to Abraham Ibn Ezra. Edited from a Manuscript in the Bodleian Library by S. R. DRIVER, D.D. Crown 8vo, paper covers, 3s. 6d.

  A Hebrew and English Lexicon of the Old Testament, with an Appendix containing the Biblical Aramaic, based on the Thesaurus and Lexicon of GESENIUS, by FRANCIS BROWN, D.D., S. R. DRIVER, D.D., and C. A. BRIGGS, D.D. Parts I and II. Small 4to, each, 2s. 6d.

  Neubauer. Book of Hebrew Roots, by Abu 'l-Walîd Marwân ibn Janâh, otherwise called Rabbi Yônâh. Now first edited, with an Appendix, by AD. NEUBAUER. 4to, 2l. 7s. 6d.

  Spurrell. Notes on the Hebrew Text of the Book of Genesis. By G. J. SPURRELL, M.A. Crown 8vo, 10s. 6d.

  Wickes. Hebrew Accentuation of Psalms, Proverbs, and Job. By WILLIAM WICKES, D.D. 8vo, 5s.

  —— Hebrew Prose Accentuation. 8vo, 10s. 6d.

I. Literature and Philology.

SANSKRIT.—Sanskrit-English **Dictionary**, Etymologically and Philologically arranged, with special reference to Greek, Latin, German, Anglo-Saxon, English, and other cognate Indo-European Languages. By Sir M. MONIER-WILLIAMS, D.C.L. 4to, 4*l*. **14s**. 6*d*.

—— Practical **Grammar of the Sanskrit** Language, arranged with reference to the Classical Languages of Europe, by Sir M. MONIER-WILLIAMS, **D.C.L.** *Fourth Edition*. 8vo, **15s**.

—— Nalopákhyánam. Story of Nala, an Episode of the Mahábhárata: Sanskrit Text, with a copious Vocabulary, and an improved version of Dean Milman's Translation, by Sir M. MONIER-WILLIAMS, **D.C.L.** *Second Edition, Revised and Improved*. 8vo, 15s.

—— Sakuntalā. A **Sanskrit** Drama, in seven Acts. Edited by SIR M. MONIER-WILLIAMS, **D.C.L.** *Second Edition*. 8vo, 1*l*. 1s.

SYRIAC.—**Thesaurus Syriacus**: collegerunt Quatremère, Bernstein, Lorsbach, Arnoldi, Agrell, Field, Roediger: edidit R. PAYNE SMITH, S.T.P. Vol. I, containing Fasc. I–V. Sm. fol. 5*l*. 5s.
  Fasc. VI, 1*l*. 1s.; VII, 1*l*. 11s. 6*d*.; VIII, 1*l*. 16s.; IX, 1*l*. 5s.

—— **The** Book of **Kalīlah** and **Dimnah. Translated** from Arabic into Syriac. Edited by W. WRIGHT, LL.D. 8vo. 1*l*. 1s.

—— **Cyrilli** Archiepiscopi Alexandrini Commentarii in Lucae Evangelium quae supersunt Syriace. E MSS. apud Mus. Britan. edidit R. PAYNE SMITH, A.M. 4to, 1*l*. 2s.

—— —— Translated by R. **PAYNE** SMITH, M.A. 2 vols. 8vo, 14s.

—— **Ephraemi Syri, Rabulae** Episcopi Edesseni, **Balaei**, &c., Opera Selecta. E Codd. Syriacis MSS. in Museo Britannico et Bibliotheca Bodleiana asservatis primus edidit J. J. OVERBECK. 8vo, 1*l*. 1s.

—— **John**, Bishop of Ephesus. The Third Part of his Ecclesiastical History. [In Syriac.] Now first edited by WILLIAM CURETON, M.A. 4to, 1*l*. 12s.

—— —— Translated by R. PAYNE SMITH, M.A. 8vo, 10s.

TAMIL. First Lessons in Tamil. By G. U. POPE, **D.D.** *Fifth Edition*. Crown 8vo, 7s. 6*d*.

—— The Nāladiyār, or **Four** Hundred Quatrains in Tamil. Edited by G. U. POPE, D.D. **8vo, 18s.** *Large Paper*, 2*l*. *half Roxburgh*.

ZEND. The Ancient **MS.** of the **Yasna**, with its Pahlavi Translation (A.D. 1323), generally quoted as J2, and now in the possession of the Bodleian Library. Reproduced in Facsimile, and Edited with an Introductory Note by L. H. MILLS, D.D. Half-bound, Imperial 4to, 10*l*. 10s. *net*.

Oxford: Clarendon Press.

SECTION VI.
ANECDOTA OXONIENSIA.
(Crown 4to, stiff covers.)

I. CLASSICAL SERIES.

I. The English Manuscripts of the Nicomachean Ethics.
By J. A. STEWART, M.A. 3s. 6d.

II. Nonius Marcellus, de Compendiosa Doctrina, Harleian MS. 2719. Collated by J. H. ONIONS, M.A. 3s. 6d.

III. Aristotle's Physics. Book VII. With Introduction by R. SHUTE, M.A. 2s.

IV. Bentley's Plautine Emendations. From his copy of Gronovius. By E. A. SONNENSCHEIN, M.A. 2s. 6d.

V. Harleian MS. 2610; Ovid's Metamorphoses I, II, III. 1–622; XXIV Latin Epigrams from Bodleian or other MSS.; Latin Glosses on Apollinaris Sidonius from MS. Digby 172. Collated and Edited by ROBINSON ELLIS, M.A., LL.D. 4s.

VI. A Collation with the Ancient Armenian Versions of the Greek Text of Aristotle's Categories, De Interpretatione, De Mundo, De Virtutibus et Vitiis, and of Porphyry's Introduction. By F. C. CONYBEARE, M.A. 14s.

VII. Collations from the Harleian MS. of Cicero 2682. By ALBERT C. CLARK, M.A. 7s. 6d.

II. SEMITIC SERIES.

I. Commentary on Ezra and Nehemiah. By Rabbi Saadiah. Edited by H. J. MATHEWS, M.A. 3s. 6d.

II. The Book of the Bee. Edited by ERNEST A. WALLIS BUDGE, M.A. 21s.

III. A Commentary on the Book of Daniel. By Japhet Ibn Ali. Edited and Translated by D. S. MARGOLIOUTH, M.A. 21s.

IV. Mediaeval Jewish Chronicles and Chronological Notes. Edited by AD. NEUBAUER, M.A. 14s.

V. The Palestinian Version of the Holy Scriptures. Five more Fragments recently acquired by the Bodleian Library. Edited by G. H. GWILLIAM, B.D. 6s.

London: HENRY FROWDE, Amen Corner, E.C.

ANECDOTA OXONIENSIA (continued).

III. ARYAN SERIES.

I. Buddhist Texts from Japan. 1. Va*grakkh*edikâ. Edited by F. MAX MÜLLER. 3s. 6d.

II. Buddhist Texts from Japan. 2. Sukhâvatî Vyûha. Edited by F. MAX MÜLLER, M.A., and BUNYIU NANJIO. 7s. 6d.

III. Buddhist Texts from Japan. 3. The Ancient Palm-leaves containing the Pra*gñâ*-Pâramitâ-H*r*idaya-Sûtra and the Ush*n*isha-Vi*g*aya-Dhâra*n*î, edited by F. MAX MÜLLER, M.A., and BUNYIU NANJIO, M.A. With an Appendix by G. BÜHLER. 10s.

IV. Kâtyâyana's Sarvânukrama*n*î of the *R*igveda. With Extracts from Sha*d*gurusishya's Commentary entitled Vedârthadîpikâ. Edited by A. A. MACDONELL, M.A., Ph.D. 16s.

V. The Dharma Sa*m*graha. Edited by KENJIU KASAWARA, F. MAX MÜLLER, and H. WENZEL. 7s. 6d.

VII. The Buddha-*K*arita of A*s*vaghosha. Edited, from three MSS., by E. B. COWELL, M.A. 12s. 6d.

IV. MEDIAEVAL AND MODERN SERIES.

I. Sinonoma Bartholomei. Edited by J. L. G. MOWAT, M.A. 3s. 6d.

II. Alphita. Edited by J. L. G. MOWAT, M.A. 12s. 6d.

III. The Saltair Na Rann. Edited from a MS. in the Bodleian Library, by WHITLEY STOKES, D.C.L. 7s. 6d.

IV. The Cath Finntrága, or Battle of Ventry. Edited by KUNO MEYER, Ph.D., M.A. 6s.

V. Lives of Saints, from the Book of Lismore. Edited, with Translation, by WHITLEY STOKES, D.C.L. 1l. 11s. 6d.

Oxford: Clarendon Press.

II. THEOLOGY.

A. THE HOLY SCRIPTURES, APOCRYPHA, &c.

COPTIC. Libri Prophetarum Majorum, cum Lamentationibus Jeremiae, in Dialecto Linguae Aegyptiacae Memphitica seu Coptica. Edidit cum Versione Latina H. TATTAM, S.T.P. Tomi II. 8vo, 17s.

—— Libri duodecim Prophetarum Minorum in Ling. Aegypt. vulgo Coptica. Edidit H. TATTAM, A.M. 8vo, 8s. 6d.

—— Novum Testamentum Coptice, cura D. WILKINS. 1716. 4to, 12s. 6d.

ENGLISH. The Holy Bible in the Earliest English **Versions**, made from the Latin Vulgate by JOHN WYCLIFFE and his followers: edited by FORSHALL and MADDEN. 4 vols. Royal 4to, 3l. 3s.

Also reprinted from the above, with Introduction and Glossary by W. W. SKEAT, Litt.D.

I. The Books of Job, Psalms, Proverbs, Ecclesiastes, and the Song of Solomon. Extra fcap. 8vo, 3s. 6d.

II. The New Testament. Extra fcap. 8vo, 6s.

—— The **Holy Bible: an exact reprint, page for page, of** the Authorised Version published in the year 1611. Demy 4to, half-bound. 1l. 1s.

—— **The Holy Bible, Revised Version***.

Cheap editions for School Use.

Revised Bible. Pearl 16mo, cloth boards, 1s. 6d.

Revised New Testament. Nonpareil 32mo, 6d.; Brevier 16mo, 1s. Long Primer 8vo, 1s. 6d.

—— **The Oxford Bible for Teachers,** containing the Holy Scriptures, together with a new, enlarged, and illustrated edition of the OXFORD HELPS TO THE STUDY OF THE BIBLE, comprising Introductions to the several Books, the History and Antiquities of the Jews, the results of Modern Discoveries, and the Natural History of Palestine, with copious Tables, Concordance and Indices, and a series of Maps. Prices in various sizes and bindings from 7s. 6d. to 2l. 2s.

---

* *The Revised Version is the joint property of the Universities of Oxford and Cambridge.*

London: HENRY FROWDE, Amen Corner, E.C.

II. Theology.

ENGLISH (*continued*).

—— **Helps to the Study of the Bible**, taken from the OXFORD BIBLE FOR TEACHERS. *New, Enlarged, and Illustrated Edition.* Crown 8vo, 4s. 6d.

—— **The Psalter, or** Psalms of David, and certain Canticles, with a Translation and Exposition in English, by RICHARD ROLLE of Hampole. Edited by H. R. BRAMLEY, M.A., Fellow of S. M. Magdalen College, Oxford. With an Introduction and Glossary. Demy 8vo, 1l. 1s.

—— **Studia** Biblica et Ecclesiastica. Essays in Biblical and Patristic Criticism, and kindred subjects. By Members of the University of Oxford. 8vo.
  Vol. I, 10s. 6d. Vol. II, 12s. 6d. Vol. III, 16s.

—— Lectures on the Book of Job. Delivered in Westminster Abbey by the Very Rev. G. G. BRADLEY, D.D. *Second Edition.* Crown 8vo, 7s. 6d.

—— Lectures on Ecclesiastes. By the same Author. Cr. 8vo, 4s. 6d.

—— The Book of Wisdom: the Greek Text, the Latin Vulgate, and the Authorised English Version; with an Introduction, Critical Apparatus, and a Commentary. By W. J. DEANE, M.A. 4to, 12s. 6d.

—— **The Five** Books **of Maccabees**, in English, with Notes and Illustrations by HENRY COTTON, D.C.L. 8vo, 10s. 6d.

—— **The Book of Enoch**. Translated from Dillmann's Ethiopic Text (emended and revised), and Edited by R. H. CHARLES, M.A. 8vo, 16s.

—— List of Editions of **the** Bible in English. By HENRY COTTON, D.C.L. *Second Edition.* 8vo, 8s. 6d.

—— Rhemes and Doway. An attempt to show what has been done by Roman Catholics for the diffusion of the Holy Scriptures in English. By HENRY COTTON, D.C.L. 8vo, 9s.

GOTHIC. Evangeliorum Versio Gothica, cum Interpr. et Annott. E. BENZELII. Edidit E. LYE, A.M. 4to, 12s. 6d.

—— **The Gospel** of St. Mark in Gothic, according to the translation made by WULFILA in the Fourth Century. Edited by W. W. SKEAT, Litt.D. Extra fcap. 8vo, 4s.

GREEK. Old Testament. Vetus Testamentum ex Versione Septuaginta Interpretum secundum exemplar Vaticanum Romae editum. Accedit potior varietas Codicis Alexandrini. Tomi III. 18mo, 18s.

—— Vetus Testamentum Graece cum Variis Lectionibus. Editionem a R. HOLMES, S.T.P. inchoatam continuavit J. PARSONS, S.T.B. Tomi V. folio, 7l.

Oxford: Clarendon Press.

GREEK (*continued*).

—— **A Concordance to the Septuagint** and the other Greek Versions of the Old Testament (including the Apocryphal Books). By the late EDWIN HATCH, M.A., and H. A. REDPATH, M.A. Parts I–III. A–ΊΩΒΗΛ. Imperial 4to, *each*, 21*s*. Part IV. *In the Press.*

—— Origenis Hexaplorum quae supersunt; sive, Veterum Interpretum Graecorum in totum Vetus Testamentum Fragmenta. Edidit FREDERICUS FIELD, A.M. 2 vols. 1875. 4to, 5*l*. 5*s*.

—— Essays in Biblical Greek. By EDWIN HATCH, M.A., D.D. 8vo, 10*s*. 6*d*.

—— An Essay on the Place of Ecclesiasticus in Semitic Literature. By D. S. MARGOLIOUTH, M.A., Laudian Professor of Arabic in the University of Oxford. Small 4to, 2*s*. 6*d*.

—— New Testament. Novum Testamentum Graece. Antiquissimorum Codicum Textus in ordine parallelo dispositi. Edidit E. H. HANSELL, S.T.B. Tomi III. 8vo, 24*s*.

—— Novum Testamentum Graece. Accedunt parallela S. Scripturae loca, &c. Edidit CAROLUS LLOYD, S.T.P.R. 18mo, 3*s*. *On writing paper, with wide margin*, 7*s*. 6*d*.

  Critical Appendices to the above, by W. SANDAY, M.A. Extra fcap. 8vo, cloth, 3*s*. 6*d*.

—— Novum Testamentum Graece. Accedunt parallela S. Scripturae loca, &c. Ed. C. LLOYD, with SANDAY's Appendices. Cloth, 6*s*.; paste grain, 7*s*. 6*d*.; morocco, 10*s*. 6*d*.

—— Novum Testamentum Graece juxta Exemplar Millianum. 18mo, 2*s*. 6*d*. *On writing paper, with wide margin*, 7*s*. 6*d*.

—— Evangelia Sacra Graece. Fcap. 8vo, limp, 1*s*. 6*d*.

—— The Greek Testament, with the Readings adopted by the Revisers of the Authorised Version:—
  (1) Pica type, with Marginal References. Demy 8vo, 10*s*. 6*d*.
  (2) Long Primer type. Fcap. 8vo, 4*s*. 6*d*.
  (3) *The same, on writing paper, with wide margin*, 15*s*.

—— The New Testament in Greek and English. Edited by E. CARDWELL, D.D. 2 vols. 1837. Crown 8vo, 6*s*.

—— The Parallel New Testament, Greek and English; being the Authorised Version, 1611; the Revised Version, 1881; and the Greek Text followed in the Revised Version. 8vo, 12*s*. 6*d*.

—— Diatessaron; sive Historia Jesu Christi ex ipsis Evangelistarum verbis apte dispositis confecta. Ed. J. WHITE. 3*s*. 6*d*.

II. Theology.

GREEK (*continued*).

—— Outlines of Textual Criticism applied to the New Testament. By C. E. Hammond, M.A. *Fifth Edition.* Crown 8vo, 4s. 6d.

—— A Greek Testament Primer. An Easy Grammar and Reading Book for the use of Students beginning Greek. By E. Miller, M.A. Extra fcap. 8vo, 3s. 6d.

—— Canon Muratorianus. Edited, with Notes and Facsimile, by S. P. Tregelles, LL.D. 4to, 10s. 6d.

HEBREW, &c. A Hebrew and English Lexicon of the Old Testament, with an Appendix containing the Biblical Aramaic, based on the Thesaurus and Lexicon of Gesenius, by Francis Brown, D.D., S. R. Driver, D.D., and C. A. Briggs, D.D. Parts I and II. Small 4to, each 2s. 6d.

—— Notes on the Hebrew Text of the Book of Genesis. By G. J. Spurrell, M.A. Crown 8vo, 10s. 6d.

—— Notes on the Hebrew Text of the Books of Samuel. By S. R. Driver, D.D. 8vo, 14s.

—— The Psalms in Hebrew without points. Stiff covers, 2s.

—— A Commentary on the Book of Proverbs. Attributed to Abraham Ibn Ezra. Edited from a MS. in the Bodleian Library by S. R. Driver, D.D. Crown 8vo, paper covers, 3s. 6d.

—— The Book of Tobit. A Chaldee Text, from a unique MS. in the Bodleian Library; with other Rabbinical Texts, English Translations, and the Itala. Edited by Ad. Neubauer, M.A. Crown 8vo, 6s.

—— Hebrew Accentuation of Psalms, Proverbs, and Job. By William Wickes, D.D. 8vo, 5s.

—— Hebrew Prose Accentuation. By the same. 8vo, 10s. 6d.

—— Horae Hebraicae et Talmudicae, a J. Lightfoot. A new Edition, by R. Gandell, M.A. 4 vols. 8vo, 1l. 1s.

LATIN. Libri Psalmorum Versio antiqua Latina, cum Paraphrasi Anglo-Saxonica. Edidit B. Thorpe, F.A.S. 8vo, 10s. 6d.

—— Nouum Testamentum Domini Nostri Iesu Christi Latine, secundum Editionem Sancti Hieronymi. Ad Codicum Manuscriptorum fidem recensuit Iohannes Wordsworth, S.T.P., Episcopus Sarisburiensis ; in operis societatem adsumto Henrico Iuliano White, A.M. 4to.

    Fasc. I.   *Euangelium secundum Mattheum.* 12s. 6d.
    Fasc. II. *Euangelium secundum Marcum.* 7s. 6d.
    Fasc. III. *Euangelium secundum Lucam.* 12s. 6d.

Oxford: Clarendon Press.

LATIN (*continued*).

—— Old-Latin Biblical Texts: No. I. The Gospel according to St. Matthew, from the St. Germain MS. (g₁). Edited by JOHN WORDSWORTH, D.D. Small 4to, stiff covers, 6s.

—— Old-Latin Biblical Texts: No. II. Portions of the Gospels according to St. Mark and St. Matthew, from the Bobbio MS. (k), &c. Edited by JOHN WORDSWORTH, D.D., W. SANDAY, M.A., D.D., and H. J. WHITE, M.A. Small 4to, stiff covers, 21s.

—— Old-Latin Biblical Texts: No. III. The Four Gospels, from the Munich MS. (q), now numbered Lat. 6224 in the Royal Library at Munich. With a Fragment from St. John in the Hof-Bibliothek at Vienna (Cod. Lat. 502). Edited, with the aid of Tischendorf's transcript (under the direction of the Bishop of Salisbury), by H. J. WHITE, M.A. Small 4to, stiff covers, 12s. 6d.

OLD-FRENCH. Libri Psalmorum Versio antiqua Gallica e Cod. MS. in Bibl. Bodleiana adservato, una cum Versione Metrica aliisque Monumentis pervetustis. Nunc primum descripsit et edidit FRANCISCUS MICHEL, Phil. Doc. 8vo, 10s. 6d.

B. FATHERS OF THE CHURCH, &c.

St. **Athanasius**: Orations against the Arians. With an Account of his Life by WILLIAM BRIGHT, D.D. Crown 8vo, 9s.

—— Historical Writings, according to the Benedictine Text. With an Introduction by W. BRIGHT, D.D. Crown 8vo, 10s. 6d.

St. **Augustine**: Select Anti-Pelagian Treatises, and the Acts of the Second Council of Orange. With an Introduction by WILLIAM BRIGHT, D.D. Crown 8vo, 9s.

St. **Basil**: The Book of St. Basil on the Holy Spirit. A Revised Text, with Notes and Introduction by C. F. H. JOHNSTON, M.A. Crown 8vo, 7s. 6d.

Barnabas, The Editio Princeps of the Epistle of, by Archbishop Ussher, as printed at Oxford, A.D. 1642, and preserved in an imperfect form in the Bodleian Library. With a Dissertation by J. H. BACKHOUSE, M.A. Small 4to, 3s. 6d.

Canons of the First Four General Councils of Nicaea, Constantinople, Ephesus, and Chalcedon. With Notes, by W. BRIGHT, D.D. *Second Edition.* Crown 8vo, 7s. 6d.

Catenae Graecorum Patrum in Novum Testamentum. Edidit J. A. CRAMER, S.T.P. Tomi VIII. 8vo, 2l. 4s.

II. Theology.

Clementis Alexandrini Opera, ex recensione Guil. Dindorfii. Tomi IV. 8vo, 3*l*.

Cyrilli Archiepiscopi Alexandrini in XII Prophetas. Edidit P. E. Pusey, A.M. Tomi II. 8vo, 2*l*. 2*s*.

—— in D. Joannis Evangelium. Accedunt Fragmenta Varia necnon Tractatus ad Tiberium Diaconum Duo. Edidit post Aubertum P. E. Pusey, A.M. Tomi III. 8vo, 2*l*. 5*s*.

—— Commentarii in Lucae Evangelium quae supersunt Syriace. E MSS. apud Mus. Britan. edidit R. Payne Smith, A.M. 4to, 1*l*. 2*s*.

—— —— Translated by R. Payne Smith, M.A. 2 vols, 14*s*.

Ephraemi Syri, Rabulae Episcopi Edesseni, Balaei, aliorumque Opera Selecta. E Codd. Syriacis MSS. in Museo Britannico et Bibliotheca Bodleiana asservatis primus edidit J. J. Overbeck. 8vo, 1*l*. 1*s*.

Eusebii Pamphili Evangelicae Praeparationis Libri XV. Ad Codd. MSS. recensuit T. Gaisford, S.T.P. Tomi IV. 8vo, 1*l*. 10*s*.

—— Evangelicae Demonstrationis Libri X. Recensuit T. Gaisford, S.T.P. Tomi II. 8vo, 15*s*.

—— contra Hieroclem et Marcellum Libri. Recensuit T. Gaisford, S.T.P. 8vo, 7*s*.

Eusebius' Ecclesiastical History, according to the text of Burton, with an Introduction by W. Bright, D.D. *Second Edition.* Crown 8vo, 8*s*. 6*d*.

—— —— Annotationes Variorum. Tomi II. 8vo, 17*s*.

Evagrii Historia Ecclesiastica, ex recensione H. Valesii. 1844. 8vo, 4*s*.

Irenaeus: The Third Book of St. Irenaeus, Bishop of Lyons, against Heresies. With short Notes and a Glossary by H. Deane, B.D. Crown 8vo, 5*s*. 6*d*.

Origenis Philosophumena; **sive** omnium Haeresium Refutatio. E Codice Parisino nunc primum edidit Emmanuel Miller. 8vo, 10*s*.

Patrum Apostolicorum, S. Clementis Romani, S. Ignatii, S. Polycarpi, quae supersunt. Edidit Guil. Jacobson, S.T.P.R. Tomi II. *Fourth Edition.* 8vo, 1*l*. 1*s*.

Reliquiae Sacrae secundi tertiique saeculi. Recensuit M. J. Routh, S.T.P. Tomi V. *Second Edition.* 8vo, 1*l*. 5*s*.

Scriptorum Ecclesiasticorum Opuscula. Recensuit M. J. Routh, S.T.P. Tomi II. *Third Edition.* 8vo, 10*s*.

Oxford: Clarendon Press.

Ecclesiastical History, &c.

Socratis Scholastici Historia Ecclesiastica. Gr. et Lat. Edidit R. Hussey, S.T.B. Tomi III. 1853. 8vo, 15s.

Socrates' Ecclesiastical History, according to the Text of Hussey, with an Introduction by William Bright, D.D. *Second Edition.* Crown 8vo, 7s. 6d.

Sozomeni Historia Ecclesiastica. Edidit R. Hussey, S.T.B. Tomi III. 8vo, 15s.

Tertulliani Apologeticus adversus Gentes pro Christianis. Edited, with Introduction and Notes, by T. Herbert Bindley, M.A. Crown 8vo, 6s.

De Praescriptione Haereticorum ad Martyras: ad Scapulam. With Introductions and Notes. By the same Editor. Crown, 8vo, 7s. 6d.

Theodoreti Ecclesiasticae Historiae Libri V. Recensuit T. Gaisford, S.T.P. 8vo, 7s. 6d.

—— Graecarum Affectionum Curatio. Ad Codices MSS. recensuit T. Gaisford, S.T.P. 8vo, 7s. 6d.

C. ECCLESIASTICAL HISTORY, &c.

Baedae Historia Ecclesiastica. Edited, with English Notes, by G. H. Moberly, M.A. Crown 8vo, 10s. 6d.

Bigg. The Christian Platonists of Alexandria; being the Bampton Lectures for 1886. By Charles Bigg, D.D. 8vo, 10s. 6d.

Bingham's Antiquities of the Christian Church, and other Works. 10 vols. 8vo, 3l. 3s.

Bright. Chapters of Early English Church History. By W. Bright, D.D. *Second Edition.* 8vo, 12s.

Burnet's History of the Reformation of the Church of England. *A new Edition.* Carefully revised, and the Records collated with the originals, by N. Pocock, M.A. 7 vols. 8vo, 1l. 10s.

Cardwell's Documentary Annals of the **Reformed Church** of England; being a Collection of Injunctions, Declarations, Orders, **Articles** of Inquiry, &c., from 1546 to 1716. 2 vols. 8vo, 18s.

Councils and Ecclesiastical **Documents** relating to Great Britain and Ireland. Edited, after Spelman and Wilkins, by A. W. Haddan, B.D., and W. Stubbs, D.D. Vols. I and III. Medium 8vo, each 1l. 1s.

Vol. II, Part I. Medium 8vo, 10s. 6d.

Vol. II, Part II. Church of Ireland; Memorials of St. Patrick. Stiff covers, 3s. 6d.

London: Henry Frowde, Amen Corner, E.C.

II. Theology.

Formularies of Faith set forth by the King's authority during the Reign of Henry VIII. 8vo, 7s.

Fuller's Church History of Britain. Edited by J. S. BREWER, M.A. 6 vols. 8vo, 1l. 19s.

Gibson's Synodus Anglicana. Edited by E. CARDWELL, D.D. 8vo, 6s.

Hamilton's (Archbishop John) Catechism, 1552. Edited, with Introduction and Glossary, by THOMAS GRAVES LAW, Librarian of the Signet Library, Edinburgh. With a Preface by the Right Hon. W. E. GLADSTONE. Demy 8vo, 12s. 6d.

Inett's Origines Anglicanae (in continuation of Stillingfleet). Edited by J. GRIFFITHS, M.A. 3 vols. 8vo, 15s.

John, Bishop of Ephesus. The Third Part of his Ecclesiastical History. [In Syriac.] Now first edited by WILLIAM CURETON, M.A. 4to, 1l. 12s.

—— The same, translated by R. PAYNE SMITH, M.A. 8vo, 10s.

Le Neve's Fasti Ecclesiae Anglicanae. Corrected and continued from 1715 to 1853 by T. DUFFUS HARDY. 3 vols. 8vo, 1l. 1s.

Noelli (A.) Catechismus sive prima institutio disciplinaque Pietatis Christianae Latine explicata. Editio nova cura GUIL. JACOBSON, A.M. 8vo, 5s. 6d.

Prideaux's Connection of Sacred and Profane History. 2 vols. 8vo, 10s.

Primers put forth in the Reign of Henry VIII. 8vo, 5s.

Records of the Reformation. The Divorce, 1527–1533. Mostly now for the first time printed from MSS. in the British Museum and other Libraries. Collected and arranged by N. POCOCK, M.A. 2 vols. 8vo, 1l. 16s.

Reformatio Legum Ecclesiasticarum. The Reformation of Ecclesiastical Laws, as attempted in the reigns of Henry VIII, Edward VI, and Elizabeth. Edited by E. CARDWELL, D.D. 8vo, 6s. 6d.

Shirley. Some Account of the Church in the Apostolic Age. By W. W. SHIRLEY, D.D. *Second Edition.* Fcap. 8vo, 3s. 6d.

Shuckford's Sacred and Profane History connected (in continuation of Prideaux). 2 vols. 8vo, 10s.

Stillingfleet's Origines Britannicae, with LLOYD's Historical Account of Church Government. Edited by T. P. PANTIN, M.A. 2 vols. 8vo, 10s.

Stubbs. **Registrum** Sacrum Anglicanum. An attempt to exhibit the course of Episcopal Succession in England. By W. STUBBS, D.D. Small 4to, 8s. 6d.

Strype's Memorials of Cranmer. 2 vols. 8vo, 11s.
    Life of Aylmer. 8vo, 5s. 6d.
    Life of Whitgift. 3 vols. 8vo, 16s. 6d.
    General Index. 2 vols. 8vo, 11s.

Sylloge Confessionum sub tempus Reformandae Ecclesiae editarum. Subjiciuntur Catechismus Heidelbergensis et **Canones** Synodi Dordrechtanae. 8vo, 8s.

D. LITURGIOLOGY.

Cardwell's Two Books of Common Prayer, set forth by authority in the Reign of King Edward VI, compared with each other. Third Edition. 8vo, 7s.

—— History of Conferences on the Book of Common Prayer from 1551 to 1690. Third Edition. 8vo, 7s. 6d.

Hammond. Liturgies, Eastern and Western. Edited, with Introduction, Notes, and a Liturgical Glossary, by C. E. HAMMOND, M.A. New Edition in the Press.

Helps to the Study of the Book of Common Prayer. Being a Companion to Church Worship. Crown 8vo, 3s. 6d.

Leofric Missal, The; together with some Account of the Red Book of Derby, the Missal of Robert of Jumièges, &c. Edited, with Introduction and Notes, by F. E. WARREN, B.D., F.S.A. 4to, half-morocco, 1l. 15s.

Maskell. Ancient Liturgy of the Church of England, according to the uses of Sarum, York, Hereford, and Bangor, and the Roman Liturgy arranged in parallel columns, with preface and notes. By W. MASKELL, M.A. Third Edition. 8vo, 15s.

—— Monumenta Ritualia Ecclesiae **Anglicanae.** The occasional Offices of the Church of England according to the old use of Salisbury, the Prymer in English, and other prayers and forms, with dissertations and notes. Second Edition. 3 vols. 8vo, 2l. 10s.

Warren. The Liturgy and Ritual of the Celtic Church. By F. E. WARREN, B.D. 8vo, 14s.

London: HENRY FROWDE, Amen Corner, E.C.

E. ENGLISH THEOLOGY.

Bradley. Lectures on the Book of Job. By GEORGE GRANVILLE BRADLEY, D.D., Dean of Westminster. *Second Edition.* Crown 8vo, 7s. 6d.

—— Lectures on Ecclesiastes. By G. G. BRADLEY, D.D. Crown 8vo, 4s. 6d.

Bull's Works, with NELSON's Life. Edited by E. BURTON, D.D. 8 vols. 8vo, 2l. 9s.

Burnet's Exposition of the xxxix Articles. 8vo, 7s.

Burton's (Edward) Testimonies of the Ante-Nicene Fathers to the Divinity of Christ. 1829. 8vo, 7s.

—— Testimonies of the Ante-Nicene Fathers to the Doctrine of the Trinity and of the Divinity of the Holy Ghost. 1831. 8vo, 3s. 6d.

Butler's Works. 2 vols. 8vo, 11s.

—— Sermons. 5s. 6d. Analogy of Religion. 5s. 6d.

Chillingworth's Works. 3 vols. 8vo, 1l. 1s. 6d.

Clergyman's Instructor. *Sixth Edition.* 8vo, 6s. 6d.

Cranmer's Works. Collected and arranged by H. JENKYNS, M.A., Fellow of Oriel College. 4 vols. 8vo, 1l. 10s.

Enchiridion Theologicum Anti-Romanum.

    Vol. I. JEREMY TAYLOR's Dissuasive from Popery, and Treatise on the Real Presence. 8vo, 8s.

    Vol. II. BARROW on the Supremacy of the Pope, with his Discourse on the Unity of the Church. 8vo, 7s. 6d.

    Vol. III. Tracts selected from WAKE, PATRICK, STILLINGFLEET, CLAGETT, and others. 8vo, 11s.

Greswell's Harmonia Evangelica. *Fifth Edition.* 8vo, 9s. 6d.

Hall's Works. Edited by P. WYNTER, D.D. 10 vols. 8vo, 3l. 3s.

Heurtley. Harmonia Symbolica: Creeds of the Western Church. By C. HEURTLEY, D.D. 8vo, 6s. 6d.

Homilies appointed to be read in Churches. Edited by J. GRIFFITHS, M.A. 8vo, 7s. 6d.

English Theology.

HOOKER'S WORKS, with his Life by WALTON, arranged by JOHN KEBLE, M.A. *Seventh Edition.* Revised by R. W. CHURCH, M.A., Dean of St. Paul's, and F. PAGET, D.D. 3 vols. medium 8vo, 1*l.* 16*s.*

—— the Text as arranged by J. KEBLE, M.A. 2 vols. 8vo, 11*s.*

Hooper's Works. 2 vols. 8vo, 8*s.*

Jackson's (Dr. Thomas) Works. 12 vols. 8vo, 3*l.* 6*s.*

Jewel's Works. Edited by R. W. JELF, D.D. 8 vols. 8vo, 1*l.* 10*s.*

Martineau. A Study of Religion: its Sources and Contents. By JAMES MARTINEAU, D.D. *Second Edition.* 2 vols. crown 8vo, 15*s.*

Patrick's Theological Works. 9 vols. 8vo, 1*l.* 1*s.*

Pearson's Exposition of the Creed. Revised and corrected by E. BURTON, D.D. *Sixth Edition.* 8vo, 10*s.* 6*d.*

—— Minor Theological Works. Edited with a Memoir, by EDWARD CHURTON, M.A. 2 vols. 8vo, 10*s.*

Sanderson's Works. Edited by W. JACOBSON, D.D. 6 vols. 8vo, 1*l.* 10*s.*

Stillingfleet's Origines Sacrae. 2 vols. 8vo, 9*s.*

—— Rational Account of the Grounds of Protestant Religion. 2 vols. 8vo, 10*s.*

Wall's History of Infant Baptism. Edited by HENRY COTTON, D.C.L. 2 vols. 8vo, 1*l.* 1*s.*

Waterland's Works, with Life, by Bp. VAN MILDERT. *A new Edition*, with copious Indexes. 6 vols. 8vo, 2*l.* 11*s.*

—— Review of the Doctrine of the Eucharist, with a Preface by the late Bishop of London. Crown 8vo, 6*s.* 6*d.*

Wheatly's Illustration of the Book of Common Prayer. 8vo, 5*s.*

Wyclif. A Catalogue of the Original Works of John Wyclif. By W. W. SHIRLEY, D.D. 8vo, 3*s.* 6*d.*

—— Select English Works. By T. ARNOLD, M.A. 3 vols. 8vo, 1*l.* 1*s.*

—— Trialogus. With the Supplement now first edited. By GOTTHARD LECHLER. 8vo, 7*s.*

London: HENRY FROWDE, Amen Corner, E.C.

III. HISTORY, BIOGRAPHY, POLITICAL ECONOMY, &c.

Arbuthnot. The Life and Works of **John** Arbuthnot. By GEORGE A. AITKEN. 8vo, cloth extra, with Portrait, 16s.

Baker's Chronicle. Chronicon Galfridi le **Baker** de Swynebroke. Edited with Notes by EDWARD MAUNDE THOMPSON, LL.D., D.C.L., F.S.A. Small 4to, stiff covers, 18s.; cloth, gilt top, 21s.

Bentham. A Fragment on Government. By JEREMY BENTHAM. Edited by F. C. MONTAGUE, M.A. 8vo, 7s. 6d.

Bluntschli. The Theory of the State. By J. K. BLUNTSCHLI. Translated from the Sixth German Edition. Second Edition, Revised. Crown 8vo, half-bound, 8s. 6d.

Boswell's Life of Samuel Johnson, LL.D.; including BosWELL'S Journal of a Tour to the Hebrides, and JOHNSON'S Diary of a Journey into North Wales. Edited by G. BIRKBECK HILL, D.C.L. In six vols., 8vo. With Portraits and Facsimiles. Half-bound, 3l. 3s.

Burnet's History of James II. 8vo, 9s. 6d.

—— Life of Sir **M. Hale**, and Fell's Life of Dr. Hammond. Small 8vo, 2s. 6d.

Calendar of the Clarendon State Papers, preserved in the Bodleian Library. In three volumes. 1869-76.
    Vol. I. From 1523 to January 1649. 8vo, 18s.
    Vol. II. From 1649 to 1654. 8vo, 16s.
    Vol. III. From 1655 to 1657. 8vo, 14s.

Calendar of Charters and Rolls preserved in the Bodleian Library. 8vo, 1l. 11s. 6d.

Carte's Life of James Duke of Ormond. A new Edition, carefully compared with the original MSS. 6 vols. 8vo, 1l. 5s.

Casaubon (Isaac), Life of, by MARK PATTISON, B.D. *Second Edition.* 8vo, 16s.

Casauboni Ephemerides, cum praefatione et notis J. RUSSELL, S.T.P. Tomi II. 8vo, 15s.

III. History, Biography, &c.

Chesterfield. Letters of Philip Dormer Fourth Earl of Chesterfield, to his Godson and Successor. Edited from the Originals, with a Memoir of Lord Chesterfield, by the late EARL OF CARNARVON. Second Edition. With Appendix of Additional Correspondence. Royal 8vo, cloth extra, 21s.

CLARENDON'S History of the Rebellion and Civil Wars in England. Re-edited from a fresh collation of the original MS. in the Bodleian Library, with marginal dates and occasional notes, by W. DUNN MACRAY, M.A., F.S.A. 6 vols. Crown 8vo, 2l. 5s.

—— History of the Rebellion and Civil Wars in England. To which are subjoined the Notes of BISHOP WARBURTON. 1849. 7 vols. Medium 8vo, 2l. 10s.

—— History of the Rebellion and Civil Wars in England. Also his Life, written by himself, in which is included a Continuation of his History of the Grand Rebellion. Royal 8vo, 1l. 2s.

Clarendon's Life, including a Continuation of his History. 2 vols. 1857. Medium 8vo, 1l. 2s.

Clinton's Fasti Hellenici. The Civil and Literary Chronology of Greece, from the LVIth to the CXXIIIrd Olympiad. Third Edition. 4to, 1l. 14s. 6d.

—— Fasti Hellenici. The Civil and Literary Chronology of Greece, from the CXXIVth Olympiad to the Death of Augustus. Second Edition. 4to, 1l. 12s.

—— Epitome of the Fasti Hellenici. 8vo, 6s. 6d.

—— Fasti Romani. The Civil and Literary Chronology of Rome and Constantinople, from the Death of Augustus to the Death of Heraclius. 2 vols. 4to, 2l. 2s.

—— Epitome of the Fasti Romani. 8vo, 7s.

Codrington. The Melanesians. Studies in their Anthropology and Folk-Lore. By R. H. CODRINGTON, D.D. 8vo, 16s.

Cramer's Geographical and Historical Description of Asia Minor. 2 vols. 8vo, 11s.

—— Description of Ancient Greece. 3 vols. 8vo, 16s. 6d.

Earle. Handbook to the Land-Charters, and other Saxonic Documents. By JOHN EARLE, M.A., Professor of Anglo-Saxon in the University of Oxford. Crown 8vo, 16s.

Elizabethan Seamen, Voyages of, to America. Edited by E. J. PAYNE, M.A. First Series. HAWKINS. FROBISHER. DRAKE. Second Edition. Crown 8vo, 5s.

III. History, Biography, &c.

Finlay. A History of Greece from its Conquest by the Romans to the present time, B.C. 146 to A.D. 1864. By GEORGE FINLAY, LL.D. A new Edition, revised throughout, and in part re-written, with considerable additions, by the Author, and edited by H. F. TOZER, M.A. 7 vols. 8vo, 3*l.* 10*s.*

Fortescue. The Governance of England: otherwise called The Difference between an Absolute and a Limited Monarchy. By Sir JOHN FORTESCUE, Kt. A Revised Text. Edited, with Introduction, Notes, &c., by CHARLES PLUMMER, M.A. 8vo, half-bound, 12*s.* 6*d.*

Freeman. The History of Sicily from the Earliest Times. Vols. I and II. 8vo, 2*l.* 2*s.*
    Vol. III. The Athenian and Carthaginian Invasions. 1*l.* 4*s.*

—— History of the Norman Conquest of England; its Causes and Results. By E. A. FREEMAN, D.C.L. In Six Volumes, 8vo, 5*l.* 9*s.* 6*d.*

—— The Reign of William Rufus and the Accession of Henry the First. 2 vols. 8vo, 1*l.* 16*s.*

—— A Short History of the Norman Conquest of England. *Third Edition.* Extra fcap. 8vo, 2*s.* 6*d.*

French Revolutionary Speeches. See STEPHENS, H. Morse.

Gardiner. The Constitutional Documents of the Puritan Revolution. 1628–1660. Selected and Edited by SAMUEL RAWSON GARDINER, M.A. Crown 8vo, 9*s.*

Gascoigne's Theological Dictionary ('Liber Veritatum'): Selected Passages, illustrating the Condition of Church and State, 1403–1458. With an Introduction by JAMES E. THOROLD ROGERS, M.A. Small 4to, 10*s.* 6*d.*

George. Genealogical Tables illustrative of Modern History. By H. B. GEORGE, M.A. *Third Edition.* Small 4to, 12*s.*

Greswell's Fasti Temporis Catholici. 4 vols. 8vo, 2*l.* 10*s.*

—— Tables to Fasti, 4to, and Introduction to Tables, 8vo, 15*s.*

—— Origines Kalendariæ Italicæ. 4 vols. 8vo, 2*l.* 2*s.*

—— Origines Kalendariæ Hellenicæ. 6 vols. 8vo, 4*l.* 4*s.*

Oxford: Clarendon Press.

III. History, Biography, &c.

Greswell (**W. Parr**). History of the Dominion of Canada.
By W. PARR GRESWELL, M.A., under the Auspices of the Royal Colonial Institute. With Eleven Maps. Crown 8vo, 7s. 6d.

—— Geography of the Dominion of Canada and Newfoundland. By the same Author. With Ten Maps. Crown 8vo, 6s.

—— Geography of Africa South of the Zambesi. With Maps. Crown 8vo, 7s. 6d.

Gross. The Gild Merchant: a Contribution to British Municipal History. By C. GROSS, Ph.D. 2 vols. 8vo, half-bound, 24s.

Hastings. Hastings and The Rohilla War. By Sir JOHN STRACHEY, G.C.S.I. 8vo, cloth, 10s. 6d.

Hodgkin. Italy and her Invaders. With Plates and Maps. By THOMAS HODGKIN, D.C.L. (A.D. 376-553).
    Vols. I-II. The Visigothic Invasions. The Hunnish Invasion. The Vandal Invasion, and the Herulian Mutiny. *Second Edition*, 2l. 2s.
    Vols. III-IV. The Ostrogothic Invasion. The Imperial Restoration. 36s.

—— The Dynasty of Theodosius; or, Seventy Years' Struggle with the Barbarians. By the same Author. Crown 8vo, 6s.

Hume. Letters of David Hume to William Strahan. Edited with Notes, Index, &c., by G. BIRKBECK HILL, D.C.L. 8vo, 12s. 6d.

Hunter (Sir W. W.). A Brief History of the Indian Peoples. By Sir W. W. HUNTER, K.C.S.I. *Eightieth Thousand*. Crown 8vo, 3s. 6d.

Jackson. Dalmatia, the Quarnero, and Istria; with Cettigne in Montenegro and the Island of Grado. By T. G. JACKSON, M.A. 3 vols. With many Plates and Illustrations. 8vo, half-bound, 2l. 2s.

Johnson. Letters of Samuel Johnson, LL.D. Collected and Edited by G. BIRKBECK HILL, D.C.L. In two volumes. Medium 8vo, half-roan (uniform with Boswell's Life of Johnson,) 28s.

Kitchin. A History of France. With numerous Maps, Plans, and Tables. By G. W. KITCHIN, D.D. In three Volumes. Crown 8vo, each 10s. 6d.
    Vol. I, to 1453. *Third Edition.*
    Vol. II, 1453-1624. *Second Edition.*
    Vol. III, 1624-1793. *Second Edition.*

Knight's Life of Dean Colet. 1823. 8vo, 7s. 6d.

Lloyd's Prices of Corn in Oxford, 1583-1830. 8vo, 1s.

Lewes, The Song of. Edited, with Introduction and Notes, by C. L. KINGSFORD, M.A. Extra fcap. 8vo, 5s.

III. History, Biography, &c.

Lewis (Sir G. Cornewall). An Essay on the Government of Dependencies. Edited by C. P. Lucas, B.A. 8vo, half-roan, 14s.

Lucas. Introduction to a Historical Geography of the British Colonies. By C. P. Lucas, B.A. With Eight Maps. Crown 8vo, 4s. 6d.

—— Historical Geography of the British Colonies. By the same Author:

    Vol. I. The Mediterranean and Eastern Colonies (exclusive of India). With Eleven Maps. 5s.

    Vol. II. The West Indian Colonies. With Twelve Maps. 7s. 6d.

Luttrell's (Narcissus) Diary. A Brief Historical Relation of State Affairs, 1678-1714. 6 vols. 8vo, 1l. 4s.

Machiavelli (Niccolò). Il Principe. Edited by L. Arthur Burd. With an Introduction by Lord Acton. 8vo, 14s.

Macray (W. D.). Annals of the Bodleian Library, Oxford, with a Notice of the Earlier Library of the University. By W. Dunn Macray, M.A., F.S.A. *Second Edition, enlarged and continued from* 1868 *to* 1880. Medium 8vo, half-bound, 25s.

Magna Carta, a careful Reprint. Edited by W. Stubbs, D.D., Lord Bishop of Oxford. 4to, stitched, 1s.

Metcalfe. Passio et Miracula Beati Olaui. Edited from a Twelfth-Century MS. by F. Metcalfe, M.A. Small 4to, 6s.

OXFORD, University of.

    Oxford University Calendar for 1894. Crown 8vo, 6s.

    The Historical Register of the University of Oxford. Being a Supplement to the Oxford University Calendar, with an Alphabetical Record of University Honours and Distinctions, completed to the end of Trinity Term, 1888. Crown 8vo, 5s.

    Student's Handbook to the University and Colleges of Oxford. *Twelfth Edition.* Crown 8vo, 2s. 6d.

    The Examination Statutes; together with the Regulations of the Boards of Studies and Boards of Faculties for the Academical Year 1893-94. Revised to June 21, 1893. 8vo, paper covers, 1s.

    Statuta Universitatis Oxoniensis. 1893. 8vo, 5s.

    Statutes made for the University of Oxford, and the Colleges therein, by the University of Oxford Commissioners. 8vo, 12s. 6d.

    Also separately—University Statutes, 2s.; College Statutes, 1s. each.

    Supplementary Statutes made by the University of Oxford, and by certain of the Colleges therein, in pursuance of the Universities of Oxford and Cambridge Act, 1877; approved by the Queen in Council. 8vo, paper covers, 2s. 6d.

Oxford : Clarendon Press.

OXFORD, **University of** (*continued*).

Statutes of the University of Oxford, codified in the year 1636 under the Authority of ARCHBISHOP LAUD, Chancellor of the University. Edited by the late JOHN GRIFFITHS, D.D. With an Introduction on the History of the Laudian Code by C. L. SHADWELL, M.A., B.C.L. 4to, 1*l*. 1*s*.

Enactments in Parliament, specially concerning the Universities of Oxford and Cambridge. Collected and arranged by J. GRIFFITHS, D.D. 1869. 8vo, 12*s*.

Catalogue of Oxford Graduates, 1659 to 1850. 7*s*. 6*d*.

Index to Wills proved in the Court of the Chancellor of the University of Oxford, &c. Compiled by J. GRIFFITHS, D.D. 3*s*. 6*d*.

Manuscript Materials relating to the History of Oxford; contained in the Printed Catalogues of the Bodleian and College Libraries. By F. MADAN, M.A. 8vo, 7*s*. 6*d*.

Pattison. **Essays by the late** MARK PATTISON, sometime Rector of Lincoln College. Collected and arranged by HENRY NETTLESHIP, M.A. 2 vols. 8vo, 24*s*.

—— **Life of Isaac Casaubon** (1559–1614). By the same Author. *Second Edition.* 8vo, 16*s*.

Payne. History of the New World called America. By E. J. PAYNE, M.A. Vol. I, 8vo, 18*s*. Vol. II. *In the Press.*

—— Voyages of the Elizabethan Seamen to **America.** Edited by E. J PAYNE, M.A. *First Series.* HAWKINS. FROBISHER. DRAKE. *Second Edition.* Crown 8vo, 5*s*.

Ralegh. Sir Walter Ralegh. A Biography. By W. STEBBING, M.A. 8vo, 10*s*. 6*d*.

Ramsay (Sir James H.). **Lancaster and York.** A Century of English History (A.D. 1399–1485). 2 vols. 8vo, 1*l*. 16*s*.

Ranke. A History of England, principally in the Seventeenth Century. By L. VON RANKE. Translated under the superintendence of G. W. KITCHIN, D.D., and C. W. BOASE, M.A. 6 vols. 8vo, 3*l*. 3*s*.

Rawlinson. A Manual of Ancient **History.** By GEORGE RAWLINSON, M.A. *Second Edition.* Demy 8vo, 14*s*.

Rhŷs. Studies in the Arthurian Legend. By JOHN RHŶS, M.A., Professor of Celtic in the University of Oxford. 8vo, 12*s*. 6*d*.

Ricardo. Letters of **David** Ricardo to T. R. Malthus (1810–1823). Edited by JAMES BONAR, M.A. 8vo, 10*s*. 6*d*.

London: HENRY FROWDE, Amen Corner, E.C.

III. History, Biography, &c.

Rogers. History of Agriculture and Prices in England, A.D. 1259-1793. By JAMES E. THOROLD ROGERS, M.A.
    Vols. I and II (1259–1400). 8vo, 2*l.* 2*s.*
    Vols. III and IV (1401–1582). 8vo, 2*l.* 10*s.*
    Vols. V and VI (1583–1702). 8vo, 2*l.* 10*s.*
    Vols. VII and VIII. *In the Press.*

—— First Nine Years of the Bank of England. 8vo, 8*s.* 6*d.*

—— Protests of the Lords, including those which have been expunged, from 1624 to 1874; with Historical Introductions. In three volumes. 8vo, 2*l.* 2*s.*

Selden. The Table Talk of JOHN SELDEN. Edited, with an Introduction and Notes, by SAMUEL HARVEY REYNOLDS, M.A. 8vo, half-roan, 8*s.* 6*d.*

Smith's Wealth of Nations. A new Edition, with Notes, by J. E. THOROLD ROGERS, M.A. 2 vols. 8vo, 21*s.*

Sprigg's England's Recovery; being the History of the Army under Sir Thomas Fairfax. 8vo, 6*s.*

RULERS OF INDIA: The History of the Indian Empire in a carefully planned succession of Political Biographies. Edited by Sir WILLIAM WILSON HUNTER, K.C.S.I. In crown 8vo. Half-crown volumes.

Now Ready:

The Marquess of Dalhousie. By Sir W. W. HUNTER.
Akbar. By COLONEL MALLESON, C.S.I.
Dupleix. By COLONEL MALLESON, C.S.I.
Warren Hastings. By CAPTAIN L. J. TROTTER.
The Marquess of Cornwallis. By W. S. SETON-KARR.
The Earl of Mayo. By Sir W. W. HUNTER, K.C.S.I.
Viscount Hardinge. By his son, VISCOUNT HARDINGE.
Clyde and Strathnairn. By Major-General Sir OWEN TUDOR BURNE, K.C.S.I.
Earl **Canning.** By Sir H. S. CUNNINGHAM, K.C.I.E.
Mádhava **Ráo Sindhia.** By H. G. KEENE, M.A., C.I.E.
Mountstuart **Elphinstone.** By J. S. COTTON, M.A.
Lord **William Bentinck.** By DEMETRIUS C. BOULGER.
Ranjit Singh. By Sir LEPEL GRIFFIN, K.C.S.I.
Lord Lawrence. By Sir C. AITCHISON, **K.C.S.I.,** LL.D.
Albuquerque. By H. MORSE STEPHENS.
Marquess of Hastings. By Major ROSS-OF-BLADENSBURG, C.B.

Oxford: Clarendon Press.

III. History, Biography, &c.

RULERS OF INDIA (*continued*).
Aurangzíb. By STANLEY LANE-POOLE, B.A.
The Earl of Auckland. By Captain L. J. TROTTER.
Lord Clive. By COLONEL MALLESON, C.S.I.
The **Marquess Wellesley, K.G.** By W. H. HUTTON, M.A.
Haidar **Alí and Tipú Sultán.** By L. B. BOWRING, C.S.I.

SUPPLEMENTARY VOLUMES.
James Thomason. By Sir RICHARD TEMPLE, Bart. 3s. 6d.
A Brief History of the Indian Peoples. By Sir
W. W. HUNTER, K.C.S.I. *Eightieth Thousand.* Crown 8vo, 3s. 6d.

Stephens. The Principal Speeches of the Statesmen and
Orators of the French Revolution, 1789-1795. With Introductions,
Notes, &c. By H. MORSE STEPHENS. 2 vols. Crown 8vo, 21s.

Stubbs. Select Charters and other Illustrations of English
Constitutional History, from the Earliest Times to the Reign of Edward I.
Arranged and edited by W. STUBBS, D.D., Lord Bishop of Oxford.
Seventh Edition. Crown 8vo, 8s. 6d.

—— The Constitutional History of England, in its Origin
and Development. *Library Edition.* 3 vols. Demy 8vo, 2l. 8s.
Also in 3 vols. crown 8vo, price 12s. each.

—— Seventeen Lectures on the Study of Mediaeval and
Modern History. *Second Edition.* Crown 8vo, 8s. 6d.

Tozer. The Islands of the Aegean. By H. FANSHAWE
TOZER, M.A., F.R.G.S. Crown 8vo, 8s. 6d.

Vinogradoff. Villainage in England. Essays in English
Mediaeval History. By PAUL VINOGRADOFF, Professor in the University
of Moscow. 8vo, half-bound, 16s.

Wellesley. A Selection from the Despatches, Treaties, and
other Papers of the MARQUESS WELLESLEY, K.G., during his Government
of India. Edited by S. J. OWEN, M.A. 8vo, 1l. 4s.

Wellington. A Selection from the Despatches, Treaties, and
other Papers relating to India of Field-Marshal the DUKE OF WELLINGTON, K.G. Edited by S. J. OWEN, M.A. 8vo, 1l. 4s.

Whitelock's Memorials of **English Affairs** from 1625 to 1660.
4 vols. 8vo, 1l. 10s.

Cannan. Elementary Political Economy. By EDWIN CANNAN,
M.A. Extra fcap. 8vo, stiff covers, 1s.

Raleigh. Elementary Politics. By THOMAS RALEIGH, M.A.
Sixth Edition. Extra fcap. 8vo, stiff covers, 1s.

IV. LAW.

Anson. Principles of the English Law of Contract, and of Agency in its Relation to Contract. By SIR W. R. ANSON, D.C.L. *Seventh Edition.* 8vo, 10s. 6d.

—— Law and Custom of the Constitution. In two Parts.
Part I. Parliament. *Second Edition.* 8vo, 12s. 6d.
Part II. The Crown. 8vo, 14s.

Baden-Powell. Land-Systems of British India; being a Manual of the Land-Tenures, and of the Systems of Land-Revenue Administration prevalent in the several Provinces. By B. H. BADEN-POWELL, C.I.E., F.R.S.E., M.R.A.S. 3 vols. 8vo, with Maps, 3l. 3s.

—— Land-Revenue and Tenure in British India. By the same Author. With Map. Crown 8vo, 5s.

Bentham. An Introduction to the Principles of Morals and Legislation. By JEREMY BENTHAM. Crown 8vo, 6s. 6d.

Digby. An Introduction to the History of the Law of Real Property. By KENELM E. DIGBY, M.A. *Fourth Edition.* 8vo, 12s. 6d.

Grueber. Lex Aquilia. The Roman Law of Damage to Property: being a Commentary on the Title of the Digest 'Ad Legem Aquiliam' (ix. 2). With an Introduction to the Study of the Corpus Iuris Civilis. By ERWIN GRUEBER, Dr. Jur., M.A. 8vo, 10s. 6d.

Hall. International Law. By W. E. HALL, M.A. *Third Edition.* 8vo, 22s. 6d.

Holland. Elements of Jurisprudence. By T. E. HOLLAND, D.C.L. *Sixth Edition.* 8vo, 10s. 6d.

—— The European Concert in the Eastern Question, a Collection of Treaties and other Public Acts. Edited, with Introductions and Notes, by T. E. HOLLAND, D.C.L. 8vo, 12s. 6d.

—— Gentilis, Alberici, I.C.D., I.C.P.R., de Iure Belli Libri Tres. Edidit T. E. HOLLAND, I.C.D. Small 4to, half-morocco, 21s.

—— The Institutes of Justinian, edited as a recension of the Institutes of GAIUS, by T. E. HOLLAND, D.C.L. *Second Edition.* Extra fcap. 8vo, 5s.

Oxford: Clarendon Press.

IV. Law.

Holland and Shadwell. Select Titles from the Digest of Justinian. By T. E. HOLLAND, D.C.L., and C. L. SHADWELL, B.C.L. 8vo, 14*s*.
    Also sold in Parts, in paper covers, as follows :—
    Part I. Introductory Titles. 2*s*. 6*d*.
    Part II. Family Law. 1*s*.
    Part III. Property Law. 2*s*. 6*d*.
    Part IV. Law of Obligations (No. 1). 3*s*. 6*d*.
    Part IV. Law of Obligations (No. 2). 4*s*. 6*d*.

Markby. Elements of Law considered with reference to Principles of General Jurisprudence. By Sir WILLIAM MARKBY, D.C.L. *Fourth Edition.* 8vo, 12*s*. 6*d*.

Moyle. Imperatoris Iustiniani Institutionum Libri Quattuor; with Introductions, Commentary, Excursus, and Translation. By J. B. MOYLE, D.C.L. *Second Edition.* 2 vols. 8vo, 22*s*.

—— Contract of Sale in the Civil Law. By J. B. MOYLE, D.C.L. 8vo, 10*s*. 6*d*.

Pollock and Wright. An Essay on Possession in the Common Law. By Sir F. POLLOCK, M.A., and Sir R. S. WRIGHT, B.C.L. 8vo, 8*s*. 6*d*.

Poste. Gaii Institutionum Juris Civilis Commentarii Quattuor; or, Elements of Roman Law by Gaius. With a Translation and Commentary by EDWARD POSTE, M.A. *Third Edition.* 8vo, 18*s*.

Raleigh. An Outline of the Law of Property. By THOMAS RALEIGH, M.A. 8vo, cloth, 7*s*. 6*d*.

Sohm. Institutes of Roman Law. By RUDOLPH SOHM, Professor in the University of Leipzig. Translated (from the Fourth Edition of the German) by J. C. LEDLIE, B.C.L., M.A. With an Introductory Essay by ERWIN GRUEBER, Dr. Jur., M.A. 8vo, 18*s*.

Stokes. Anglo-Indian Codes. By WHITLEY STOKES, LL.D. Vol. I. Substantive Law. 8vo, 30*s*. Vol. II. Adjective Law. 8vo, 35*s*.

—— First Supplement to the above, 1887, 1888. 2*s*. 6*d*.

—— Second Supplement, to May 31, 1891. 4*s*. 6*d*.

—— First and Second Supplements in one volume, price 6*s*. 6*d*.

Twiss. The Law of Nations considered as Independent Political Communities. By SIR TRAVERS TWISS, D.C.L.
    Part I. On the rights and Duties of Nations in time of Peace. New Edition, Revised and Enlarged. 8vo, 15*s*.

London: HENRY FROWDE, Amen Corner, E.C.

V. PHILOSOPHY, LOGIC, &c.

Bacon. Novum Organum. Edited, with Introduction, Notes, &c., by T. FOWLER, D.D. *Second Edition.* 8vo, 15s.

—— Novum Organum. Edited, with English Notes, by G. W. KITCHIN, D.D. 8vo, 9s. 6d.

—— The Essays. Edited, with Introduction and Illustrative Notes, by S. H. REYNOLDS, M.A. Demy 8vo, half-bound, 12s. 6d.

Berkeley. The works of GEORGE BERKELEY, D.D., formerly Bishop of Cloyne; including many of his writings hitherto unpublished. With Prefaces, Annotations, and an Account of his Life and Philosophy, by ALEXANDER CAMPBELL FRASER, LL.D. 4 vols. 8vo, 2l. 18s.

The Life, Letters, &c., separately, 16s.

Berkeley. Selections. With Introduction and Notes. **For the** use of Students in the Universities. By ALEXANDER CAMPBELL **FRASER**, LL.D. *Fourth Edition.* Crown 8vo, 8s. 6d.

Bosanquet. Logic; or, The Morphology of Knowledge. By B. BOSANQUET, M.A. 8vo, 21s.

Butler's Works, with Index to the Analogy. 2 vols. 8vo, 11s.

Fowler. The Elements of Deductive Logic, designed mainly for the use of Junior Students in the Universities. By T. FOWLER, D.D. *Ninth Edition,* with **a Collection of** Examples. Extra fcap. 8vo, 3s. 6d.

Fowler. The Elements of Inductive Logic, designed mainly for the use of Students in the Universities. *Fifth Edition.* Extra fcap. 8vo, 6s.

—— The Principles of Morals (Introductory Chapters). By T. FOWLER, D.D., and J. M. WILSON, B.D. 8vo, boards, 3s. 6d.

—— The Principles of Morals. Part II. By T. FOWLER, D.D. 8vo, 10s. 6d.

Green. Prolegomena to Ethics. By T. H. GREEN, **M.A.** Edited by A. C. BRADLEY, M.A. *Third Edition.* 8vo, 12s. 6d.

Hegel. The Logic of Hegel; translated from the Encyclopaedia of the Philosophical Sciences. By WILLIAM WALLACE, M.A., LL.D. *Second Edition, Revised and Augmented.* Crown 8vo, 10s. 6d.

The Volume containing the Prolegomena is under Revision, and will be issued shortly.

Hume's Treatise of Human Nature. Reprinted from the Original Edition in Three Volumes, and Edited by L. A. Selby-Bigge, M.A. Crown 8vo, 9s.

Oxford: Clarendon Press.

Locke's Conduct of the Understanding. Edited by T. FOWLER, D.D. *Third Edition.* Extra fcap. 8vo, 2s. 6d.

Lotze's Logic, in Three Books; of Thought, of Investigation, and of Knowledge. English Translation; Edited by B. BOSANQUET, M.A. *Second Edition.* 2 vols. Crown 8vo, 12s.

—— Metaphysic, in Three Books; Ontology, Cosmology, and Psychology. English Translation; Edited by B. BOSANQUET, M.A. *Second Edition.* 2 vols. Crown 8vo, 12s.

Martineau. Types of Ethical Theory. By JAMES MARTINEAU, D.D. *Third Edition.* 2 vols. Crown 8vo, 15s.

—— A Study of Religion: its Sources and Contents. *Second Edition.* 2 vols. Crown 8vo, 15s.

VI. PHYSICAL SCIENCE AND MATHEMATICS, &c.

Acland. Synopsis of the Pathological Series in the Oxford Museum. By Sir H. W. ACLAND, M.D., F.R.S. 8vo, 2s. 6d.

Aldis. A Text-Book of Algebra: with Answers to the Examples. By W. S. ALDIS, M.A. Crown 8vo, 7s. 6d.

Aplin. The Birds of Oxfordshire. By O. V. APLIN. 8vo. with a Map and one coloured Plate, 10s. 6d.

Archimedis quae supersunt omnia cum Eutocii commentariis ex recensione J. TORELLI, cum nova versione latina. 1792. Fol. 1l. 5s.

Baynes. Lessons on Thermodynamics. By R. E. BAYNES, M.A. Crown 8vo, 7s. 6d.

BIOLOGICAL SERIES. (Translations of Foreign Memoirs.)

I. Memoirs on the Physiology of Nerve, of Muscle, and of the Electrical Organ. Edited by J. BURDON-SANDERSON, M.D., F.R.SS.L. & E. Medium 8vo, 1l. 1s.

II. The Anatomy of the Frog. By Dr. ALEXANDER ECKER, Professor in the University of Freiburg. Translated, with numerous Annotations and Additions, by GEORGE HASLAM, M.D. Medium 8vo, 21s.

IV. Essays upon Heredity and kindred Biological Problems. By Dr. AUGUST WEISMANN. Authorised Translation. Edited by EDWARD B. POULTON, M.A., F.R.S., SELMAR SCHÖNLAND, PH.D., and ARTHUR E. SHIPLEY, M.A., F.L.S. Crown 8vo.

Vol. I. *Second Edition*, 7s. 6d.
Vol. II. Edited by E. B. POULTON and A. E. SHIPLEY. 5s.

BOTANICAL SERIES.

History of Botany (1530-1860). By JULIUS VON SACHS.
Authorised Translation, by H. E. F. GARNSEY, M.A. Revised by ISAAC BAYLEY BALFOUR, M.A., M.D., F.R.S. Crown 8vo, 10s.

Comparative Anatomy of the Vegetative Organs of the Phanerogams and Ferns. By Dr. A. DE BARY. Translated and Annotated by F. O. BOWER, M.A., F.L.S., and D. H. SCOTT, M.A., Ph.D., F.L.S. Royal 8vo, half-morocco, 1l. 2s. 6d.

Outlines of Classification and Special Morphology of Plants. By Dr. K. GOEBEL. Translated by H. E. F. GARNSEY, M.A., and Revised by ISAAC BAYLEY BALFOUR, M.A., M.D., F.R.S. Royal 8vo, half-morocco, 1l. 1s.

Lectures on the Physiology of Plants. By JULIUS VON SACHS. Translated by H. MARSHALL WARD, M.A., F.L.S. Royal 8vo, half-morocco, 1l. 11s. 6d.

Comparative Morphology and Biology of Fungi, Mycetozoa and Bacteria. By Dr. A. DE BARY. Translated by H. E. F. GARNSEY, M.A., Revised by ISAAC BAYLEY BALFOUR, M.A., M.D., F.R.S. Royal 8vo, half-morocco, 1l. 2s. 6d.

Lectures on Bacteria. By Dr. A. DE BARY. Second Improved Edition. Translated by H. E. F. GARNSEY, M.A. Revised by ISAAC BAYLEY BALFOUR, M.A., M.D., F.R.S. Crown 8vo, 6s.

Introduction to Fossil Botany. By Count H. ZU SOLMS-LAUBACH. Translated by H. E. F. GARNSEY, M.A. Revised by ISAAC BAYLEY BALFOUR, M.A., M.D., F.R.S. Royal 8vo, half-morocco, 18s.

Index Kewensis; an enumeration of the Genera and Species of Flowering Plants from the time of Linnaeus to the year 1885 inclusive. Edited by Sir J. D. HOOKER and B. D. JACKSON. Part I. 4to. Price to Subscribers, 2l. 2s. net.

*** *The Work will be completed in Four Parts, to be issued to Subscribers at Eight Guineas net.*

Annals of Botany. Edited by ISAAC BAYLEY BALFOUR, M.A., M.D., F.R.S., SYDNEY H. VINES, D.Sc., F.R.S., D. H. SCOTT, M.A., Ph.D., F.L.S., and W. G. FARLOW, M.D.; assisted by other Botanists. Royal 8vo, half-morocco, gilt top.

Vol. I. Parts I–IV. 1l. 16s.   Vol. II. Parts V–VIII. 2l. 2s.
Vol. III. Parts IX–XII. 2l. 12s. 6d.   Vol. IV. Parts XIII–XVI. 2l. 5s.
Vol. V. Parts XVII–XX. 2l. 10s.   Vol. VI. Part XXI–XXIV. 2l. 4s.
Vol. VII. Part XXV. 12s.   Part XXVI. 12s.

Oxford: Clarendon Press.

VI. Physical Science and Mathematics.

Reprints from the 'Annals of Botany.'
A Summary of the New Ferns which have been Discovered or Described since 1874. A Supplement to the *Synopsis Filicum*, bringing that work up to 1890. By J. G. BAKER, F.R.S. Royal 8vo, with one Plate, price 5s. *net.*

A Revised List of the British Marine Algae. With an Appendix, by E. M. HOLMES, F.L.S., and E. A. L. BATTERS, B.A., LL.B., F.L.S. Royal 8vo, paper covers, price 2s. 6d. *net.*

Bradley's Miscellaneous Works and Correspondence. With an Account of Harriot's Astronomical Papers. 4to, 17s.

Chambers. A Handbook of Descriptive Astronomy. By G. F. CHAMBERS, F.R.A.S. *Fourth Edition.*
> Vol. I. The Sun, Planets, and Comets. 8vo, 21s.
> Vol. II. Instruments and Practical Astronomy. 8vo, 21s.
> Vol. III. The Starry Heavens. 8vo, 14s.

Clarke. Geodesy. By Col. A. R. CLARKE, C.B., R.E. 8vo, 12s. 6d.

Cremona. Elements of Projective Geometry. By LUIGI CREMONA. Translated by C. LEUDESDORF, M.A. *Second Edition.* 8vo, 12s. 6d.

—— Graphical Statics. Two Treatises on the Graphical Calculus and Reciprocal Figures in Graphical Statics. By the same Author. Translated by T. HUDSON BEARE. Demy 8vo, 8s. 6d.

Daubeny's Introduction to the Atomic Theory. 16mo, 6s.

Dixey. Epidemic Influenza, a Study in Comparative Statistics. By F. A. DIXEY, M.A., D.M. Medium 8vo, 7s. 6d.

Donkin. Acoustics. By W. F. DONKIN, M.A., F.R.S. *Second Edition.* Crown 8vo, 7s. 6d.

Emtage. An Introduction to the Mathematical Theory of Electricity and Magnetism. By W. T. A. EMTAGE, M.A. Crown 8vo, 7s. 6d.

Etheridge. Fossils of the British Islands, Stratigraphically and Zoologically arranged. Part I. PALAEOZOIC. By R. ETHERIDGE, F.R.SS.L. & E., F.G.S. 4to, 1l. 10s.

EUCLID REVISED. Containing the Essentials of the Elements of Plane Geometry as given by Euclid in his first Six Books. Edited by R. C. J. NIXON, M.A. *Second Edition.* Crown 8vo, 6s.

> Supplement to *Euclid Revised.* 6d.
> Sold separately as follows:—
> Book I. 1s.   Books I, II. 1s. 6d.
> Books I–IV. 3s.   Books V, VI. 3s.

VI. *Physical Science and Mathematics.*

Euclid. Geometry in Space. Containing parts of Euclid's Eleventh and Twelfth Books. By R. C. J. NIXON, M.A. Crown 8vo, 3s. 6d.

Fisher. Class-Book of Chemistry. By W. W. FISHER, M.A., F.C.S. Second Edition. Crown 8vo, 4s. 6d.

Galton. The Construction of Healthy Dwellings. By Sir DOUGLAS GALTON, K.C.B., F.R.S. 8vo, 10s. 6d.

—— Healthy Hospitals. Observations on some points connected with Hospital Construction. With Illustrations. 8vo, 10s. 6d.

Greenwell. British Barrows, a Record of the Examination of Sepulchral Mounds in various parts of England. By W. GREENWELL, M.A., F.S.A. Together with Description of Figures of Skulls, General Remarks on Prehistoric Crania, and an Appendix by GEORGE ROLLESTON, M.D., F.R.S. Medium 8vo, 25s.

Gresswell. A Contribution to the Natural History of Scarlatina, derived from Observations on the London Epidemic of 1887–1888. By D. ASTLEY GRESSWELL, M.D. Medium 8vo, 10s. 6d.

Hamilton and Ball. Book-keeping. New and enlarged Edition. By Sir R. G. C. HAMILTON and JOHN BALL. Cloth, 2s. *Ruled Exercise books adapted to the above may be had, price 1s. 6d.; also, adapted to the Preliminary Course only, price 4d.*

Harcourt and Madan. Exercises in Practical Chemistry. Vol. 1. Elementary Exercises. By A. G. VERNON HARCOURT, M.A., and H. G. MADAN, M.A. *Fourth Edition.* Crown 8vo, 10s. 6d.

—— Madan. Tables of Qualitative Analysis. By H. G. MADAN, M.A. Large 4to, paper covers, 4s. 6d.

Hensley. Figures made Easy. A first Arithmetic Book. By LEWIS HENSLEY, M.A. Crown 8vo, 6d. Answers, 1s.

—— The Scholar's Arithmetic. 2s. 6d. Answers, 1s. 6d.

—— The Scholar's Algebra. Crown 8vo, 2s. 6d.

Hughes. Geography for Schools. By ALFRED HUGHES, M.A. Part I. Practical Geography. With Diagrams. Crown 8vo, 2s. 6d.

Johnston. An Elementary Treatise on Analytical Geometry. By W. J. JOHNSTON, M.A. Crown 8vo, 10s. 6d.

Maclaren. A System of Physical Education: Theoretical and Practical. By ARCHIBALD MACLAREN. Extra fcap. 8vo, 7s. 6d.

Maxwell. A Treatise on Electricity and Magnetism. By J. CLERK MAXWELL, M.A. *Third Edition.* 2 vols. 8vo, 1l. 12s.

—— An Elementary Treatise on Electricity. Edited by WILLIAM GARNETT, M.A. 8vo, 7s. 6d.

Oxford: Clarendon Press.

VI. Physical Science and Mathematics. 69

Minchin. A Treatise on Statics with Applications to Physics.
By G. M. MINCHIN, M.A. *Fourth Edition.*
  Vol. I. Equilibrium of Coplanar Forces. 8vo, 10s. 6d.
  Vol. II. Non-Coplanar Forces. 8vo, 16s.

—— Uniplanar Kinematics of Solids and Fluids. Crown 8vo, 7s. 6d.

—— Hydrostatics and Elementary Hydrokinetics. Crown 8vo, 10s. 6d.

Müller. On certain Variations in the Vocal Organs of the Passeres. By J. MÜLLER. Translated by F. J. BELL, B.A., and edited by A. H. GARROD, M.A., F.R.S. With Plates. 4to, 7s. 6d.

Nixon. Elementary Plane Trigonometry. By R. C. J. NIXON, M.A. Crown 8vo, 7s. 6d. (See EUCLID REVISED.)

Phillips. Geology of Oxford and the Valley of the Thames. By JOHN PHILLIPS, M.A., F.R.S. 8vo, 21s.

—— Vesuvius. Crown 8vo, 10s. 6d.

Powell. The Surgical Aspect of Traumatic Insanity. By H. A. POWELL, M.A., M.D. 8vo, stiff cover, 2s. 6d.

Prestwich. Geology, Chemical, Physical, and Stratigraphical. By JOSEPH PRESTWICH, M.A., F.R.S. In two Volumes.
  Vol. I. Chemical and Physical. Royal 8vo, 1l. 5s.
  Vol. II. Stratigraphical and Physical. With a new Geological Map of Europe. Royal 8vo, 1l. 16s.
  New Geological Map of Europe. In case or on roller. 5s.

Price. Treatise on Infinitesimal Calculus. By BARTHOLOMEW PRICE, M.A., F.R.S.
  Vol. I. Differential Calculus. *Second Edition.* 8vo, 14s. 6d.
  Vol. II. Integral Calculus, Calculus of Variations, and Differential Equations. *Reprinting.*
  Vol. III. Statics, including Attractions; Dynamics of a Material Particle. *Second Edition.* 8vo, 16s.
  Vol. IV. Dynamics of Material Systems. *Second Edition.* 8vo, 18s.

Pritchard. Astronomical Observations made at the University Observatory, Oxford, under the direction of C. PRITCHARD, D.D. No. 1. Royal 8vo, paper covers, 3s. 6d.

—— No. II. Uranometria Nova Oxoniensis. A Photometric determination of the magnitudes of all Stars visible to the naked eye, from the Pole to ten degrees south of the Equator. Royal 8vo, 8s. 6d.

—— No. III. Researches in Stellar Parallax by the aid of Photography. Royal 8vo, 7s. 6d.

—— No IV. Researches in Stellar Parallax by the aid of Photography. Part II. Royal 8vo, 4s. 6d.

London: HENRY FROWDE, Amen Corner, E.C.

VI. Physical Science and Mathematics.

Rigaud's Correspondence of Scientific Men of the 17th Century, with Table of Contents by A. de MORGAN, and Index by J. RIGAUD, M.A. 2 vols. 8vo, 18s. 6d.

Rolleston and Jackson. Forms of Animal Life. A Manual of Comparative Anatomy, with descriptions of selected types. By GEORGE ROLLESTON, M.D., F.R.S. *Second Edition.* Revised and enlarged by W. HATCHETT JACKSON, M.A. Medium 8vo, 1l. 16s.

Russell. An Elementary Treatise on Pure Geometry. With numerous Examples. By J. WELLESLEY RUSSELL, M.A. Crown 8vo, 10s. 6d.

Rolleston. Scientific Papers and Addresses. By GEORGE ROLLESTON, M.D., F.R.S. Arranged and edited by WILLIAM TURNER, M.B., F.R.S. With a Biographical Sketch by EDWARD TYLOR, F.R.S. 2 vols. 8vo, 1l. 4s.

Selby. Elementary Mechanics of Solids and Fluids. By A. L. SELBY, M.A. Crown 8vo, 7s. 6d.

Smyth. A Cycle of Celestial Objects. Observed, Reduced, and Discussed by Admiral W. H. SMYTH, R.N. Revised, condensed, and greatly enlarged by G. F. CHAMBERS, F.R.A.S. 8vo, 12s.

Stewart. An Elementary Treatise on Heat, with numerous Woodcuts and Diagrams. By BALFOUR STEWART, LL.D., F.R.S. *Fifth Edition.* Extra fcap. 8vo, 7s. 6d.

Strabo, Selections from. With an Introduction on Strabo's Life and Works. By H. F. TOZER, M.A., F.R.G.S. With Maps and Plans. [*Immediately.*]

Swinhoe. Catalogue of Eastern and Australian Lepidoptera Heterocera in the Collection of the Oxford University Museum. By Colonel C. Swinhoe, F.L.S., F.Z.S., &c. Part I. Sphinges and Bombyces. 8vo, with eight Plates, 21s.

Thomson. Notes on Recent Researches in Electricity and Magnetism, intended as a sequel to Professor CLERK MAXWELL'S 'Treatise on Electricity and Magnetism.' By J. J. THOMSON, M.A., F.R.S., Professor of Experimental Physics in the University of Cambridge. 8vo, 18s. 6d.

Van 't Hoff. Chemistry in Space. Translated and Edited by J. E. MARSH, B.A. Crown 8vo, 4s. 6d.

Vernon-Harcourt. Treatise on Rivers and Canals, relating to Control and Improvement of Rivers, and Design, Construction, and Development of Canals. By L. F. VERNON-HARCOURT, M.A. 2 vols. 8vo, 1l. 1s.

—— Harbours and Docks; their Physical Features, History, Construction, Equipment, and Maintenance. 2 vols. 8vo, 25s.

Oxford: Clarendon Press.

Walker. The Theory of a Physical Balance. By JAMES WALKER, M.A. 8vo, stiff cover, 3s. 6d.

Watson. A Treatise on the Kinetic Theory of Gases. By H. W. WATSON, D.Sc., F.R.S. *Second Edition.* Crown 8vo, 4s. 6d.

Watson and **Burbury.** A Treatise on the Application of Generalised Co-ordinates to the Kinetics of a Material System. By H. W. WATSON, D.Sc., and S. H. BURBURY, M.A. 8vo, 6s.

—— The Mathematical Theory of Electricity and **Magnetism.** Vol. I. Electrostatics. 8vo, 10s. 6d.
Vol. II. Magnetism and Electrodynamics. 8vo, 10s. 6d.

Westwood. Thesaurus Entomologicus Hopeianus. By J. O. WESTWOOD, M.A., F.R.S. With 40 Plates. Small folio, 7l. 10s.

Williamson. Chemistry for Students. With Solutions. By A. W. WILLIAMSON, Phil. Doc., F.R.S. Extra fcap. 8vo, 8s. 6d.

Woollcombe. Practical Work in Heat. By W. G. WOOLLCOMBE, M.A., B.Sc. Crown 8vo, 3s.

VII. ART AND ARCHAEOLOGY.

Butler. Ancient Coptic Churches of Egypt. By A. J. BUTLER, M.A., F.S.A. 2 vols. 8vo, 30s.

Head. Historia Numorum. A Manual of Greek Numismatics. By BARCLAY V. HEAD, D.C.L., Keeper of the Department of Coins and Medals in the British Museum. Royal 8vo, half-morocco, 42s.

Jackson. Dalmatia, the Quarnero and Istria; with Cettigne in Montenegro and the Island of Grado. By T. G. JACKSON, M.A. 3 vols. 8vo. With many Illustrations. Half-bound, 42s.

—— Wadham College, Oxford; Its Foundation, Architecture and History. With an Account of the Family of Wadham, and their seats in Somerset and Devon. By T. G. JACKSON, M.A., A.R.A. 4to, half-persian, 2l. 2s. net.

Gardner. Catalogue of the Greek Vases in the Ashmolean Museum. By PERCY GARDNER, M.A., Litt.D. Small folio, linen, with 26 Plates. Price 3l. 3s. net.

Three hundred and fifty copies only printed, all of which are numbered.

MUSIC.—**Farmer.** Hymns and Chorales for Schools and Colleges. Edited by JOHN FARMER, Organist of Balliol College. 5s.

☞ *The Hymns without the Tunes,* 2s.

Hullah. Cultivation of the Speaking Voice. By JOHN HULLAH. *Second Edition.* Extra fcap. 8vo, 2s. 6d.

MUSIC (*continued*).

    Ouseley. Treatise on Harmony. By Sir F. A. GORE OUSELEY, Bart. *Third Edition.* 4to, 10s.

    —— Treatise on Counterpoint, Canon, and Fugue, based upon that of Cherubini. *Second Edition.* 4to, 16s.

    —— Treatise on Musical Form and General Composition. *Second Edition.* 4to, 10s.

    Troutbeck and Dale. Music Primer. By J. TROUTBECK, D.D., and F. DALE, M.A. *Second Edition.* Crown 8vo, 1s. 6d.

Robinson. A Critical Account of the Drawings by Michel Angelo and Raffaello in the University Galleries, Oxford. By J. C. ROBINSON, F.S.A. Crown 8vo, 4s.

Tyrwhitt. Handbook of Pictorial Art. With Illustrations, and a chapter on Perspective by A. Macdonald. By R. St. J. TYRWHITT, M.A. *Second Edition.* 8vo, half-morocco, 18s.

Upcott. Introduction to Greek Sculpture. By L. E. UPCOTT, M.A. Crown 8vo, 4s. 6d.

Vaux. Catalogue of the Castellani Collection in the University Galleries, Oxford. By W. S. W. VAUX, M.A. Crown 8vo, 1s.

VIII. PALAEOGRAPHY.

Allen. Notes on Abbreviations in Greek Manuscripts. By T. W. ALLEN, M.A., Queen's College, Oxford. Royal 8vo, 5s.

Gardthausen. Catalogus Codicum Graecorum Sinaiticorum. Scripsit V. GARDTHAUSEN Lipsiensis. With Facsimiles. 8vo, *linen*, 25s.

Fragmenta Herculanensia. A Descriptive Catalogue of the Oxford copies of the Herculanean Rolls, together with the texts of several papyri. Edited by WALTER SCOTT, M.A. Royal 8vo, 21s.

—— Thirty-six Engravings of Texts and Alphabets from the Herculanean Fragments, taken from the original Copper-plates executed under the direction of the Rev. JOHN HAYTER, M.A., and now in the Bodleian Library. With an Introductory Note by BODLEY'S LIBRARIAN. Folio, *small paper*, 10s. 6d.; *large paper*, 21s.

Herculanensium Voluminum Partes II. 1824. 8vo, 10s.

Oxford:
AT THE CLARENDON PRESS.
LONDON: HENRY FROWDE,
OXFORD UNIVERSITY PRESS WAREHOUSE, AMEN CORNER, E.C.

www.ingramcontent.com/pod-product-compliance
Lightning Source LLC
Chambersburg PA
CBHW020304240426
43673CB00039B/703